YOSEMITE FALLS.

THE

GREAT WEST

AND

PACIFIC COAST;

OR,

FIFTEEN THOUSAND MILES BY STAGE-COACH, AMBULANCE, HORSEBACK, RAILROAD, AND STEAMER — ACROSS THE CONTINENT AND ALONG THE PACIFIC SLOPE — THROUGH THE ROCKY MOUNTAINS, DOWN THE COLUMBIA RIVER, OVER THE SIERRA NEVADAS — AMONG INDIANS, MORMONS, MINERS AND MEXICANS.

BY ORDER OF UNITED STATES GOVERNMENT.

With a Map of Entire Route and Eight full-page Engravings.

BEING SKETCHES OF MEN AND THINGS FROM NEW YORK TO ST. LOUIS — IN MISSOURI, KANSAS, NEBRASKA, COLORADO, DAKOTA, WYOMING, UTAH, MONTANA, IDAHO, OREGON, WASHINGTON, CALIFORNIA, ARIZONA, NEVADA, MEXICO, AND CENTRAL AMERICA. WITH A CHAPTER OF ADVICE TO EMIGRANTS AND SETTLERS.

BY JAMES F. RUSLING,

BREVET BRIGADIER-GENERAL U. S. V.

"I hear the tread of pioneers,
Of nations yet to be;
The first low wash of waves, where soon
Shall roll a human sea."

SHELDON & COMPANY, NEW YORK.

CROCKER & STICKNEY, BOSTON, MASS.
H. W. KELLY, PHILADELPHIA, PA.
BRYAN, BRAND & CO., ST. LOUIS, MO.
P. W. GARFIELD, CLEVELAND, OHIO.
M. M. BURNHAM, SYRACUSE, N. Y.
A. ROMAN & CO., SAN FRANCISCO, CAL.
A. G. NETTLETON & CO., CHICAGO, ILL., AND CINCINNATI, O.

LIST OF ILLUSTRATIONS.

PREFACE.

IN the summer of 1866, having lately concluded a tour of inspection through the West and South, and awaiting orders in Washington, it was my fortune one morning to receive the following:

"QUARTERMASTER-GENERAL'S OFFICE,
"WASHINGTON, D. C., *July* 10, 1866.

"GENERAL:—You will immediately enter upon a tour of inspection of the affairs of the Quartermaster's Department, as administered at Fort Leavenworth, Kansas, and thence west *via* Denver City and Salt Lake City to the Pacific Coast, inspecting all intermediate Posts while *en route*. At Denver City you will confer with Brevet Col. Howard, A. Q. M., as to the practicability of breaking up that depot, and removing the stores to other points where needed. Thence to Salt Lake City, where a rigid inspection is needed. Thence to San Francisco, Cal.

"Upon reaching the Pacific Coast, you will confer with the Commanding General and Chief Quartermaster of the Military Division of the Pacific, and having procured necessary information relative to the locality, importance, etc. of the various Posts, you will proceed upon a careful inspection throughout California, Oregon,

Nevada, and Washington and Arizona Territories. Upon completing this duty, you will return to this city, *via* the Isthmus, and report in person to the Quartermaster-General.

"It will be necessary to keep this Office fully informed, in advance, as to your probable whereabouts, so that instructions may be telegraphed to you at the stations where you are on duty when necessary.

"You are authorized to take a clerk with you.

* * * * * *

"Very respectfully,
"Your ob't. serv't.,
"M. C. MEIGS,
"*Quartermaster-General,*
"*Brevet Maj.-Gen., U. S. A.*"

"*Brevet Brig.-Gen. James F. Rusling,*
"*Inspector Q. M. Dep't.*"

These, my orders, were subsequently endorsed as follows:

"HEADQUARTERS OF THE ARMY,
"WASHINGTON, D. C., *July* 18, 1866.

"Commanding officers will, on the requisition of Gen. Rusling, furnish the necessary escorts to enable him to make the within directed inspections.

"By command of Lieut.-Gen. Grant,
"GEO. K. LEET,
"*Ass't. Adj't.-Gen.*"

The general object of this tour, perhaps I should explain, in a word, was to examine into the condition of our various depots and posts West, and consider then bases and routes of supply, with a view to reducing if possible the enormous expenditures, that then everywhere prevailed there. How well or ill *this* was accomplished, it is not for me to say, nor is this volume the place—my Reports at the time speaking for themselves.*

The route thus roughly indicated was long, and in parts reputed dangerous; but for years I had cherished a desire to see something of that vast region in the sunset, and here at length was the golden opportunity. I need scarcely say, therefore, that I obeyed my orders with alacrity, and in the execution of them was absent in all about a twelvemonth. During that period, crossing the continent to San Francisco, among the Mountains, along the Pacific Coast, and thence home by the Isthmus, I travelled in all over 15,000 miles, as per accompanying Map; of which about 2,000 were by railroad, 2,000 by stage-coach, 3,000 by ambulance or on horseback, and the remainder by steamer. This book, now, is the rough record of it all, written at odd hours since, as occasion offered. Much of this journey, of course, was over the old travelled routes, so well described already by Bowles, Richardson, Nordhoff, and others. But several hundred miles of it, along and among the Rocky Mountains, a thousand or so through Utah and Idaho, and perhaps two thousand or more through Southern California and Arizona, were through regions that most overland travellers never see; and here,

* Mostly published by Congress in 1867-8, and among the Pub. Docs. for those years.

at least, I trust something was gleaned of interest and profit to the general reader. Moreover, my official orders gave me access to points not always to be reached, and to sources of information not usually open; so that it was my duty, as well as pleasure, to see and hear as much of the Great West and the Pacific Coast everywhere, as seemed practicable in such a period.

The completion of the Pacific Railroad, it will be noted, made this long tour of mine, by stage-coach and ambulance, through the Great West and along the Pacific Coast, about the last, if not *the* last, of its kind possible; and, therefore, under all the circumstances, it has seemed not unfitting to give these pages to the world.

Writing only for the general public, it will be noticed, I have tried everywhere to avoid all military and official details, as far as practicable, and to confine myself mainly to what would seem of interest, if not value, to everybody. So, too, I have aimed to bridge the interval from 1866–7 to 1877 by such additional facts as appeared necessary; but without, however, modifying my own observations and experiences materially. If some persons, and some localities, are spoken of more flatteringly (or less) than usual, it is at least with truthfulness and candor, as things seemed to me. No doubt errors of fact have been committed, but these were not intended; and some of these, of course, were simply unavoidable in a book like this. So, too, as to style, no pretension whatever is made; but I claim merely an honest endeavor to convey some useful, if not interesting information *currente calamo*, in the readiest way possible, and a generous public will forgive much accordingly.

In brief, if what is here roughly said will lead any American to a better love of his country, or to a truer pride in it, or any foreigner to a kindlier appreciation of the Republic, verily I have my reward.

J. F. R.

CONTENTS.

CHAPTER I.

New York to Fort Riley, Kansas.

CHAPTER II.

From the Kansas to the Platte.

CHAPTER III.

Up the Platte to Denver.

CHAPTER IV.

Up the Platte to Denver (concluded).

CHAPTER V.

Denver and the Mines.

CHAPTER VI.

Among the Mountains.

CHAPTER VII.

Among the Mountains (continued).

CHAPTER VIII.

The Indians—Gen. Sherman—Kit Carson, etc.

CHAPTER IX.

Denver to Salt Lake.

CHAPTER X.

At Salt Lake City.

CHAPTER XIII.

Salt Lake to Boisè City.

CHAPTER XIV.

Boisè City to the Columbia.

CHAPTER XV.

Down the Columbia.

CHAPTER XVI.

Fort Vancouver to San Francisco.

CHAPTER XVII.

San Francisco.

CHAPTER XVIII.

San Francisco (continued).

CHAPTER XXIV.

Tucson to Prescott (continued).

CHAPTER XXV.

Prescott, the Apaches, etc.

CHAPTER XXVI.

Prescott to Los Angelos.

THE GREAT WEST

AND

THE PACIFIC COAST.

CHAPTER I.

FROM NEW YORK TO FORT RILEY, KANSAS.

ACROSS America, from New York to San Francisco, may be roughly estimated as three thousand miles. The first third of this occupied us only about three days and three nights, though the whole trip consumed just less than a twelve-month. From New York to St. Louis, *via* Cincinnati, was our first stage, and of course by railroad. We left New York, Tuesday, July 24, 1866, by the Erie Railway, and on the following Thursday afternoon reached St. Louis in time for a late dinner. Tarrying here a day or two, to pick up some information about the Plains, we passed on to Leavenworth; and thence, after a longer pause to Fort Riley. The Union Pacific Railroad, Eastern Division (or Kansas Pacific, as it is now generally called), halted then at Waumega, some thirty miles from Fort Riley, whence we reached Riley by stage-coach. The coach itself was a lumbering, weather-beaten vehicle, with sorry teams of horses; it was a hot August afternoon, with rolling clouds of dust;

we had nine passengers inside and three outside, with freight and baggage everywhere; and altogether this little stage-ride was a good initiation into the mysteries and miseries of stage-coaching across the continent.

From New York to St. Louis is already a series of towns and cities, with the country as a whole well settled up, for America. The Great West, it is soon seen, is no longer the valley of Ohio and the prairies of Illinois. It has long since crossed the Mississippi, and emigrated beyond the Missouri. What used to be called the "West" has already become the centre; and "out west" now means Kansas or Colorado, if anything at all. The Erie road, with its broad-gauge coaches, takes you through the picturesque, as well as rich and fertile regions of northern New Jersey, and western New York, whence the ride through Ohio, down the lovely valley of the Miami to Cincinnati, is substantially as through a garden. Over much of this region, it is plain to be seen, New England has left her mark, never to be effaced. Her school-houses and churches, her intelligence and thrift, are all reproduced (only slightly westernized), and one can see that he is in Yankee-land still at a glance. You might know it, by the omnipresence of white paint and green blinds, if nothing else. You see it in the average inhabitant and detect it in his speech. And yet it is Yankee-land, with enlarged freedom and independence of thought and action, and therefore doubly welcome. Southern Indiana and Illinois, you find rapidly filling up; but they still seem much behind that sunny heart of Ohio, the Miami Valley. Populated largely by the overflow from Kentucky and Tennessee—chiefly the "poor whites" of those former slave states—the results are everywhere unmistakable. Evidently, even to the passing traveller, the average Hoosier or Sucker, as yet.

is much behind the average Buckeye, and he will find it a hard task to overtake him. The lineal descendant of the Cavalier and the Corncracker, how can he expect to compete successfully with the regular representative of the Roundhead and the Yankee?

Cincinnati and St. Louis strike you as large and growing cities; but they do not impress you like Chicago, at least as she did before the great fire. They seem to have taken Quaker Philadelphia, as their type and model, rather than buoyant New York. Many of their streets, you find similarly named, and a like atmosphere pervades much of their business. In talking with their magnates of trade and finance, you note a conservative tone, that illy accords with your ideas of the West, and you are inclined to wonder whether the far-famed push and pluck of that romantic region are not myths after all. Buffalo and Toledo, Cleveland and Chicago, however, would soon undeceive you—especially, Chicago. The push and drive, the enterprise and *elan* of New York, that are reproduced so well along our northern tier of cities, all culminated at Chicago—at least before the fire—until she seemed New York incarnate or even intensified. The metropolis and brain of the northwest, how a day in her busy streets braced and inspired one! With all her brave memories of the past, no wonder she still believes enthusiastically in herself, and even in her ashes doubted not her future!

St. Louis, long her rival in trade, we found just beginning to recover from the benumbing effects of slavery and the rebellion. The rebellion, sealing up her railroads and extinguishing her down-river trade, had given her a bad set back. But she was already fast picking up the broken threads of her commerce, and was again preparing to contend with Chicago for the palm of supremacy. Seated on the Mississippi, with a vast river trade up and down, and an immense region back of her, her geographical position could scarcely be surpassed, and no doubt she has a grand and noble future before her. Her levees, we found, thronged with steamers, some up for New Orleans 1,200 miles south; others for Fort Benton 3,100 miles north and west. Her population already exceeded a quarter of a million. Her suburbs were steadily filling up, in spite of numerous sinkholes in the limestone formation there. Her streets were already well gridironed with horse-railroads. Her facilities for business were large and increasing. And with her vast system of rivers, north to the British Dominion and south to the gulf, and her rapidly developing back country—even to the Rocky Mountains and New Mexico—nature seems to have destined her to become the great and abiding metropolis of all that region. Her vast bridge and tunnels were not yet begun, but she was already prophesying great things for the future.

From St. Louis, three hundred miles through Missouri, to Leavenworth, Kansas, you find a noble region, that needs only a live population to make it a garden. It is mostly rich rolling prairie, but with more timber and streams than in Illinois, and with limestone abounding nearly everywhere. All along the route, it was plain to be seen, Missouri had suffered sadly from slavery. Both in population and business, in town and country, clearly "the trail of the serpent" had been over her all. But the wave of immigration, now that slavery was dead, had already reached her, and we found its healthful cur rents everywhere overflowing her bottoms and prairies. The new-comers seemed to be largely Yankee and German, almost everywhere. France once so predominant here, was already supplanted by Germany, and the Teuton bade fair to rule Missouri soon, even then. At Hermann, where we stopped for dinner, a German Hebe tendered us excellent native wine, and the culture of the grape, we learned, had already become a leading industry of this section of the state. The sturdy Rhine-men, as true to freedom as in the days of Tacitus, were already everywhere planting vineyards, and in the near future were sure of handsome returns from petty farms, that our old time "Pikes" and "Border Ruffians" would have starved on. Throughout the ride, the Missouri or Big-Muddy, as the Indians call it, was often in sight, a broad tawny stream; and many of its bends and reaches were so beautiful, that it hardly seemed to deserve that savage criticism of Bayard Taylor's, as being "too lazy to wash itself." Its banks as a rule are higher and better, than those of the Mississippi anywhere below Cairo, and its bottom lands seemed unsurpassed in fertility.

Leavenworth, on the Missouri, where it takes a final bend north, was still the entrepôt for New Mexico and the plains. Omaha had already tapped the Colorado and Utah trade and travel, and has since mainly absorbed them, by the completion of the Union Pacific railroad. But Leavenworth still had a large trade and travel of her own, as a point of departure for New Mexico and the Plains, and seemed destined to maintain it. Only a decade or so before, she was without a house or inhabitant; but now she claimed thirty-thousand people, and was rapidly increasing. We found many handsome stores and elegant residences everywhere going up. Her streets were fast being graded and macadamized, and the guttering especially was most solid and substantial. She had several daily papers already, with weekly editions of a large circulation. Many of her stores were doing a wholesale business of a million of dollars annually. A fine Catholic church was being erected, which when completed promised to be the chief ornament of the city. But the largest and showiest building there then was a combined brewery and dance house, which augured badly for the town. Off on the suburbs of the city, we passed a park of wagons or "prairie-schooners," acres in extent, tangible evidence that we had already struck the commerce of the Plains.

By Lawrence and Topeka, already towns of several thousand people, over the historic plains of Kansas, we sped along up the valley of the Kaw or Kansas to Waumega; and thence, as I have said, by stage to Fort Riley. Junction City, just beyond Fort Riley, at the confluence of the Republican and Smoky Hill rivers, we found to be a hamlet of several hundred people, and already growing rapidly. It had been projected, with the expectation that the railroad would bend north here, and ascending the Republican go thence to Denver, which would have made Junction the last station and grand depot for all New Mexico and much of the Rocky Mountain region. But, as it had been decided afterwards to keep on up the Smoky Hill instead, Junction had missed of much of its importance. Its location, however, was good, at the confluence thus of two rivers; and with its single street of straggling houses, of all styles of architecture, and in every stage of construction, it was a good specimen of a frontier town, in the first year of its settlement.

The country as a whole, thus far through Kansas, much surpassed our expectations. Not only were the broad bottoms of the Kaw everywhere dotted with farms, but even the high rolling prairies beyond were fast settling up. Of course, settlements grew more scattering the farther we progressed westward; but they were always in sight and everywhere rapidly increasing. Herds of horses and cattle grazed along the bottoms, and grouse and sage-hens whirred up by the roadside as we sped along. At one point, a brace of oxen, yoked together, got upon the track, and our engine mangled the poor beasts dreadfully before they escaped. The road, as yet, was poorly ditched, and without fences on either side, so that horses and cattle strayed across it quite at will. The wheat-crop had everywhere been fair, and Indian corn was promising to be magnificent. Corn had looked well, all through Ohio and Indiana, Illinois and Missouri; but in the Kansas bottoms it was superb in its "embattled glory," and seemed to be a great favorite with the farmers. Indeed, Kansas, both in soil and climate, is a rare state, and well worth to freedom all the blood and treasure she cost us. True she lacks timber; but so far she had got along, and the weight of testimony seemed everywhere to be that her growth of timber improved with the reclamation and settlement of the country. The Indian was everywhere retiring before the pale faces, and the autumnal fires ceasing with his departure, bushes and trees soon appeared, and we heard repeated instances of springs even breaking out, where none had been known before. As an offset to her want of timber, coal had been discovered in many places, and all through the valley of the Kaw, she has a cream-colored limestone in the bluffs, that works up beautifully for building purposes. When first quarried, it is so soft that a common hand-saw or chisel can dress it into any shape desired; but exposure to the atmosphere soon hardens it, and then it continues so. In appearance it resembles the Milwaukee free-stone, that used to make Michigan Avenue, Chicago, so handsome and stately, and as a building material will prove immensely valuable through all Southern Kansas. At Junction City it was being got out by machinery, and fashioned into blocks by horse-power. A company controlled the business, and as they could furnish this elegant stone at a much less cost than lumber or brick, they were anticipating very handsome profits.

The scenery of Kansas possesses many points of interest, but as a whole lacks grandeur and sublimity. The view from Prospect Ridge, back of Leavenworth, up and down the Missouri, is good; but the landscape from Indian Point, near Junction City, up the Smoky Hill, has more scope and variety, and was the finest we saw. Here, and at other points, are some superb specimens of river terraces. We counted four and five separate "benches," as they call them there, or terraces, in many places, and the ancient water-marks of past geologic ages seemed very evident. The rounded appearance of the country generally, cropping out here and there into rough and misshapen ridges, indicated pretty clearly the former water-line, and we often interested ourselves in tracing it for miles.

Kansas, of course, abounds in enterprise and thrift. Saved to freedom by Sharpe's rifles and the Bible, she invested largely in the school-house and the church, and already reaps her fit reward. Her Yankees whittle away just as cutely as they used to in New England, and her Western men spread themselves hugely as elsewhere. Since the war, she had received quite a large accession of population from our ex-officers and soldiers. We found specimens of the Boys in Blue scattered almost everywhere, and usually they were doing well. A fine *esprit du corps* animated them, and will keep them knit together for the future. At various points we found them just "squatted" on a quarter-section, and with the very rudest surroundings, but ever plucky and hopeful. At Junction we met a late Paymaster, U. S. Vol's., who was half-owner of the chief grocery and liquor-store, as well as partner in a stone-quarry, and was about establishing a National Bank. He was a man of spirit and enterprise, and seemed to have enough surplus energy left for several more employments.

At Leavenworth, up at the old Fort, we saw our first Indians—a party of Delawares. They consisted of Fall-Leaf, war-chief of the Delawares, his nephew General Jackson, and a handful of other braves. They were dressed in the usual rough costume of the border, but with an eagle-feather or two in their broad-brimmed sombreros trailing in the wind. Fall-Leaf was a noble specimen of the Indian in a half-civilized state. He was a brawny, athletic, powerful fellow, five feet eleven inches high, weighed one hundred and ninety-six pounds, and was fifty-five years old. A perfect mass of bone and muscle, without an ounce of superfluous flesh, his frame was a sight to look upon—especially the massive splendor of his neck and chest. A Hercules of the Plains, we could well believe the stories told of his great strength and powers of endurance. General Jackson was a lithe, light-built man, about thirty-six years of age, and in physique almost the opposite of his brawny uncle. Three of them had just been engaged as guides to a military expedition about leaving for the Indian country, and a fourth was going along as interpreter. Fall-Leaf had long served the government, with marked fidelity, as guide on the Plains and in the far Indian country, and received one hundred and fifty dollars per month and rations when absent on such duty. He was familiar with the whole country west, as far as the Rocky Mountains, and southward to

New Mexico, and was reputed as invaluable in his way. He told me the Delawares numbered about a thousand souls yet, and had stood at those figures for several years. They occupy a Reservation of several thousand acres on the Missouri just below Leavenworth, and are engaged generally in farming and stock-raising. They have a church, pretty generally attended, and a good school, well-patronized. He said his people were fully impressed with the importance of education and religion, and generally there was an earnest desire among them to have their children learn all "Pale-Face ways." He said he took a drink of "fire-water" himself occasionally, on cold or wet days, and rather liked it; but that, as a rule, drunkenness was on the decrease among the Delawares, and he was glad of it. He had a wife and eight children, and said they allowed "only one wife at a time in his tribe." He said he was born far away toward the rising sun, on a river among the mountains; and when I showed him a map, he immediately pointed out the head-waters of the Delaware. When I told him I had just come from there, and that my "wigwam" stood upon its banks, he seemed greatly interested. The first steamboat he ever saw, was many years before at St. Louis, and he thought it "Very good," because "It went itself! Puff! Puff! No paddle!" His first locomotive, was quite recently at Leavenworth, and he thought it "Much good! Went whiz! Beat buffalo or pony!" Of the telegraph, he said, "I no understand; but very much good! Heap swift! Like arrow or bullet between wide places; only heap better!"

He said, the Delawares believed in the Great Manitou, who made earth, and sky, and everything; but many did not believe in the Evil Manitou. He himself seemed to be a pretty good Universalist. He thought God "very much good," and could'nt imagine how any lesser being could interfere with Him. "Perhaps, Evil Manitou somewhere; but Fall-Leaf know only Good Manitou." He admitted some of his people believed in spirits; but he himself had never seen any, and was skeptical on the whole subject. Some medicine-men, he said, claimed to have seen them, and to be able to control them; but he thought the whole thing "a heap humbug."

Fall-Leaf, as I have said, was then War Chief of the Delawares. In his time he had been quite a noted warrior, and was proud of his reputation for bravery and prowess. His last fight against the Plains Indians had been about two years before, when he covered the retreat of a squad of infantry, from a body of mounted Cheyennes and Arrapahoes, and brought them all safely off. His last fight at the head of the Delawares had been some ten years before, when with less than fifty warriors he encountered and fought over two hundred Pawnees, and whipped them well. Altogether, he supposed, he had killed and scalped two or three hundred Indians, in his time; but never a pale-face. He was a dignified and quiet enough looking Red Skin to talk to through an interpreter, and occasionally would grunt out a little broken English himself; but when roused, and with the fury of battle upon him, no doubt he would be an ugly customer to deal with. His face was full of smothered force and fire, of latent power and fierceness, like a tamed tiger's; and notwithstanding his peaceful demeanor, he all the while suggested that a single war-whoop, or a scalping-knife flashing through the air, would speedily transform the gentle Fall-Leaf into a hideous savage again.

Beyond Topeka we passed St. Mary's, a Catholic Mission among the Pottawotamies. These Indians had a Reservation there then thirty miles square, of as fine land as there was in Kansas. Stock-raising seemed to be their chief occupation, though they had some fields well fenced, and their corn crops were looking well. They lived in one-story log-cabins, and by dint of years of hard work the missionaries had succeeded in reducing them to a sort of semi-civilization; but the aborigine survived still, and cropped out fearfully everywhere. It was an anomaly and an anachronism to see them driving teams and threshing grain; and they themselves seemed to confess it by their awkwardness. Beyond Manhattanville we met *en route* a large party of them—braves, squaws and papooses—returning from a Buffalo hunt on the Plains. Some were in wagons with their spoils of buffalo meat and robes; but the majority went careering along on horseback. Most of them were in semi-civilized costume, not much rougher than an average borderer, though their head-gear usually ran much to feather. A few of their young squaws were decidedly pretty and piquant, and, as they ambled by on their gaily-caparisoned ponies, created quite a sensation among us; but the older ones were hideous looking hags.

In all this part of Kansas, the Indian had already had his day, and everywhere was being fast eliminated. The valleys of the Kaw and its two chief tributaries, the Republican and Smoky Hill, had already heard the whistle of the white man's locomotive, and the whole region there was beginning to shake with the tread of the onward march of civilization. As "Bleeding Kansas," she had had her dark days; but these, happily, were past, and the tide wave of eastern immigration was now surging and swelling all up and down her borders. We met cheery voices and friendly hands at every stage of progress; and could not but bid Kansas a hearty God-speed as we journeyed on.

CHAPTER II.

FROM THE KANSAS TO THE PLATTE.

IT was the middle of August, before I was ready to leave Fort Riley; and now a word about my *compagnons du voyage.* These were two, Mr. J. D. L. of Boston, my well-tried clerk and friend; and Dr. B. E. M. of New York, then recently Ass't. Editor ———— Magazine. Mr. L. had been with me for several years in the field and at post; was active, intelligent, alert; and was as capital a shot, as he was rare a penman. Dr. M. I knew but slightly; but he came well-recommended, as a *litterateur* and gentleman, and I was glad to have his company. He had been considerable of a traveller in Europe, and was now desirous of crossing the Continent to San Francisco, whence he might go over to Japan and China. Another gentleman had also talked much of joining us; but his heart failed him at the last hour, and he preceded us to California, *via* the Isthmus.

My inspections at Leavenworth and Riley being completed, we left Fort Riley just after sunrise Aug. 16th, and soon were fairly afloat on the Plains, and off for the Pacific. Hitherto the railroad had still served to connect us with the East. But now we bade good-bye to cars and locomotives, and did not see them again until we heard their tramp and whistle two thousand miles away, in the cañon of the Columbia. "Afloat," I think,

2*

is the only right word for the Plains; because the first impression they give you is that of the sea, so vast is their extent, and even the wagons that cross them—huge, lumbering, fore-and-aft vehicles, with from eight to ten yoke of oxen each—in border parlance are called "Prairie-Schooners."

My orders were to proceed from Fort Riley on the Kaw or Kansas, to Fort Kearney on the Platte; and, as the shortest and most direct route, we were now off, across the country, in execution of them. Our route lay northwest across the high "divide" between the Kansas and the Platte, through central Kansas; and as there was no stage-line here, we had to go by ambulance. Neither was there any well-defined road; but we were told that at Marysville, some sixty miles north, we could strike the great Overland Route, from Atchison, Mo. and afterwards travel westward by that. Our "outfit" consisted of one ambulance for ourselves, one army-wagon for our escort of five infantry-men, and another for baggage, forage, and rations. Our friends at Riley knew little about the intervening country, except that Indians were reported there; and as their cavalry was all out scouting, could furnish only the infantry escort, as above. Even this seemed small; but we were all well-armed ourselves; and what with our repeating rifles and revolvers, few as we were, felt good for fifty red skins or more, come as they would.

For the first seventy-five miles or so, we were seldom out of sight of scattered ranches; but long before reaching Fort Kearney—some two hundred and thirty miles from Riley—they had dwindled away to only the occasional stage-stations, every ten or twelve miles or so apart. Along the creeks and streams, we found farms rapidly springing up; but the "divides" between these were generally barren and withered up. Oftentimes we could find no water for ten or twelve miles, and wood was even rarer. Of course, we "camped-out" during the whole trip, and frequently had to carry our necessary fire-wood fifteen and twenty miles. In the spring, all these "divides," as well as the bottoms, are clothed with luxuriant verdure; but in summer, the rainless atmosphere there sweeps over them, like a sirocco, and everything soon perishes. At night, we found the air grew rapidly cold, and we shivered under our blankets; but in the middle of the day, the sun fairly blazed from a cloudless sky, and I have seldom felt its effects more severely. When we struck the Overland Route, we found its roadway a mass of impalpable dust, black and stifling. With the breeze dead-ahead, or athwart our course, we got along very well; but when it chopped around behind us, the black prairie soil rose in clouds, and our poor mules suffered terribly. Two of them, indeed, died outright, from heat and dust, before reaching the Platte, though we drove very carefully, seldom averaging over thirty-five miles per day. Evidently this part of Kansas must grow more trees, and thus secure more rain and moisture, before these high "divides" or ridges between the Kansas and the Platte will amount to much for farming purposes.

After a week of travelling like this, our first sight of the Platte, with its broad and luxuriant bottoms waving with verdure, was refreshing to the eye. Our jaded animals snuffed the water and grass afar off, and of their own accord broke into a trot as we neared them. We struck the river at Valley Ranche, a collection of a dozen or so sod-houses, some seven or eight miles below Fort Kearney. The Platte here is a mile or more wide, and looks like a noble stream; but it is shallow and treacherous with shoals and quicksands, as well as tainted with alkali, and altogether is about as thorough a swindle as a river can well be. Its northern bank was still fringed with cottonwoods, but its southern had scarcely a bush to break the monotony. Ascending it to Fort Kearney, we found its broad bottoms literally swarming with countless millions of Plains grasshoppers. They really covered the ground, a moving army; they filled the air, coming in all directions, their white wings twinkling like a snow-squall. Egypt's plague of locusts could scarcely have been worse, for they swept a broad tract of country clean of everything, as they moved eastward. We found the settlers complaining of them bitterly, as the greatest pests of the region, destroying all vegetation and forbidding all attempts at farming, some seasons. Said a butternut Missourian, in speaking of them: "The pesky varmints! They eat up all my corn, and tobacco. And then when I cussed 'em for it, they coolly sat on the Shanghai-fence thar, and squirted tobacco juice at me!" But they have been almost as bad in other new states, at first, and it was thought the advance of our line of settlements would soon subdue or extirpate them.

On leaving Riley, we had anticipated some good shooting *en route;* but game generally proved rare, or else quite shy. Prairie-chickens or grouse abounded until we got beyond the settlements, when they disappeared almost entirely. They are a timid bird, and hard to approach on foot; but on horseback or in a wagon you may get close upon them very easily. Feeding in the grass or reeds, in small flocks, at the first sound they pop their heads up erect, as if inviting the sportsman to crack away at them. This we did continually from our ambulance or behind it, and seldom went into camp the first few days without prairie-chickens enough for all. We expected to see deer and buffalo, but were unable to catch sight of even one, being too far east yet. As we approached the Platte, we saw a solitary antelope, gazing at us from a distant bluff; but when we drew nearer he wheeled about and dashed quickly out of sight among its sand-hills. Doves and cow-birds appeared in quite considerable numbers when we struck the Overland Route, and, of course, the crow or buzzard also—the omnipresent scavenger of the Plains. Our first prairie-dogs turned up on the Little Blue, just beyond Thompson's. Here was quite a village of the little fellows, with their sentinels duly out; but as we came nearer, the alarm was sounded, and soon "whisk" went a hundred tails, as they plunged head downwards into their holes. A few noses peeped cautiously out as we drove by; but the most of their dogships continued *perdu*. Just above one hole a diminutive owl still stood guard in the deepening twilight, and the settlers insisted that the old yarn about the prairie-dog, the owl, and the rattlesnake being tenants in common—all keeping house in one and the same hole—is really true. We overheard our teamsters (all old Plainsmen) disputing about this one night, around their camp-fire, as we lay awake; but their final conclusion, and the weight of frontier testimony, seemed to be in favor of this Happy Family.

Of Indians we heard a great deal, but saw none. Rumors of them increased as we moved north and west; but, if about, they gave us a wide berth. At Virginia Station, about half way, the station-keeper reported the Pawnees in force on the Little Blue; and at Big Sandy the last stage-driver through from Fort Kearny reported Fort Reno taken, Fort Laramie besieged and Kearny itself in danger. He said, one settler had already been lanced and killed on the Little Blue; that the Pawnees there—six hundred lodges strong—were moody and hostile; and, as our party was too small for effective resistance advised our return. Farther on we found ranches here and there abandoned, with the crops left growing; and one day we descried a solitary horseman in the distance galloping rapidly towards us, that we were sure must be a red skin. But as he came nearer he proved to be a settler's half-grown boy, who had been up the road several miles helping a neighbor move. He, too, had heard "Big Injun" stories, but said his people did not mind them much. These reports, at first, I confess, were rather startling, as we had no idea of losing our scalps; but as our safe advance day by day exploded one after another of them, we soon became quite skeptical on the Indian question. The chief effect was to increase our prudence and vigilance. We looked well to our arms morning and evening, and seldom halted, even briefly, without posting a guard. In due time we reached and passed the valley of the Little Blue without seeing a Pawnee—they had all gone off a fortnight before to the Republican and Smoky Hill to hunt buffalo—and finally arrived at Fort Kearney in safety. There they laughed at the idea of Indians south or east of them, but confessed to ugly reports about Reno and Laramie. Ultimately, as we got farther west, these also proved false; and our conclusion as to Big Injun stories in general, was not very favorable.

The few settlers along the route consisted chiefly of New Englanders, with a goodly sprinkling of Germans. They generally had milk and eggs to sell, but seldom butter or vegetables. We camped one night on Fancy Creek, near a Mr. Segrist's, where we got tomatoes and onions, as well as eggs and milk; and as we had shot several prairie-chickens during the day, we supped luxuriously. Our mess-kit was rather a primitive affair, not much to speak of, and our cook quite a worthless fellow, as it turned out; but L. developed a talent that way very surprising, and so we got along comfortably. This Segrist himself was quite a character in his way. A Pennsylvania Dutchman by birth, he was bred in Indiana, but emigrated to Fancy Creek during the Kansas troubles, to help save the territory to freedom. Squatting on a quarter-section there, he first built himself a log-cabin, and then subsequently enlarged and improved this by a "lean-to;" now he had just completed a good two-story stone house, of magnesian limestone, and aspired to luxury. He had flocks and herds well about him; he was a hearty, cheery man, not afraid of hard work, nor a spice of danger; and, it was plain to be seen, would soon be a rich man, if he kept on. Of course, he was a Republican in politics, and took the St. Louis *Westliche Post.*

On Wild-Cat Creek, the first day out from Fort Riley, we struck a Mr. Silvers, who proved to be a minister of the United Brethren. He had a half-section of land there, and his son-in-law as much more just adjoining. They were both living in rude shanties put up by themselves, but seemed happy and contented. During the war, he had sent one son to the army, and when Price invaded Kansas he himself shouldered his Plains rifle, and marched to the defence of Lawrence and Topeka. When at home, he worked upon his farm; but he had a frontier circuit, with preaching places a hundred miles in every direction, which took him away most of the time. He seemed to be a veritable missionary, looking up the lost sheep scattered along the Border, and we bade him God-speed. His "gude wife" gave us a bowl of buttermilk fresh from the churn, and we paid her in the latest eastern newspapers.

CHAPTER III.

UP THE PLATTE TO DENVER.

THE Union Pacific Railroad had then just reached Fort Kearney from Omaha, and was the sensation of the hour. With a large force of men, it was being pushed rapidly up the north bank of the Platte; but as our road lay up the south bank, we did not cross to see it. There was little to prevent its rapid progress of a mile and even two miles per day, as the Platte valley ascends gradually, and for railroad purposes is almost everywhere practically a level. We now dismissed our ambulance and escort, with instructions to return to Fort Riley, and transferred ourselves, bag and baggage, to Holliday's Overland Stages, which here connected with the railroad.

This stage-line was long one of the first enterprises of America, and, as the forerunner of the railroad did its part well in carrying civilization across the continent. It was then owned and controlled by Mr. Ben Holliday, an enterprising Missourian, but then living in New York. It had originally fallen into his hands for debt, but he had since greatly enlarged and extended it. It then ran from Fort Kearney to Denver, with branches to the mining regions; thence across the Rocky Mountains to Salt Lake;* thence through Idaho to the Columbia, with branches through Montana; extending in all, nearly three thousand miles, employing six thousand horses and

* The line thence to California was run by Wells, Fargo & Co.

mules, and more than three hundred coaches. He paid his general superintendent ten thousand dollars per year; his division superintendents, half that; and lesser employees proportionately. His hay, and grain, and provisions, he had to haul hundreds of miles, distributing them along the route, and his fuel frequently one hundred and fifty. To offset all this, he carried the U. S. Mail, daily each way, and for this service alone received over half a million of dollars per year from the government. In addition, his passenger fares from Fort Kearney to Denver were one hundred and fifty dollars; to Salt Lake, three hundred; to Nevada, four hundred and fifty; to California, five hundred; and to Idaho and Montana, about the same.

We found his stages to be our well-known Concord coaches, and they quite surpassed our expectations, both as to comfort and to speed. They were intended for nine inside—three seats full—and as many more outside, as could be induced to get on. Their teams were either four or six horses, depending on the roads, and the distance between stations. The animals themselves were our standing wonder; no broken-down nags, or half-starved Rosinantes, like our typical stage-horses east; but, as a rule, they were fat and fiery, and would have done credit to a horseman anywhere. Wiry, gamey, as if feeling their oats thoroughly, they often went off from the stations at a full gallop; at the end of a mile or so would settle down to a square steady trot; and this they would usually keep up right along until they reached the next station. These "stations" varied from ten to twelve miles apart, depending on water and grass, and consisted of the rudest kind of a shanty or sod-house ordinarily. Here we would find another team, ready harnessed, prancing to be gone, and in fifteen minutes or so would be off on the road again. Halts were made twice a day for meals, forty minutes each, and with this exception we kept bowling ahead night and day. Our meals were fair for the region; generally coffee, beef-steak or bacon, potatoes, and saleratus-biscuit hot; but the prices — one dollar and one dollar and a half per meal—seemed extortionate. In this way, we often made ten and twelve miles per hour, while on the road; and seldom drove less than one hundred, and one hundred and twenty-five miles, per day and night.

We talked a good deal, or essayed to, with the drivers; but as a rule, they were a taciturn species. Off the box they were loquacious enough; but when mounted, with four or six in hand, they either thought it unprofessional to talk, or else were absorbed too much in their business. I remarked this to a Division Superintendent, when he replied, "You bet! A talking driver is like a whistling girl or crowing hen, always of no account!" They each had their drive of fifty or sixty miles, up one day, and back the next, and to the people along the route were important personages. Many we found were from New Hampshire, and Western New York. Usually they were a roving class; but when they once settled down to stage-driving, they seldom left it permanently. There seemed to be a fascination about the life, hard as it was, and we found many of these Jehus who had been driving for years, and never expected to quit it. They were fond of tobacco and whiskey, and rolled out ponderous oaths, when things did not go to suit them; but as a rule, they were hearty and generous fellows, and were doing the world good service. As bearers of the U. S. Mail, they felt themselves kings of the road, and were seldom loth to show it. "Clar the road! Git out of the way thar with your bull-teams!" was a frequent salutation, when overtaking or meeting wagon-trains; and if this was not complied with quickly, they made little hesitation in running into the oxen, and swearing till all was blue. I have a vivid recollection of one instance of the kind, when we ran into an ox-team, and the justly exasperated teamster sent us his compliments, in the shape of a bullet whizzing through the air, as we whirled away again.

In fellow-passengers we were remarkably lucky. Col. B. was a good specimen of the ups and downs of an average Westerner. He was a graduate of West Point, or at least had been a cadet there, and afterwards served some years in the Regular Army. Retiring to civil life, he subsequently was elected Lieut.-Governor of a western state, and afterwards became Governor — the incumbent dying. When the war broke out, he turned up as Colonel of a volunteer regiment; and now, like the Irishman, having been "promoted backward," was vegetating as sutler at a post on the Plains. He was a man of rare wit and intelligence, of infinite jest and humor (his own worst enemy), and we were sorry to part when he reached his post. Then we had a Swiss artist, M. Buchser, sent over by his government to make a grand painting illustrative of our late war, embracing our most famous statesmen and generals, for the Capitol at Berne. Having a month or two of leisure, he was spending it wisely in making a run to the Plains and the Rocky Mountains. Now he was hurrying on to join Gen. Sherman at Julesburg, whence he was to accompany him and his brother, the Ohio Senator, on a tour of inspection to Fort Laramie, Buford, Denver, and then east again *via* the Arkansas. He was a close observer, had travelled much on both continents, and was very chatty and companionable, speaking English like a native. He sketched constantly *en route*, making "studies" of the Platte valley from the top of the stage-coach, and when we parted at Fort McPherson, it was with the mutual hope of meeting again at Denver. Next we had a Doctor of Divinity from Illinois, of the Methodist persuasion, *en route* to Golden City and the Mountains, in search of health, and to look after certain mining interests of some company in the east. Then we had a banker from New York, of copperhead tendĕncies, bound for Idaho City, also in quest of mines; but his wife was a staunch Republican, and more than offset his political heresies. We had others besides, merchants, miners, telegraph-men, etc., and really not one disagreeable person.

As to the weather, we found that intensely hot in the middle of the day (it being the last of August and first of September), but the mornings and evenings were delightful, and the nights always superb. Most of the passengers preferred the inside; but Dr. M. and I chose the outside, which with some inconveniences had its advantages after all. By day it gave us a wider view of the country; and at night we used to give our blankets a "shake down" on the flat top (first borrowing an armful of hay from some station), and then go luxuriously to sleep. At first when we tried this, not understanding the philosophy of the situation, we came near rolling off when the coach would pitch into a chuck-hole, or give a lurch from heel to 'port; but we soon learned to boom ourselves on, with a rope or strap from railing to railing, and thus managed to secure not a little of "tired nature's sweet restorer, balmy sleep," while our fellow-passengers down below (nine inside), packed like sardines in a box, got seldom a wink.

The most of the time, the moon was at the full or about that, and superb in her unveiled glory. The sky was packed with a myriad of stars, far beyond what we ever see east. The air, pure and dry, free from both dew and frost, was a perpetual tonic to lungs and brain. Every hundred miles or so we stopped over a day or two to inspect some Military Post, and so got rested. The scenery from day to day was ever fresh and changing, abounding in new sensations. And, in short, in all my experiences of life, I have few pleasanter recollections than in thus staging it outside, across the Plains, and up the Platte to Denver. One night, however, a wind-storm from the summit of the Rocky Mountains struck us, and for hours raged furiously—raw and gusty, piercing to the bone. But at midnight we rolled into Fort Morgan, and halting in its hospitable quarters, waited until the wind blew itself out.

The sunsets now and then were magnificent, and one particularly beyond Fort Sedgwick or Julesburg deserves further mention. We were rolling rapidly along, when the sun went down behind a cloud, that formed the huge segment of a circle on the horizon, and from around and behind this his rays came flashing forth with a beauty—a glory and a gorgeousness—that we had never seen equalled. Heavy, sombre clouds hung about the west, while over head and off to the east they thinned out into fleecy mottled masses almost invisible, until his reflected rays illuminated them. Up among these, across the whole dome of the heavens, the colors flamed and went, as tremulous as a maiden's blushes—now crimson and gold, then purple and violet, and now again a dreamy, hazy, half-pink, half rosy light, that baffles description. I had seen gorgeous sunsets elsewhere—on the Hudson, among the Alleghanies, by the sea—but never any so full of glory and majesty, and sublimity as this. The fleecy masses overhead seemed to hang in curtains, one behind the other, like the top scenes at a theatre, and the shifting light playing about among them added to the illusion. Nature seemed here to enrobe the heavens in her most magnificent and gorgeous tapestry, as if trying to show what glorious fabrics her noiseless looms could weave; and over all brooded that mysterious silence of the Plains, that seems like the hush of eternity. It must have been some such scene, that flamed through the poet's brain when he wrote:

> "All the west was washed with fire;
> Great clouds were standing round the setting sun,
> Like gaping caves, fantastic pinnacles,
> Citadels throbbing in their own fierce light,
> Tall spires that came and went like spires of flame,
> Cliffs quivering with fire-snow, and peaks
> Of pilèd gorgeousness, and rocks of fire
> A-tilt and poised, bare beaches, crimson seas."

A singular part of it all was, that passengers in the next stage-coach, a hundred miles east, were struck with the same magnificent sunset, and followed us into Denver with similar accounts of its grandeur and sublimity, at the point where they had been.

CHAPTER IV.

UP THE PLATTE TO DENVER (*Concluded*).

THE Platte Valley itself is a great furrow or groove in the heart of the Plains proper, extending substantially due west from the Missouri to the Rocky Mountains. On the line of our tier of northern cities, and so in the track of northern ideas across the continent, it is as if nature intended it for a great natural highway, and already it had come to its fulfilment. Its early selection by our army of emigrants to Colorado, Utah, California, etc., was because of its supplying the three great desiderata of wood, water and grass, better than any other route; and its easy grades, as well as accumulating trade and travel, made it the predestined pathway of the Pacific Railroad. It varies in breadth from five to ten miles, and is bounded on either side by abrupt bluffs two or three hundred feet high, whence outstretch the Plains proper. Extending from the foot of these bluffs, for a mile or more usually, is a level plateau or "bench" (in Plains parlance), composed of sand and gravel, and worthless for agricultural purposes from want of moisture. To be sure, during the spring a meagre herbage is sustained here, but long before summer ends everything green parches and withers up. Then come the bottoms proper, on either side of the river, of rich loam and clay, which produce grass in goodly quantities all summer, and we saw no reason why they should not also grow most cereals and vegetables.

Perhaps it is too far north for Indian corn; but wheat, barley, oats and rye ought to flourish there, except in localities where the soil may be too strongly impregnated with alkali or soda. Their natural adaptation, however, is for grass, and I apprehend we shall soon have our flocks and herds, by the acre, feeding all up and down by the Platte. When you reach the North Platte the valley of course subdivides, and you continue on up the valley of the South Platte to Denver. The fertile and cultivable bottoms, of course, narrow as you advance; nevertheless, they maintain a considerable breadth nearly everywhere, despite encroaching bluffs, and around and beyond Denver are made highly productive by occasional irrigation as needed. Utilize the unfailing waters of the Platte by windmills or otherwise, as they do their streams in Italy, Egypt and China, and the Platte valley throughout its length will yet become a garden.

The Platte itself to the eye is a broad and lusty stream, and in places, as near Fort McPherson, expands into a sea of islands, most refreshing to behold after days of dusty travel. But while in volume sufficient for a first-class river, its banks are so shifting and its sand-bars so numerous and variable, that it has always proved practically unnavigable, notwithstanding our western rivers swarm with stern-wheelers, many of which it is said only require a respectable ditch or half decent dew. Unbridged and without ferries, we found it crossed only at a few well-defined fords, and even these were so cursed by quicksands, that trains in crossing stood in great danger of bringing up at Jeddo or Pekin. Its waters were considered healthy and sweet, notwithstanding a trace of alkali, and with all its shortcomings, it seemed nevertheless a perfect God-send to that particular region. Its banks and islands were usually fringed with cottonwoods and poplars, and furnished almost the only supply of fuel to passing emigrants and travellers. The settled residents there, however, the station-keepers and ranchmen, depended more on the stunted cedars, that abounded generally in all the ravines and cañons, with which the side-bluffs of the valley are more or less seamed. Here also they procured the most of their lumber, and from here supplied thousands of ties for the Union Pacific Railroad. We were surprised to find these cedars so abundant in the cañons, where nothing tree-like was visible until you entered. Then we found the whole bottom and sides frequently lined with them to the top; but there they abruptly ceased, as if close shaven by the winds, which in certain months sweep over the Plains mercilessly.

In both wood and lumber, however, we found the Platte valley sadly lacking, and the whole Plains country generally. Good peat had been found at Julesburg, and bituminous coal was reported near Fort Morgan; but our posts were depending for both fuel and lumber mainly on the Platte and its side cañons. At Fort Sedgwick, near Julesburg, they had been hauling wood nearly a hundred miles, at a cost to the government of over a hundred dollars per cord, there being none nearer or cheaper. Lumber cost one hundred and seventeen dollars per thousand, and shingles fifteen dollars per thousand, and were held cheap at that. The year before, lumber had cost two hundred and five dollars per thousand, and shingles in proportion. Grain (corn and oats) was wagoned from the Missouri, and cost the government, put down at Sedgwick, about seven dollars per bushel. Hay was cut in the vicinity, and cost thirty-four dollars per ton. Recently they had made a contract with shrewd operators in Denver, for lumber at ninety dollars per thousand, and wood at forty-six dollars per cord, both to come from the Rocky Mountains, over two hundred miles away; but the contractors availed themselves of cheap freights by eastward-bound wagon-trains, otherwise returning empty. At Julesburg, we were told, there was not a tree even for fifty miles; formerly there had been a scrubby cottonwood, on the south bank of the Platte there —a lone star in solitary splendor—which was regularly shown to tourists as one of its lions. But this had recently fallen down and floated away, and now Julesburg mourned its loss as "the last of the Mohicans." There was some talk of erecting a monument to its memory; but even this would have to be of "adobe," as stone was equally a rarity there.

Down in the valley proper, the field of vision is limited by the side bluffs, and you see but comparatively little of the country generally. But ascend the bluffs on either side, and the vast ocean of the Plains stretches boundlessly before you—not flat, but billowy with swells and ridges, an illimitable plateau, with only here and there a solitary "butte," sharply defined against the clear sky. In spring this whole vast extent is a wilderness of verdure and flowers; but the summer skies, untempered by rain, as elsewhere said, scorch and burn the ground to cinders, and long before autumn comes all vegetation there practically perishes. Even the hardy buffalo-grass becomes brown and tinder-like, and the only grazing there is in the cañons and valleys. Nevertheless our Plains have hitherto sustained buffalo by the million, and do it still, although these shaggy monsters have of late mostly disappeared from the Platte region. We did not see one in our entire trip to Denver; but a friend, who came through a month or so later, over the Smoky Hill route, where there was less travel, reported buffalo there yet by the horizon full—the whole country being substantially black with them. The short and sweet buffalo-grass is indigenous through all this region, and is said to be nutritious, even when dried up, the year round. What a magnificent range for stock these great Plains will yet afford, when the country becomes more thickly settled up! Much of this region is marked on the old maps as the "Great American Desert;" but from all we saw and heard I doubt not, as a whole, it will yet become the great stock-raising and dairy region of the Republic, whence we shall export beef and mutton, leather and wool, in exchange for cloth and steel.*

We had several fine rides with brother-officers among the cañons and bluffs while stopping over to inspect our military posts *en route*, and a grand gallop one bright September morning over the Plains and far away after antelope. In the cañons and along the bluffs we started plenty of jack-rabbits; but the antelope were shy and apparently always on the run, so much so we could never get within shot of them. We formed a long line across the country, and as we swept forward started two or three small herds; but they were all too fleet for Uncle Sam's coursers. Subsequently we halted, and lying down tried the old hunter's trick of enticing them with a handkerchief on a ramrod, with our rifles ready to blaze away as they drew near; but they were too cunning to be caught by any such rascally flag-of-truce arrangement, and it seemed a shame to attempt it. The ride itself, however, was a great satisfaction, full of excitement, exhilaration, enjoyment. The sky was a perfect sapphire, without cloud or haze. The clear atmosphere braced one's nerves like wine, and revealed distant objects with a pre-Raphaelite distinctness. A

* See Appendix.

pyramid-like "butte," off to the southwest, seemed near at hand, though more than twenty miles away. The ground was baked hard, with a thin covering of dry-grass, except in the occasional buffalo-wallows; and altogether our horses seemed to enjoy the gallop quite as much as we did ourselves. There was just a spice of danger in the ride, too, as Indians were reported prowling about, but none appeared. We left the Platte with its bluffs and cañons behind us, and out into the boundless Plains we rode, on and on, and only drew rein when we discovered that we had lost our reckoning, and were without a compass. The person charged with providing this had forgotten it, and suddenly we found ourselves at sea, without guide or headland. Fortunately we had the well-worn buffalo-trails, that there run almost due north and south—the old paths over which they formerly went to and from the Platte for water—and following up one of these, after an hour or two, we found ourselves in sight of the river again. These "trails" are no wider than ordinary cow-paths, but they are worn deep into the soil, and show by their great number and depth what countless herds of buffalo must have roamed here in other days. They are a sure guide up and down the bluffs, many of which are so precipitous that safe ascent or descent elsewhere seems impossible. But the buffalo, by a wise instinct, seems to have hit just the right point, and deserves credit for such skillful engineering.

The population of the Platte Valley was yet mostly *in futuro*. The little *in esse* was grouped sparsely around the several Military posts—Forts Kearney, McPherson, Sedgwick and Morgan—the intervening stage-stations, and at Julesburg. The largest hamlet, perhaps five hundred inhabitants or so, was near Fort Kearney, having grown up on the outskirts of that post, and bearing the same name. Julesburg consisted of a blacksmith-shop, a grocery, a billiard-saloon, and a half-dozen houses all of adobe. It was on the South Platte, at the point of crossing for the Utah and Montana travel, which here bore away northwest for Bridger's Pass, and so did a considerable business already in canned-fruits and tangle-foot whiskey. A year afterwards, it was the terminus for awhile of the Union Pacific Railroad, went up speedily to two or three thousand inhabitants, and figured largely in eastern journals. But, presently, with the ongoing of the railroad, its importance ceased, and its inhabitants,

> "Folded their tents like the Arabs,
> And silently stole away."

The stage-stations usually had a ranch or two adjoining, though these grew more infrequent, as we got farther west. These were only rude huts of sod or adobe, with dirt-roofs, divided into two apartments—one for sleeping purposes, and the other for a cross-roads grocery. The stock on hand usually consisted largely of tobacco, canned-fruits and vegetables, and the worst varieties of "needle-gun" whiskey, warranted to kill a mile away. Hay and wood were also kept on hand, for sale to passing trains, and many ranchmen managed thus to pick up considerable money in the course of the year. Generally two men occupied a ranch thus together, though sometimes squaws were found serving as "brevet"-wives. Much of their time was spent, especially at night, in playing "poker," "old-sledge," "seven-up," etc. for the want of something else to do; and a newspaper, a Congressional speech, or even a Pub. Doc., was always welcome. Farther west, the stage-stations and ranch-huts were built more substantially, and often were regularly bastioned and loop-holed for a siege. One of the most notable of these was Fort Wicked, about half-way between Julesburg and Denver. It was built of sods and adobe, with a thick wall of the same on three sides, and was really an arrow and bullet-proof block-house. A year or so before, it had been attacked by a party of Cheyennes and Arrapahoes; but the owner and his men showed fight—killed several of the red-skins, and put the rest to flight—whereupon some one christened the place "Fort Wicked," and the name stuck.

Wagon-trains going west or returning east, we met frequently, but not to the extent we anticipated. They usually consisted of from ten to twenty wagons each, with from eight to twelve pairs of mules or yokes of oxen to each wagon. Going up from the "River," as the Missouri was always called, these trains being loaded all had their full complement of wagon-masters, teamsters, cooks, etc. But, returning empty, several wagons were often coupled together—the surplus employees stopping over in the mines. By day, these trains stretched their huge length along, the great white-sheeted wagons or "prairie-schooners" carrying each from ten to twelve thousand pounds; but, at night, their wagons were formed into a "corral," with the animals inside to prevent the Indians stampeding them, and the picturesque effect of such encampments was always pleasing. Even here on the Plains, about the last place we would suppose, the inherent aristocracy of human nature cropped out distinctly. The lords of the lash *par excellence* were the stage-drivers. The next most important, the horse or mule teamsters; and the lowest, the "bull-drivers." The horse or mule teams made from twelve to fifteen miles per day; the ox-trains eight to ten. For real vagabondage, pure and simple, life with one of these

PLAINS INDIANS.

trains seemed hard to beat. An Arab of the desert, or a Gaucho of the pampas, could ask for nothing more nomadic. And if anybody is sick of Sybaris, and anxious to get away from all trace of civilization, here is the place for him. It seemed to be going down to "bed-rock" in the social scale, and afforded a splendid opportunity to study first principles. A school-friend of mine, a man of fine culture, tried it formerly, and his experiences were racy and rare. Subsequently, as miner, land agent, speculator, and lawyer, at Pike's Peak and Denver, he made two or three fortunes and lost them; then emigrated to San Francisco, where he made another as army contractor; and then wisely forsook the fickle goddess, and settled in New York.

Rumors of impending troubles with the Indians thickened as we advanced. The settlers and stage-people said the Indians appeared but little on the road, which was a sure sign that a storm was brewing. Further they said the tribes had had a grand pow-wow recently on the Smoky Hill and the Republican, in which they had agreed to bury the hatchet and make common cause against the pale-faces. Subsequently, later in the autumn, they did attack some stations on the Smoky Hill route, and a stage or two on the Platte route; but we reached Denver unmolested. East of Julesburg, at Baker's ranch, we passed an encampment of Sioux, perhaps two or three hundred, papooses and all, in cone-shaped wigwams, evidently the original of our army "Sibley." While changing horses, we strolled into several of their wigwams, and found them full of braves, squat upon their hams, intently engaged in playing cards. In Indian pantomime, they warmly invited us to participate, but we were obliged to decline the distinguished honor. The squaws were mostly at work on moccasins or blankets, and their tawny little papooses (stark naked, except a breech-cloth) were either practising with bows and arrows, or "lying around loose." The entire party seemed utterly poverty-stricken, even to their ponies and dogs, and, generally, about as wretched as human beings could well be. Their main provisions seemed to be rusty army-rations, which had recently been issued to them at one of our neighboring posts, and without these they would have been practically destitute. Dirty, squalid, indecent, and half-starving, they seemed but little removed above the brute creation, and gave a terrible shock to all preconceived ideas about the "Noble Red Man," if we had any. They were the first real savages—pure and simple—we had met, and our poetry and romance, born of Cooper and Longfellow, shivered at the spectacle. Some miles farther on, we encountered two young "bucks," gaily attired in blankets, beads, feathers, etc., jogging along on their ponies to the camp at Baker's. They had given a big scare to a poor German we overtook—a blacksmith, travelling alone from station to station, in a light two-mule buggy, to shoe the Company's horses. The appearance of our coach, however, made him feel his scalp more secure, and falling in behind he followed us up for miles, singing at the top of his voice "Annie, dear Annie of the vale!" Our stage was full inside and out, and we were all well-armed—in fact, fairly bristled with repeating-rifles and revolvers—and had we been attacked no doubt would have given a good account of ourselves. Our experiences up to Denver, however, inclined us to be somewhat skeptical on the Indian question, and our subsequent observations did not greatly change this. The whole region, indeed, seemed to be over-sensitive on the subject. The air was everywhere thick with rumors, that one by one disappeared as we advanced, and we hardly knew which to wonder at the more—the veracity or credulity of the Plains. In fact, that prince of romancers, Baron Munchausen, seemed to preside over the country, or the people to be his lineal descendants, almost everywhere.

CHAPTER V.

DENVER AND THE MINES.

WE reached Denver Sept. 5th, and remained there several days. Approaching by the South Platte, you catch sight of the town a mile or two away, when crossing a "divide," and are surprised at its size and importance. Ten years before, there was not an inhabitant there; but now she claimed seven thousand or more, and boasted with reason, of two hundred and fifty houses erected that year. Moreover, the new buildings were chiefly of brick or stone, while the old ones were log or frame. At the junction of the South Platte and Cherry Creek her streets are well-laid out, mostly at right-angles, and for suburbs she has the boundless Plains. Apparently on a plateau, she is nevertheless really a mountain city; for at St. Louis you are only three hundred feet above the sea, at Omaha nine hundred feet, while at Denver you have got up imperceptibly to four thousand feet above the sea, or higher than our average Alleghanies. Her climate is pure and dry, without rain or frost for many months in the year—the paradise of consumptives—and for scenery, she has the ever-glorious Rocky Mountains. Already she had six churches, two seminaries, two daily papers, a banking-house with a business of twelve millions a year, a U. S. Mint, a theatre, and hotels and saloons unnumbered, though these last it was thought were diminishing. Until recently, gambling-hells had also flourished openly on her streets, with their usual concomitants of drunkenness and affrays. But some months before, a Judge Gale—backed by a strong public opinion—had taken hold of the gamblers, and squelched them effectually. Like other "peculiar institutions," they died hard, raising large sums of money to prolong their evil life—threatening some men and bribing, or trying to bribe, others; but Judge Lynch came to the support of Judge Gale, with the counter-threat of "a cottonwood limb and a rope," and so gamblers ceased to rule in Denver. The happy change was freely commented on, and now that it had come, people wondered why they had endured the blacklegs so long. Denver was now evidently aspiring to better things—to "sweeter manners, purer laws." Her merchants and bankers were building themselves homes, sending east for their families, and settling down, as if to stay. Though not so law-abiding and Sabbath-loving, as our eastern cities, yet her churches were well-attended; and her Episcopal Bishop (Randall), we found scouring the country with all the earnestness and zeal of an old-time missionary, or Methodist itinerant. Band and gown, stole and chasuble, and other ritualistic millenery, he affected but little; but he preached Christ and Him crucified with a tenderness and power, that touched all hearts, and Colorado already had come to love and honor him. "Seek ye first the kingdom of God and His righteousness, and all these things shall be added unto you," was his text for as sound and appropriate a discourse the Sabbath we were in Denver, as we had heard in a long while. Every sentence struck home, like a rapier or a bullet, at some sin most prevalent in Colorado, and Denver might well "make a note of it." Subsequently we heard of him in the mines and among the mountains, preaching in quartz-mills and by the roadside—wherever he could gather a handful of hearers—always engaged in the Master's work, and always leaving a deep impression behind him.

Denver, with water and coal both near, yet had neither water nor gas works then, and scarcely a tree or shrub growing anywhere. Numerous trees had been planted, and much shrubbery; but the long and rainless summers had proven too much for them. The winter before, a company had been chartered to bring water from the mountains, for irrigating and other purposes, and they already had one ditch completed—three or four feet wide, by one or two deep—and were projecting others. This one irrigated several farms, turned a grist-mill or two, and then, with a branch to the fair-grounds, emptied into the Platte. But Denver must have such ditches, all around and through her, if she wants trees and shrubbery and then she may have streets and suburbs unsurpassed anywhere. Salt Lake, we afterwards found, had done this; and Denver will, when she has once been well scourged by fire. Then she was powerless against the fire-fiend, and a large conflagration well under way would have swept the town.*

Though the largest town in Colorado, and of commanding influence there, yet Denver we found was not the capital, but Golden City instead—a hamlet of five hundred inhabitants or so, fifteen miles farther west, at the base of the mountains. The Territorial Legislature convened there every winter, as required by law; but immediately adjourned to Denver, where all business was really transacted, and where the governor and other territorial officers resided, when not absent in the states, as some often were. In location, Denver itself

* See Appendix.

was, no doubt a geographical blunder, as the business of the country was really among the mines and mountains; but as gold had been first discovered here, it got the start, and bade fair to maintain its supremacy. The sharpest and shrewdest men in Colorado, we found were all settled here. All enterprises, of much pith and moment, began and ended here. All capital centred here. And Denver brains and Denver capital, it was plain to see, ruled and controlled our whole Rocky Mountain region, north to Dacotah and south to New Mexico.

Denver had two real "sensations," while we were there—one, the alleged usurpation of Gov. Cumming, the other the arrival of Gen. Sherman. It seemed there had been a territorial election, for delegate to Congress, and the returns not being clear, Gov. Cumming assumed to give the certificate of election to Hunt, an Andrew Johnson man, rather than to Chilcott, a radical Republican—notwithstanding the Board of Canvassers decided otherwise. The governor claimed that the law and facts were with him, but the Board of Canvassers protested to the contrary, and popular opinion seemed to sustain them. There was a breezy time in Denver for awhile. The papers savagely denounced the governor's conduct, as an outrage and usurpation, and fell into a vein of coarse vituperation they seemed incapable of before. The saloons were filled with excited crowds at night; knots gathered on the streets by day; and presently, one morning out came the papers with the old-time suggestion of "a cottonwood limb and a rope," if His Excellency did not yield. An explosion was now hourly expected, but it did not come. Denver evidently had grown in grace. The mob-spirit of her early days could not be revived, and all good citizens rejoiced to see it. No doubt she liked Judge Lynch still; but she liked Eastern immigration and English capital better, and would do nothing to startle either. The governor wisely appeared in public but little, and for several nights found it convenient to sleep elsewhere than at home. Finally, it was given out, that the military were on his side, as in duty bound, and the storm presently blew over. Subsequently it appeared, that said military consisted of only *two* officers, without a single soldier; but His Excellency attributed his safety to them, all the same. General Sherman's arrival immediately after was just in the nick of time. It followed on the heels of the election imbroglio, and was a good salve to the public sore. All Denver turned out to welcome him and his distinguished brother (the Ohio Senator), and a cavalcade of horsemen and carriages met them miles away. Next night there was a reception, banquet, speeches, ball, etc. and hundreds assembled to do them honor. There was a lamentable lack of ladies; but brighter, keener men, you could find nowhere. What there were of ladies, were intelligent and sprightly, and all were richly attired and adorned; but Denver needed more of them. Everybody vied in doing Sherman honor, as a great soldier who had fought nobly for the country. They did not know his views yet on the Indian question, which a few months afterwards they denounced so severely. By an ambulance tour of two thousand miles, from post to post, through the heart of the Indian country, he was trying to study the Indian question for himself, as *the* great question of his Military Division; and yet Denver, fond of contracts, claimed to understand that *quæstio vexata* better than he!

We left Denver one bright September morning for Central City and the Mines. A stage ran daily, but wanting to travel more leisurely we went by ambulance. Across the Platte, and over the Plains again for fifteen miles, brought us to the mountains and Golden City, just within the foothills. Clear Creek dashes through the "city," a broad swift stream, furnishing fine water-power for several mills already, with plenty to spare for more. Coal, iron, lead, copper and kaolin were said to exist in the mountains adjacent, and this water-power was therefore justly esteemed very valuable. Four or five miles farther on, the mountains seem to close up—a solid rampart—before you; but suddenly the road shifts and at Gate City, through a narrow rocky cañon you again pass on. The road here follows up a diminutive mountain stream, crossing and re-crossing its bed every few yards, and by a very sinuous course slowly makes its way forward between abrupt masses of red and purple rock, that everywhere seemed to block its progress. Farther on, the hills open out, and wild currant and gooseberry-bushes appear, with pines and firs here and there—many charred by former fires. The road gets wilder the farther you proceed, and the mountain views become more and more superb. You catch glimpses of the great Snowy Range from time to time; but after awhile you cross the first range, and then you have the great white-capped Sierra almost always before you. Three peaks there are especially superb—Old Chief, Squaw and Papoose—their white and glittering summits flashing gloriously in the sunshine. Sometimes we got long views of the Snowy Range, for miles on miles; and then again, deep down in some wild gorge, its rocky sides would suddenly expand, and there would stand these three grand peaks projected against the clear sky, framed in like a picture. A right "kingly spirit throned among the hills," Old Chief seemed to be keeping watch and ward over these Rocky Mountain fastnesses in solemn and solitary grandeur; but the Yankee and the miner had been too much for him.

We dined *en route*, getting a good meal for seventy-five cents, and reached the Conner House at Central City, about 6 P. M., forty miles from Denver. What a strange place was this, and how surprising it all seemed! A busy, active, bustling town, with all the appliances of eastern civilization, in the very heart of the Rocky Mountains—our *ultima thule* but a few years ago! Or, rather, four towns—Black Hawk, Gregory Gulch, Mountain City, and Central City—all now grown into one. It never was any place for a town; but there had to be one there, and so American genius and pluck went to work and created it. Imagine a narrow, winding mountain-gorge, with Clear Creek flashing through it, with scarcely standing-room on either side for an antelope even, and you have about all Nature has done for a town-site there. Yet our miners had stuck mills, and stores, and saloons, and dwelling-houses, and churches here, almost everywhere, in the most delightful and picturesque confusion. Some were astride of Clear Creek, as if wading up stream. Others were propped up on its edges, as if about to topple in. Others again were mounted on lofty stilts, all along the mountain side, as if just ready to start and walk away. About and through them all, following the general course of Clear Creek, wound one long and narrow street—too narrow for side-walks—and here in this bizarre place, walled in on all sides by the Rocky Mountains, lived and flourished six thousand souls, all apparently busy and well-to-do—with banks, schools, churches, newspapers, telegraphs, theatres, and pretty much all the institutions and destitutions of modern society. There only remained one need, a railroad, and that was already in contemplation, down Clear Creek to

Golden City, and so away to Denver. This would bring the ores and coal together at Golden City, for fuel was becoming scarce among the mines; would save much of the cost of travel and transportation by the wild mountain roads; and be a great blessing to the mining regions every way.* After tea, we strolled through the town for a mile or more, and found the streets full to overflowing. The theatres were crowded, and the drinking and gambling-saloons in full blast; yet the streets were comparatively orderly. The population seemed of a better class than one would suppose, all things considered. There were scarcely any women, it is true, and what there were had better been elsewhere, as a rule; but the men carried keen, clear-cut, energetic faces, that well explained the enterprise and *elan* of this audacious town. Of foreigners, there were far fewer than one ordinarily meets east, and the Americans as a rule were athletic and live men—fit to be the pioneers of empire. The inevitable African, of course, cropped out here and there; but usually he had risen from the dignity of a barber or a bootblack, to be a merchant or a miner. Everybody talked of "feet," and "claims," and "dust;" and bets were made, and drinks paid for, in "ounces" and parts of an ounce, as determined by the universal scales and weights. Greenbacks were still taken, but they were regarded as a depreciated currency, unworthy of the Mines and Mountains.

Indications of mining operations appeared first at Denver, where gold was first discovered at the junction of the South Platte and Cherry Creek. But the "diggings," or placer mines, here were soon worked out, and then the miners naturally ascended Cherry Creek tc Clear Creek, and so into the heart of the mountains. All

* This road since built and now in operation.

along North Clear Creek, you see where the stream has been turned aside, and its bed "panned" over, and as we approached Black Hawk we found a few miners still humbly at work this way. But placer-mining in Colorado had mostly been abandoned as no longer profitable, and now the chief labor and capital were applied to the quartz mines—the parents of the "diggings." These seemed to occur, more or less, all through the Rocky Mountains, wherever quartz cropped out; but the richest of them thus far had been found in the narrow defile about Central City. The sides of the ranges there had been "prospected" all over, until they seemed honey-combed or like pepper-boxes, so ragged and torn were they with the process. Here and there they were divided up into infinitesimal lots, rudely enclosed, embracing a few hundred feet or so, denoting mining "claims." Many of these had shafts sunk some distance, with a board up, proclaiming name of mine and the ownership thereof, but others were without these. The favorite mine in Colorado just then seemed to be the Gregory Consolidated, near Central City. We went down into this some three hundred feet, exploring its various galleries, and it seemed to be all that was represented. The gold here was so much diffused through the quartz as to be imperceptible to the eye, and was further mingled badly with silver, copper, and sulphur. The company had erected no mill as yet, but were contenting themselves with developing the lode, and getting out "pay-ore." Their plan was to sink the main shaft straight down on the lode, and every twenty feet or so follow up the indications by lateral galleries, to see whether the vein held out or not. So far it was doing well, and the ore continued of an excellent quality. But it was so difficult to reduce, there was no mill in Colorado that could save a fair proportion of the gold; so that what ore they cared to work was shipped east, or to Swansea, Wales, even, for reduction. The superintendent of the mine was a sturdy young Englishman, once a humble miner with his pick and candle, but afterwards sub-superintendent of a great silver mine in Mexico, and now for two or three years here—a man of rare energy and intelligence. No wonder the stock of the Gregory Consolidated was steadily rising, with such a policy and such a superintendent. Too many of the companies organized in the east were pursuing just the contrary course. They were putting up mills at once at great expense, with steam engines and stamps complete, and then when they came to sink down upon their veins, lo! they had no "pay-ore" there, or at least none worth working. A signal instance of this had occurred a year or two before. A New York Wall street Company had been organized, on a broad basis, and with great expectations. With a West Point ex-army officer superintendent and plenty of capital, their stock soon went soaring up like a rocket; but presently it came down again like a stick—*a la* their superintendent during the war. He erected a splendid mill of dressed stone at a cost of thousands of dollars, and went in wildly for all the latest and most improved machinery; but when afterwards he came to test their lode thoroughly, alas! he discovered they had only a poor sickly trace of ore, that soon "petered out," and so that fine company of gold and silver miners incontinently collapsed—or, as Mr. Mantilini would have said, "went to the demnition bow-wows!" Machinery that cost the company thirty-three thousand dollars in New York, was afterwards sold by the Colorado sheriff for thirteen hundred dollars, to pay freight bills; and other property in proportion. Other instances were reported to us, but none quite so bad as this. But from the large number of mills and mines standing idle—fully fifty per cent., it seemed—we could well believe that mining machinery could be bought cheaper in Colorado than New York, and that steam-engines and boilers were a drug. A foundry-man beyond Golden City, we were told, found it more profitable to buy up old machinery and recast it, than to work a rich iron mine, though the former was scattered through the mountains and the latter was just at his door.

The trouble with the Colorado ores was, they were refractory sulphurets, which we had not yet learned how to reduce at a profit. They assayed very readily two hundred and even three hundred dollars per ton, or more; but when you came to mill them out in large quantities, you were lucky if you got twenty-five or thirty dollars per ton. The problem Colorado then wanted solved was how to desulphurize these rich ores of hers at a profit. Various "processes" were continually being tried at great expense, but none of them seemed yet to be the "success" she desired. Stamp-mills, with copper-plate and quicksilver amalgamators, seemed to be the process in use generally, though not saving over twenty-five per cent. of the precious metals usually. Many companies were using these and saving their "talings," or refuse, with the expectation of yet realizing goodly sums from working the "talings" over by some new process by-and-by. A "process" just introduced was saving from twenty-five to fifty per cent more from these "talings;" but it was too costly for general use, or, perhaps, to pay. Individual mine-owners and the lighter companies seemed mostly to have suspended, or like Mr. Micawber to be waiting for "something to turn up"—for the strong companies to go on and find the much coveted "new process," when they would resume operations. Another trouble evidently was the great number of companies organized to sell stock east, rather than to mine successfully. Companies, with a property worth a hundred thousand dollars, had frequently issued stock for a million, and of course could not expect to make regular dividends on such an overplus. On a basis of a hundred thousand dollars, or real value, with an experienced honest superintendent, they might have got along well, if content to creep at first and walk afterwards. But as a rule they had preferred to "water" their stock, after the most approved Sangrado method; and the result, after a year or two's operations, was disappointed stockholders and the old, old cry of "bogus" and "wild-cat." Many of the companies, too, were heavily in debt, and what was called in Colorado parlance "freezing out" was taking place largely. That is to say, a company gives a mortgage for say twenty thousand dollars on property worth perhaps a hundred thousand, or at least represented by that amount of stock. When due it is not met, the treasury being empty, and the stockholders discouraged from want of dividends, or by "bear" reports about the mine; whereupon the mortgage is foreclosed, and the "bear" directors buy the property in for a song, thus "freezing out" the feebler and more timid brethren. This operation may lack the essential feature of old-fashioned honesty, but is no doubt a paying one—pecuniarily—for the new owners, who can now well afford to go bravely on. "Others may sink; but what's the odds, so we apples swim!"

No doubt Colorado is rich, immensely rich, in mineral resources—gold, silver, copper, iron, coal, etc.,—but she was scarcely making much decided headway as a mining community, so far as could be seen, in 1866.

Considerable of her population, indeed, had gone off to Montana and Idaho, to the reputed rich gold-fields there, and many of the rest were waiting patiently for the Pacific Railroad and a market. Great results were anticipated from the oncoming of the railroad, and it is to be hoped she has realized them. Her yield of the precious metals in 1862, it was estimated by good authority, amounted to ten millions of dollars; but in 1863 it fell to eight millions, in 1864 to five millions, and in 1865 to four millions. Ross Browne, in 1866, in his report of *Mineral Resources of the United States*, with characteristic exaggeration, estimated her yield for that year at seventeen millions; but more accurate observers regarded this as a California joke, and pronounced his estimate at least four or five times too high. The large yield in 1862 represented the maximum from gulch or placer mining, and the soft outcroppings of the quartz veins. But in 1866 placer mining, as I have said, had mostly ceased, and our quartz-miners had to go down so deep, and then got only the hardest and most refractory sulphurets, that the business greatly languished. Yet, it was plain to be seen, the gold and the silver were all there, in inexhaustible quantities, practically speaking; or as Mr. Lincoln once remarked, in speaking of our western mines, "We there hold the Treasury of the world!" All Colorado wanted, as elsewhere said, was the right "process" to subdue these rebellious sulphurets and compel them to release their imprisoned deities. Science surely holds the key somewhere, and waits only the coming man to hand it over to him. Millions of our countrymen are watching and praying for him. A half a continent calls for him. And when this coming man does come, who shall estimate the untold treasures he will here unlock and outpour upon the world! He will but have to strike the naked rocks, and abundant streams of wealth will gush forth. He will but have to touch the rugged mountain sides, and gold and silver by the million will obey his bidding—enough not only to pay our own National Debt, but the National Debts of the world. Let Colorado, then, be of good courage. The Pacific Railroad will cheapen supplies, and swell the volume of her immigration. The Yankee hand and brain are busily at work, conning over her knotty problem; and we may be sure, that the right hour will bring the necessary man.

From Central City we crossed the range at an altitude of nine thousand feet above the sea, and thence descended to Idaho, on South Clear Creek. A fine hotel here, in good view of the Snowy range, boasted itself the best in Colorado, and we found none better. Here also were several fine mineral springs, that bubble up quite near to each other, and yet are all of different temperatures. A bath-house had been erected, where you might take a plunge in hot or cold water, as you chose; the walks were romantic, with a possibility of deer or bear; the sights, what with ravine, and ridge, and peak, were magnificent; and Idaho, already something of a summer resort, expected yet to become the Saratoga of Colorado. Up South Clear Creek, above Idaho, were the new mining districts of Georgetown and Mill City, then but recently discovered and reputed quite rich; but we had not time to visit them. Down South Clear Creek, and thence to Denver, is a wild and surprising ride of forty-five miles, that well repays you. Much of the way Clear Creek roars and tumbles by the roadside, with the rocky walls of its cañon towering far above you; and when at length you cross the last range and prepare to descend, you catch a distant view of Denver and the Plains, that has few if any equals in all that region. The sun was fast declining, as we rounded the last crag or shoulder of the range, and the Plains—outstretched, illimitable, everlasting—were all before us, flooded with light as far as the eye could reach, while the mountains already in shade were everywhere projecting their lengthening shadows across the foot-hills, like grim phantoms of the night. A cloudless sky overarched the whole. Denver gleamed and sparkled in the midst twenty miles away, the brightest jewel of the Plains; and beyond, the Platte flashed onward to the east a thread of silver. It was a superb and glorious scene, and for an hour afterward, as we descended the range, we caught here and there exquisite views of it, through the opening pine and fir trees, that transferred to canvas would surely have made the fortune of any painter. With our Pacific Railroad completed, our artists must take time to study up the Rocky Mountains, with all their fine effects of light and shade—of wide extent and far perspective, of clear atmosphere, blue sky, and purple haze—and then their landscapes may well delight and charm the world.

Mining is, of course, the chief business of all that region, from the Missouri to the Mountains, and the habits and customs of the miner prevail everywhere. He digs and tunnels pretty much as he wills—under roads, beneath houses, below towns—and all things, more or less, are made subservient to his will. His free-and-easy ways mark social and political life, and his slang—half Mexican, half miner—is everywhere the language of the masses. A "square" meal is his usual phrase for a full or first-rate one. A "shebang" means any structure, from a hotel to a shanty. An "outfit" is a very general term, meaning anything you may happen to have, from a stamp-mill complete to a tooth-pick—a suit of clothes or a revolver—a twelve-ox team or a velocipede. A "divide" means a ridge or water-shed between two valleys or depressions. A "cañon" is Mexican or Spanish for a deep defile or gorge in the mountains. A "ranch," ditto, means a farm, or a sort of half-tavern and half-farm, as the country needs there. To "vamose the ranch" means to clear out, to depart, to cut stick, to absquatulate. A "corral," ditto, means an enclosed horse or cattle-yard. To "corral" a man or stock, therefore, means to corner him or it. To go down to "bed-rock," means the very bottom of things. "Panned-out" means exhausted, used-up, bankrupt. "Pay-streak" means a vein of gold or silver quartz, that it will *pay* to work. When it ceases to pay, it is said to "peter out." Said a miner one day at dinner, at a hotel in Central City, to a traveller from the east, "I say, stranger," pointing to a piece of meat by his side, "is there a *pay-streak* in that beef thar?" He wanted to know if there was a piece of it worth eating or not. The short phrase "You bet!" is pure Californice, and has followed our miners thence eastward across the continent. We struck it first on the Missouri, and thence found it used everywhere and among all classes, to express by different intonations a great variety of meanings. For example, meeting a man you remark:

"It is a fine day, my friend!"

He answers promptly and decidedly, "You *bet!*"

You continue, "It is a great country you have out here!"

He responds, "You BET *ye!*" sharp and quick.

"A good many mills standing idle, though!"

"Wa'll, yes, too many of them! You bet!" with a knowing shake of the head.

"Miners making much now-a-days?"

"Oh, yes! Some of us, a heap! *You* bet!" rather timid.

"Going back to the states one of these days?"

"When I make my pile! *You* BET!" firm and decided.

"Get married then, I suppose?"

"Won't I? Just that! *You* BET *ye*!" with his hat up, his eyes wide open, and his face all aglow with honest pride and warm memory of "The girl I left behind me!"

In Central City they told us a story of a miner, who was awakened one night by a noise at his window, and found it to be a burglar trying to get in. Slipping quietly out of bed, he waited patiently by the window until the sash was well up, and the burglar tolerably in, when he placed his revolver against the fellow's head, and sententiously remarked, "Now you *git!*" The story ran, the burglar looking quietly up surveyed the situation, with the cold steel against his brow, and as sententiously replied, as he backed out and dropped to the ground, "*You* BET!"

CHAPTER VI.

AMONG THE MOUNTAINS.

THE Plains after awhile became somewhat of a bore, they are so vast and outstretched, and you long for a change, something to break the monotony. To us this came one evening, just beyond Fort Morgan, when a hundred and fifty miles away, just peeping above the horizon, we descried the cone-like summit of Long's Peak, all pink and rosy in the sunset. "Driver, isn't that the Mountains?" said some one. "You bet!" was his answer, of course. "'Tisn't often you can see the Peak this fur; but it is mighty clar to-day!" The night soon afterwards shut down upon us, during which we bowled rapidly along from station to station, and the next morning were early awake. Soon the sun rose bright and clear; but the air was keen, with a stiff breeze eastward in our teeth. We were down in a wide depression of the Plains; but presently we rose up out of it, and as we struck the summit of the "divide," lo, the Rocky Mountains were before us in all their grandeur and sublimity. To the north rose Long's Peak, fourteen thousand feet above the sea, heaven-kissing, but with his night-cap still on; to the south, was Pike's Peak, eleven thousand feet above the sea, snow-crowned; while between, a hundred miles or more, swelled and towered the Mountains—at the base mere foot-hills, then ridge mounting on ridge and peak on peak, until over and above all the Snowy Range cropped out sublime. Patches of pines dotted their surface here and there, but the general effect was that of nakedness and barrenness. Clouds hung about their summits, or lingered along their sides; but the uprising sun soon dissipated these, or sent them careering aloft, as if bound for heaven. In the course of the morning we whirled into Denver, and there for a week or more—by sunlight, by moonlight—the Mountains were ever before us, in all their thousand varieties of tint and shadow. They never seemed precisely the same. Some new point was ever looming up, or flashing out—and yet they always realized one's best conceptions of beauty, grandeur, vastness, and sublimity.

Subsequently, accepting an invitation to accompany Gen. Sherman and Gov. Cumming to Southern Colorado and an Indian treaty there, we spent nearly a month among the Rocky Mountains, following down their eastern base and crossing them to Fort Garland, some two hundred and fifty miles, and thence returning to Denver again through the heart of them, *via* San Luis Park, Homan's Park, and South Park. This trip we made by ambulance, camping out at night, and rationing ourselves, as there were no stages on the route and very few settlements. Our little party, by the addition of officers and others at Denver, had swelled to seven, exclusive of cook and teamsters. Our "outfit" consisted of two four-horse ambulances and an army-wagon, with spare animals for saddle or other purposes, as occasion required. We took a tent along, but seldom had occasion to use it. We had blankets and buffalo robes for the night; some stray books and magazines for the day, when weary of the scenery; pipes and tobacco for all; and other supplies, it seemed, *ad infinitum*. In the matter of arms, what with our repeating-rifles and revolvers for Indians, and a brace of fowling-pieces for game, our ambulances were travelling arsenals. And from reports on leaving Denver, (Sept. 13th) we did not know but we should want all, and more. With the usual exaggeration of the border, the story current there was, that a Mexican belonging to one of the settlements down below had quarrelled with a Ute about a squaw, and wound up by killing him; that the Utes were consequently up in arms, stealing stock and murdering the inhabitants; that Fort Garland was already practically besieged; and that the United States was of "no account, no how," because we did not send more troops to Colorado. However, we started for Garland, well-armed as above; we did not meet a hostile Indian on the way; and when we arrived there, we found there hadn't been a settler molested, or mule stolen; and the whole yarn had come from a Ute found dead, supposed killed by lightning. When first discovered, near one of the settlements, the Utes were considerably ruffled; but when the post-surgeon at Garland and their medicine-man had examined him and found no marks of violence, the chiefs laid their heads together and sagely concluded the Great Spirit had called him.

Our course from Denver was about due South, following the trend of the mountains, and always near them. For several days our road was substantially over Fremont's old trail of 1843, across the high "divide" between the Platte and Arkansas, and so down the dashing *Fontaine qui Bout* to the Arkansas. This "divide" bears an unenviable reputation, as a storm-region. Coloradoans aver, that it rains, hails, snows, or blows there, when it is fair weather all around it, and we were warned of it accordingly. It is a high rolling region, running well up into the mountains, with Pike's Peak frowning over it, and I suppose the configuration of the country is such as to attract and concentrate storms there. We made haste to get across it, but sure enough encountered both rain and hail, though we found the country both north and south of it basking in a dreamy, autumnal atmosphere, that seemed like the very wine of life. That night we camped near "Dirty Woman's Ranch," close into the mountains, and slept delightfully in a hay-yard. The sun went down in a cloudless sky, transfiguring the snow-clad summit of Pike's Peak with a glory all its own, whose pink and crimson faded into purple, and this again to blue, as the day died out. So, too, the rest of the range, from purple and blue, came out sharp and black against the star-thick sky, and night shut down upon the Plains with scarcely a sound to break the silence.

During the day, the blank monotony of the Plains was broken by numerous "buttes," some of which were very surprising. The chief one, "Castle-Rock," was an abrupt precipitous mass, well bastioned and castellated, that rose sheer into the air several hundred feet, as if the work of hammer and trowel. At a distance, it seemed almost squarely perpendicular, but two of our party, who had galloped on ahead, found an accessible path to the summit on its southeast side. As we drove up abreast of it, we descried them on its dizzy edge, but took them to be eagles or buzzards, until they out with their handkerchiefs and fired off their pistols. The smoke curled away on the breezy air, but the sound was inaudible down by the roadside as we drove by. These "buttes" dot the country over there for miles, standing solitary and alone—wholly disconnected from each other—and are a strange feature of the Rocky Mountain region.

The next day we struck Monument Creek and followed this down to the *Fontaine qui Bout.* Here the country for miles is marked by great masses of sandstone and limestone, chiseled by wind and rain into the most fantastic shapes and forms. Some are slender columns of gray or red rock, a hundred feet or more in height, worn and smooth; while others are cut and carved so curiously, that it seems they must be the deft handiwork of man. Right under the shadow of Pike's Peak, they seem to culminate, and here is Colorado's famous Garden of the Gods. Entering from the roadside we passed through a little ravine, that rapidly widened into a *bijou* of a valley, and there near its centre uprose two tremendous rocks, red dashed with gray, six hundred feet long by two hundred high, tapering to a knife-like edge. They were both inaccessible to man, but the elements had bored a hole through the summit of one, that looked for all the world as if a round shot or shell had knocked its way through there. A score of swallows were twittering about this, as we passed by, and their nests were visible all up and down the rocks. A little distance off stood three red sandstones, ten or twelve feet in diameter, by a hundred or more high, like the surviving columns of some ruined temple—one somewhat splintered and shattered, but the others still uplifting their capitals sublime against the sky. Farther on the whole country here is studded for miles, with these wedge-shaped and columnar masses of red and gray rock, some even on a grander scale, as though it were a cemetery of Titans, marked by Cyclopean tombstones. It is a vast meadow, rich with herbage, with Monument Creek meandering through it, vocal with the song of birds, the whole lying close up under the overshadowing Mountains; while over all, breaking sharp and clear against the faultless sky, stands Pike's

Peak, imperial in his majesty, dark below with pines and firs, but his bald head crowned with eternal snows, looking calmly down, as if God's sentinel keeping watch and ward over all below. Altogether the grouping of the landscape there is very fine, as if the gods had done their best; and on the glorious morning when we saw it, beneath a perfect September sky, we thought Colorado had indeed here much to be supremely proud of.

Some three miles farther on, near the banks of the *Fontaine qui Bout,* which here comes boiling down from the foot of Pike's Peak, there are several fine natural soda-springs. They come bubbling up on either side of the stream from the far depths below, and their overflow during the long ages has deposited large rocks of calcareous tufa or carbonate of soda all about them. We tried this soda-water, and found it as cool, and as sharp and titillating as that from a city-fountain; and when treated with an acid, it effervesced and vanished quite as freely. H—— and B—— tried it with lemons and whiskey and reported their cocktails quite unequalled since leaving New York. Col. Chivington, of Sand Creek memory, had recently purchased these springs and the land adjacent for three thousand dollars; but he was now asking ten thousand, though there had not been a dollar expended for improvements yet. Combined with Pike's Peak, the Garden of the Gods, and all the unique and romantic scenery from there to Denver, as well as the general Plains and Mountains, the investment did not seem to be a bad one, and no doubt will pay handsomely some day. But it was then waiting the completion of the Pacific Railroad, and the in-pouring of population, that all Coloradoans then devoutly hoped and prayed for.*

* I believe these are now called Colorado Springs, and much resorted to, and Manitou is somewhere about the Garden of the Gods.

Just beyond the Soda Springs, stood or rather *slept* Colorado City. We had been so unfortunate as to break our ambulance-tongue in pulling out of a mud-hole, and halted there to have a new one made. In the days of 1857–60, when mining centred at Pike's Peak, Colorado City was the Denver of southwestern Colorado, and must have been a place of considerable importance. But the "diggings" there long since gave out, and C. C. was now in a bad way. Corner-lots were for sale, dirt-cheap. It had plenty of empty shanties, but scarcely any population; and what it had, were the sleepiest-looking Coloradoans we had yet seen anywhere. The "hotel" or tavern, was forlorn and dirty; the people, idle and listless; and the "City," as a whole, was evidently hastening fast to the status of Goldsmith's Deserted Village. Cañon City, farther up in the mountains, they told us, was even worse off—having no inhabitants at all. It had good buildings, some even of brick and stone, equal indeed to any in Colorado; but all stood empty, like "some banquet-hall deserted," and the once busy "City" was now as silent as Thebes or Petræ. Such is life in our mining regions. Population comes and goes, as restless as the sea, according as the "diggings" promise good "pay-dirt" or bad. And what are prosperous and busy centres this year, next year may become empty and deserted.* At sunset we went into camp on the banks of the *Fontaine qui Bout,* while a snow-squall was careering around Pike's Peak. Several of these had been prancing about his summit during the afternoon, and about five P. M., one of them swept down over the

* The Denver and Santa Fe narrow-gauge railroad, now in operation, following the mountains down, has doubtless done much to revive and stimulate this whole region again. But it halts, I believe at Pueblo for the present.

foothills and valley, with far out-stretched wings, giving us a taste of its icy breath as we journeyed by. At sunset the hues along the mountains and among the snow-peaks were magnificent and glorious; but the air became keen and nipping as night fell, and all the evening we hugged the fire closely. Just before dark, while supper was cooking, two or three of us tried the *Fontaine qui Bout* for trout, and caught—not a nibble even!

Soon after leaving Colorado City the mountains trend away to the southwest, while the road to Fort Garland continues on down the *Fontaine qui Bout* to the Arkansas. Fording this at Pueblo, and subsequently its two affluents, the Greenhorn and the Huerfano, you again strike the mountains, a hundred miles farther south, at the foot of Sangre del Christo Pass. The high ridges or "divides" between all of these streams are barren and sterile, to an extent little imagined in the east; but the streams themselves are bordered by broad valleys, rich and fertile, that as a rule need only irrigation to produce luxuriantly. In some seasons they do not require even this, as their proximity to the mountains affords them rains enough. Still, no farmer is safe there without his system of *acequias* or water-ditches, to irrigate if necessary; and we found these everywhere constructed, if not in use, where settlements had been made. In all of these valleys we already had scattered ranches—some of them very large—and raised wheat, barley, corn, oats, etc. in considerable quantities. Colorado had formerly imported all her grain and flour from the Missouri, at an enormous cost; but latterly she had drawn large supplies from these fertile valleys, and in '66 considered herself about self-sustaining. Not more than one-tenth, or less, of her arable land here, however, seemed to be under cultivation, and agriculture even then was of the rudest and simplest. The ranchemen were mainly Americans or Germans, but the labor was all performed by Mexican peons, subjected for generations to but one remove from slavery. It was the threshing season, and in many places we saw them treading out their wheat and barley by mules, with a Greaser on the back of each, lazily whiffing his cigarrito, while his donkey dozed around. Elsewhere, their threshing done, we saw them winnowing their grain by hand, as the breeze chanced along. We did not see or hear of a threshing-machine or a fanning-mill in the whole region there, and doubt if there was one. The Mexicans do not comprehend these nineteenth century new-fangled notions, and will have none of them. They prefer by far their old-time *dolce far niente*. *Festina lente* is their national maxim, and your thorough-bred peon would choose a broncho rather than a locomotive any day. And naturally enough, the American settlers here, we found, were mostly from the south, and during the war had been none too ardent for the Union.

Most of the farms here were large in size, and in crossing the Greenhorn we passed through a noble ranch, twelve miles wide by eighteen long, owned by a Mr. Zan Hincklin. In '65 he sold his crop of grain for eighty thousand dollars, and in '66 expected to do even better. He had on hand a thousand horses, three thousand head of cattle, and six thousand sheep, all of which he grazed the year round. He lived very plainly, in a rude adobe hut, that we should think hardly fit for a canal-laborer east; but was as hospitable and generous as a prince. We had scarcely gone into camp, on the banks of the rippling Greenhorn, before he sent us over butter, eggs, and vegetables, and bade us welcome to his heart and home. He acquired his great estate by marrying one of the half-breed daughters of the celebrated John Brent, who used to hunt and trap all through this region, and who lived so long among the Indians that he became himself half Red-Skin. He died possessed of vast tracts of land here, acquired chiefly through trading with the Indians, but his children it appeared, as a rule, had turned out poorly. One of his sons had returned to Indian life, joining a wandering tribe, and others still hung about the settlements, of small account to anybody.

From the Arkansas, the country gradually but constantly ascends, until you strike the mountains again at the foot of Sangre del Christo Pass. Here you follow up a dashing rivulet, that courses away to the Huerfano, and advantage is taken of a depression in the main ridge to cross into San Luis Park. We camped the night before in a sheltered nook among the foot-hills, surrounded on three sides by gnarled piñon trees, while the fourth opened on a little plateau sloping down to a noisy brook, that afforded water and grass in abundance. The next morning we breakfasted early, and were off up the Pass soon after sunrise. The morning air was nipping, and as we advanced we found the mists rolling down the mountains, and so off over the Plains eastward. The teams being a little slow that morning in packing up and getting off, some of us concluded to walk on; but we had not proceeded far, before some one suggested this might be dangerous, as Indians were reported about, and our arms were all behind in the ambulances. Halting, therefore, for the rest to come up, two of us then secured our Spencers and six-shooters, and mounting one a horse and the other a mule pushed on ahead again. The ascent, though gentle, we found nevertheless very constant, and gradually the ambulances dropped much behind. The road led over a shelving plateau, and up a pretty sharp hill, and then plunged by a rapid descent into a little valley again. Here we met several men, with a drove of indifferent cattle and sheep, *en route* from Culebra to Denver and a market. Climbing out of this valley, we struck a sharp ascent, that led southward along and up the ridge, and then turning west by south struck straight across the summit. As we raised the summit, a keen, fierce wind met us from the west, and soon set our teeth to chattering in unison with it. On the tip-top we found a contractor's train, *en route* to Fort Garland with supplies, doubling up ox-teams and doing its "level best" to forge slowly ahead. The summit or ridge, the tip-top of the Rocky Mountains—the very backbone of America here—we found only a few hundred yards across; and then we came out on the western slope, with all the glories of the San Luis Park nestling at our feet, or uprising gorgeously before us. Below, the Park lay wrapped in a dreamy haze, with the Sangre del Christo creek flashing onward through it; above, peak on peak—huge, snow-white, and sublime—rimmed it round, as with a crown. Over all, hung one of those blue and faultless skies, for which the Rocky Mountains are so world-famous, with the sun sweeping majestically through it, while God himself seemed ready to speak on every side. This was to the west. Turning to the east, the view there seemed, if possible, even more grand and sublime. Peak and ridge, plateau and foot-hill, stretched away beneath us; in the distance the brace of Spanish Peaks, two bold "buttes" passed the day before, shot up abruptly six thousand feet into the sky, from the dead level of the Plains around them; while beyond and around to the dim horizon, east, north, and south, for hundreds of miles, outstretched the illimitable Plains.

The elevation of the Pass is given, as about ten thousand feet above the sea. At our feet, the fog was breaking up and rolling off eastward in sullen masses, which the morning sun gilded with glory, or here and there pierced through and through down to the earth beneath. Soon it passed away into airy clouds, careering along the sky, and presently vanished altogether. And then the Plains! The Plains! How their immense outstretch absorbed and overwhelmed the eye! It was not the ocean, but something much grander and vaster, than even the ocean seems. If you could view the sea from the same altitude, doubtless the impression would be much the same. But what is the loftiest mast-head, compared with the summit of Sangre del Christo? The grandeur and sublimity of the scene awed one into silence, as if in the presence of Deity himself, and the great and holy thoughts of that hour well repaid us for all our toil and fatigue. Say what we may, there is something gracious and ennobling in such mountain scenery, which men can illy dispense with. How it deepens and widens one's feelings! How it broadens and uplifts one's thoughts! How it strengthens—emboldens—one's manhood! What Switzerland is to Europe, and New England to the Atlantic States, this and more, the whole Rocky Mountain region will yet become to America.

Descending the mountains westward, a ride of a mile or two brought us to a spring, where a Mexican was taking his noon-day meal of tortillas, while his inevitable mule was cropping the grass near by. H. dismounted and scooped up a drink with his hands, Indian fashion, but I was not yet thirsty enough for that. A mile or two farther, still descending, brought us to the head of Sangre del Christo creek, a dashing rivulet fed by snow streams, that runs thence to the Rio Grande. A winding defile or cañon, of steady though not very rapid descent, affords a bed-way down the Pass and out into the San Luis Park, and down this the wild little creek shoots very serpentinely. It crosses the road no less than twenty-six times in ten miles, and constantly reminds you of the famous Yankee fence, which was made up of such crooked rails, that when the pigs crept through it they never exactly knew whether they were inside or out! We jogged leisurely down the creek, until we judged we were some six or seven miles from the summit, and perhaps half way down the mountain, when we halted for the teams to come up. The wind blew sharply up the Pass still, though it was now much after noon, and we found the shelter of a neighboring ravine very welcome. Here we unsaddled our animals, and turned them loose to graze. They fed up and down the ravine, cropping the rich herbage there, but would never stray over a hundred yards or so away, when they would turn and graze back to us again. On such mountain trips saddle-animals become attached to their riders, and will seldom leave of their own accord. So, also, they are unerring sentinels, and always announce the approach of Indians or others with a neigh or bray. Building a royal fire with the dry fir-trees there, we next spread our saddle-blankets on the ground, and then with our saddles under our heads, and our feet Indian-fashion to the fire, smoked and talked until the rest arrived. About two P. M. I noticed Kate (my mule) stop grazing and snuff the air, very inquiringly; presently, with a whisk of her tail and a salutatory bray, she darted down the ravine, as if thoroughly satisfied; and in a minute or two along came the ambulances, with our friends chilled through, despite their robes and blankets. All tumbled out to stretch their benumbed limbs, and we ate lunch around our impromptu fire grouped very picturesquely.

Meanwhile about everybody nearly had got "trout on the brain." We had caught frequent glimpses of the speckled beauties, as we crossed Sangre del Christo creek or rode along its banks, and concluded to go into camp early, so as to try our luck with a fly or two. A good camping place was found a mile or two farther on, near the foot of the Pass, and here while supper was preparing, several of us rigged up our lines and started off. H. and I were most unfortunate; we whipped the stream up and down quite a distance, but came back fishless. H. caught a bite, and I several nibbles, but neither of us landed a trout. We could see plenty of them, young dandies, darting about in the black pools, or, old fogies, floating along by the banks; but they were Arcadian in their tastes, and disdained the fancy flies we threw them. Dr. M. and L., however, had better luck. The spirit of good Isaak Walton seemed to rest upon and abide with them. They caught a dozen or more, of handsome mountain trout, weighing from two to three pounds each, and the next morning when brought on our rude table for breakfast, hot and smoking from the fire, nothing could have been more savory and delicious. Gen. B. and L. turned cooks for the occasion, and judged by the result Delmonico might have envied them. Their broiled trout, fresh from the brook and now piping hot, buttered and steaming, assailed both eye and palate at once, and we awarded them the palm, *nem. con.*

The weather that day, from noon on, had grown steadily colder, though the sun shone unclouded most of the time, and before we got our camp well pitched a snow-squall struck us. The flakes came thick and fast for awhile, but presently passed away, though more or less continued sifting downward until nightfall. Farther up the Pass, around the crest of the mountains, snow-squalls marched and countermarched most of the afternoon, and at sunset the air grew nippingly cold, even down where we were. We soon pitched our tent, and built a glorious fire in front of it; but that not sufficing, supper once over, we carried our sheet-iron cooking-stove inside, and all huddled about that. When bed-time came, blankets, buffalo-robes and great-coats were all in demand; yet in spite of all, we passed a sorry night of it, and morning dawned at last much to our relief.

We reached Fort Garland next day (Sept. 20) about one, P. M., without meeting a single Indian, either hostile or friendly. Denver, as before said, had warned us to be on our guard, and we tried to be; but all reported dangers vanished as we advanced—Munchausen after Munchausen exploding in turn. From the Huerfano across the mountains to Garland, some fifty miles or more, there was but a single ranch, and scarcely anybody on the road. A Mexican on foot and another on a donkey were emigrating to the Huerfano, and at one point we encountered a whole family similarly engaged. Paterfamilias, whiffing his cigarito, led a diminutive broncho (Mexican for jackass) about the size of a spring calf, on which sat his household gods, to wit, his Señora also smoking, with a child before and another behind her—all of them astride. Another broncho of about the same size followed on behind, loaded down with clothing, bedding, and various domestic utensils until there was but little to be seen of him except his legs. What the locomotive is to the Yankee, and the horse to the borderer, that the broncho is to the Mexican, and the two seem alike fitted for each other and inseparable. His patient little beast costs but little, and when stopping browses by the way-side the best it may, while Don Quixote himself sits basking in the sunshine. The serene and infinite content of a Mexican peon, as he sits thus wrapped in his poncho or serape, sucking his everlasting cigarrito, no American can imagine. His dignity is as perfect as that of a Castilian; but the stolidity of his brain, who shall describe?

Some fifteen miles or so from Fort Garland, in the heart of the San Luis Park, lies San Luis de Culebra, a hamlet of five or six hundred people, and I believe, the most considerable "city," there. You strike the Park proper some distance east of Fort Garland, and from there to Culebra the country is substantially a dead-level. Culebra was then a genuine Mexican town without an atom of the Yankee in or about it, and seemed a thousand years old, it was so sleepy, though comparatively a new settlement. Its houses were all one-story adobes, with chimneys in the corner, in the true Mexican style, and were all grouped about a central "plaza," of course, or the town would not be Mexican. All Southern Colorado, it will be remembered, formerly belonged to New Mexico, and hence these Mexican settlements here and beyond. The people raised wheat, barley, and oats to some extent; but depended on their flocks and herds chiefly for support. We entered Culebra at dark, amidst a multitudinous chorus of dogs, and halted at the house of Capt. D. a bright German, formerly an officer of New Mexican Volunteers, but who had recently married a Culebra señorita and settled there. He gave us an excellent supper, after which we all adjourned to a "baille," or Mexican Ball, gotten up especially in honor of Gen. Sherman and Gov. Cumming, but which Sherman was unable to attend. Several of his staff-officers, however, and the governor were present, and these with the rest of us made up quite a party. These *bailles* are great institutions among the New Mexicans, who retain all the old Spanish fondness for music and dancing, and are ready for a "baille," any time. The Culebrans had already had two or three that week, but got up the Sherman-Cumming one on short notice and in grand style. The only thing necessary was to engage a room and music, and send a runner through the village, to announce a baille was on the tapis, and the whole population—men, women, children, dogs, and fleas—were sure to be there. At the primitive hour of eight P. M. the people began to assemble, and by nine P. M. the baille was in full blast. The ball-room itself was an adobe building, one-story high, perhaps fifty feet long by thirty wide, with a dirt floor, and seats all around. At the farther end was a rude bar, with a transparency over it, bearing the motto, "Limonade and Egg-nog," at which each cavalier was expected to treat his lady from time to time. Near this was a rough platform for the musicians, who consisted of three or four violinists, led by an irrepressible guitarist—blind and quite a character in his way. As the evening progressed, he worked himself up into an ecstacy of enthusiasm, and then, with his eyes "in fine phrensy rolling," improvised words to every piece they played. He appeared perfectly absorbed and carried away with playing and singing, and when a dance ended seemed quite exhausted. No bone-ist, or tambourine-ist, in a troupe of minstrels east, ever performed with more thorough and reckless abandon. His head was thrown back; his eye-balls rolled wildly: his coarse, matted, coal-black hair swept his shoulders: his long and bony fingers fairly flew up and down his quivering guitar: while his shrill, piping, tenor voice rose and fell above the music, in thorough unison with the general scene. Later in the evening, after frequent potations of egg-nog, Don Jesus, (for that was his name) became immensely funny, and his gyrations amused us greatly.

With the first sound of the violins, the couples took the floor, and kept it up vigorously to the "wee sma' hours." The older people participated less, but young and old were all there, apparently the whole population, in their best "bib and tucker." Women came carrying their infants, and others held the babies while their mothers danced. The younger people, down to mere boys and girls, of course, all danced. First came some slow, stately Spanish dances; but presently they slid into schottisches and polkas, and performed these with a vigor worthy of New York or Paris. Many present were dressed humbly, and but few comparatively were well dressed; but ornaments abounded, and the baille or fandango seemed to put all on an equality. Most of our party selected partners, and soon were lost in the maze and whirl. True, they could not speak a word of Spanish, nor their señoritas any English; but that did not matter, as the Mexicans regard it as a mark of ill-breeding to converse while dancing. Their manner of saluting each other, when first they met, was unique and original, to wit: the sexes poked their heads over each other's shoulders, and took a good old fashioned hug. Throughout the evening, of course, there was a total absence of indecorum. As a whole, they seemed to be honest, simple folk, who took life as it came, without fret or worriment, and enjoyed themselves greatly. There was less beauty among the women, but more intelligence among the men, than we expected; their hospitality was hearty and generous—they did their best to give us a pleasant evening; and altogether the baille at Culebra was an event long to be remembered. I left Gov. C. at 11 P. M., looking on and enjoying it, and went to sleep on a good wool bed—the only kind used there—in a comfortable room, for the first time since leaving Denver.

CHAPTER VII.

AMONG THE MOUNTAINS (*Continued*).

RETURNING next day from Culebra to Fort Garland, we proceeded thence subsequently up the Park to the Indian treaty on the Rio Grande; and from there *via* Homan's Park and Poncho Pass north to Fair Play in South Park. These "parks," so called, are a peculiar feature of the Rocky Mountains and play an important part in the scenery. There are five of them—North, Middle, South, Homan's, and San Luis—of which we passed through the last three. They constitute in reality a great system of plateaus or valleys, morticed as it were into the very heart of the mountains, from twenty-five to fifty miles long by half as many wide, disconnected by intervening ranges, yet all alike in their general features. One of the main ranges of the Rocky Mountains bounds them on the east; but *the* main range, the real Sierra Nevada or Mother Range—the great Snowy Range or real water-shed of the continent, dividing the waters of the Pacific from those of the Atlantic—runs along the west. True, this is disputed by enthusiastic Coloradoans; but the facts seem nevertheless, as above. The North Platte, South Platte, Arkansas, and Rio Grande, all take their rise there, and piercing the eastern range flow thence to the Atlantic or the Gulf, while no considerable stream flows thence to the Pacific. Kit Carson, whom we met at Fort Garland, the best geographer of that region, took this view of the subject, and I humbly concur.

The largest of these Parks, by far, is the San Luis, and we found it fairly gridironed with trout streams, and rimmed around with mountains. Its general elevation is from six to seven thousand feet above the sea, with its surrounding peaks and ridges about as much more, which is too cold for Indian corn, though the other cereals—such as wheat, barley, oats, etc.—may readily be grown there. Volcanic agencies have had much to do with its formation, as its wide-spread igneous rocks and pebbles still plainly show. Along the Rio Grande and its numerous affluents wide bottoms have been formed, that are very rich—the very washings of the mountains; but elsewhere you have only rocks and gravel, sage-brush and grease-wood. It contains no timber, except a fringe of cottonwoods and poplars along most of the larger streams; but cedar, pine, and fir are found in the neighboring cañons and mountains. Cattle and other live stock find good grazing in summer along the streams, and in winter they were said to thrive well on the coarse bunch-grass, with which the surrounding cañons all abound. The broad bottoms of the Rio Grande, waving with tall grass and fatter than the prairies of Illinois, ought to make magnificent meadows, and will some day when more of our Anglo-Saxon population overflows there. The population of the Park was grouped mainly in two or three Mexican hamlets, and was computed by Kit Carson (then Colonel of New Mexico Volunteers and Post Commandant at Fort Garland) at about five or six thousand only. A noted citizen of Denver, who owned a large part of the Park, had reported it to us as about twenty thousand. Not that he intended to be inexact; but his imagination was naturally very vivid, and his language apt to be poetic. In purchasing property there, under an old Spanish grant, he certainly acquired any quantity of magnificent mountain, and a wide stretch of plain; but we suspected, he would wait some time before he saw his money back again.

Our general ride up the San Luis Park, and so through Homan's to Poncho Pass, was unique and perfect in its way. Our route on leaving Fort Garland was first across several mountain brooks, where the trout were so abundant, that the soldiers at the fort caught them with blankets and feasted on them at will, and then directly up the Park, with the Sierra Blanca or Snowy Range towering on our right. Striking the Rio Grande, we found it alive with geese and ducks, and when we went into camp, L. — our champion sportsman — caught several noble trout, weighing from five to six pounds each. Singularly enough, the streams flowing to the Rio Grande all abound in trout, while those going to the Mississippi, we were told, all lack them. We halted two days here, attending the Indian Treaty before alluded to, and then proceeded on. At Fort Garland, we were advised to return to Denver by the same route we had come, as the season was already advancing and nobody had come through by Poncho Pass since the previous spring. Moreover, the trail was reported impracticable for ambulances, and even Kit Carson shook his head, unless we went by pack-mules. But as the pack-mules were not to be had, and we were all averse to returning over the old route, we resolved to push ahead by Poncho Pass, and get through the mountains that way, if possible. From the Treaty-Ground, our route lay nearly due north, with the snowy crest and peaks of the Sierra Blanca on our right and about parallel. Bidding our friends good-bye, we set out early (Sept. 24), with the wind dead-ahead and bitter cold. Toward noon, the weather moderated somewhat; but snow-squalls chased each other along the mountains all day, and once we counted nine in view —one careering along behind the other—at the same time. Now and then one would expand its wings, and sweep across the Park; and several times in the course of the day we were thus in the midst of real winter. The range to the west was more or less broken into foot-hills and ridges; but the Sierra Blanca to the right seemed a solid rampart, rugged, inaccessible, sublime. Its serrated crest, white with perpetual snow, rose five or six thousand feet above the level of the Park; its tree-line was distinctly marked, as with a rule; and the whole seemed so near and so gorgeous, when the sunset swallowed up the snow-squalls, that we could scarcely realize it was yet miles away. As we got farther up the Park, the soil grew thinner, and more volcanic in its origin; but we crossed several handsome streams, that might be made to irrigate considerable land there.

We found only one ranch, however, north of Fort Garland—a Mr. Russell's, at the extreme north-eastern end of the Park. We camped there one night, and found the proprietor to be a good specimen of the average Coloradoan. Born in Illinois and bred a blacksmith, the gold-fever had taken him to California, where he worked partly in the mines and partly at his trade. When he failed in the mines, as he usually did, he again resorted to his trade; and had he stuck to his anvil, he verily believed, he would have been well-off long before. But as soon as he had hammered out a little money, his evil genius led him back to the "diggings;" and so he had wandered all up and down our mining regions—California, Nevada, Colorado, etc.,—until 1861, when he found himself in Denver, without a cent in his pockets. Mining happened to be dull there, a regiment of volunteers was then forming for service against the Indians, and so he turned soldier. Before his three years were up, he had saved a moderate "pile," and when he was finally mustered out and discharged, he came here and "squatted" on a quarter-section. The money saved while thus soldiering started him in farming, and he now thought his future secure. This was his first year there, but he had got along very well so far. The Indians had not disturbed him, though frequently there, and his Mexican peons had proved faithful laborers, though a little slow. He had raised fine crops of oats, barley, and potatoes, which he would sell to the garrison at Garland at good prices; but his wheat was a failure—he feared, for want of sufficient warmth. He had a good adobe house, which he meant to enlarge and improve, and a fine flock of sheep, besides considerable cattle. The worst feature of his ranch was, that he had to irrigate; but he said he had plenty of water for this, and the cost was small. His nearest neighbor was eighteen miles off, and that was too near; his post-office, sixty miles; and church, two hundred. It is strange, that men can be content to bury themselves thus, in the heart of a wilderness, when God and nature are so bountiful elsewhere. It is the everlasting itching, I suppose, that we Americans have for change, which comes to little good after all. No doubt plenty of Coloradoans would emigrate to the moon, or even to Le Verrier, if there were a practicable "trail" there.

The next day crossing a low ridge, through a forest of gnarled cedars, we entered Homan's Park, and found it to be nearly a duplicate of the San Luis, on a smaller scale. It is about thirty miles long, by perhaps half as many wide, and its essential features are about the same as those of the San Luis, though its soil seemed deeper and more generous. About half way up, a lusty mountain-stream crosses from west to east, lined with cottonwoods, and here four Germans had each "pre-empted" a quarter-section, all lying together. They had all been officers of Colorado Volunteers, and when mustered out came and "squatted" here together, in this picturesque little valley. The last year of their service, being stationed at Fort Garland, they had been up that way on a scout after Indians; and, falling in love with the Park, selected it for their future homes. One of them was married, and his wife—a tidy young German woman—kept house for all. They began operations the previous year, and already had accomplished large results. They put in seven thousand dollars as joint-capital, and with this purchased all the necessary animals, implements, provisions, seeds etc., to start well with. Among the rest, they bought a hundred and forty cows, which the following spring brought them in nearly as many calves, all of which they were now raising. Pasturage was abundant in summer, and in the winter the adjoining cañons supplied bunch-grass, etc. They milked all their cows, and converted the milk into butter and cheese, which two items alone had paid their current expenses so far, with a small margin over. A sluice-way from the brook carried the water into their milk-house, where instead of tin or earthen pans, they had long milk-troughs hollowed out of logs, around which the water flowed, and then passed back into the stream again. A bowl of buttermilk, that they tendered us, fresh from the churn, was an unlooked-for luxury in the heart of the Rocky Mountains, that none of us could refuse. The ensuing winter they proposed to build a water-churn, and sc make their friendly brook serve them still further.

They had had tolerable crops of barley, oats, and potatoes, all of which that could be spared they were husbanding for seed the coming year. They had tried some corn and wheat, but neither had matured well, and they would hardly venture them again. Their butter and cheese they sold to the miners over in South Park, and some they sent even to Denver and a market. They called their place *Kerber's* Ranch, after their leading partner, who seemed to be a live Dutchman all over. Of course, we had to stop to dinner, though it was not yet noon; and when that meal was announced, they conducted us to a table Denver might have envied. Trout, venison, grouse, krout, with all the vegetables of the season, and lager-beer home-brewed, made up a meal not to be despised anywhere, least of all in the fastnesses of the Rocky Mountains. They had seen no officers and hardly any body else, for months, and would take no pay for anything; but gratefully accepted an armful of "literature," as we bade them good-bye—the last of our newspapers, magazines, and books still left from our supply on leaving Denver. Their nearest neighbor was eighteen miles off, and nearest post-office seventy-five. To Denver was a hundred and fifty miles, and it took a team a month or more to go there and return *via* Poncho Pass. They pronounced the Pass, in response to our eager inquiries, entirely practicable, with careful driving, if we crossed by daylight; and with their kindest wishes, we went on our way rejoicing.

Some miles after leaving Kerber's, we began to ascend the mountain, but the ascent was so gradual you scarcely noticed it. There was no well-defined road any where —only an old Indian trail for saddle and pack animals, along which only a few wagons had ever passed before. We continued to ascend until dusk, hoping to reach and cross the summit before going into camp; but after sunset, the trail became so faint and our animals so leg-weary, we were compelled to halt at the first wood and water we came to. This we did on the bank of a beautiful stream, that washed the base of a high bluff or rather "butte," and rushed thence *via* Homan's Park to the Rio Grande. Several of us had rode on ahead on horseback, but the teams did not get up until after dark. Meanwhile, we had gathered wood, and built a roaring fire; and when the rest arrived, we soon had camp pitched, and the coffee boiling. We had shot some ducks on the Rio Grande, and brought along some excellent beef-steaks; and these H. and L. now broiled before the fire, on sharpened sticks, in a style the Parker House could hardly have beaten. We found excellent grass here, although so far up the Pass, and our poor tired animals cropped it eagerly. The moon was at the full that night, and the sky cloudless; but before morning the air grew bitter cold. We shivered through the night, in spite of our blankets and buffalo-robes; and the next morning at breakfast, the ice formed in our tin-cups between the intervals of eating and drinking. We were camped, in fact, on the summit of the Rocky Mountains, at a height of nine or ten thousand feet above the sea, with snow-peaks all about us, and the only wonder is that we got through the night so well. For the first time since leaving Denver, we felt a sense of loneliness and danger; and the occasional yelping of the wolves around us, in the still midnight air, did little to allay this. Our animals, also, seemed fretful and uneasy, and we suspected Indians about, but nothing came of it. We looked well to our arms before retiring, and talked much of the night away—it was so cold; and the next morning broke camp early, and were off up the Pass again.

A half an hour's ride or so brought us to the summit, which surprised us, as the ascent had been so gentle all the way up from Kerber's—far less than that of Sangre del Christo from Fort Garland. The view from the summit we found limited, compared with that from Sangre del Christo ; and soon after we descended into a sheltered nook knee deep in grass, with wood and water both just at hand, where we had been advised to camp the night before, if able to reach it. Following the banks of a diminutive brook, we descended gradually to Poncho Creek; and here our really bad road began. So far, the Pass had been excellent, all things considered, and we were astonished at its bad reputation; but after we crossed Poncho Creek, and got started down its wild cañon, we soon found ample cause for it all. A narrow defile, with precipitous banks on either side from five hundred to a thousand feet high, furnished the only road-way, which here found room first on one side of the creek and then on the other, the best it could, and in many places it had to take to the bed of the creek itself, in order to round the rocky bluffs. The trouble with the Pass was, it had had no work done on it, and needed grading badly at several points. A few hundred dollars judiciously expended would have made it much superior to Sangre del Christo, we all thought. It is not so high by a thousand feet or more, nor nearly so steep, and we judged it would yet become one of the favorite routes to and from San Luis Park.

While the teams were working through, L. and I passed on ahead, with our rifles at our saddle-bows, hoping to start a bear or shoot a buck-tail deer, but saw no game of any kind. Our experience among the mountains on this trip, indeed, was unfavorable to the stirring accounts we had heard and read of great game there.

The lack of trees there, except in the cañons, and especially of nut-bearing trees, and likewise of fruit-bearing bushes, must be unfavorable to animal life, as a rule, and I doubt if there ever was much there, except an occasional deer or bear, eagle or buzzard. We were surprised to find so few birds, and scarcely any squirrels, except a little red species no bigger than our ground-squirrels east. We met two of Kerber's teams toiling wearily up the Pass, as we descended it, and gave them the first news they had had from the ranch in weeks. We got several miles ahead, before we knew it, and did not halt until we reached the foot of the Pass, where it debouches into the valley of the Little Arkansas. It was an hour or more before the ambulances overtook us, and then we received a rough account of their experiences. In several places, they had had to lash ropes around them and edge them along the hillsides the best they could. In others, they only managed to keep them on their wheels by walking and pushing very carefully, and so finally got through safe and sound. The wagon, however, being heavier and clumsier, had capsized badly, and they had driven ahead and left it, with instructions to follow on as soon as possible. Crossing the valley of the little Arkansas and a high range beyond, late in the afternoon we descended into the valley of the Arkansas proper, and at sunset went into camp on its banks, near Schwander's ranch. The Arkansas, we found, was here already a very considerable stream, but we forded it without difficulty. Our unfortunate wagon, perhaps it should be added, got along after dark, much the worse for wear; and jaded and weary with the day's journey, we were glad to pass a quiet night of it.

The next morning we crossed another lofty range, the ascent of which was wild and picturesque, and thence descended into South Park. Less in size than the San Luis, and more broken in surface, the South Park nevertheless has the same general characteristics, though more nearly circular. Its enclosing mountains are abrupt and bold, and the views from many points are very striking and charming. Passing out of it to Denver, we ascended the range from which Leutze is said to have conceived his well-known painting in the Capitol at Washington, "Westward the star of Empire takes its way." The facts are little like the painting aforesaid, because no emigrant train would ever attempt to pass over such an impossible road, as Leutze has painted: but the landscape from the point referred to is nevertheless noble and grand. The range there, I believe, is about eight thousand feet above the sea. South Park, at your feet, extends say, thirty miles north and south, by twenty east and west; down in its bosom nestles a necklace of exquisite little lakes, with streams flashing onward from the mountains to them; while beyond—all along the west, in fact—runs the perpetual Snowy Range, notched and peaked, clear cut and beautiful against the sky, though not so grand and stately as we had seen it farther south. To the north of the road the range shoots up nearly a thousand feet higher, but the view from there did not compensate us for our toil in ascending it. The whole view here, though fine in its way, lacks breadth and sublimity, as a specimen of Rocky Mountain scenery, and Leutze would have done better (in my judgment) had he gone to Sangre del Christo or perhaps Poncho Pass. The sky and general coloring of his painting are good; but how inadequately, how feebly they express the exquisite serenity and unapproachable glory of the Mountains! Bierstadt's skies, though thought impossible east, are nearer to the

TWIN LAKES (South Park).

truth, as our critics will yet learn, when they come to know more of Colorado.

In South Park, we had struck a new civilization, the evidences of which grew constantly more apparent. The Mexican and the herder had given way to the Yankee and the miner, and the contrast was most striking. Ranches and settlements were more numerous, and the spirit of enterprise was everywhere observable. First we struck some saline springs, where extensive salt-works had already been erected, and they were reported to be paying well. They were said to furnish a superior article of salt, at a less price than it could be imported from the east, and the company expected thus to monopolize the salt-market of Colorado and the adjoining regions. Beyond these, ranches thickened up all the way to Fair Play, and we found some splendid duck-shooting in the marshes, that now and then skirted the road. Some of the flocks, however, carried off an immense amount of lead, or else H. and L. were indifferent shots—we were never quite able to decide which. They were our champion sportsmen, and though they bagged a number of fine ducks *en route*, they never were entirely satisfied. They both fired simultaneously at a great flock that rose up as we drove by, and when none dropped H. protested, " I know I hit a dozen that time, but these confounded Rocky Mountain ducks don't know what shot is. They fly away with enough honest lead in them to kill an ordinary eastern duck twice over." L. of course, confirmed this, and adduced the abundant feathers as proof of their joint achievement. B. suggested that the Indians had charmed their fowling-pieces, and meekly inquired of H, " Didn't the ducks carry off your shot-pouch also?" At Fair Play, in the northwest corner of the Park, we found a mining town of four or five hundred inhabitants, apparently busy and prosperous. Timber grew plentifully in the neighboring cañons, and now adobe huts gave place to frame and log shanties. The South Platte skirts the town, and is already a considerable stream here, although it cannot be far away from its source. At Fair Play it heads north up into the great Snowy Range, or water shed of the continent, which feeds it perpetually, and runs thence east to join the North Platte near Fort McPherson, where we had struck it by stage-coach a month before. Good "gold diggings" had been found here long before, and its entire banks about Fair Play have been dug over, "panned out," and ransacked generally. They presented a torn and ragged appearance, as if a young earthquake or two had recently broken out there, and this was not materially improved by the long and high flumes then going up. When these were completed, they expected to turn the Platte considerably aside, and to find rich "placer mines" in its sand-bars and bed again. The principal mining then in South Park, however, was farther up the Platte, at Empire, Buckskin Joe, and other euphoneously named places, none of which had we time to visit. The business generally seemed to be settling down to quartz-mining, as at Black-Hawk and Central City, and to be passing more and more into the hands of Companies. We met several huge boilers on the road, *en route* to various mills, and it seemed marvellous how they could ever wagon them so far across the Plains, and up into the very heart of the Mountains. Progress with them must have been slow and tedious anywhere; but when they struck a slough, or reached the mountain ranges, then came the whacks and oaths.

Judge Costello, of the Fair Play House, entertained us while there, and gave us excellent accommodations.

There had been several inches of snow at Fair Play a few days before, and arriving just at nightfall after a long day's drive, we felt the cold very keenly. But the Judge soon had a roaring fire blazing on his hearth, and welcomed us to Fair Play right royally. In due time he gave us a substantial dinner, piping hot—roast-beef, chicken-fricasee, potatoes with their jackets on, dried-apple-pie and coffee—a meal that seemed supremely Sybaritic, after "roughing it" by the roadside for over a fortnight. We did ample justice to it, having breakfasted nearly twelve hours before, and then adjourned to a common bed-room, where we smoked and read the papers until midnight. We had seen none since leaving Denver, nearly a month before; but Judge C. happened to have just received a large supply, which we devoured eagerly. The elections in California and Oregon had just been held, and the North was again rocking with enthusiasm. Andrew Johnson's apostacy, it was clear, promised to be a losing game after all. The spirit of a free people at last was aroused, as after the firing on Sumter, and evidently the nation meant again neither to be bribed nor scared. True, the November elections were yet to come; but we took increased faith in the virtue and intelligence of the masses, and rejoiced that Congress was still true to Liberty. Absence from "the states" is a great purifier of one's political ideas. We see things at home clearer, and reverence the Union more, the farther we get away from New York and Washington. We forgot all the wretched hair-splitting east, by one side or the other; and came to love only the old flag, in its highest and best significance, as the symbol of freedom and justice, for each and for all men, the broad continent across and the wide world over.

The next morning, a young miner invited us out to

take a look at a fine specimen of the American black-eagle, which he had caught a few days before, while "prospecting" along the Snowy Range. He was comparatively a young bird still, yet measured some six feet from tip to tip of wings, and was as brave and fierce as a tiger. He was kept chained by the leg in a dark stable; but he was as wide awake as he could be, and screamed and flew savagely at every one who came near him. It was intended to forward him to the great Fair soon to be held at St. Louis, as a specimen of the feathered tribe from Colorado, where no doubt he created a sensation. His eyes were bright and keen as a falchion, and his talons ugly looking grappling-irons. So, too, his legs were massive, compact columns, that seemed made for strength and endurance. And altogether he was not a bad representative of the Rocky Mountains, where his species have their birth-place and home.

From Fair Play we descended the South Platte direct to Denver, following the course of the river wherever practicable. In some places, its narrow and precipitous cañons prevented this, but we always returned to its banks again as soon as possible. Some miles from Fair Play, we passed several gems of lakes, which H. declared to be "the natural home of the wild-duck;" but though the ducks were there, he failed to bag any, greatly to his disgust. L. more fortunate, got one, and killed several others, but failed to reach them because of the marshes. Our road led over several ranges, some of them quite precipitous, but in the main followed the windings of the Platte, as before said. Here and there the wild cañons, through which the Platte sped like an arrow, became picturesque in the extreme. Frequently our course ahead seemed barred by impenetrable fastnesses, yet somehow we always got through. High and rocky cliffs towered all about us, and all up and down these, wherever they could secure a foothold, the fir, pine, maple, ash, etc. grew densely. As we neared Denver, ranches became more frequent, and saw-mills multiplied, the lumber from which was shipped far and near, among the mines and across the Plains, even to Julesburg and Fort Riley. The road in the main was a natural way; but here and there it had been blasted out of the bluff, or built up on the edge of the Platte, at large expense, and I believe is a chartered turnpike from Fair Play down. The Platte alone makes such a road practicable, and South Park and all its dependencies would be virtually inaccessible, were it not for this great natural highway into the very heart of the Mountains. Altogether, it is a remarkably good road, all things considered, and so are the majority of the roads there. As a rule, they follow the streams that seem to lead almost everywhere among the ranges, as if purposely chiseled out from the beginning, as future pathways of civilization. Our miners, taking the hint, carry their roads over heights, and through depths, and among peaks, that would appal most eastern engineers, and thus enable us to conquer nature in her mightiest strongholds.

The last day out from Denver, we ascended Bradford's Hill—our last serious climb—about noon. This is in reality the first range of the mountains, and gets itself up to some 8,000 feet above the sea; but is yet termed a "Hill," in Colorado parlance. We all got out or dismounted and walked up, to relieve our worn animals, and became well blown ourselves before reaching the summit—the atmosphere grew so rare. As we rounded its western shoulder, we caught a grand view of the Snowy Range again, solemn and sublime over and above all intervening peaks and ridges; but with one accord, all hastened forward to behold once more the Plains, the Plains! Yes, there they were, in all their immeasurable extent! We were out of the Mountains—our long jaunt almost over. No more cañons. No more forests. No more snow-squalls. No more rides, hour by hour, through narrow valleys and defiles, where the whole man feels "cabined, cribbed, confined." No. There were the Plains, illimitable, grand, in all their immensity and sublimity. We thought the view from Sangre del Christo fine, and so it is; but as a view of the Plains proper, without the Mountains thrown in, this view from Bradford's Hill, I think, perhaps surpasses it. There is no end to the vast outstretch and outlook, and in the serene atmosphere of that region the eye ranges over it all with an ease and freedom, only equalled by the eagle himself when poised in mid air. To say that the Plains are visible for miles on miles—north, south, east—is but a feeble description of the wonderful panorama, that there unfolds before you. To the south appeared Castle Rock and its sister buttes, that we had passed three weeks before, looking now like mole-hills beneath us. Issuing from the Mountains at our feet, we could trace the South Platte and Cherry Creek to where they unite near Denver, and then follow the Platte on and on to the east, till lost in the far horizon. Denver lay like a toy-city, seemingly at the base of the Mountains, though really twenty miles away. Over all, was one of those perfect days,

> "So cool, so calm, so bright,
> The bridal of the earth and sky."

as old George Herbert wrote, which no Bostonian or Gothamite ever truly witnesses—with not a cloud or haze even visible, the air so pure it was joy to breathe it and ecstacy to gaze abroad through it. Verily, here in Colorado, if anywhere.

"The sky *is* a drinking cup,
That was overturned of old,
And it pours into the eyes of men
Its wine of airy gold;
We drink that wine all day
Till the last drop is drained up,
And are lighted off to bed,
By the jewels in the cup."

Off to the southwest, just shouldering over the range, presently a white cloud loomed up, no bigger than a man's hand; but the dry atmosphere east was too much for it, and faded away as fast as it toppled over. As we stood gazing at the immensity before us, some one incidentally said, "I think I now understand how Balboa felt, when from the summit of the Andes he beheld the Pacific;" and it is a good illustration of the identity of thought under like circumstances, that half-a-dozen others quickly responded, "You bet! Just thinking of the same thing!"

We reached Denver the same evening, jaded and travel-stained, but full of enthusiasm over our trip among the mountains. We had traversed nine counties, some as large as a moderate state east, and been absent nearly a month in all. We had been reported captured and slain by the Indians, as much as two or three times, but from first to last did not see a hostile aborigine. We drove the same animals down and back, over five hundred miles continuously, without the loss of a mule, and seldom made less than thirty or forty miles a day, when on the road. Our ambulances proved very convenient and serviceable, but in crossing the ranges or in bad cañons I always preferred a mule. My favorite was Kate, a noble jenny, as large as a horse and a splendid walker. that carried me over many a mile delightfully. She was as gentle as a kitten, and as faithful as a dog—it sometimes seemed almost as knowing as a man—obeying every whim of her rider, and following him everywhere. If any mule ever attains immortality and a sort of heaven hereafter, surely Kate deserves to. In crossing the ranges or threading the cañons thus, on horse or mule back, several of us would often get miles ahead, and the time thus gained afforded ample leisure for observation and reflection. We were seldom at a loss for conversation, there was so much to investigate and discuss; but when all else failed, we amused ourselves by organizing (on paper) two monster Mining Companies, with fabulous capitals, in which we divided off and took stock. I believe I belonged to the Grand Sangre del Christo Rocky Mountain Mutual Benefit Gold and Silver Mining Association; capital, $20,000,000! H. and C. and others constituted a rival company, with like assets and name equally pretentious. We set up these financial fictions early in the trip, when somebody fell to talking about "feet;" and what with selling "short," operating for a "rise," "corraling the market," "declaring dividends," and abusing each others' "Company," they served to while away many an idle interval. The last afternoon out, we "consolidated," shook hands over the "union," elected a full "Board of Officers," and adjourned to receive our "joint dividends," at New York; but hitherto have never been so fortunate as to get a "quorum" together there, and doubt now if we ever will.

CHAPTER VIII.

THE INDIANS—GEN. SHERMAN—KIT CARSON, ETC.

AT Fort Garland, in San Louis Park, Sept 21st, Gov. Cumming, Gen. Sherman, and the famous Kit Carson (then Bv't. Brig. Gen. U. S. Vols.), met in council, concerning the Utes and the Indian question generally. Sherman, as elsewhere intimated, was then in the midst of a long tour by ambulance, through the heart of the Indian country embraced in his then Military Division, and as he had already travelled about 1200 miles, with no escort except a couple of staff-officers and the necessary teamsters, without seeing a hostile Red Skin, he was getting to be somewhat skeptical on the whole Indian subject. The grand Treaty with the Utes was to come off Sept. 22d and 23d on the banks of the Rio Grande, some thirty miles northwest from Fort Garland; but as Sherman had decided to leave Garland on the 22d for his return east *via* the Arkansas, a preliminary council was called at Fort Garland on the 21st. Runners had been sent out a day or two before, and the Big Chiefs of the Utes kept arriving all that day. The council was held late in the afternoon, in a large room back of the commandant's quarters. The chiefs were grouped on one side of the room, squat upon their haunches, grave and dignified; while on the other sat Sherman in loose uniform, puffing a cigar, with Gov. Cumming on one side and Kit Carson on the other.

Carson served as interpreter, speaking Mexican well, which the chiefs mostly understood. After some preliminary skirmishing, Sherman said he had called them together to ascertain whether the Utes were willing to quit their nomadic life and settle down on a Reservation. He urged this upon them, as their true interest, if they wished to maintain their tribal existence, and said he had only come among them to promote their happiness and welfare. He added, he had recently been visiting many other tribes with the same object and purposes, and as a friend to their race was convinced their only hope for the future lay in going on a Reservation. The chiefs debated the matter among themselves for awhile, and presently made answer, that they thanked the Big Warrior for his suggestions and approved them; but that their young men were opposed to such a policy, and they feared it would be difficult to persuade the Utes of its wisdom, until the Cheyennes and Comanches—their hereditary foes—had first adopted it. The council lasted an hour or more, with much skillful fencing and adroit diplomacy on the part of Ooray and Ancantash, the head-chiefs; but this was the substance of all that Sherman could worm out of them. He tried to explain and reason with them in various ways, but at last broke up the council in disgust, and blurted out in his peculiar way, as he strode back to his quarters, "They will have to freeze and starve a little more, I reckon, before they will listen to common sense!" Subsequently he told us of a council that he had held about a fortnight or so before, at Fort Laramie or somewhere up there, with the Arrapahoes or the Sioux. He had urged upon the chiefs, that their white brothers were opposed to war and desired peace, and he hoped there would be no more bloodshed in that region between the Red

Man and the Pale Face. The chiefs presently replied, with a wariness worthy of Talleyrand, that they reciprocated his Quaker sentiments, and would do all in their power to enforce them; but that their young men were rash and fiery sometimes, and it might be difficult to hold them in. "Well, then," said Sherman to the interpreter, firing up, "Tell the rascals so are *mine;* and if another white man is scalped in all this region, it will be *impossible* to hold *mine* in." The chiefs saw the point, and no doubt sagely concluded they would have trouble, if ever they got Tecumseh Sherman fairly after them.

The grand Treaty with the Utes came off, as I have said, Sept. 22d and 23d, on the banks of the Rio Grande, some thirty miles or so northwest from Fort Garland. We left Garland early in the morning by ambulance, and reached the treaty ground soon after noon. Gov. Cumming and Indian Agent Hunt had preceded us, and on arriving we found them just sitting down to discuss a Rio Grande trout, nearly as large as an eastern shad. The Utes had pitched their lodges a mile or so away, in a bend of the river, but they were constantly passing to and fro on horseback and afoot. Apparently none of them ever walked, if he could afford the luxury of a pony, and often one puny pony was made to carry two or three lubberly fellows at a time. Evidently the Plains Indians are as averse to walking, as the traditional Texan, who is said never to leave his door-sill without mounting a mustang. These Ute ponies are hardy, sagacious little fellows, some of them very handsome, and are of course, the lineal descendants of the wild horses of the Plains. Ooray, their head chief, rode a bright little bay, that would have taken a first-class premium almost anywhere. Of course, they get no grain, but subsist exclusively on grass. They constitute their owners' chief wealth, and a Ute will part with almost anything sooner than his pony. Braves, squaws, papooses, all ride astride, and generally at a gallop. They seldom use the spur, but rarely mount without a whip, and this they keep going pretty steadily while on the road. Their saddles are rude affairs of wood, with very short stirrups; but their bridles are better made, and usually have some kind of an iron bit, if at all obtainable.

In the course of the afternoon, hundreds of the Indians thronged our little camp, in all varieties of costume, though chiefly in breech-cloth and blanket or buffalo-robe. Both sexes dress much alike, and at first it was difficult to distinguish one from the other, though you soon came to know the squaws from their smaller stature. The paraphernalia of some of them was ludicrous in the extreme. One young buck had managed to secure an old-style artillery hat, with long scarlet horse-hair plume, and a dilapidated white shirt; and as he strutted about in these (only these and nothing more!) considered himself wholly *en regle*. Another, the princess and beauty of the tribe, a dirty belle of seventeen, resplendent in paint and feathers, was arrayed in much gorgeousness of beads and buckskin, and whiffed her cigarritos by the hour together. During the morning she had ridden her thirty miles, man-fashion, with the chiefs from Fort Garland, and in the afternoon she lolled about camp in magnificent indolence. Her laugh was rich and musical, and she seemed indeed quite a pet with the tribe.

The afternoon was passed in preliminary arrangements for the Treaty, and towards evening a number of us walked over to the Indian village to return our calls. We found it to consist of perhaps three hundred wigwams, arranged pretty regularly in streets, and containing in all some twelve hundred souls. The wigwams or lodges were made of skins and hides, stretched over circularly inclined poles—rude originals evidently of our army Sibley tents—with an opening at the top for the smoke to escape through. At the door were planted their spears or lances, and shields; inside, on skins or blankets, the braves were fast asleep or playing cards; without, the youngsters were playing ball or practicing with the bow and arrows. We wandered through the streets until nightfall, striking up a talk or barter in our broken Ute the best we could, and had some interesting experiences. Just then the village was all agog with excitement and joy. The day before, their Agent had given them several beeves, which they had at once slaughtered and partly eaten; the surplus was now hanging all about on lariats and poles, curing in the dry atmosphere. "Jerked-beef," I suppose, our Plains-men would call it. A flock of sheep had also been given them, and the squaws were now busy "corraling" these, as we happened along. A few refractory ewes refused to enter the corral—a slight enclosure of brush—and these were being hotly pursued by the boy-braves and dogs. The dogs headed them off on all sides, while the boys lassoed them one after another, until the squaws came up and caught them. It was fine practice for the lasso, and the youngsters seemed to enjoy it greatly. Dogs abounded everywhere. Each wigwam seemed to have a goodly supply, and the village at large a brigade besides. They were small wolfish-looking curs, as a rule, and the most vociferous and incessant yelpers I ever listened to. They had no regular bark—only a wild yelp, like their savage ancestors, the cayotes of the Plains. It is only the civilized dog, that "bays deep-mouthed welcome"—that has a full, open "bark"—and this he loses when he relapses to savagery again. There was no moving anywhere about the village, without having a score or more of them yelping at your heels; but this seemed to be the extent of their hostile intentions. When they became rather noisier than usual, some passing squaw would dash at them with a stick and a shower of "God dams," and that would scatter them for the time. Most of our Indians have all learned to swear the rough oaths of the Border, and always swear in English, as they have no corresponding words in their own language. In describing cavalry, they put the thumb and forefinger of one hand on the palm of the other, and then move them along in imitation of a gallop. In speaking of ox-trains, they stretch out their arms, and say, "Whoa-Haw! Git!" But when they come to mule-teams, they invariably speak of them as "God dams! Go 'long!" because of the copious oaths our teamsters hurl at them. Indeed, the average Indian always speaks of the donkey, as a "God dam," and thinks that the correct name. These Utes in general, I must say, seemed to be much more thrifty and comfortable than we had anticipated, though doubtless some of this was due to the recent generous issue of supplies by the Agent.

Our party scattered pretty well through the village, one after another halting to palaver with acquaintances we had picked up; but as it grew dark, we gradually drifted together and prepared to return. Dr. M. was still bargaining with a chief for a fancy shield he wanted as a souvenir, when the rest began moving off, and begged me to wait a minute until he was through. Several minutes passed by, and then his bargaining ended in failure—the Big Chief refusing to "swop"—their universal word for selling or trading. Then we started to overtake the rest, but they had passed out of view in the deepening twilight, and though we hallooed to them could get no answer—the hubbub of the village evidently drowning our voices. Emerging from the wigwams, we soon discovered, that neither of us had taken any proper notes of the landmarks, as we came over, being busy talking with the rest, and consequently neither knew the way back. Here was a pretty predicament, surely, for two ambitious young men—cast away in a village of a thousand savages, unable to speak a sentence of their language intelligibly or they ours, night already come, and no hint of how to extricate ourselves. To make it doubly absurd, we presently discovered, that our only belligerent weapons, whether for offence or defence, consisted of a Rogers' penknife apiece. We had been so remiss, as to leave camp without our revolvers—a precaution that no Mountain or Plains-man ever neglects. While pondering the "situation," we luckily caught sight of the Sierra Blanca glistening in the moonlight, and as we knew this to be southeast of our camp we concluded our route lay toward it. We set off accordingly, and had made perhaps a quarter of a mile, across sloughs now dry and through the rank grass, when one of us suggested, that we could not be going right, or our camp-fires would appear. This seemed reasonable, the country was so level; so a halt was ordered, while we scanned the horizon for fires elsewhere. Presently far away to the left, we descried a fire blazing loftily up, and concluded this must be ours, and that our comrades had put on extra fuel to guide us the better home. The direction seemed wrong, judging by the position of the Sierra Blanca; but as it was the only fire visible, except those at the Indian village, we concluded it must be ours, and changing our course struck for it accordingly. A trudge of a mile or more, with an occasional tumble into a dry slough, at length brought us to the fire, when to our disappointment we found it to be only the camp-fire of two rough-looking customers, who said they were out "prospecting" for mines. They said they had reached there just at nightfall, from a long trip through the Mountains, and as yet had seen nothing of our camp, and of course knew nothing of its whereabouts. Two Utes were squatted before the fire, who they said had just rode over from the village, and we asked one of the men, who had been talking with them in Mexican, to inquire the way to "Kit Carson's Camp" for us. He did so, and the Indians jumping up responded, they would conduct us there. We thought now we were in luck, surely, and thanking the miners for their kindness prepared to follow our copper-colored friends. Unloosing a little pony, that was picketed near by, they both clambered upon him, and then with grunts and mutterings to each other, of which we only understood an occasional "God dam," they rode along ahead for perhaps a quarter of a mile, when suddenly they turned round on the pony without stopping, chattered and gibbered away at us for a minute or two like monkeys, and then with a wild whoop, that for a moment quite dazed us, galloped wildly off toward the Indian village.

We were now worse off than ever, and our affairs were evidently coming to a crisis. Of course, we halted again, and called another "council of war." M. advised going back to the miners' camp-fire, and trusting our fortunes for the night with them. I objected that we knew nothing about them; that they were suspicious looking customers anyhow—hadn't the air of genuine miners; and suggested that we camp down where we were, on the banks of a bayou, as there was plenty of dry wood there for a fire, and when morning came we would hunt up the

Rio Grande, and follow it down to our lost camp. He assented to this, but on reflection I further suggested, whether it wouldn't be better, after all, to go boldly into the Indian village, and govern ourselves by circumstances. We knew Ooray and Ancantash, the head chiefs, and why not ask for them? If we could find *them*, our troubles would be over. If we couldn't, at the worst, we could claim the hospitality of some other chieftain, and quarter for the night in a Ute wigwam. I urged that the Indians already knew where we were anyhow, and also knew that we were unarmed and lost; that it would be disagreeable to hear their arrows whizzing around us there, or perhaps be scalped and tossed into the bayou before morning; and that, in short, I would risk the Utes, if he would. M. approved the plan, as the best we could do under such dismal circumstances; so off we trudged again for the Indian village, which by that time we were beginning to wish we had never seen. We tried to keep our courage up by discussing Mark Tapley, and his philosophy of the "jolly;" but the result could hardly be called a success. Perhaps the two braves who had so suddenly deserted us, with such unearthly whoops, were lying in wait for us somewhere ahead! Perhaps the next step we would hear an arrow whiz by, or over us—perchance *through* us! Nevertheless, I remember also a ludicrous feeling at the idea—after escaping unscathed from the rebellion—of falling ignominiously there, on the banks of the Del Norte, by the hand of a Ute, with only a pocket-knife to defend myself with!

However, we proceeded cautiously forward, with many a halt and "hist," and presently without molestation reached the village again. The dogs, of course, challenged our approach with a multitudinous yelping, as before: but some friendly squaws appeared, and soon dispersed them with a copious shower of "God dams." Approaching a lodge in which we saw a number of Indians reclining around a fire, we tried to make them understand, that we were lost and wanted to find the way to "Kit Carson's Camp;" but met with the same poor success as before. Then we inquired for Ooray and Ancantash, but they either did not comprehend, or else were unwilling to bother with us, as their only answer was a grunt—"Ugh"—or a stare. Evidently, on reflection, they concluded we were *bores*, for they soon resumed their pipes, and the low drawling song they were crooning when we entered. We tried two or three more lodges, with the same result, and had about made up our minds to camp down for the night, where we were, when M. suggested that we try one more wigwam, and if we failed there to give it up. This seemed almost providential; for as we entered the lodge-door, up sprang a lithe young chief, whom we had met during the day, and came smiling toward us with the greeting, "How, Gen-e-ral! How, Doc-tor! Know me? Me, Wellington!" (*How* is all the Indian has learned yet of How do you do? or How are you?) Greasy and dirty as the fellow was, we could have hugged him with delight; for now we knew our troubles were all over. We answered him, "O yes! Know Wellington, of course! In our wigwam to-day! But lost now! No find wigwam! Kit Carson's Camp?" He comprehended our lingo, and "the situation," in a moment, and quickly replied, "Yes! Wellington go!" and then, with an eye to the main chance, shrewdly added, "How much?" We answered, "Two paint, and some tobacco." He held up three fingers, and bargainingly responded, "Three paint, and 'baccy a heap?" By "paint" he meant little packages of Indian paint—blue, vermillion, yellow—such as some in camp had brought along for barter, and we readily acceded to his terms. As it was growing late, he asked another young buck to go along, who demanded the same terms, which of course we cheerfully granted. Then they took up their bows and arrows, drew their blankets around their shoulders, and bidding the rest "*bueno noche*" we moved off.

We soon observed, that they were conducting us toward the Sierra Blanca, in the same direction that we took originally. We questioned Wellington about this, but he persisted it was right; and so we pushed on, though not without some misgivings. A half hour or so, however, brought us safely to camp, where we found our friends discussing our absence, and wondering what had become of us. We cautioned each other to say nothing about our adventure; but the joke was too good to keep, and the facts all came out in the course of the evening, as we sat around the camp-fire and smoked our fatigue away. However tame it may read now, it was exciting and romantic enough at the time, and I record it here for the moral involved, to wit: 1. Mind your topography, on leaving camp; 2. Never quit camp, without your rifle or revolver!

Of course, we paid Wellington and his friend their paint and tobacco, and dismissed them with hearty thanks. We won their hearts by inviting them both to lunch next day, and continued fast friends during the rest of our stay there.

The next day (Sept. 23d) having been set apart for the Treaty, Indians of both sexes and all ages at an early hour began to swarm through our encampment. All, of course, were naturally on hand, to hear the Big Talk and share the many presents. The chiefs and braves were there first, gorgeous in paint and feathers; but long before the Council assembled, the poor squaws also arrived, freighted with their papooses. The spot selected was a sloping lawn on the banks of the Rio Grande, and but a short distance therefrom. Blankets were spread on the grass for the Commissioners and head chiefs: the young chiefs and braves formed a rude circle around these; and beyond these still were the women and children. The four leading men seemed to be Ooray, *Arrow*, Sha-wa-she-wit, *Blue Flower*, Ancantash, and Chi-chis-na-sau-no, also abbreviated into Shauno. The head chief of the tribe, and the finest looking Indian we had yet seen, was Ooray. He was a medium sized, athletic looking man, of about forty, with as fine an eye and head, as you will see anywhere. Moreover, he was very neat and clean in his person, as if he believed in the saving virtues of soap and water—something wonderful for a Red Skin. Two or three years before, he had made the tour of Washington and the East, and to-day wore the handsome silver medal, that President Lincoln then gave him. Kit Carson said he had made good use of this eastern trip, and being already a rising man, the knowledge and experience then acquired had since raised him to the king-ship, notwithstanding his want of age—several of the chiefs being older, but none so shrewd as he. The head-warrior, however, was Ancantash, and he was certainly one of the coolest and bravest looking men I ever met. He was a reticent, reflective, but very observant man, with many of the calm characteristics of our own Grant, and no doubt is quite as desperate and obstinate a fighter in his small way. Kit Carson cited instances of his prowess, that showed supreme manhood and courage; but there is not room for them here. Shauno, taller and more dignified, had a face and form much like Tecumseh's, and altogether was about as fine a looking specimen of the savage as history makes mention of.

The Council opened, as usual, with a general smoke, the pipe being passed for a whiff or two from one to another all around, and then Gov. Cumming proceeded to address his copper-colored friends. He said the Great Father at Washington had made him Big Agent for Colorado*, and as such he had come down from Denver, to bring them their annual presents, hear their grievances, if any, and have a general talk about their future welfare. This was interpreted by Kit Carson into Mexican, with profuse pantomime, after the Indian fashion, and then reinterpreted by Ooray into Ute for the benefit of his red brethren. It was received with a general grunt of satisfaction all round, and then Ooray replied:

"Good! Let the Big Chief speak on!"

"Our Father at Washington has many children, both white and red, and the Great Spirit bids him regard all alike. He has watched his red children, the Utes, a long time, and generally found them peaceable and friendly. Therefore, he loves them very much, and is pained to see them diminishing in numbers from year to year. He thinks this is because of their wars with other tribes, and increasing scarcity of game, and believes if they would settle down in one place, like his pale-face children, they would be much better off. Then they could raise cattle, and sheep, and barley, and have comfort and plenty always."

To which, Ooray:

"True! So; a heap! Utes got plenty now. Hunt give. But soon all gone, and then Utes starve a heap. Long time ago, Utes always had plenty. On the prairie,

* As Governor he was *ex-officio* Superintendent of Indian Affairs there.

antelope and buffalo, so many Ooray can't count. In the mountains, deer and bear, everywhere. In the streams, trout, duck, beaver, everything. Good Manitou gave all to red man; Utes happy all the year. White man came, and now Utes go hungry a heap. Game much go every year—hard to shoot now. Old man often weak for want of food. Squaw and papoose cry. Only strong brave live. White man grow a heap; Red man no grow—soon die all."

To which, Gov. C.:

"Our Great Father knows all this, and it grieves him very much. But he can think of no way to remedy it, except by the Utes quitting their wandering life, and settling down on a Reservation. If they will do this, and will stop fighting the Cheyennes and Comanches, he will have a good Reservation set apart for them, with water, wood, and grass in abundance. He will give them cattle, sheep, seeds, and implements. And he will send good white men among them, to teach them farming, etc. By this means, the Utes will soon have houses and fields, flocks and herds, the same as white men, and all will be better off and happier.

To which, Ooray:

"Yes! So! Much true! Ooray and Big-Chief understand, and know Utes must go on Reservation some day—raise beef, pony, and barley—or perish. But young braves no understand; hard to make 'em. Some, too, say, if Utes go on Reservation, Cheyennes and Comanches—enemies of Utes always—will know where to find. Then some night, when Utes all asleep, will come like a squaw and kill a heap. Utes hate Cheyenne—Comanche—God dam!"

"But our Great Father will prevent that. He will

build forts, and station his blue coats near you, and they will keep off the Cheyennes and Comanches."

When this was interpreted to Ooray, for the first time he lost his savage dignity, and laughed outright. When he reinterpreted it to the Utes, there was a general chorus of laughter, which lasted several minutes. Evidently, they had little respect for the average soldier of the Plains, whether infantry or cavalry. Presently, however, Ooray recovering his dignity replied:

"Why don't our Great Father's blue-coats keep off the Cheyennes and Comanches some now? Last snow the Comanches came right by the forts, found the Utes in one place, and killed many. Utes killed Comanches back a heap. Now Utes move about much—hunt buffalo on the prairie—build wigwam in the mountains—fish in Del Norte. Utes stop not in one place, and Comanches no find. But Utes settle down; then Comanches come and kill. Tell Great Father, Cheyennes and Comanches go on Reservation *first*; then Utes will. But Comanches first."

This was about the same answer substantially, that they had given Gen. Sherman down at Fort Garland; and with all his diplomacy, Gov. C. could not extract more from them. There was a deal of good common sense in it, too—the instinct of self-preservation—and the governor could not help admitting this, much as he desired to enforce the views of the Government. He rehashed his arguments, and presented them anew in various ways; but to all of them, Ooray steadily made answer:

"Ooray has spoken!" And there the matter ended.

Subsequently, after some considerable talk with his brother chiefs, Ooray resumed:

"Suppose Utes go on Reservation, and bad pale-face

come and shoot Indian; what will our Great Father do then?"

"Why," answered Gov. C., "Our Great Father will have him arrested and tried in his courts; and, if found guilty, will hang him. If the Great Father's own brother, he would hang him all the same."

Ooray had great difficulty in understanding this. Gen. Carson had to repeat and explain it a number of times, before he could comprehend what a court and jury were, and even then he seemed somewhat dazed. Doubtless he found it hard to believe, that we would hang any white man for killing an Indian, let alone our Great Father's brother, after what he had seen and heard of law and justice on the border. But after much questioning back and forth, he appeared to catch some glimpse of the idea, and after pondering it awhile, sorrowfully answered:

"Yes! So! Ooray comprehend! Much good! But my people no comprehend. No make them now."

He seemed to think there was no use, in even trying to get such an idea into their heads, and communicated to them some short answer, which apparently satisfied them.

Again, after much deliberation, he warily asked:

"Suppose pale-face steal pony from red-man, what will Great Father do?"

To which Gov. C.:

"He will compel the pale-face to restore the pony. And if the thief can't be found, and his red children prove their loss, the Great Father will pay for it in goods or money."

This seemed to give great satisfaction, when he first interpreted it; but presently the chiefs became excited, and a hot discussion spread among them. Kit Carson said, as well as he could make out, they were canvassing among themselves, whether on the same principle the government would not compel them to restore or pay for what *they* stole from the whites; and as their thefts were evidently much the larger, they speedily directed Ooray to dodge this question, without further talk.

There was some other desultory conversation, and much repetition necessarily; but the above is about the substance of it all. The council lasted two or three hours, and finally wound up with a dignified expression of thanks by Ooray, for the interest the Great Father and Gov. C. took in them. This was followed by a general expression of "Bueno! Bueno!"* by the rest of the Indians, and so the pow-wow ended. The governor managed his side of the affair with much shrewdness and ability, but failed to secure the positive pledges the government so much desired. On the other hand, Ooray certainly conducted himself with great dignity and good sense, for an "untutored savage," and fully realized our old-time notions of an Indian chieftain. Should he live, he will yet make a figure among the Indians, and go down to history as a Logan or a Red-Jacket. His trip to Washington, he told me, convinced him, it was idle for his people to contend with the pale-faces, and his counsels were always for peace and civilization. Subsequently, some months afterwards, when the Utes rose in hostilities against his advice, he deliberately repaired to Fort Garland and gave himself up, refusing to have anything to do with the tribe, until they laid down their arms again. All honor and praise to this dusky son of the Plains and Mountains!

After the council broke up, there came a grand distribution of presents, the most sensible of which were a

* Good! good!

flock of sheep and a small herd of cattle. The balance amounted to but little in a practical point of view, though the Utes of course were delighted with their beads, paint, scarlet blankets, gilt trinkets, etc. The Agents seemed to deal fairly and honestly by their savage wards, and I doubt not Mr. Hunt (since Gov. of Colorado) did his duty in the premises very faithfully.

During the day, and indeed most of the time we were there, there was considerable bartering going on between some of us and the Indians, though in a petty way. We were eager for Indian relics and trophies, to send East as souvenirs, and they were equally eager for some articles we possessed; so that barter was not difficult. Neither party knew much, if any, of the language of the other, but the bargaining went steadily on for all that. The Utes came into camp, with such articles as they wished to dispose of. If we desired them and had anything to exchange, we laid it on the ground, and then —pointing to the Indian articles—uttered the classic word "Swop?" If they assented, the bargain ended, and the exchange took place immediately. But if they refused, or wanted more, they shook their heads and answered "No swop!" These words, "Swop" and "No swop," are about the only English necessary in trading with them, and we found them current everywhere among our Indians, from the Missouri to the Pacific. In this way, our party succeeded in securing a few lances and shields, bows and arrows, grizzly-bear skins, buffalo-robes, etc., though their stock of skins had been mostly disposed of to the regular traders some time before. We found them, as a rule, fond of trading, and keen at a bargain, but averse to parting with their ponies or their bows and arrows. Their ponies they held in special regard, and asked extravagant prices for them. Their bows and arrows were made of tough, elastic wood, very scarce in that region, and they were loth to sell them, except for a pistol or a "carabina." In this matter of trading, however, a young chief named Jack Cox seemed to be a marked exception. He had a handsome wolf-skin quiver, beautifully finished and embroidered—the finest we saw there—and I was desirous of securing it, if he cared to part with it. Various offers were tendered him, but all were refused. He had set his heart on one of our repeating-rifles, and his constant answer was, as he patted the barrel, "Me take carabina! Nothing else!" Subsequently, others pressed him with various offers; but they could not shake his resolution. At last he rose up, as if vexed and irritated, and pointing to a group of Utes, who were crowding around all eager for barter, indignantly exclaimed, "Mean Indian swop — pony, bow, quiver, robe, any thing! Jack Cox no swop!" Instinctively I handed him a pipe, and begged him to join in a smoke. Accepting the courtesy, he sat down again, and as he spoke a little broken English we managed to talk some on several subjects. But, all the while, he watched the "swopping," that was going on about him, and when he saw any one about to make what he considered a foolish or bad bargain, he would sneer at his want of judgment, and set all the rest of the Indians to laughing at him—a trick which usually broke up the bargain. Subsequently, he went off to the village for a fancy buffalo robe, which he said he would "swop" me for something that pleased him, and kept his promise by returning with it an hour or so afterwards. This Jack Cox was a bright, shrewd young fellow—lithe, sinewy and straight as an arrow—about seventeen or eighteen years of age; and, if he live, will doubtless yet distinguish himself among the Utes. He was already much deferred to among those of his age, and was decidedly the keenest one among them. He had heard of Washington and the east, and asked many curious questions concerning them. I inquired if he would not like to make a trip east, as Ooray and others had done. He answered, after reflecting a little:

"How long be gone?"

I replied at hap-hazard:

"Perhaps five snows," meaning five years.

He rejoined,

"O, no! No! Not *five* snows! One snow! Then Jack Cox go!"

He interested us very much at the time, and we all augured well of his future.

The same evening Wellington and Jack Cox sent word, that they were going to have a Big Dance over at the village, and invited us all over. Accordingly soon after dark their tom-toms began to beat, and at about 8 P. M., several of us walked thither. The dance had already commenced, on a natural lawn that sloped down from the village to the Rio Grande. Here were perhaps a hundred or so young braves, with hand locked in hand and shoulder pressed to shoulder, moving slowly round in a circle facing inward, while back of them were gathered the whole village gazing on. Two or three of them beat time on rude drums or tom-toms, while all joined in a wild chant or song. The music was barbarous, and their movements not much of a dance; but they went through it all with much gravity and earnestness, whatever they meant by it. Jack Cox left the crowd as we approached, and invited us to participate, which several did. One was allowed to beat the tom-tom, as a special favor; but his performance proved to be not a "success," as he failed to keep time. We spent an hour with them, and no doubt the Utes will long remember the occasion, when their pale-face friends from the east danced with them by moonlight on the banks of the Rio Grande. Altogether, it was rather a unique experience, and we wondered what would come next. As we strolled back to camp, the moon had mounted above the Sierra Blanca, and was flooding the whole Park with a sea of light. The notched and jagged peaks of the Mountains all about us, tipped with snow, glittered in her beams. And the hour and the place seemed, for all the world, more like a chapter from fairy land, than sober reality.

As already intimated, we found some striking characters among the Utes—Ooray, Ancantash, Jack Cox, etc.—but they were few and far between. The great mass of the tribe were small, undersized men, with coarse, animal faces, that looked as if they went hungry half the time, if not more. Their dress in general consisted of the usual breech-cloth, a blanket or buffalo-robe, and deer-skin leggings and moccasins. The nights and mornings were already sharp and chilly; but they had a knack of twisting a robe or blanket about them, even when on horseback at a gallop, that I have never seen equalled, and they declared they were not uncomfortable. In winter, however, especially their winter, we would suppose they must suffer from the weather severely. They seemed to treat their poor squaws about as shabbily as all other Indians—that is to say, about as bad as bad can be. They compelled them to wait upon and serve them on every possible occasion, no matter how degrading. In coming to and going from our encampment, the braves always galloped or trotted along on horseback, while the squaws as a rule trudged wearily by on foot, with their papooses at their backs. It was the squaws, who made their bows and arrows, spears and shields—dressed their skins—pitched and struck camp—saddled and unsaddled their ponies—and, in short, performed all other menial or laborious offices, that Indian life is heir to. They carried their papooses strapped to a board, with a wicker-work at the top to protect the child's head—the whole swung over the shoulders or across the forehead by a rude thong. This board was made round at the lower end, to rock backward and forward when necessary, and thus serve as a sort of cradle. In camp it is hung up on a tree, which places the child out of danger, while at the same time the wind sways it to and fro. On the march, the whole dangles from the mother's shoulder. Some of these Ute cradles were quite neatly adorned with paint and bead-work, and made as soft and cosy as buck-skin and buffalo-robe or beaver-fur could make them. The papooses occupying them, with their jet-black eyes and copper-colored cheeks, seemed to be model babies; for they never even whimpered. The wretched and degraded condition of their women, however, is everywhere the reproach of savage life. There was a forlorn and hopeless look in the faces of these Ute squaws, as if all their womanhood was crushed out, that would have touched a heart of stone. A father, we are told, may chastise any of his children, but a mother only her daughters. She must not lay a finger on a boy-brave, on pain of death; and this is only a specimen of her disabilities. On the whole, I must say, we were not favorably impressed with Ute life, as a rule. It had its romantic features, but their universal "shiftlessness," their long matted hair sweeping loosely about their faces or hanging in heavy plaits around their shoulders, their general squalor, raggedness and dirt, and above all, their neglect and abuse of their poor squaws—all made a bad impression and dispelled many of the poetic ideas about the "Noble Red Man," "Lo, the poor Indian, etc." that we cherish in the east. In spite of our preconceived notions, we could not help regarding the great majority of them, as but little above the wild animals, that roam over the Plains and through the Mountains with them; and as a whole—for all practical purposes of citizenship—infinitely below the colored race, even of the cotton states. Of course, there were some noble exceptions, such as Ooray and Ancantash, but then they only proved the rule. In point of intellect and character, and promise of improvement, the African will certainly beat the Red Man all to pieces, as the future will show. Nevertheless, I must say, we found the Utes truthful and honest in their way, and Kit Carson—a good judge—credited them with being the bravest and best Red Skins he had ever met, in all his wide wanderings.

I have spoken several times of Kit Carson, and as he is a real historical character, perhaps can not conclude this chapter better, than with a word or two more in regard to him. We met him first at Fort Garland, where we found him in command of a battalion of New Mexico Volunteers, and Brevet Brigadier-General. When the war broke out, and most of our troops were withdrawn from the Plains and Mountains, he applied to Mr. Lincoln for permission to raise a Regiment of Volunteers in New Mexico, to protect our settlements there, and the "good President" very properly granted it. At the head of these, Kit did excellent service during the war, on one occasion taking 9,000 Navajoes prisoners with less than 600 men, and at its close was ordered to Fort Garland and given command of a wide region there. We found him in log quarters, rough but comfortable, with his Mexican wife and half-breed children around him. We had expected to see a small and wiry man, weather-beaten and reticent; but met a medium sized, rather stoutish, florid, and quite talkative person instead. He certainly bore the marks of exposure, but none of that extreme "roughing it," that we had anticipated. In age, he seemed to be about forty-five. His head was a remarkably good one, with the bumps of benevolence and reflection well developed. His eye was mild and blue, the very type of good nature, while his voice was as soft and sympathetic as a woman's. He impressed you at once as a man of rare kindliness and charity, such as a truly brave man ought always to be. As simple as a child, but brave as a lion, he soon took our hearts by storm, and grew upon our regard all the while we were with him. He talked and smoked far into the night each evening we spent together, and we have no room here for a tithe of what he told us. Born in Kentucky, he emigrated to the Plains and Mountains when a child, and attached himself to a party of trappers and hunters, when he was so small that he couldn't set a trap. When he became older, he turned trapper himself, and as such wandered all over our possessions, from the Missouri to the Pacific, and from British America to Mexico. Next he became a government scout and guide, and as such piloted Fremont and others all over the Plains and through the Mountains. He confirmed the accounts, we had heard, that Fremont, as an explorer, was somewhat of a charlatan, and said the worst time the Pathfinder ever had was, when on one of his expeditions, he disregarded his (Kit's) advice, and endeavored to force the Mountains northwest of where Fort Garland now stands. Kit told him he could not get through or over them at that period of the year, and, when Fremont nevertheless insisted on proceeding, he resigned as guide. The Pathfinder, however, went sternly forward, but got caught in terrible snow-storms, and presently returned, with half of his men and animals perished outright, from cold and hunger. Subsequently, Kit became a U. S. Indian Agent, and one of the best we ever had. Familiar with their language and customs, he frequently spent months together among them, without seeing a white man, and indeed became sort of half Indian himself. In talking, I observed, that he frequently hesitated for the right English word; but when speaking bastard Spanish (Mexican) or Indian, he was as fluent as a native. Both Mexican and Indian, however, are largely pantomime, which may have helped him along somewhat. The Utes seemed to have the greatest possible confidence in him, and invariably called him simply "Kit." Said Sherman, while at Garland, "These Red Skins think Kit twice as big a man as me. Why his integrity is simply perfect. They know it, and they would believe him and trust him any day before me." And Kit returned this confidence, by being their most steadfast and unswerving friend. He declared all our Indian troubles were caused originally by bad white men, and was terribly severe on the barbarities of the Border. He said he was once among the Indians for two or three years exclusively, and had seen an Indian kill his brother even, for insulting a white man in the old times. He protested, that in all the peculiar and ingenious outrages for which the Indians had been so much abused of late years, they were only imitating or improving on the bad example of wicked white men. His anathemas of Col. Chivington, and the Sand Creek massacre of 1864, were something fearful to listen to. He pleaded for the Indians, as "pore ignorant creatures," whom we were daily despoiling of their hunting grounds and homes, and his denunciations of the outrages and wrongs we had heaped upon them were sometimes really eloquent.

Said he, "To think of that dog Chivington, and his hounds, up thar at Sand Creek! Whoever heerd of sich doings among Christians! The pore Injuns had our flag flyin over 'em, that same old stars and stripes thar we all love and honor, and they'd bin told down to Denver, that so long as they kept that flyin they'd be safe. Well, then, here come along that durned Chivington and his cusses. They'd bin out several days huntin hostile Injuns, and couldn't find none no whar, and if they had, they'd run from them, you bet! So they just pitched into these friendlies, and massa-*creed* them—yes, sir, literally massa-*creed* them—in cold blood, in spite of our flag thar—women and little children even! Why, Senator Foster told me with his own lips, (and him and his committee investigated this, you know), that that thar d——d miscreant and his men shot down squaws, and blew the brains out of little innocent children—even pistoled little babies in the arms of their dead mothers, and worse than this! And ye call *these* civilized men—Christians; and the Injuns savages, du ye?

"I tell ye what; I don't like a hostile Red Skin any better, than you du. And when they are hostile, I've fit 'em—fout 'em—as hard as any man. But I never yit drew a bead on a squaw or papoose, and I loathe and hate the man who would. 'Tain't nateral for brave men to kill women and little children, and no one but a coward or a dog would do it. Of course, when we white men du sich awful things, why these pore ignorant critters don't know no better, than to follow suit. Poor things! I've seen as much of 'em as any white man livin, and I can't help but pity 'em! They'll all soon be gone anyhow."

Poor Kit! He has already "gone" himself to his

long home. But the Indians had no truer friend, and he would wish no prouder epitaph, than this. He and Sherman were great friends, and evidently had a genuine regard for each other. They had known each other in California in '49, when Sherman was a banker there, and Kit only an Indian guide. In '65, when Kit was at Leavenworth on a visit, Sherman sent for him to come down to St. Louis, and they spent some time together very pleasantly. Now Sherman returned his visit, by coming to Fort Garland, in the heart of the Rocky Mountains. It will be betraying no secret to say, that Sherman had but a poor opinion of the Plains country, especially of New Mexico and Arizona; for he did not hesitate to say so anywhere. While at Garland, he told the following good story one night, as we all sat smoking around the fire, and he will pardon me for repeating it here. He said the Quartermaster General during the summer had written him several letters, calling his attention to the enormous cost of our posts on the Plains, in New Mexico, etc., and begging him if possible to suggest some plan, that would reduce expenses, etc. "At first," said Sherman, "I paid no attention to these letters, because I could not help the matter. The Posts were there—established by order of the Hon. Secretary of War—and he knew it. Moreover, the people would have them there, and I could not help it, if they did cost a 'heap.' Above all, I was *ordered* to keep them up, and I always obey orders; so what could I do? So, at first, I did not answer his letters, but let him write away! But finally they got to coming so thick and long, that one day I sat down and replied, that the Posts were all there, and ordered there, as he knew, and we were bound to supply them, no matter what it cost. But that, in my judgment, of the whole vast region there, the greater portion was not worth a Confederate note to us, and never would be; and if he wished my opinion as to the best way of reducing expenses, I would respectfully recommend, that the United States sell New Mexico, and all the region round about, to Maximilian for $15,000,000, and lend him the greenbacks to pay with!

"I must say, the government don't seem to have considered my recommendation favorably yet. But neither have I received any more letters from the Q. M. Gen'l. So, I suppose, he is satisfied!"

He told this with infinite gusto, as if he enjoyed the joke hugely, and presently added:

"The idea, however, wasn't wholly my own, but was suggested by an old story we used to hear about Gen. Sumner. You knew Sumner, I suppose, in the East? We used to call him Bull Sumner, in old times, because he was so obstinate, and so thoroughly a soldier. Well, some years ago, he was sent out to command in New Mexico, and he certainly entered upon his duties with great alacrity and enthusiasm. He was going to explore the country, he said, make known its vast resources, pacify the Red Skins, induce immigration, settle up the country, and thus do away with our costly Posts, and all that. Of course, he was sincere in the matter—always was sincere—one of the honestest men I ever knew. So, he went to work, and for two or three years worked hard, summer and winter—did a vast amount of work. But, finally, he came to the same conclusion I have—viz. that the whole region was worthless—and reported to the Secretary of War, that in his judgment, the wisest thing we could do, would be to buy out the New Mexicans and pay them to emigrate —to old Mexico, if possible—and then throw the whole country open (and keep it open) to the buffalo and the Indians!

"Sumner, they say, recommended this seriously, and thought it a good thing. But I have never heard that the government agreed with him, any more than it will with me!"

These were the stories substantially; but it is impossible to give the twinkle of his eye, the jocular toss of his head, and the serio-comic twitch of his many-wrinkled features, as he got them off. Meanwhile he smoked furiously, and kept up that everlasting long stride of his up and down the floor, with his hands deep in his trowsers' pockets, as if he would never weary. Sherman is a great talker and smoker, and beyond doubt a great man and original thinker in many ways. At the Denver banquet, he made a better speech than his distinguished brother (the Senator from Ohio); and it is no wonder he outwitted Joe Johnston, and smashed Hood as he pleased, when "marching through Georgia." Neither is it any wonder, when you come to scan him closely, that he should sometimes err a little, as he did at Raleigh. Evidently, with all his great talents, now and then he needs a "governor" to steady him, as much as any other steam-engine does. Then, he is a hundred horse-power or more; and as General of the Army, long may he live!

The Treaty over, we returned to Denver through the heart of the Mountains, as related in the preceding chapter; and now for Salt Lake and beyond.

CHAPTER IX.

DENVER TO SALT LAKE.

FROM Denver, we shipped eastward by express the various Indian trophies, we had secured—shields, lances, bows and arrows, grizzly bear-skins, etc.—and rested for a day or two. We found the weather there hot and oppressive, compared with what we had experienced in the Mountains, and the change to the dry atmosphere of the one, from the moist air of the other, affected us very sensibly. Here they were still wearing summer clothing, though in the Mountains we needed our great-coats, and Denver mocked at winter as weeks yet to come. From Denver the Mountains as a whole seemed grander than ever; and the view of them at sunset from our hotel windows could scarcely be finer, as the snowy range and the heaven-kissing peaks one by one faded away, through orange, crimson and purple into night. The majesty and grandeur of the general range impress one more there at Denver, I think, than elsewhere; and then, there is always something new about these mighty Mountains—they never seem the same for an hour together. A difference of clouds, or of atmosphere, or of your own point of vision, makes all the difference in the world; and to me, I confess, the Rocky Mountains from Denver were always a constant joy and perpetual delight. So calm, so grand, so superb, such stately rest, such profound peace. As if they upheld the sky, and steadied the earth, and did it easily. If there be no God, no being of infinite wisdom and goodness, there ought to be one, to account for the might and majesty, the beauty and sublimity, with which the universe is filled, when it might so easily have been monotonous and commonplace.

Finally, Oct. 4th, we closed up our duties at Denver, and started for Salt Lake. The stage left at 8 P. M., and after much hearty hand-shaking and kindly good-byes, we were at last off for the Pacific. For the first time we fully realized, that we had definitely cut loose from the Atlantic States, and had a long and toilsome trip now before us. I remember a feeling of sadness, as this conviction came sharply upon me; but we were soon whirling across the Platte, and off for Laporte. The fare through to Salt Lake, some 600 miles, with 25 pounds of baggage, was $150, currency; meals extra, at $1,00 and $1,50 each. Our coach, "Red Rupert," was a mountain mud-wagon, with a low canvas top, so as to be less liable to capsize in crossing the range, than a regular Concord Coach, and was intended for ten passengers—nine inside and one outside. As we had only half that number of passengers, however, we thought we would get along very comfortably. We had gamey, spirited horses, that carried us along quite rapidly, until near midnight, when we stuck fast in a mudhole, and all hands were ordered up to help shift baggage and lift the coach out. Next morning early we rolled into Laporte, having made seventy-five miles since leaving Denver. It was a bright clear morning, with a crisp bracing air, and we sat down to an excellent breakfast of fried elk, potatoes, eggs, etc., as hungry as wolves. In the corner of the room, at a rude table, sat a little bearded man, eyeing us occasionally as he bent over his maps and papers, whose face seemed familiar; and presently I recognized him as Gen. Dodge, an old acquaintance of war times in Tennessee in 1864. Now he was Chief Engineer of the Union Pacific Railroad, and was here comparing maps and surveys, to see whether they couldn't find a shorter route to Salt Lake, than the somewhat circuitous one by Bridger's Pass. He recognized me about the same moment, and we had a hearty hand-shake and chat over old times.

Past Laporte, our road speedily entered the foot-hills, or "hog-backs" as the Coloradoans call them; and all day long we were bowling ahead, either between or across these. These abrupt ridges hid our view of the Plains and Mountains usually, so that the day's ride as a whole proved dull and monotonous. We were well armed, but saw no Indians, nor any game worth mentioning. It was plain, that the road was gradually ascending, but there were no sharp ascents, and but little to indicate, that we were actually crossing the Rocky Mountains. The country, as a whole, was rocky and barren in the extreme. Here and there the old red sandstone cropped out, and had been fashioned by the elements into all sorts of curious forms, which travellers had named Castle Rock, Steamboat Rock, Indian Chief, etc. The day's ride ended at Virginia Dale, where we got a tolerable dinner, and found an exquisite little valley, as if nature was trying just there quite to outdo herself. Abrupt mountains tower all around and shut it in like a picture, while the entrance to and exit from the vale are bold and precipitous. With its limpid stream, green sward, and bristling pines, it seemed like an oasis in the desert of the foot-hills there; and a party of miners encamped there for the night, *en route* from Montana to the States, appeared to enjoy its freshness and beauty to the full. We met several such parties of miners between Denver and Salt Lake, all bound east to winter, expecting to return in the spring. They said the difference in the cost of living would more than pay them for the trip, while at the same time they would be with their families and friends. They moved in parties of a dozen or so, and said they considered themselves safe against all hostile comers, whether Road Agents or Indians. They were all well-mounted, and literally bristling with rifles, revolvers, and bowie-knives. Their baggage and "traps" generally were usually piled high on pack-horses or mules, that they drove along ahead of them. They all carried their own provisions, and when night came camped down by the nearest stream, where there was wood, water, and grass. Such a life has its hardships and risks, but is not without its enjoyments also; and many an eastern cockney might well envy the big-bearded, bronzed, weather-beaten, but apparently thoroughly happy fellows, that we met *en route*.

We left Virginia Dale about 6 P. M. and the same night about 10 P. M. reached Willow Springs, one of the most desolate stage-stations on the road. It was a raw chilly night, and while the stage-men were changing horses, all of the passengers except myself got out and strolled off to the station-house—a hundred yards or so away—to get warm. Weary with the stage ride of two days and nights continuously, I remained half-dozing in the coach, wrapped in my buffalo-robe, when suddenly I was aroused by a distant noise, that grew rapidly louder and nearer, and presently came thundering down the road directly toward the station. While pondering what it could be, half-sleepy still, all at once the station-keeper, who was helping with the horses, broke out with:

"I say, Tom (our driver), hark! Do you hear that?"

"Yes, Billy! What the deuce is it?"

"Why, good heavens, it must be the infernal Injuns, shure as you live! The d—d Red Skins, I reckon, hev jest stampeded that Government-train down the road thar; and they'll all be yer, licketty split, quicker than lightnin', you bet!"

I was wide awake in a second, now. They pushed the horses quickly back into the stable, and shouted to me to seize all the arms and hurry to the station-house. I was not certain, that it was not better to stand by the coach, and "fight it out on that line," come what might; but concluded the stage-men knew more about such encounters than I did, and so followed their directions. Out I tumbled, gathered up all the rifles and revolvers I could lay my hands on, and rushed to the station-house, shouting "Indians! Indians!" Soon the driver and stock-tenders came running in from the stable, as fast as their legs could carry them; and for a few mimutes we thought we had the Indians upon us at last, sure enough. The pluck of the party, I must say, was admirable. L. and M. stood to their guns. Nobody thought of flight or surrender. But all quickly resolved, as we grasped our rifles and revolvers, to make the best stand we could, and to fight it out in that shanty, if it took all summer. But presently, as the mules thundered up the road and past us, just as we were about to fire on one of their pursuers, we saw him tumble from his horse all sprawling, as it stumbled across a chuck-hole, and as he gathered himself up heard him break out swearing in good vigorous English, that stamped him as a Pale Face beyond a question. The swearing probably saved his life, however objectionable otherwise, and we were soon at his side. We found him more stunned, than hurt, and presently his comrades succeeded in stopping the herd. They were unable to say what had caused the stampede; but as no Indians appeared, we were soon off on the road again.

These "stampedes" of animals are not uncommon on the Plains, and sometimes prove very embarrassing. A herd of mules, well stampeded, will run for miles, over every thing that opposes them, until they tire themselves thoroughly out. Had we been on the road, they would probably have stampeded our stage-horses—thundering up so behind us—and then there would have been a break-neck race by night, among the Rocky Mountains, that would have been rather exciting, not to say more. It is a favorite trick of the Indians, when they want to steal stock, to stampede them thus at night, and then run off the scattered animals. A large freight-train, that we subsequently heard of, had lost all its mules a few nights before by such a stampede, and been compelled to send back to the nearest settlement for others.

Thence on to the North Platte, our route wound over and between foot-hills and ridges, where the general ascent was indeed perceptible, but never difficult. One by one we flanked the main ranges, and at old Fort Halleck, 8,000 feet above the sea, found a natural depression or cañon through the Mountains, in the absence of which a wagon-road there would be seemingly impossible. It really appeared, as if nature had cleft the range there expressly to accommodate the oncoming future; and we swung through it, and so down to the North Platte, at a steady trot. Here and there, in crossing the ridges, we caught exquisite glimpses of snowy peaks off to the west, and of the far-stretching Laramie Plains off to the east; but the country, as a whole, was barren and desolate. We reached the North Platte just at dusk, having made 104 miles in the last 24 hours. This seemed a good day's drive, considering we were crossing the Rocky

Mountains; but it was not quite up to the regular schedule. We had hoped to get down into the Platte valley before dark, but daylight left us before we reached the station. We had caught long stretches of the valley, as we came over the ridges and down the bluffs; but darkness fell so suddenly, we saw little of it close at hand. Parts of it, we were told, are well adapted to farming, and nearly all of it could be made cultivable by proper irrigation; but it seemed too cold for anything but grass, and the more hardy cereals. No doubt it could be made available for grazing purposes, and the cañons of the neighboring Mountains would afford shelter and grass for winter. Antelope and elk were reported quite abundant still in the valley. We saw a herd of antelope feeding quietly, a mile away, soon after we struck the valley, and at the station they gave us elk-steaks for dinner—"fried," of course, as usual. Gold was reported in the Mountains beyond, but little had been done there yet in the way of mining. No doubt the Rocky Mountains are penetrated nearly everywhere by gold-bearing veins, and where these crop out, and water runs, "placer mines"—more or less lucrative—will be found. We found the North Platte a very considerable stream, though readily fordable then and there. It had already come a long distance through and out of the Mountains, and now struck eastward by Fort Laramie, for its long journey through the Plains to the Missouri. What a delightfully lazy, dreamy, lotus-eating voyage it would be, to embark upon its waters in an Indian canoe, far up among the Mountains, and float thence day by day, and week after week, adown the Missouri, *via* the Mississippi, to the sea!

At North Platte, we changed our mountain mud-wagon, for a coach lighter and less top-heavy still, and pushed on continuing to ascend. We left Colorado near Fort Halleck, and were now in Wyoming. At Bridger's Pass, we were at last fairly across the Rocky Mountains—had left the east and the Atlantic slope behind us—and turned our faces fully Pacificwards. The North Platte was the last stream flowing east, and about 3 A. M., after leaving it we struck the headwaters of Bitter Creek, a tributary of Green River, that flows thence *via* the great Rio Colorado and the Gulf of California two thousand miles away to the Pacific. The Rocky Mountains, the great water-shed of the continent, were thus over and past; but we had crossed the summit so easily we were not aware of it, until our driver informed us. Our first introduction to the Pacific slope was hardly an agreeable one. At our great elevation the night was bitterly cold, and we had shivered through its long hours, in spite of our blankets and buffalo-robes. Routed out at 3 A. M., for breakfast, we straggled into the stage-station at Sulphur Springs, cold and cross, to find only dirty alkali water to wash in, and the roughest breakfast on the table we had seen yet, since leaving the States. Coffee plain, saleratus-biscuit hot, and salt pork fried—only this and nothing more—made up the charming variety, and we bolted it all, I fear, as surlily as bears. A confused recollection of cold, and discomfort, and misery, is all that remains in my memory now of that wretched station at Sulphur Springs, and may I never see the like again!

Long before daylight we were off on the road again, and now had fairly entered the Desert of the Mountains, the famous or infamous "Bitter Creek Country," accursed of all who cross the continent. Here, when the sun got fairly up, the sharp keen winds of the night hours changed to hot sirocco breezes, that laden with the alkali dust there became absolutely stifling. Alkali or soda—

the basis of common soap—abounds throughout all this region for two or three hundred miles, and literally curses all nature everywhere. It destroys all vegetation, except sage-brush and grease-wood, and exterminates all animals, except cayotes and Indians. The Indians even mostly desert the country, and how the cayotes manage to "get on" is a wonder and astonishment. The wheels of our coach whirled the alkali into our faces by day and by night, in a fine impalpable dust, that penetrated everywhere—eyes, ears, nose, mouth—and made all efforts at personal cleanliness a dismal failure. The only results of our frequent ablutions were chapped hands and tender faces—our noses, indeed, quite peeling off. In many places the alkali effloresced from the soil, and at a little distance looked like hoar-frost. It polluted the streams, giving the water a dirty milky hue and disgusting taste, and in very dry seasons makes such streams rank poison to man and beast. The plains of Sodom and Gomorrah, after the vengeance of Jehovah smote them, could not have been much worse than this Desert of the Mountains; and good John Pierpont must certainly have had some such region in his mind's eye, when he wrote so felicitously:

> "There the gaunt wolf sits on his rock and howls,
> And there in painted pomp the savage Indian prowls."

One wretched day, while traversing this region, one of our passengers, from whom we expected better things, unable to "stand the pressure" longer, indulged too freely in Colorado whiskey; and that night we had to fight the *delirium tremens*, as well. He tried several times to jump out of the coach, and made the night hideous with his screams; but we succeeded finally in getting him down under one of the seats, and thus carried him safely along. As if to add to our misfortunes, soon after midnight one of our thorough-braces broke, and then we had to go bumping along on the axle-tree for ten or twelve miles, until we reached the next station. This no doubt was a good antidote to John Barleycorn; but it scarcely improved our impressions of "Bitter Creek."

At Laclede, in the heart of the Bitter Creek Country, we halted one day for dinner, and were agreeably surprised by getting a very good one. This station had once been famed for the poorness of its fare, and so great were the complaints of passengers, that Mr. Holliday resolved to take charge of this and several others himself. He imported flour and vegetables from Denver or Salt Lake, and employed hunters on the Platte to shoot antelope and elk, and deliver them along at these stations as required. The groceries, of course, had all to come from the Missouri or the Pacific. We found a tidy, middle-aged, Danish woman in charge at Laclede—a Mormon imported from Salt Lake—and she gave us the best meal we had eaten since leaving Laporte or Denver. We complimented her on the table, and on the general cleanliness and neatness of the station; and she seemed much gratified, as she had a right to be.

Our ride through the Bitter Creek region, as a whole, however, was thoroughly detestable, and how the slow-moving emigrant and freight trains ever managed to traverse it was surprising. The bleaching bones of horses, mules, and oxen whitened every mile of it, and the very genius of desolation seemed to brood over the landscape. Nevertheless, the station-keepers averred, there were cañons back of the bluffs, where grass grew freely; and they pointed to their winter's supply of hay in stack, as proof of this. So, too, at Black Buttes station, we found good bituminous coal burning in a rude grate, and were shown a bluff a hundred yards away where it was mined. Elsewhere we heard of petroleum "showing" well, and one day I suggested to our driver, that as the Creator never made anything uselessly, there must be some compensation here after all.

"Bother, stranger!" he rejoined; "The Almighty'd nothin to du with this yer region. 'Tother fellar (pointing downward) made Bitter Creek, ef it ever war made at all; tho, I reckin, it war just *left!*"

"But what about the coal?" I said.

"Dunno ef there's enny thar! But ef thar be, Providence only 'lowed it, jist to help in the last conflaggerration—you bet! He did n't mean enny human critter to live yer, and mine it—not by a long shot—you bet!"

At several points, however, we observed the bluffs abounded in slate shales, and other coal-bearing earths; and as we suspected then, the Union Pacific Railroad has already developed a vast deposit of coal there. Bitter Creek itself flowed sluggishly by us for a day or so, and was a little miserable stream, that just managed to crawl—usually at the bottom of a deep gulch or abrupt cañon—its chalky color proclaiming its alkali taint even before you tasted it. We must have followed it for a hundred miles or more, and yet it continued very nearly the same in size throughout. What water it drained in one locality was largely evaporated in another, and its wretched, villainous character made it everywhere an eye-sore, instead of a pleasing feature in the landscape as it should have been. But enough of Bitter Creek, and its God-forsaken region.

Past Green river, here a considerable stream, we entered the Butte region, and one evening just before sunset approached Church Butte, the most famous of them all. It was too late in the day to explore it, but we had a grand view of it in the shifting sunlight, as we drove slowly by. On the box with the driver, a portion of it was pointed out, that resembled a colossal Dutchman, about lifting to his mouth a foaming beaker. Further on, as we rolled westward, the Teuton faded out, and the church-like character of the Butte more fully appeared. Seen from the west, it presents a very wonderful likeness to an old-time cathedral, of the Gothic type, and at a distance might well be taken for the crumbling ruins of some such edifice, though of cyclopean proportions. Porch, nave, dome, caryatides, fluted columns, bas-reliefs, broken roof and capitals—all are there in shapes more or less perfect, and the illusion was very striking in the shadowy twilight. The Butte itself, like most others there, is a vast mass of sandstone, covered with tenacious blue clay, both of which are being constantly chiseled down by wind and rain. These buttes all seemed either to have been upheaved from the dead level around them, or else to be the surviving portions of great mountain chains, from which the earth has been washed or blown away, leaving their skeletons—so to speak—behind in solitary grandeur. The latter theory seemed more probable, judging by the general direction of the buttes themselves. Much of the scenery about here for a hundred miles or so, was enlivened by sandstone bluffs, cut and chiseled by the elements into castles, fortresses, etc., that frowned majestically at us in the distance; but we were only too glad to quit their grandeur and sublimity, that turned only to barren rocks as we approached, and to hail some signs of cultivation again as we neared Fort Bridger. No doubt the wind has been an important agency in fashioning all these, though scarcely to the extent that is claimed by some travellers. In Bowles' "*Across the Continent*," he tells a story about a wind-storm down in Colorado, that dashed the sand against a window so furiously, that a common pane of glass was converted into "the most perfect of ground glass," in a single night! We met a good many Coloradoans, who were laughing at this "yarn," and were told to set it down among other good "Rocky Mountain' stories. The fact is, people who live out there on those vast Plains, or among those great Mountains, become demoralized with the amplitude of everything; and when they attempt to narrate, unconsciously—I suppose—get to exaggerating. Not intentionally; of course not. But bigness "rules the hour," and we early learned to distrust—and discount largely—most of the extraordinary stories we heard.

We reached Fort Bridger late at night (Oct. 8th), and found ourselves pretty well jaded, both in body and mind. We had been four days and nights continuously on the road since leaving Denver, and in that time had made four hundred and eighty miles. This was the hardest ride by stage-coach we had had yet, and altogether was a pretty fair test of one's power of endurance. We became so accustomed to the coach, that we could fall asleep almost any time; but slumber in a stage-coach, or rather "mountain mud-wagon," is only a poor apology for "tired nature's sweet restorer," after all. The first night out, there being but five of us, four each "pre-empted" a corner, while the fifth man "camped down" on the middle seat. Along about 11 P. M. we struck a piece of extra good road, the conversation gradually wound up, each settled back into his great-coat and robe, and presently we were all fairly off into dreamland. A half hour or so rolls by, when bump goes the coach against an obstinate rock, or chuck into a malicious mud-hole; your neighbor's head comes bucking against you, or you go bucking wildly against him; the man on the middle seat rolls off and wakes up, with a growl or objurgation, that seems half excusable; your friends on the front seat get their legs tangled and twisted up with yours, or you get yours twisted and tangled up with theirs—you don't exactly know which; and, in short, everybody wakes up chaotic and confused, not to say dismal and cross. Of course you try it again after a while, you wrap your robes still better about you, you adjust your legs more carefully than before, and settling down again into your corner, think now you will surely get a good sleep. However, you hardly get to nodding fairly, before there comes a repetition of your former dismal experiences, and so the night wears on like a hideous dream. A series of unusual jolts and bumps disgusts every one with even the attempt to sleep, and presently all hands drift into a general talk or smoke. The history of one night is the wretched history of all—only each successive one, as you advance, becomes "a little more so." Long before reaching Fort Bridger, we were in a sort of a half-comatose condition, with every bone aching, and every inch of flesh sore, and with the romance of stage-coaching gone from us forever. Now, if a man's body were made of india-rubber, or his arms and legs were telescopic, so as to lengthen out and shorten up, perhaps such continuous travelling would not be so bad. But, as it is, I confess, it was a great weariness to the flesh, and looking back on it now, with the Pacific Railroad completed—its express trains and palace-cars in motion—I don't really see how poor human nature managed to endure it. Conversation is a good thing *per se*, but most men converse themselves out in a day or two. So, a good joke or a popular song helps to fill the hiatus somewhat, and accordingly we buried "John Brown," and "Rallied round the flag," and "Marched through

Georgia," day after day, until they got to be a "bore,' even to the most severely patriotic among us. Our only constant and unfailing friends were our briar-wood pipes, and what a *corps de reserve* they were! Possibly smoking has its evils—I don't deny it—but no man has thoroughly tested the heights and depths of life, or shall I say its altitudes and profundities, its joys and its sorrows, its mysteries and miseries—especially stage-coaching—who has not bowed at the shrine of Killykinnick, and puffed and whiffed as it pleased him. There is such comfort, and solace, and philosophy in it, when sojourning on the Plains, or camped down among the Mountains, or cast away in a stage-coach, that all the King Jameses and Dr. Trasks in the universe, I suspect, will never be able to overcome or abolish it.

Our horses were usually steady-going enough, the splendid teams of the Plains; but one night, just before reaching Fort Bridger, we had a team of fiery California mustangs, never geared up but once before, and, of course, they ran away. The road was slightly descending, but pretty smooth, and for the time our heavy, lumbering mountain mud-wagon went booming along, like a ship under full sail. Presently, too, the lead-bars broke, and as they came rattling down on the heels of the leaders, we had every prospect for awhile of a general over-turn and smash-up. But our driver, a courageous skillful Jehu, "put down the brakes," and at length succeeded in halting his runaways, just as we approached a rocky precipice, over which to have gone would have been an ugly piece of business. We expected an upset every minute, with all its attending infelicities; but luckily escaped.

We halted at Fort Bridger two or three days, to inspect this post and consider its bearings, and so became pretty well rested up again. Some miles below the

Fort, Green River subdivides into Black's and Smith's Forks, and the valleys of both of these we found contained much excellent land. Judge Carter, the sutler and postmaster at Bridger, and a striking character in many ways, already had several large tracts under cultivation, by way of experiment, and the next year he expected to try more. His grass was magnificent; his oats, barley, and potatoes, very fair; but his wheat and Indian corn wanted more sunshine. The post itself is 7,000 feet above the sea, and the Wahsatch Mountains just beyond were reported snow-capped the year round. Black's Fork runs directly through the parade-ground, in front of the officers' quarters, and was said to furnish superb trout-fishing in season. In summer, it seemed to us, Bridger must be a delightful place; but in winter, rather wild and desolate. Apart from the garrison, the only white people there, or near there, were Judge Carter and his employees. A few lodges of Shoshones, the famous Jim Bridger with them, were encamped below the Fort; but they were quiet and peaceable. The Government Reservation there embraced all the best lands for many miles, and practically excluded settlements; otherwise no doubt quite a population would soon spring up. Sage-hens abounded in the neighboring "divides," and we bagged several of them during a day's ride by ambulance over to Smith's Fork and return. We found them larger and darker, than the Kansas grouse or prairie-chicken; but no less rich and gamey in taste. Maj. Burt, in command at Bridger, was an enthusiastic sportsman; but our ambulance broke down seven miles out, and we had to foot it back after dark.

We were now in Utah proper, and Judge Carter was Probate Judge of the young county there. A Virginian by birth, from near Fairfax Court-House, he enlisted in the army at an early age, and served as a private for awhile in Florida. It was a romantic freak, and his friends soon had him discharged; but he still continued with the army, as purveyor or sutler. Subsequently, he accompanied our troops to California; but afterwards returned east, and followed Albert Sidney Johnston to Utah in 1858. When in that year Fort Bridger was established, he was appointed sutler, and had continued there ever since. Gradually his sutler-store had grown to be a trade-store with the Indians, and passing emigrants; and in 1866 he reported his sales at $100,000 per year, and increasing. He was a shrewd, intelligent man, with a fine library and the best eastern newspapers, who had seen a vast deal of life in many phases on both sides of the continent, and his hospitality was open-handed and generous even for a Virginian.

We left Fort Bridger October 12th, at 10 P. M., in the midst of gusty winds that soon turned to rain, and reached Salt Lake City the next night about midnight; distance 120 miles. We halted for breakfast at the head of Echo Cañon, and were at a loss to account for the air of neatness and refinement, that pervaded the rude station, until we noticed Scott's Marmion and the Bible lying on a side shelf. Two nice looking ladies waited on the table, and it is safe to conclude a taste for literature and religion will keep people civilized and refined almost anywhere. Echo Cañon itself proved to be a narrow rocky defile, some thirty miles long through the heart of the mountains there, with a little brawling creek flowing through it. Its red sandstone walls mostly tower above you for several hundred feet, and in places quite overhang the road. Here in 1857–8, Brigham Young made his famous stand against the United States, and flooded the cañon by damming the creek at various points. The remains of his dam, and of various rude fortifications, were still perceptible; but Judge Carter reported them all of small account, as Johnston's engineers knew of at least two other passes, by either of which they could have flanked the Mormon position, and so entered the valley. He said, our troops should have marched at once on Salt Lake, without halting at Bridger as they did; but the Mormons showed fight, and our commanding officer—not liking the looks of things—called a council of war, after which, of course, we did nothing. Councils of war, it is well-nigh settled, never do. Clive, that brave soldier of his time, never held a council of war but once, and then made his fortune by disregarding its decision. When Sidney Johnston assumed command, late in the fall of 1857, he had no orders to advance; and, therefore, inferred he was wanted merely to maintain the *status quo!* Accordingly he made haste to do nothing, and soon after went into winter-quarters. Meanwhile, Brigham—unmolested by our show of force—waxed fat and kicked. The next spring a compromise was effected, which like most other "compromises" decided nothing, and left the "saints" as saucy as ever. Judge C. knew all the men of that troubled period well, especially Army people; and said he had long thought, that the reason why the troops were not ordered forward was, because Davis, Floyd, & Co., were already looking ahead to secession in the near future, and did not care to establish *coercion* as a precedent. They feared such a precedent might be quoted against their own "sovereign" States, in such a contingency, and so managed to have the Army instructed How *not* to do it, until Brigham found a convenient loop-hole, and crept out of the scrape himself. Verily, the ways of politicians are "past finding out!"

Past Echo Cañon, we struck Weber Valley, and here

found ourselves at last thoroughly among the Mormons. Fine little farms dotted the valley everywhere, and the settlements indeed were so numerous, that much of the valley resembled rather a scattered village. The little Weber River passes down the valley, on its way to Great Salt Lake, and its waters had everywhere been diverted, and made to irrigate nearly every possible acre of ground. Fine crops of barley, oats, wheat, potatoes, etc., appeared to have been gathered, and cattle and sheep were grazing on all sides. The people looked like a hardy, industrious, thrifty race, well fitted for their stern struggle with the wilderness. Everybody was apparently well-fed and well-clad, though the women had a worn and tired look, as if they led a dull life and lacked sympathy. Children of all ages and sizes flocked about the gates and crowded the doorways, and to all appearances they were about the same frolicking youngsters that we have east, though they seemed less watched and cared for. Near the head of the valley, we saw several coal-drifts that had already been worked considerably, and were told that these mines supplied all the coal then used in Utah, though it was thought coal would soon be found elsewhere. It was of a soft bituminous character, far from first-class, but nevertheless invaluable in the absence of something better.

Just at dark, we found ourselves at the head of Parley's Cañon, and still several miles distant from Salt Lake City. Snow-flakes had sifted lazily downward all day, but at night-fall they changed to sleet, which thickened presently into a regular snow-storm, and soon the roads usually so good became heavy and slushy. In many places the track was merely a roadway, quarried out of the rocky bluffs, with a swollen and angry rivulet below; and as we wound cautiously along this, both the coach and horses were constantly slipping and sliding

Only a week before, in a similar snow-storm, the stage-horses lost their foot-hold here, and a crowded coach—team and all—went crashing down into the creek below. I had no fancy for this sort of an experience; but when, soon after dark, we saw the driver light up his side-lamps for the first time since leaving the Missouri, I concluded that our chances for an "upset" at last were perhaps improving. L. got nervous, and being somewhat mathematical in his turn of mind, fell to calculating how far it was down to the water and rocks, and what would be the probable results of plunging down there quite miscellaneously. But I was half sick and thoroughly tired out—in that worn and jaded condition, where a man becomes fairly indifferent as to what may happen—and at length, as L. averred, went soundly to sleep, though I had no recollection afterwards of anything but dozing. I only know that when the horses again struck a trot, as we began to descend the cañon westward, I roused up shivering with cold; and was only too glad, when far away in the distance our driver pointed out the lights of Salt Lake City, twinkling through the darkness. It seemed then, as if the coach never would get there. But at last the farms thickened into suburbs, and the houses into streets, and a little before midnight we drew up and halted at the Salt-Lake House. A smart-looking colored man, acting both as porter and night-clerk, showed us to a comfortable room, and I need scarcely say we retired at once. What a luxury it was, to get between clean sheets once more, and stretch our cramped up limbs wholly out again, *ad libitum!* No one but an Overland stage-passenger can fully appreciate the downy comfort of a bed, or truly sleep almost the sleep that knows no waking. How we *did* sleep and stretch ourselves, and stretch ourselves and sleep that night! It seemed almost as if to sleep was the chief end of life, and we made the most of our pillows accordingly.

CHAPTER X.

AT SALT LAKE CITY.

OUR first day in Salt Lake city (Oct. 14) was Sunday, and of course we rose late—I to find myself stiff and ill. A package of letters from the east, and a bath near noon, set me up somewhat, and when the gong sounded at 1, P. M. we went down to dinner. Here everything was profuse and excellent, the vegetables and fruits especially. But apart from the table, the Salt Lake House proved indifferent, though the only hotel in the city. Its rooms were small and dingy, and its appointments of the plainest, though its rates for every thing were all-sufficient. The policy of the saints had been opposed to Gentile travel, and hence no hotels at all were allowed at first. But subsequently Brigham Young built the Salt Lake House, and leased it to a Mr. Little—our three-wived landlord—and that paid so well, he was about erecting a new and enlarged one, commensurate with the wants and business of the city.

After dinner, as the sun was out brilliantly and the air bracing, we concluded to take a short stroll. Our snow-storm of the day before in the mountains had been only an affair of an inch or two here, and what had fallen was already fast disappearing. A walk of a square or two soon revealed the unique and wonderful beauty of this far-famed town. Its streets, eight rods wide with broad foot-walks, cross each other at right angles, and down each side course clear and rippling streams, fresh from the neighboring mountains. These spacious streets divide the city into squares or blocks of ten acres each, which are in turn subdivided into homestead lots of an acre and a quarter each, except in the heart of the city, where of course it is built up pretty solidly for several blocks. Standing back from the street in these goodly lots are their houses, built of frame or adobe, usually only one story high but sometimes two, and with as many doors ordinarily as the owner has wives. These were literally embowered in shrubbery and fruit trees, the grounds having been made wondrously fertile by irrigation, and as we walked along we could see the apple, peach, plum, pear, and apricot trees loaded down with their ripening fruit. The snow of the day before did not seem to have injured any of them materially, it was so unseasonable and soon gone. So, too, roses and flowers in rich profusion crowned the door-yards, while the gardens beyond seemed heaped with vegetables exquisite in their perfection and development. Lofty mountains, their snow-capped summits glittering in the sun-light, rimmed the valley in, whichever way you turned; while in the distance, tranquil as a sapphire, flashed the expanse of Great Salt Lake. To the traveller worn with stage-coaching, or weary from Bitter Creek, no wonder Salt Lake seems like Rasselas's Happy Valley, or Paradise Regained. Imagine to yourself a valley say fifty miles north and south, by thirty east and west, crowned above with snow-clad peaks, thick below with clustering farms, its interlacing streams flashing in the sun-light, with a fair city of fifteen or twenty thousand people gleaming in the midst, embowered in fruit and shade-trees, and you may form some conception of the prospect that greets you, as you rattle down the Wahsatch range, and out into the valley of Great Salt Lake. I doubt if there is a more picturesque or charming scene anywhere, not excepting the descent from the Alps into Italy. You involuntarily thank heaven, that "Bitter Creek" is over and past, and congratulate yourself on having struck civilization once more, Mormon though it be.

We took in much of this scene, as we strolled along, with senses keenly alive to its beauties and felicities. Flowers never seemed more fragrant; fruits never so luscious. In the clear atmosphere how the mountains glowed and towered! How crisp and elastic was the air! How the blood went coursing through one's veins! The streets seemed alive with people, and as they were moving mainly in one direction we followed on, and presently found ourselves at the Mormon Tabernacle. This was an odd-looking, oblong structure, built of adobe, and with no pretence evidently to any of the known orders of architecture. Its side-walls were low, and between these sprang the roof in a great semi-circle, with narrow prison-like windows near the line where the walls and roof came together. Outside, the walls were of the usual dun adobe color; inside, plain white—the whole utterly devoid of ornamentation whatever. The organ and choir occupied the end near the street; opposite was a raised platform, extending entirely across the audience-room, and on this sat fifty or more plain-looking men—the priests and chief dignitaries of "the Church of Jesus Christ of Latter Day Saints." The audience consisted of perhaps two thousand people—men women, and children—all dressed respectably, and though the average of intelligence was not high, yet as a whole they were a better appearing people than we had been led to expect. This edifice was their old tabernacle; the new tabernacle, an enormous structure on much the same plan, but with a capacity of ten or twelve thousand souls, was not yet completed, though well under way. Their great Temple had not yet progressed beyond the foundation stones, and there seemed to be much doubt whether it ever would. Its plan, however, is on a magnificent scale, and if ever completed, it will doubtless be one of the greatest edifices on the continent.

Religious services had already begun, and we found a Mr. Nicholson, a returned missionary from England, expatiating at the desk with much fervor. We were too late for his text, but found him discussing at length the evidences and undeniability of their peculiar doctrines. He was a fluent, but vapid speaker, and, with all our curiosity to hear him, soon became very tiresome. The gist of his argument was, that the saints knew for themselves, in their own hearts, that Mormonism was true, and, therefore, that no Gentile (or outside unbeliever) could possibly disprove it. He said, "My brethren, we *know* our doctrines to be true, yea and amen, forever. They have come to us by express revelation from heaven, and we have tested them in our own experience; and, therefore, to argue against them is the same as to argue against the multiplication-table, or to doubt logic itself. Yes, our priesthood, from Brother Brigham down, is God's own appointed succession, and whoever rejects its teachings will be damned for time and eternity." He iterated and reiterated these crude and common-place ideas for an hour or more *ad nauseam*, until finally Brigham Young (who presided) stopped him, and ordered the sacrament administered. This consisted only of bread and water, passed through the audience, everybody partaking of the elements. This over, singing followed, in which all participated, the chief functionaries leading.

Now came another "returned missionary," whose name we missed. He talked for twenty minutes or more, in a very loose and rambling way, about the work in England and Wales, and evidently was regarded as a rather "weak brother," to say the least of him. The next speaker was George Q. Cannon, a leading dignitary of the church, and a man of decided parts in many ways. He is an Englishman by birth, and for awhile after arriving here served Brigham Young as secretary. Now he was a stout, hearty looking man, in his prime, with good frontal developments, and impressed us as the smartest Mormon on the platform—Brigham, perhaps, excepted. He spoke for nearly an hour, delivering a calm, connected, methodical address, and evidently moved his audience deeply. The substance of his discourse was, that they as a church were blessed beyond and above all other churches, because they had a genuine priesthood, appointed by God himself, and in constant communication with Him. "Other churches," he said, "in their decadence had dropped this doctrine, and accordingly had lost their spirituality and power. But Joseph Smith, in the fulness of time, found the Book of Mormon, where God had concealed it, and so became His vice-gerent on earth. Brother Joseph selected Brigham Young, Heber Kimball, and Orson Pratt, as his co-workers, and through these and others Jehovah now communicates his unchanging will to the children of men. These great and good men speak not themselves, but the Holy Ghost in and through them. What we shall speak, we know not, nor how we shall speak it; but God inspires our hearts and tongues. Ofttimes we are moved to declare things, that are seemingly incredible. If left to ourselves, we would prefer *not* to declare them. But Jehovah speaks through us—we are but his mouth-pieces—and what are we to do? We *must* proclaim His solemn revelations, and to-day I tell you, brothers, what Brother Brigham has often said before, that the time is not distant—nay, is near at hand—when the North and South will both call upon Brigham Young and his holy priesthood to come and help them re-establish free constitutional government there. We, here in Utah, have the only free and christian government upon the earth, and God has revealed it to us, that His holy church shall yet occupy and possess the continent. Some of you may doubt this, and Gentiles especially may mock at and deride it. But Jehovah has so spoken it, to Brother Brigham and others, and many now here will yet live to see this fulfilled. Heaven and earth may pass away, but my words shall not fail, saith the Lord!" All this, and much more of the same purport, he uttered with the greatest solemnity, as if devoutly believing it, and his audience received it with a hearty chorus of "amens." There was more singing, and then Brigham, who had presided over the meeting as a sort of moderator, dismissed the congregation with the usual benediction. We had hoped to hear him speak also, as their great chief and leader; but he was ailing that day, and so disappointed us.

The speaking, as a whole, scarcely rose above mediocrity, except perhaps Mr. Cannon's. It was noisy and common-place, without logic or symmetry, and would have provoked most eastern audiences to ridicule, rather than led to conviction. Mr. Cannon evinced much natural ability; but all seemed quite illiterate, their rhetoric limping badly, and their pronouns and verbs marrying very miscellaneously. But little was said about their "peculiar institution" of polygamy, though it was alluded to once or twice, and its sacredness assumed. The singing was strong and emotional, and swept through the tabernacle a mighty wave of praise. Of course, it lacked culture; but then there were passionate and glowing hearts back of it, for all sang "with the spirit," if not "with the understanding also." Their fine organ we missed hearing, as it was then out of order. A new and much larger one was building for the new tabernacle, by workmen from abroad, and this it was claimed was going to be bigger, if not better, than the great one at Boston. Let the Hub look to her laurels!

The next morning I found myself down, with what is termed out there the Mountain Fever. And so this was the explanation of what had troubled me occasionally, even before leaving Denver. I had struggled desperately against it for a fortnight, but now surrendered at discretion, and was taken to Camp Douglas—the military post north of the city—where I found sympathizing comrades and a hearty welcome. This Mountain Fever seems to be an ugly combination of the bilious and typhoid, with the ague thrown in, and often pays its respects to overland travellers, unless they are very careful. In my own case it yielded readily to calomel and quinine, but only after liberal and repeated doses of each. For over a fortnight I wrestled with it there, sometimes hardly knowing which would conquer; but a resolute determination *not* "to shuffle off this mortal coil" in Utah, if I could help it, and a kind providence at last brought me safely through. At first, this loss of time was greatly regretted, as I was eager to complete my duties at Salt Lake, and push on; but ultimately, I was not sorry, as it afforded an opportunity to observe and study the Utah problem, much more fully than I should otherwise have done.

My first day out again, a beautiful October day and perfect of its kind, the Post-Surgeon advised a ride in the open air. Accordingly Major Grimes, the Post-Quartermaster, brought round his buggy, and together we drove down to the city, and thence out to the hot Sulphur Springs. These are on the Bear River road, some two or three miles north of the city. The water here bursts out of the ground at the foot of a bluff or mountain, as thick as a man's leg, and runs thence in a considerable stream to Great Salt Lake. It has a strong sulphur color and taste, and a temperature sufficient for a warm bath. Some miles farther north there are other Springs —we were told—hot enough to boil an egg. In the bath-house adjoining, we found a number of men and boys enjoying the luxury of a sulphur plunge, and the place appeared to be a considerable resort already, especially on Sundays. Most passing travellers and miners endeavor here to get rid of the accumulated dirt of their journey hitherward, and to depart cleaner if not better men. A refreshment-saloon near by furnished superb apples and peaches fresh from the trees, and most other American edibles, including our inevitable "pies;" but no drinkables, except tea and coffee. The patrons of the springs, it was said, complained bitterly of Brigham's stern, prohibitory liquor laws, but with little result. Even in Salt Lake City itself, a town of fifteen or twenty thousand souls, (1866), there were but two or three drinking-saloons, and these, we were told, were either owned or strictly regulated by the church *i. e.* Brigham Young. Whatever else the saints may be, Brigham intends that they shall at least not be drunkards, if he can help it.

Returning we drove by the ruins of the old city-wall, erected by the Mormons soon after they settled here, of concrete and adobe, as a defence against the Indians. The growth of the town and the disappearance of the Indians, rendered it useless years ago, and it was now fast falling to pieces, though no doubt of service in its day. It was one of Mr. Buchanan's Salt Lake scarecrows in 1857, but would not have stood a half-dozen shots from an ordinary field-piece, or even mountain-howitzer. The labor of erecting it, however, must have been prodigious, as it enclosed originally several square miles, and its remains even now speak well for the industry and enterprise of the saints in those early times.

Thursday, Nov. 1st, was a great gala-day at Salt Lake, and we were fortunate to be there still. It was the chief day of their annual militia muster, and the whole country-side apparently turned out. The place selected was a plateau west of the Jordan, some three miles from Salt Lake city. Proceeding thither, we found a rather heterogenous encampment, with not much of the military about it, except in name. The officers were mainly in uniform, but the men generally in civilian dress, and many without either arms or accoutrements. As we passed through the encampment, they were all out at company drill. Of course, there were many awkward squads, but the so-called officers were the awkwardest of all. In many instances, they were unable to drill their men in the simplest evolutions; but stood stupidly by, in brand-new coats, resplendent with brass-buttons, while some corporal or private, in civilian dress, "put the company through!"

Soon after noon, a cloud of dust and a large accompanying concourse of people heralded the approach of the chief Mormon dignitaries—in carriages. The flag of the "State of Deseret" floated in the advance; then came the standard of the old Nauvoo Legion; and as the procession neared the parade-ground, the "Lieutenant-General Commanding the Militia of Utah" and a brilliant staff (chiefly of Brigadier-Generals) moved out to meet and escort the hierarchs in. In the carriages, were most of the leading Mormons then at Salt Lake. Brigham himself was reported absent sick, but he sent his state-carriage instead, with Bishops Kimball and Cannon in it. The Lieutenant-General and staff, with the carriages following, now rode by in review, after which the troops formed column and marched by in review. They moved by company front, and being near the reviewing station, we made a rough count as they straggled by, and estimated the total force at about a thousand infantry, five hundred cavalry, and a battery of artillery. The cavalry was tolerably mounted; but the artillery was "horsed" with mules, and consisted of mere howitzers, no two of like calibre. The personnel of the force was certainly good; but everything betrayed an utter lack of discipline and drill. Nevertheless the Mormon officials seemed greatly elated by the martial array, and much disposed to exaggerate its numbers. Having been introduced to his excellency the Commander-in-chief, "Lieutenant-General etc.," I took occasion incidentally to ask him how many troops were on the field. He replied, he could not exactly tell, but he "reckoned" about three thousand! Afterwards, in reply to a similar question, his Adjutant-General—a son-in-law of Brigham Young's, and, of course, a Brigadier-General—answered, he guessed about four thousand! Other Mormon dignitaries computed them at from five to six thousand, even. I said nothing, of course, about my own passing "count;" but on returning to Camp Douglas, found it substantially confirmed by a very accurate count, made by another U. S. officer present, who had a better opportunity.

The true *status* of this Salt Lake militia appears pretty clearly, I judge, from the following conversation with the said Lieutenant-General. We were still "on the field," and I had casually asked him, whether this was the militia of the Church or of the Territory?

"O, of the Territory, of course!" he replied, with a smile that was child-like and bland.

"But its officers are all Mormons, and its men mostly so, I believe?"

"Why, yes, sir!" sobering down.

"Its chief officers, especially, I observe, are men high in the church, like yourself, Generals C—— and Y——, and others I see here; are they not?"

"Well, yes sir!" becoming more grave.

"Are these troops, then, the quota of Utah, or only of a single county?"

"Only of Salt Lake County. The other counties have similar organizations, but smaller; and all are required to spend at least three days per year in camp, for drill and review."

"To whom, however, does your militia report?"

"To myself only. By act of the Territorial Legislature, I am Commander-in-Chief of the Utah Militia, and of course they take orders only from me."

"Then his excellency, the governor of the Territory, though its chief executive, has no power to call out the territorial militia, or in any way to control it?"

"Why, no—no—sir! I believe—not!" very hesitatingly, and as if a good deal confused.

By this time, he began to see the drift of things somewhat, and suddenly remembered he had important business elsewhere. This was not surprising; for had he not already virtually acknowledged, that this whole militia force—such as it is—was nothing more nor less, than an auxiliary of the Mormon church, organized and held well in hand to do her bidding? Gov. Durkee, the territorial governor, a few days afterwards confirmed this view of the subject, and added, that in his judgment this militia was a standing menace to our authority in Utah, and would make us trouble there yet. He said, in his last Annual Message, he had called the attention of the Legislature to its anomalous character, and recommended that the militia laws be amended, so that the troops should report to him, and that he be provided with the usual staff—Adjutant-General, Quartermaster-General, Inspector-General, etc.—the same as in all our other Territories. The Legislature, however, being wholly Mormon, paid no attention to his recommendations, and he did not suppose it would very soon. No doubt this militia from its Lieutenant-General commanding, down, is a mere creature of Brigham Young's—Mormon in composition and organization—Mormon in spirit and purpose—Mormon in body, brain, and soul—and what Brother Brigham proposes to *do* with it, it remains for our good-natured Uncle Samuel yet to see. In case of a future collision in Utah, between United States and Mormon authority, we shall probably soon learn.

Two days afterwards the encampment broke up, and the troops marched into Salt Lake City, and so past the Bee-Hive House, for Brigham's inspection in person. Having business with his excellency or reverence (whichever you choose to call him), accompanied by Major Grimes, I called that morning, and thus chanced upon quite an assemblage of their chiefs and dignitaries. Among them, were Heber C. Kimball, George Q. Cannon, Bishop West, Lieut.-Gen. Wells, Brig.-Gen. Clawson, Brig.-Gen. Young, (Brigham, Jr.), Col. Young—another son—and others, whose names were not noted. Brigham himself met us at the door, with an ease and dignity that well became him, and after shaking hands very cordially, introduced us all around. Our object was to obtain certain information for the War Department, about the region between Salt Lake and the Rio Colorado (then little known), with a view to supplying Camp Douglas, and possibly Fort Bridger also, by that route hereafter, if practicable, *via* the Gulf of California. The Salt Lake merchants and others had given us a mass of facts, or supposed facts, concerning it; but we had been told, that the Church had made surveys and maps of all the country between, and that Brigham Young knew more about the region there, than any other white man living. The problem was to extract his information, for the public benefit, if possible. I began by congratulating him on the general appearance of industry and thrift in Utah—the wide-spread evidences of their prosperity—(which one might safely do)—and then, having thus paved the way, casually asked him why it was, that with all their shrewdness and intelligence, they still persisted in wagoning their goods and merchandise twelve hundred miles from the Missouri, across the Plains and Mountains, when they might strike navigation—it was alleged—on the Colorado at less than half that distance? He answered instantly, with perfect frankness, as if delighted with the question:

"It *is* extraordinary, surely! For ten year now, and more, I've bin tryin' to talk it into our people, that the Colorado is our true route. But Californy has done nuthin to open it, or *draw* us toward her, while New York keeps tight hold of us; and it is mighty hard to change the course of trade and travel." And then he added, by way of comment, "When things git *set*, it takes a heap to alter 'em, you bet!" which was certainly excellent "horse-sense," to say the least of it. A philosopher—not even the elder Weller—could have said it better. We discussed the subject very generally for some minutes, he appearing full of interest; but presently, when I began to inquire more minutely about the intervening country, its roads, resources, distances, etc., suddenly, with a flash of intelligence, he seemed to divine some sinister object, and at once began to "disremember" (his own word) nearly everything asked him. He was positive there were no maps or surveys of that region in the Record Office of the Church, though subsequently I received copies of several there; and drew back into his shell on the subject generally, as far as possible. One of the Bishops present, not perceiving the studied ignorance of his chief, answered several of the questions, which Brigham "disremembered," but presently caught his cue and relapsed into silence. On most other topics, Brigham talked with much fluency and politeness; but as to Southern Utah, we soon found he had no idea of giving any information he could suppress, and so changed the conversation. We talked for perhaps an hour, on a variety of subjects, and he impressed me as anything but an ignorant man, though slimly educated. He believed their religion to be the latest revelation of God's will to man, and that it would yet reform or supplant all others. He thought "plurality of wives" a Divine arrangement, and essential to Utah, whatever it might be elsewhere. It had given them the most frugal and thrifty, the most honest and moral population on the earth; and what more could be desired? If Congress didn't like it, they could lump it. God Almighty would stand by them. He said, Utah now numbered about a hundred thousand souls, and they were rapidly increasing. They had gained three thousand that year (1866), by immigration alone, mostly English and Welsh; some years they got more, seldom less. He said their soil and climate were all that could be desired, and claimed that by judicious irrigation they could beat the world, especially in fruits and vegetables. He thought they had coal, iron, and salt in abundance; but did not believe their gold and silver amounted to much, and hoped to Heaven they never would. Subsequently, I learned from other sources, that silver and copper had been discovered in considerable richness, at Rush Valley and elsewhere; but mining operations in Utah, as yet, had been feeble. The Church was averse to an influx of Gentile miners, for obvious reasons; and, accordingly, did all she could to discourage mining, as a business.

This conversation, though lacking in the results desired, yet afforded an opportunity for observing Brigham pretty well. Though then about sixty-five, he looked at least ten years younger, and evidently had many years hard work in him yet. He was of medium height, stoutly built every way, and of late years inclining to corpulency. His hair was a sandy red, now well sprinkled with gray, and somewhat disposed to curl. His eyes, a pale blue, were resolute and sagacious; but had a steely look in them at times, that might mean any depth of cruelty or tyranny. His nose, though not so pronounced as his career would indicate, was nevertheless very characteristic; while his mouth, though large and firm, had less of the animal about it, than would naturally be expected. His under-jaw would, perhaps, strike you more than any other one feature. Heavy and strong, full and massive, it looked like cast-iron, and at times, when he talked of Congress or of his enemies, it would shut with a snap like a gigantic nut-cracker. His dress was plain black, and his manners altogether unexceptionable. His position as head of the Mormon people has bred the habit of power, while his contact with representative men from abroad has imparted much of the elegance and *suaviter in modo* of the man of the world; so that he would pass for a pretty good diplomat almost anywhere. To take Brigham Young for a fool, or a mere fanatic, it was plain to be seen, would be a great mistake. It is true, he knows nothing about grammar or rhetoric, and but little about the dictionary; but his knowledge of all the country there, and of human nature, we found to be full and exact, and no man west of the Rocky Mountains knows better how make a good bargain, or fill a paying contract. However illiterate, he has patience, shrewdness, cunning, and abundance of hard common-sense—"horse-sense," as we used to say of Grant in the army—and doubtless would have made his way in the world, in whatever sphere he happened to drop. If he had not become "Brother Brigham," great hierarch of the Mormon Church and autocrat of all Utah, worth $25,000,000 in his own right, (as reported), owning countless lands and herds, no doubt he would have gravitated into a first-class hotel-keeper, or a money king on Wall Street, or a great railroad-contractor, or something of that sort, requiring keen perceptions and fine executive abilities. To deny him some such qualities, is evidently preposterous. Discredit him in every way; call him charlatan and humbug, if you please; the fact still remains, that he has changed an isolated desert into a land flowing with milk and honey, and created a community of a hundred thousand souls devoted to his will, holding their lives and fortunes absolutely at his bidding—and surely no mere imbecile, or blunderer, could have achieved such results.

We saw Brigham again, a few days afterwards, one night at the theatre. The Salt Lake Theatre is really a fine building, and very creditable to the city. Its scenery, and ap-

BRIGHAM YOUNG.

pointments generally, are unsurpassed in this country, outside of a few of our great cities East, and but few of our play-houses indeed equal it even there. Nearly everything about it has been imported from England, at large expense, and Englishmen in the main manage it now. The play the night we were there was of the kind yclept Moral Drama, but it was put on the stage with considerable ability. Two "stars" from San Francisco took the leading characters; the minor ones were sustained by the stock-company, most of whom were Mormon residents of Salt Lake. Among these a sprightly looking girl of seventeen was pointed out to us, as a daughter of Brigham Young's, though on the bills she bore a high-sounding theatrical name. What corresponds to the "pit" in most theatres, is their dress-circle, and this was well-filled with families—chiefly women and children. The rest of the theatre was occupied mostly by Gentiles and soldiers. What impressed one particularly, was the domestic or family character of the whole thing, Men, women, and children, were all there, down to the last baby, and young misses came and went at will, quite unattended, as at church East. Between the acts, paterfamilias and all munched their apples and nuts, and promenaded about quite *ad libitum;* but during the performance everything was very decorous. In the very centre of the house were four long seats, handsomely upholstered, and "reserved" for Mrs. Brigham Young. There were "sixteen of her," as poor Artemus Ward used to say, there that night, all ordinary looking women, apparently from thirty-five to fifty years of age, and dressed rather plainly. A fine large rocking-chair, abreast of the seats, was pointed out to us as Brigham's place when he sits with them. Ordinarily he occupies a private box, with his favorite wife, and did so that evening with his dear

Amelia. He paid but little attention to the play, but most of the time was sweeping the audience with an opera-glass, or conversing with a gentleman by his side. Mrs. Amelia was well-dressed, but not richly, and was scarcely better looking than the other sixteen, whom she had displaced in Brigham's affections. Evidently the Prophet has no taste for female beauty, or else is indifferent to it. Sometimes, between the acts, he comes down and chats a little with his domestic flock below, but retires to his box again when the play resumes. That evening, however, he continued faithful throughout to Mrs. Amelia.

Flanking the stage were two long seats, upholstered somewhat better than the rest, and here sat some twenty or more of Brigham's children—of all sizes and both sexes. They were mostly maidens from ten to fifteen years of age, though some were only prattling infants on their mothers' knees. They were better dressed and brighter looking, than most of the young people present; but the sight was a singular one for the nineteenth century, and in christian America. Altogether, Brigham was said to have over fifty children—mostly girls. Heber Kimball was credited with about the same number, but his were chiefly boys—whereat he was inclined to joke Brigham. Their wives so-called, were reported at the same number, about twenty-five each. Recently Brigham had said, that he had "about a dozen or twenty, he was not certain which—it was nobody's business but his own." But public opinion at Salt Lake credited him with twenty-five or more, regular and "brevet" together, when we were there; and he has probably increased the number one or two per year, ever since.

Our main object, however, in going to the Theatre, was to get a good look at the general audience. On the surface, I must say, this was genteel and respectable. There was no fashion or "style" about it, of course; but the people as a whole were well-dressed—always comfortably—and in the main looked contented and well-to-do. Here and there a woman's face however, showed, unmistakable signs of grief and anguish; but there were not nearly so many of these, as might be expected. What the women's faces chiefly lacked, was that air of sprightliness and grace, of culture and refinement, that characterizes the majority of theatre-going ladies East and elsewhere. There was an ugly subdued look about many of them, as if they felt themselves trodden down and inferior to the men—much such as we used to see in the negro's face down South—and too little of that calm, masterful, rounded equipoise of self-respect, which is the true glory of either man or woman. Prolong polygamy for a century, with all such downward forces constantly at work, and what may not our Utah dames and damsels become? The men, on the other hand, looked heavy and coarse, and while there were keen sharp faces among them, here and there, that could have belonged only to men of character anywhere, yet in too many instances the animal was evidently creeping over them, and in the end would surely predominate. It was pitiful to think how inexorably their higher nature must suffer, if polygamy continued, unless all history is false, and physiology a lie. But there are some things, that need not be said; it is enough to intimate them.

CHAPTER XI.

MORMON OUTRAGES—POLYGAMY, ETC.

AS to the alleged outrages and wrongs by Mormons against Gentiles, we found public opinion at Salt Lake much divided. The Mormons, as a class, of course, all repudiated and denied them; while the Gentiles, as a class, were equally earnest in affirming them. Before arriving there, we were very skeptical on this subject; but before leaving, and afterwards, heard so many ugly stories, that we were compelled to believe somewhat in them. It is a delicate subject to touch at all, and I would fain avoid it; but no account of Salt Lake would be complete without some allusion thereto. Space would fail me to speak of them at length; so that I shall content myself with recording only a case or two, and from them the reader must judge for himself. The Mountain Meadow massacre, and the Brassfield murder, were old stories; but just previous to our arrival, a party of Gentiles had been threatened with drowning in the Jordan, and indeed, while we were there, the atrocious murder of Dr. Robinson occurred. The editor of the little *Vidette*, the plucky Gentile paper then at Salt Lake, was one of the Gentiles above referred to, and his story was that a band of masked men seized them on the street one night, and taking them out to the Jordan tied them hand and foot, and then gave them the option—either to leave Utah in one week, or to be tossed in and drowned.

Their only offence was, that they had been too bitter against Mormonism, and Salt Lake they were informed was "an unhealthy place" for such people. They all agreed, we believe, to emigrate. But the *Vidette* man, on getting home, concluded such a promise under duress was not very binding, and proceeded to strengthen his conclusion by securing a guard from Camp Douglas. Loaded down with revolvers, he went about his business as usual in the day time, but at night kept within doors, and so far had remained unmolested. The others, however, as a whole, thought it safer to keep their agreement, and accordingly duly quitted Utah.

The murder of Dr. Robinson (Oct. 22d), it must be admitted, was a cold-blooded atrocity, worthy only of fanatics or savages. He had come to Salt Lake originally, as Surgeon or Ass't-Surgeon of a regiment of volunteers, ordered there from California during the war, to replace the Regulars sent east. When his regiment was mustered out, he concluded to settle at Salt Lake, and soon after "pre-empted" the quarter-section containing the Hot Sulphur Springs. Associating a Dr. Williamson with him, who had also been in the army, they put up a bath-house and refreshment-saloon at the Springs, and by liberal advertising were soon in a fair way to make some money. Now, all at once, two Mormons living near suddenly discovered that the property belonged to them, although they had never claimed it before, or regularly "pre-empted" it, or made any "permanent improvement" there, as required by our pre-emption laws. They accordingly brought suit in ejectment against Messrs. Robinson and Williamson, in the U. S. District Court there; but before the cause reached trial, became convinced there was nothing in their case, and concluded to abandon it. Now, however, Salt Lake City itself stepped in as plaintiff in the cause, and claimed the Springs also as corporation property, by virtue of some old ordinance, though two or three miles beyond the city limits. Immediately, without waiting for the Court, Messrs. R. and W. were declared trespassers, and the Mayor ordered the city police to eject them from the premises, which was done one night by tearing down the buildings over their heads, and dragging them both off bodily. This summary proceeding, no better than a riot, naturally created much excitement among the Gentiles, and was still being talked of when we reached Salt Lake. Meanwhile, Dr. Robinson took it very coolly, and moving into Salt Lake, opened an office for practice there, proposing to abide the judgment of the Court. Shortly, however, before this could be reached, he was roused up one night by a man at his door, with the plausible story, that a friend down the street had broken his leg and needed his immediate services, being already in great agony. His wife, newly married, fearing treachery, begged him not to go. But the Doctor felt bound by the vows of his profession, and while proceeding forth upon this supposed errand of mercy and benevolence, he was waylaid on one of the most public streets, knocked down, and shot through the head, three or four times, as if his assassins meant to make sure work of their victim. From the testimony of those awakened by the shots and his loud outcries, it appeared there were over a half a dozen of his assassins and their accessories —some doing the bloody work, while others stood guard on the adjacent corners—and yet not one of them was arrested, though it was a bright moonlight night, and a fresh fall of snow on the ground. The city police, when sought, were all found collected at the Central Police Station, as if purposely out of the way, and no serious or concerted attempt was made to track the murderers. His watch was untouched; his pockets, unrifled; there was no evidence that he had a personal enemy; and the almost universal conviction of the Gentiles then at Salt Lake was, that he had fallen a victim to the Mormons, at the bidding or instigation of the Church—they preferring to end their action of ejectment thus summarily, rather than abide "the law's delay," or its "glorious uncertainties." Subsequently, a leading Mormon, a son-in-law of Brigham Young's, *admitted* to me, indeed, that Robinson had probably been "silenced" by some ignorant or bigoted brother; but repudiated, of course, all connection of the Church therewith, or responsibility therefor.

The morning after the assassination, as the facts got known, the Gentile population became greatly excited, and for a day or two there was hot talk of a "Vigilance Committee," etc. Happily, however, this last suggestion was abandoned, or the Mormons would have exterminated them, as they outnumbered the Gentiles fully six to one in the city, and immensely more than that outside in the Territory. To pacify them, however, a coroner's inquest was ordered, and, as the excitement grew, the City Government came out ostentatiously with a reward of $2,000, for the apprehension and conviction of the murderers. So intense was the feeling, Brigham Young himself thought it wise to start a private subscription, and raised $7,000 more among the Mormon merchants and "tender-footed" Gentiles. The sturdier Gentiles, however, and many of the U. S. officials, refused to have anything to do with this; and one, at least, of the U. S. Judges, when asked to sign it, unhesitatingly branded the whole movement, as only "a cheat and swindle to throw dust into the eyes of people East." It was, however, a shrewd dodge, worthy of such an old fox, and

Brigham immediately telegraphed to Gen. Sherman, at St. Louis, then commanding that Department, "We have offered $9,000 reward for Dr. Robinson's murderers. The church nothing to do with it!" No doubt, when interrogated by tourists about such outrages and wrongs hereafter, he will refer to that "$9,000 reward," for many a day, with great unction, and extol his saints to the skies accordingly. Of course, it was perfectly safe to "subscribe" it; for it was never meant, that any body should be caught. The coroner's inquest made a show of sitting several days, but nothing came of their labors. Some Gentiles, indeed, went so far as to retain Ex-Gov. Weller, of California, who happened then to be at Salt Lake, and he prosecuted the inquiry with some vigor; but the verdict of the jury was, "Killed by some person or persons unknown." The effect of it all was, to deepen the sense of insecurity in the minds of all Gentiles there, as to both person and property, and to intensify the general feeling against Mormonism, which we found everywhere throughout Colorado, Idaho, Oregon, Nevada, and the Pacific Coast generally. It became at once another wall of division, another root of bitterness, between Gentiles and Mormons throughout all that region; and will be sure to be treasured up "as wrath against a day of wrath," when that dark day comes. And justice, against even Brighamdom, we may depend, will not sleep forever.

Mrs. Robinson, it should be added, subsequently returned to her friends in California, and Dr. Williamson left for the East, both abandoning their undoubted property, after such convincing arguments. The City immediately leased the Springs and their appurtenances for $2,000 per year; and thus this cruel assassination was apparently a "paying" operation for the Saints, whatever may be its barbarism, or however others fared.

This case I have given somewhat in detail, because it occurred under my own eye—so to speak—and I endeavored to sift its facts pretty thoroughly for myself. In my Official Report on Utah, attention was called to it; and whatever else may be said or thought of it, one thing seems clear, to wit, that such unlawful and wicked acts are but *the logical fruit of the habitual teachings of the Mormon chiefs and leaders.* Said Brigham Young some time before, in one of his pulpit discourses, "Brethren, if any body comes here, and goes to interfere with our lands or women, my advice is to send 'em to hell across lots." Said the editor of the *Salt Lake Telegraph*, the chief Mormon paper there, one day in my hearing, "If a man comes here, and don't like our institutions, all he has to do is to leave. If he stops here, and minds his own business, he will get along well enough—nobody will molest him. But if he goes to denouncing President Young, or interfering with our domestic relations, of course he will get into trouble mighty quick, you bet!" I thought *that* a fair statement of their position; but failed to see wherein it differed from the hideous despotism down South, which we had just had to break as with a rod of iron, and dash in pieces as a potter's vessel. He indignantly denied, that Gentiles were ordinarily ill-treated or tabooed; but his own statement, it seemed to me, confessed away the whole case substantially of *Gentile vs. Mormon*, involving as it does a thorough surrender of our cherished freedom of speech and of the press. This editor was a bluff and hearty Englishman, about forty years of age, and was reported engaged to a daughter of Brigham Young's, only about seventeen. The current criticism of him was, that he really believed no more in Mormonism, than the most incorrigible Gentile but he had found the institution, or rather "destitution," (as Theodore Parker called its "twin relic," and would much more have branded *it*), to "pay," and so eulogized and defended it.

Perhaps I can not do better, than relate just here a rather remarkable conversation I had with a high judicial officer of the Territory, on this and kindred subjects. He had been there several years, was a man of ability and character, and I give the conversation at length, because it seemed trustworthy, and also because it will probably answer a variety of questions the reader may want to ask. It took place in his own chambers, while I was at Salt Lake; and as no injunction of secrecy was imposed, or apparently desired, I see no objections to publishing it. He said he had come to Utah unprejudiced against the Mormons, but at length had become convinced, however reluctantly, that they had a secret organization—call it "Thugs," "Danites," "Destroying Angels," or what you will—whose sworn duty it was to "put out of the way" any person, who became hostile or obnoxious to their views or interests. For a long while after coming there, he had refused to credit this; but at length was compelled to, by the most indubitable evidence, to wit, his own multiplied observations and experiences as a U. S. judge. He continued:

"I can't help believing, sir that poor Dr. Robinson was killed in this way, and when Brigham Young's hypocritical subscription-paper, for a reward for the arrest of the assassins, was presented for my signature, I indignantly spurned it. I told the committe in charge, that it was only another of Brigham's tricks to throw dust into the eyes of the people at Washington, and I would have nothing to do with it."

"Do you think his murderers will ever be discovered?"

"Suppose they are, they will never be convicted. No Mormon jury would convict a brother Mormon, in such a case, even if indicted, as everybody knows here. I know very well who murdered poor Brassfield some time ago, and where the Church sent him abroad to keep him out of the way. I suppose England would return him, under our extradition laws, if requested. But *cui bono?* Our juries here are all summoned by the Mormon sheriffs, and the jurors, of course, are either Mormons, or dough-face Gentiles, worse than Mormons; so that, it would be hopeless to expect a righteous verdict."

"Then you really think, the accounts we get East of outrages and crimes by Mormons, against Gentiles or apostate Mormons, are, on the whole, true?"

"Why, yes, I am sorry to say, I fear so—the most of them—as true as holy writ. But the half of them never come to light. 'Dead men tell no tales.' And what do we know of the mysteries and miseries of their barbarous polygamy?"

"Do you think Brigham Young has much to do with such outrages?"

"In some cases, yes, directly. In others, only indirectly, by his sermons and addresses. No doubt he advised, or at least suggested, the 'taking off' of Brassfield and Dr. Robinson, to save trouble and serve as examples. So, also, he was directly responsible for the Mountain Meadow massacre, that occurred several years ago, when a whole train of Gentile emigrants, *en route* to California, were murdered in cold blood, and their property and little children distributed around among the Mormons. They had offended the Saints while passing through Salt Lake, and this was their revenge. This murder by wholesale they have always charged upon the Indians; but I myself have seen the secret orders for their massacre, signed 'By order of President Young, D. H. Wells, Adj't.-Gen.' I was in Washington in the autumn of 1865, and was at the White-House one day, when these orders were shown to Andrew Johnson. He took the tattered and discolored papers to the window, scanned them closely for awhile, and when he returned them said, with much feeling, it was "high time something was done to *clean out* such scoundrels." It was a generous impulse, while it lasted, and he meant it, too. But subsequently, when I saw him again, in the winter, he had become embroiled with Congress, and dismissed the Utah question with the curt remark, that there was "practical polygamy in Massachusetts too, as well as Utah." The property of these Mountain Meadow emigrants, I repeat, was divided up, and distributed around among the Mormons. Some of their furniture is in Salt Lake now, and can readily be identified. Many of their mules were sold by Capt. H. —subsequently our delegate to Congress—to the U. S. Quartermaster then here, and the proceeds shared by himself, Young, Wells, and others. There is plenty of evidence of all this, that I can put my finger on at any time; but it would be ridiculous to submit it to a Mormon jury, with any hope of a conviction now. And so, the case rests."

"I suppose, this also is why our anti-polygamy laws prove to be a failure?"

"Certainly, sir! It is an old adage, 'Dog won't eat dog!' There didn't use to be much polygamy here. But as soon as Congress made it a misdemeanor and a crime, Brigham and his Bishops set to work to get as many of their people into it as possible, so as to make the enforcement of the new law difficult, if not well nigh impracticable. They argued very shrewdly, 'You can't indict and try a whole people.' Polygamy, indeed, used to be only a matter of taste, and but little talked about; but now it is constantly preached, as a civil and religious duty, and all who can support more than one wife are proceeding to take others. The women objected a good deal, at first, and do still; but they were told, it was a New Revelation, 'thus saith the Lord,' and submission would make them 'Queens in Heaven' etc., and so they yielded. What else could they do in these mountain fastnesses, with Gown and Sword both against them?"

"Well, judge, you must have seen a good deal of the 'peculiar institution.' What are its practical workings?"

"Bad, and only bad—every way. It tends to make the men petty despots and mere animals, of course, while it degrades American women to the level of the Oriental harem. Their husbands, so-called, already habitually think and speak of them, as their 'women'—not *wives*—as you may have noticed, as a part of their goodly possessions, somewhat more esteemed perhaps than their flocks and herds, but not so much more either. Affection, sympathy, confidence—the finer instincts and feelings—all true delicacy between husband and wife—are fast dying out, and we have nothing half so good to show for them. Sometimes, however, a first wife gets the bit into her teeth, and then the others have to stand around, or leave. *Per contra*, sometimes the first wife herself gets ejected. One of Heber Kimball's sons married a second wife some time ago, and soon after she persuaded his first wife—a wife of many years, with several children—to vacate, by three shots from a revolver, and then installed herself as *first* wife instead! No doubt, the Saints have many a little "unpleasantness," like this, to mar their domestic felicity; but they hush them up, and keep quiet about it."

"What about their polygamous children?"

"Why, they are inferior of course, in many ways, *ex necessitate*, as the fruits of such a practice always are, and must be. Go to the City Cemetery, and you will find it a perfect Golgotha of infant graves. If not feeble and tainted already in constitution, they must speedily become so; or else all History is false, and Science a slander."

"And yet those we have seen on the road, and about the streets here, seem bright and spry enough."

"No doubt. It is a good climate, and there has not been time enough yet. But, then, have you considered the whole foul brood of downward influences at work here, and what must be the logical result in due season, by the very nature of things? Why, with our population of a hundred thousand souls, we have not a *Free* School yet in all Utah, and outside of this city scarcely a *School*-House. Here, we have a few Ward Schools; but the teachers are inferior, and the rates of tuition, cost of books etc., so high, that only the children of the better classes can attend. Brigham Young has a school of his own, in his seraglio grounds, where his numerous progeny are taught music, dancing, and some of the commoner branches; but the great bulk of our rising generation here are growing up in a state of ignorance and superstition so dense, as to be absolutely inconceivable elsewhere. So, too, many of the Saints have two or more sisters for wives, at the same time. Others, again, marry their own blood-cousins, and some even their own step-daughters. And instances exist, where they have had mother and daughter for wives, at the same time. Now, where all this is to end, it seems to me, it is not difficult to predict, unless Nature suspends her laws, and Evil becomes our Good."

"It is certainly very shocking, judge. But what do you propose to *do* about it?"

"Well, I would do something, or at at least *try* to. I have thought a good deal about it, since I got my eyes open; and, first of all, I would have Congress authorize and instruct the U. S. Marshal here to summon the jurors for the U. S. Courts direct. By some strange oversight, I suspect by Mormon intrigue (for they watch Congress closely, and boast they control it on all Utah matters usually), this was omitted in our Organic Act, and consequently our jury-lists are now taken from the county-lists, which are of course made up by Mormon sheriffs. Therefore, all open and avowed Gentiles, who have any back-bone in them, are left off, and we get nobody in our U. S. jury-boxes even, except Mormons and doughface Gentiles. Of course, such juries won't indict or convict for polygamy, or any other offence worth mentioning, if a Mormon is to be mulcted for it. But if our jurors were summoned by our Marshal direct, out of the whole body of the Territory, as they are everywhere else, I believe, he could take good care to put only reliable citizens on the lists, and thus give us juries that *would* indict and convict in all necessary or flagrant cases.*

* Senator Wade's Bill (1867) met the Utah Question somewhat like this, and I suspect Judge —— had a finger in it. So, Senator Cragin's Bill subsequently, and others since. The present imbroglio in Utah hinges on this Jury Question, more than anything else, and Congress ought to settle it speedily, on a just and right basis. Judge McKean may be in the wrong technically; but substantially, he is fighting for truth and justice, and if he lacks the necessary weapons, should be furnished them. This is what Senator Frelinghuysen's Bill, now pending, (1874) proposes well to do.

"But would the Saints meekly consent to be thus overslaughed, and ignored?"

"Of course, not! The first verdict we got and attempted to enforce, there would be a riot, or threatened riot, and then we would have to fall back on the Military. The Utah Militia, of course, could not be depended on; for it is all officered and controlled by the creatures of the Church. Therefore, we would have to call on the United States, and it would be for Uncle Sam to decide at last. This, of course, would necessitate an increase of troops here; for, if the garrison were small, the Saints might make trouble. But give us a couple of batteries, a regiment of cavalry, and say two regiments of infantry, such as Sherman 'went marching through Georgia' with; and Brighamdom can be made to obey the laws, the same as Dixie, or be ground to powder."

"But, judge, will not the Pacific Railroad solve the problem in a more excellent way—peaceably and quietly—by bringing in such an influx of Gentiles, that Mormonism will be neutralized? This is what we all hope East?"

"Perhaps so, if this 'influx' is *big* enough, and *good* enough. But, you see, the Saints claim to have pre-empted about all the land here, that is worth anything, and they won't sell or lease to Gentiles, unless the Church says so. Besides, with the heavy immigration the Mormons are constantly receiving—about three thousand this year, to next to nothing by the Gentiles, and their naturally rapid increase, I fear they will keep greatly ahead of all outsiders, who won't be likely to come and stay long where they will be ostracised and outlawed. It isn't natural, that they should. Won't it be the same, as it was down South before the war, and has been ever since? Northern brain and capital wouldn't go there, and won't, because they believe in perfect freedom of speech and of the press—absolute security of person and property—and won't settle where these are wanting. How then can we expect them to emigrate here, where we have no true enjoyment of either? What sensible man would come to Utah, or bring his wife and children here, when he could go just as well to Colorado or Montana, Oregon or California, and escape the dismal drawbacks we have here? I admit I have great hopes of the Railroad, in time; and yet I confess, I fear, our *quæstio vexata* here in Utah, like its "twin" question down in Dixie, will find its solution only in gunpowder, if it is to find it soon. When nothing else will do, I have great faith in the moral power of bayonets—especially, when used on the right side."

"But, judge, is not Brigham Young the main cohesive power; and when he dies, what then?"

"Well, when that happens they may split up, on the question of his successor; but I suspect Brigham is too shrewd and far-seeing for that. He already has Brigham Young, Jr., his smartest son, in training for the succession—sent him missionary to England, and now he is a Brigadier-General in the Mormon Militia here—and the probability is, a "Revelation" will designate him for the Presidency, if death don't come too suddenly. Brigham will undoubtedly keep the succession in his own family, if he can; but he will not hesitate a moment to designate some other person, if the seeming interests of the Church require it. Of course, he is very illiterate; but he is a very able and sagacious man, for all that—devoted to Mormonism, and "dangerous" in every sense of that word."

"Have you no fear of him, yourself, judge? You speak your mind pretty plainly."

"No, I think not. He would hardly strike so high. Besides he is reputed to be a coward, personally, and I guess *that* is so. I have seen him charged with complicity in the Mountain Meadow massacre, and his shirking and cringing then was pitiful. No doubt, my life is always in danger here, more or less, as would be that of any other upright and fearless judge. Indeed, I have good reason to know, that they cordially hate me. After Dr. Robinson's assassination a friendly Mormon came to me at night, and told me confidentially my turn would come next. But I keep indoors after dark, or else go out only in company, or when heavily armed, and am prepared to sacrifice my life, if need be, at any time. I have lived too long in this world, to be much afraid of leaving it; and I don't know as I could die better anyhow, than in upholding and enforcing the laws of my country here in Utah."

"Do your Courts ever meet with real opposition to their ordinary courses of procedure?"

"Why, no—not formally; though I never have much confidence in a verdict, where one of the parties is a Gentile. Where plaintiff and defendant are both Mormons, our verdicts are usually righteous enough; though these are liable to be overruled or set aside, by the High Council of the Church—a body of irresponsible ecclesiastics, of course, unknown to the laws. This Council is composed of Brigham Young, and a number of the chief dignitaries of the Church, and is often appealed to by "big" Mormons, when the civil courts have gone against them."

"No! Really? But is not this mere rumor, judge?"

"No, indeed! I could cite several such cases, but will only trouble you with one. Not long ago, down in one of our Southern counties, a laboring man—a Mormon—was working in a barn, for and with a Mormon Bishop. In some way or other, they got into a quarrel, which ended in a fight, and in the course of this the Bishop hurt the poor fellow very badly. Among other things, he struck him with a pitchfork, harpooning him —so to speak—through the leg, so that the poor man was laid up for months, and made a cripple indeed for life. After his recovery, the outrage was so atrocious, and the community so generally with him, he mustered up courage enough to bring an action against the Bishop. The cause was tried in the Probate or County Court, where of course, all were Mormons. But the jurors, being neighbors of the injured man and cognizant of all the facts, resolved to do justice, and accordingly without much delay returned a verdict for $3,500 damages. The Bishop being rich, as the high dignitaries all are, appealed the case to my court, where I, after a full hearing, of course, affirmed the judgment of the court below, with heavy costs.

"Well, now, I supposed this settled the case, as there was no higher court here. But judge of my astonishment, when some weeks after the plaintiff came to me one day, and said the Bishop had further appealed the case to the High Council of the Church, where they had tried it over again, and awarded him only $1,000 damages; and he wanted to know if this was right and "good law" here? Of course, I could do nothing for him myself, with the facts in that shape. But I referred him to one of our Gentile lawyers here, and told him if he would put the case in his hands, and have the facts brought regularly before me, so that I could get hold of the matter judicially, I would soon teach this "High Council of the Church" a lesson, as to their rights and duties, as against a United States Court, that they would be apt to remember for awhile. He thanked me, and took my advice. But before the papers got regularly before me, the Mormons somehow got wind of the matter, and hastened to settle with the man. I believe they gave him $2,000, or something like that, and I suppose frightened him into silence. Now, to think once of these insolent villains, presuming—without law and in violation of law—to review and overrule the solemn decision of a United States Court! I tell you, it made my Quaker blood boil, when I heard of it.* I would just like to have laid my hands on that "High Council of the Church," in a case like that. I feel right sure, I would have taught Brigham Young and his lawless associates a wholesome lesson, they wouldn't have forgotten very soon, if it had cost me my life to do it."

There was something grand and heroic—almost sublime—about this man's talk at times, and I only reproduce it here very faintly. He knew I was seeking official facts, and doubtless unburdened his whole soul to me. He had had unusual opportunities for observation; he seemed to be well-informed; and certainly was thoroughly honest. Further than this, I cannot vouch for him, but report the conversation substantially as it occurred, from notes made the same evening. I must, however, do him the justice to add, that his views in the main were everywhere corroborated by almost all the Federal officers I met—both civil and military—as well as the vast majority of Gentile settlers, throughout all that region. Such were the views of Judge——; and subsequent events there, it must be confessed, have pretty well illustrated them.

* He was originally from Pennsylvania.

CHAPTER XII.

MORMONISM IN GENERAL.

IN the two previous chapters, I have discussed Utah pretty thoroughly, touching most of the mooted questions there; and now, to sum up. Without doubt, it must be said of the people of Utah, that they are an industrious, frugal, and thrifty race. By their wonderful system of irrigation, they have converted the desert there into a garden, and literally made the wilderness, "bloom and blossom as the rose." Their statistics (1866) showed, that they had already constructed over a thousand miles of irrigating canals and ditches, watering 150,000 acres of land, at a cost of nearly $2,000,000. Each family has its own few acres, and these are cultivated so thoroughly, that the total annual product is surprising. In Salt Lake City many families almost live on their acre-and-a quarter lots, and many of their farms elsewhere do not exceed forty or fifty acres, with many much smaller. With their system of careful culture and general double-cropping, one man cannot well manage over ten or twelve acres per year; nor is more necessary for an ordinary family, the land proves so bountiful. Fifty and sixty bushels of wheat per acre, we were told, was not an unusual yield. So, since leaving the Missouri, we had nowhere seen more comfortable and apparently well-to-do homes. We must say, they were much superior to the average homes of our people in Colorado. Evidently, these

Utahans had come there to *stay*, and from the first had "governed themselves accordingly;" while the Coloradoans, it was plain, were too many of them, only "birds of passage," like so much of our population in the West generally. Their towns and villages are well laid out, and in the main neatly built. In the country, their little farms are well-fenced or walled, with comfortable adobe houses clustering with vines and flowers, or surrounded with fruit and shade trees, while a throng of hay and grain-stacks encircle their barns. So, too, the Mormons, whatever else may be said of them, are certainly a sober race of people. Many of them no doubt keep liquor about their premises, and drink when they choose to; but drunkenness as a vice, or habitual drinking as a practice, is unknown in Utah, comparatively speaking. So, too, they allow no gambling there, except "on the sly;" and no houses of prostitution, unless you regard every "much-married" Mormon's as such, which it seems hardly fair to do—the women considered. On the whole, it is safe to say, that the Mormons deserve marked commendation and praise for what they have accomplished in Utah, in redeeming a barren wilderness and building up a prosperous community there, and full credit should be awarded them accordingly. They brag constantly, and largely, about Great Salt Lake City, and surely they have a right to. In the essential points of beauty, comfort, cleanliness, and good order, it has few equals, and perhaps no superiors of its age and size anywhere, and all things considered is indeed a perfect miracle for Utah. In the very heart of the great internal basin of the continent, and the centre of a busy and thriving people, it really seemed to be a natural metropolis there, and was everywhere talked of as the future workshop and mart of that region.

On the other hand, it is due to truth to say, that impartial as I tried to be, the more I studied affairs there, the more Mormonism impressed me as, in many respects, a huge mass of thorough iniquity. It did not strike me as a Religion at all, *per se*, and I suspect there is less of the purely "religious" about it, than any other ecclesiastical organization on the earth. Their sermons were not so much theological discourses, as they were sectarian stump-speeches. The whole Church, "so-called," struck me ordinarily, as a coarse utilitarianism, not to say rude materialism. Their missionaries seemed to be sent out, not so much to spread the gospel (even according to J. Smith and B. Young), as to induce and hasten immigration to Utah. It is true, they have Bishops and other subordinate clergy; but their main duty appeared to be to preside over and direct colonization, rather than to cure souls. They had indeed their regular dioceses; but these were so arranged as to make the Bishop the chief man in each town or settlement, and judging by those we saw these dignitaries were selected rather for their shrewd business talents, than any special piety or virtue. They were almost invariably sharp smart Americans, while the great majority of the Mormons were English, Welsh, Danes, etc., of the very lowest and poorest classes. In every community, the Bishop's word was law and gospel, as he claimed to receive "revelations" direct from heaven on most knotty questions, and he virtually inspired and directed all its business. Usually he owned the mill, store, and hotel, and he who controls these three essentials of a new community ordinarily controls the community itself. Observation shows, that nearly everybody in a new country becomes mortgaged, sooner or later, to the miller, store-keeper, or hotel-keeper; and hence as the Bishops are all three of these in one, their chances for amassing wealth are simply enormous. The result is, that all or nearly all of the Mormon Bishops have become immensely rich, while Brigham himself is reported worth a fabulous amount in his own right, independently of the vast property he holds, as "Trustee in trust for the Church of Jesus Christ of Latter Day Saints."* Indeed, to sum it up in one word, the whole institution of Mormonism—polygamy and all—apart from its theological aspects, impresses you rather as a gigantic organization for collecting and consolidating a population, and thus settling up a Territory rapidly, whatever else it may be; and its success, in this respect, has certainly been notable and great.

As a whole, the Mormons are no doubt a very ignorant, and, therefore, very bigoted people, and the whole tendency of their pulpit-teachings is to lawlessness and violence, so far as Gentiles are concerned. They affect to despise mere intellect and sentiment, and to pride themselves on being plain-spoken and practical. They will not "fellowship" with open and avowed Gentiles, if they can avoid it; and boldly proclaim their hostility to and contempt for the Government of the United States, as on the Sunday we were at their Tabernacle. No doubt, if opportunity offered, they would assail or embarrass it, though now they are more wary and circumspect, than they were before the South learned a lesson on this score. So, Brigham Young is governor *de facto* in Utah, and has been always, no matter who is governor *de jure*, and will be, while that other "twin relic of barbarism," polygamy, endures. The evidence on all these points, I must say, seemed fairly overwhelming, though no more can be given here. So, too, they believe, or affect to believe,

* His account in the Bank of England was said to be *fourth* on the list, in point of magnitude, and his wealth estimated any where from $25,000,000 to $50,000,000.

that the United States dares not touch their "peculiar institution," and brand all our laws against it as acts of "National wickedness," "Federal tyranny," invasions of their "sacred rights," etc. It seemed to me, that we had heard such complaints before; but not from a part of the country, that led us to respect them greatly, when reiterated there in Utah. The true test is, what are the results to Humanity, and how do they affect us as a People? And I am sure, the answer in all candor must be, a bigoted and seditious race of *men*, a degraded and inferior class of *women*, an ignorant and degenerate herd of *children;* and does not the inevitable, and inexorable, logic of things necessitate just these? If these be the elements of progress and the seeds of empire, then Utah should be let alone; if otherwise, then let us lay the strong hand of the Government upon her, and teach her respect for and obedience to the laws, the same as all other parts of the Union.

No doubt their poor women are already relapsing into a condition, that is truly pitiable, as elsewhere intimated, and their tendency must be rapidly to the worse. Evidently the Saints take care to seclude them from Gentile gaze, as much as possible; but a more dreary, homely, pokey set of women, as a whole, were never seen. I may have been unfortunate, but in all Utah, I did not see a truly happy and sunny countenance, or noble and serene, on a mature Mormon woman; nor did I anywhere hear of one, who would fully realize our old and fond ideal of

> "A perfect woman nobly planned,
> To warn, to comfort, and command;
> And yet a spirit—still and bright—
> With something of an angel's light!"

But, what else could be expected in a country, where a husband signifies only the fractional part of a man, and a wife—any number of women you please? Beyond controversy, their "peculiar institution" of polygamy *is* a "relic of barbarism"—yea, verily, a "twin-relic" to slavery—as the Republican party in 1856-60 had the manliness and courage to pronounce it. "Peculiar" institutions, of whatever character, have no business in a republic; they mean inequality, and inevitably tend to violence and disorder. No doubt, had Abraham Lincoln lived, when we had finished our first "twin" right thoroughly, he would have found a way to look well after the other. We owe this to our mothers and sisters, to our wives and daughters,

> "The graces and the loves, that make
> The music of the march of life—

to all of womankind, the broad continent across and the wide world over; and Congress should take care, that we lend not the sanction of our flag to this hideous crime, an hour longer than we must. Our age, so far, has largely honored itself, in honoring and respecting womankind, and it is too late now to let Christian America barbarize any portion of herself, with the exploded savagery of pagandom. We *must* have freedom of speech and of the press there, security of person and property—absolute and perfect—the same as in New York or Massachusetts, or our flag is a lie. We must maintain and execute our national laws against polygamy, the same as everywhere else, no matter who opposes, or our government is a sham. And if Mormon juries wont do this, refusing to indict or convict, and nothing else will do, so that we have to fall back on the bayonet, why then I see nothing in Utah so sacred, that we should not give Brighamdom the bayonet, the same as we did Jeffdom. I believe in the Pacific Railroad, and hope much from its civilizing and refining influences; I have great faith in the locomotive and the telegraph; but I also believe, with Judge —— in "the moral power of bayonets, when nothing else will suffice—especially when used on the right side." We have just had to use them against one "twin-relic," when nothing else would do, in spite of our Railroads there; now let them charge down upon the other, if Utah will not obey the laws, and that right speedily. Were Mormonism merely a religion, as a republic we should be the last to touch it. But polygamy, its baleful flower and fruit, and the source of all Utah's woes, is an unmitigated barbarism; an outrage and crime, not only against woman, but humanity; an organized insult to the christianity and civilization of the age; and we Americans, of this generation, owe it to ourselves and to history, to end it—to stamp it out if need be—*sans* ceremony and instanter. Let us not dally with it, as we did with Southern slavery. Else may God, in his just wrath, break us again with a rod of iron, or haply dash us in pieces as a potter's vessel. Let Congress and the President but do their duty in the premises, and Brigham Young I predict will receive a "new revelation," that will quickly end the whole trouble. The power is with them, and History will hold them justly responsible.

CHAPTER XIII.

SALT LAKE TO BOISÈ CITY, IDAHO.

IT was our intention originally to proceed from Salt Lake to San Francisco direct, *via* Nevada; but our long sojourn at Salt Lake induced us to go *via* Boisè City and the Columbia instead. When arranging for our departure, we happened to meet Mr. Ben Holliday, the great stage-proprietor of the Plains there, and he advised us to inspect Idaho first, or we would be caught there in winter. He was then temporarily at Salt Lake, on one of his semi-annual inspections of his vast stage-lines. The Pacific Railroad has supplanted these now, in the main; but they were then the only means of rapid transit, and a great and important agency of civilization throughout all that region. His line of stages commenced then at Fort Kearney on the Platte, and ran thence to Denver, about five hundred miles; thence to Central City, in the heart of the Colorado mines, about forty miles; returning to Denver, thence along and across the Rocky and Wahsatch Mountains to Salt Lake, about six hundred miles; thence through Idaho and Oregon, to Umatilla on the Columbia, about seven hundred miles, with a branch at Bear River, through Montana to Virginia City, about four hundred miles more. In all, his stage-lines then footed up about two thousand two hundred and forty miles, through the great frontier heart of the continent. From Kearney to

Salt Lake, he ran a daily stage each way; over the balance of his routes, only a tri-weekly. From Salt Lake to California, about seven hundred and fifty miles more, there was also a daily stage each way, but this line was owned and run by Wells, Fargo & Co., then and still the great Express Company of the Pacific Coast. Mr. Holliday, in anticipation of the Railroad, with his wonted sagacity, was just completing the sale and transfer of all his stage-lines to Wells, Fargo & Co., whose stage-business alone thus became one gigantic enterprise, reaching from the Missouri to the Pacific, and from Salt Lake to the Columbia. What a prodigious undertaking! How colossal in its proportions! It was estimated that these lines would then foot up over three thousand miles, and to operate them would require about five hundred coaches, and fully ten thousand horses and mules, first and last. Mr. Holliday said his lines had been very profitable some years, but in others again he had lost heavily. Sometimes the Indians stole or destroyed a quarter of a million's worth of his property per annum, and then again his expenses were always necessarily enormous. Stations had to be erected and maintained, ten or fifteen miles apart, along all the routes. Grain had to be hauled, in the main, from either the Missouri or Salt Lake, although Colorado and Idaho had begun to yield something. Hay had to be transported often fifty miles, and fuel sometimes a hundred and fifty. He paid his General Superintendent ten thousand dollars per year, and his Washington Agent about the same; his Division Superintendents about half that sum; his drivers and station-keepers from seventy-five to a hundred dollars per month and their board; and then there were ten thousand and one incidental expenses besides. One would have supposed, that the oversight and management of his vast stage-enterprises would have been enough for one man to carry. But, in addition, he owned and ran a line of steam-ships on the Pacific from San Francisco to Oregon and Alaska, another to Lower California and Mexico, and was planning to get more business still. He was a man apparently of about forty-five, tall and thin, of large grasp and quick perceptions, of indifferent health but indomitable will, fiery and irascible when crossed, and a Westerner all through. Apparently he carried his vast business very jauntily, without much thought or care; but he crossed the continent twice each year, from end to end of his stage-routes, and saw for himself how matters were getting on. When he went through thus, extra teams and coaches were always held in readiness, and he had made the quickest Overland trip recorded. Time was everything with him then; horse-flesh and expense —nothing. Once he drove from Salt Lake to the Missouri, over twelve hundred miles, in six days and a half, and made the total trip from San Francisco in twelve days. The locomotive beats this now, but nothing else could. The usual schedule-time was about twenty days; but it often took two or three more.

Mr. Holladay, however, was beginning to show signs of his hard work, and on this trip had found it necessary to bring his physician along with him. Subsequently, we met him in San Francisco, still an invalid, but as hard at work as ever, and there seemed to be no end to his teeming schemes. Of course, we found these great stage-lines not always popular, because they were rapacious monopolies, *ex necessitate*. Nevertheless, on the whole, they accomplished a great work in their day; and, all things considered, did it cheaply and well. They have a history of their own, full of incident and adventure, that will read like romance a few years hence; and the man who will gather up all the facts, and give us a full account of them, will do the future a real service. Now, if ever, is the time to do this; for the Railroad has already done away with the main lines, and soon over all our American stage-coaching will be written "Ichabod"—its glory has departed.

Mr. Halsey, Mr. Holladay's general superintendent at Salt Lake, was about going to Boisè City to look after stage-affairs generally, and politely invited us to share his special coach. I was still feeble, and it was some days before I could leave; but finally Nov. 7th, we bade good-bye to Camp Douglas and Salt Lake, and were off for the Columbia. Once out of the city, our route struck due north, and skirted the shores of Great Salt Lake for a day or so. This great inland sea, fifty miles long by twenty wide, was on our left, while to the right rose abrupt mountains barren to the summit. The Lake itself was surrounded by marshes, abounding in water-fowl, and just then afforded excellent duck-shooting to frequent parties from the city. It was dotted with islands, several of them large and mountainous, which furnished rich pasturage for large herds of horses and cattle, belonging chiefly to Brigham Young. These beautiful islands had been "granted" to him by the Utah Legislature, as well as the exclusive right to numerous streams and cañons in other parts of the Territory, that were esteemed especially valuable. Among others, they had granted to him City Creek cañon, which contained about the only valuable timber within many miles of Salt Lake City, and now every man, who chopped a load of wood there, had to pay tribute to Brother Brigham to the tune of one dollar per cord. Along the base of the mountains, we frequently came across hot Sulphur Springs, steaming in the sharp November air, and Mr. Halsey pointed out several said to be hot enough to boil an egg. The sulphur and heat from them destroyed all vegetation around them, and also for a considerable distance along the issuing streams, that flowed thence into Great Salt Lake. Every few miles we crossed dashing rivulets, that came roaring and foaming out of the cañons, all making their way ultimately to the Lake—the common reservoir of all that basin. Great Salt Lake drains many hundreds of square miles there, receiving streams from all directions, but giving out none. Its only relief is evaporation, which of course must be enormous during the long and dry summer there. Hence its saltiness and great specific gravity, a man floating in it—it is said—very readily. Its volume that year was greater than usual, owing it was thought to a heavy rain-fall; but this year (1873), I see it reported as several feet higher, than ever before. This would seem to confirm the favorite theory of many pioneers, that as the country became settled up and cultivated, the average rain-fall constantly increased. Between the mountains and the Lake, along its whole extent, there was usually a fine broad plateau of land, and this was dotted thickly with farms to Ogden and beyond.

Ogden, now the stopping point on the Pacific Railroad for Salt Lake City, and about forty miles north of it, was then a smart little town of perhaps 1200 inhabitants, and rapidly growing larger. It was Salt Lake City over again, on a reduced scale, but evidently patterning after it, both in plan and detail. Its streets were broad and rectangular; its irrigating streams, clear and cold from the neighboring cañons; its houses, adobe or frame; and its yards and gardens, a mass of beauty and luxuriance. A general air of industry and thriftiness pervaded the little community. Everybody appeared to be constantly at work, though not very hard work. And, indeed, so far as material comfort was concerned, there seemed little ground for criticism. The supervisor and main-spring of the whole was Bishop West—a burly active man of forty, with three buxom wives, and a house-full of well-graduated children. He was a live, go-ahead business man, with little or nothing of the sacerdotal about him—owned the mill, store, and hotel there, and managed them all with rare shrewdness and energy. His hotel was a comfortable two-story adobe house, with shingle roof, and was remarkably well kept for a country tavern, all things considered. He was a heavy contractor with the stage-line, to deliver grain along at the stations between Salt Lake and Boisè City, and Mr. Halsey concluded to stop over one night to see and confer with him. He received us with generous hospitality, and was soon conversing freely upon all matters relating to Utah, aside from Mormonism. He little suspected then the good luck in store for him, by the oncoming of the Pacific Railroad, which has doubtless made him a millionaire, if he was not approaching that before. Salt Lake was then depending on the Railroad coming there, and doubtless was grievously disappointed, when it left her "out in the cold"—forty miles to the South.*

The Bishop's partner in many of his operations was Mr. Joseph Young, the eldest son, I believe, of Brigham. He happened at Ogden that night, and we saw considerable of him. Mr. Halsey said he was "some married" already, having four wives, and as he was still a comparatively young man—about thirty-five—might have a good many more yet. He was a tall, well-knit, resolute

* But she has already filled this gap with a branch Road, which ultimately she will push north to the Columbia, and south to the Gulf of California.

looking young fellow; but did not seem to be overly wel. stocked with brains or judgment. Nevertheless, in addition to his investments with Bishop West, he owned sawmills in the mountains beyond Salt Lake, and was a heavy contractor with the stage-company besides for supplies elsewhere. He spoke carelessly, not to say disrespectfully, about Mormon affairs in general, and left the impression, that he might abjure the faith some day yet, when the fit occasion came. Brigham, it appears, had discarded him for the succession some time before, in favor of his younger brother, Brigham, Jr., who was said to be a much abler and discreeter man; and this, it was thought, had something to do with "Joe's" free and easy thinking.

From Ogden to Brigham City, about half way to Bear River, the country continued much the same, except that the mountains trended away more to the east, and the plateau thence to the Lake consequently became broader. Settlements continued most of the way, but the farms grew more scattered, and ran more to grazing. Wherever a stream issued from the cañons, it had been caught up and carried far up and down the plateau, to irrigate a wide breadth of land, and its application appeared always to have met with a generous return. Brigham City was a clever little town, of a thousand inhabitants or so, and in its general plan and make up was as much like Ogden as two peas. It lies on a higher bench or plateau, however, and affords a much finer prospect of the bottom country below. We halted there for dinner, and while waiting in the office a Ute Indian came in, with a noble wild goose for sale, that he had just shot in the marshes. He was a splendidly built young fellow, with nothing in the way of clothing, however, except a ragged blanket and the inevitable breech-cloth. His feet and limbs were entirely naked, and would have served well as models for a Belvidere Apollo. It was a cold raw day, with alternating rain and sleet, and no wonder the poor wretch mumbled, "Me cold; much cold!" as he huddled up to the fire. He sold his goose for two "bits," and the last we saw of him he was purchasing "smoke-tobacco" at the nearest store. We saw many lodges of Utes, while *en route* from Ogden to Bear River, and they all seemed to be pitiably off. As we left Brigham City, we observed a dozen squaws or more loitering around a slaughter-house on its outskirts, waiting to secure the entrails or other refuse, that the butchers might throw away. Just beyond, several more crossed the road, loaded down with great bundles of sage-brush, that they had been out gathering for fuel, while their "braves" loafed at home. "Mr. Lo" (the poor Indian!), as our borderers satirically call him, in brief, has certainly sadly deteriorated in Utah, whatever he may be elsewhere. These Utes seemed to be a taller and better class of savages naturally, than their cousins on the Rio Grande; but from contact with the Mormons they were fast disappearing, and would soon become extinct. Brigham Young was credited with saying, with his wonted shrewdness, "I can kill more injuns with a sack of flour, than a keg of gunpowder;" and no doubt he was correct. When left to themselves, as children of nature, they manage to get along somehow, on the old principle of "root pig, or die!" But when they mix with the whites, they acquire our habits and tastes in part, without learning how safely to gratify or benefit by them; and consequently, when left to themselves again, sicken and die.

From Brigham City to Bear River, the country was wilder and more unsettled; but ranches—the true forerunners of settlements—were starting up in various places. The mountain streams were smaller and fewer, but still there were enough to irrigate thousands of broad acres there yet, and to spare. Indeed, the whole country from Salt Lake to Bear River, as a rule, needs only population, to become prosperous and flourishing. The mountain streams did not seem to be a quarter utilized; and, apart from these, vast tracks of land were unused, where grazing would certainly prove profitable.

We crossed Bear River, here a broad deep stream, on a rude bridge, and were now fairly off for Boisè City. Here, eighty-three miles from Salt Lake, the road forked —one branch going to Virginia City, Montana, and the other continuing on to Boisè. The Montana travel was then much the larger, and the stages thus far went full. But the Idaho travel was light—most of her miners preferring the Columbia as a base. From Bear River quite through to Boisè, the country as a whole proved wild and sterile, with but little to recommend it, until we struck the valley of the Boisè. There were some good grazing lands here and there, judging by the "bunch" grass; but Idaho, as a rule, seemed to be a high volcanic plateau, barren and desert-like. Much of it reminded us of Bitter Creek, though here there was less alkali and old red sand-stone. There were no settlements anywhere, except the isolated stage-stations, and but little travel beyond the tri-weekly stages. The lonely stations occurred as usual, every ten or fifteen miles; but they were most dreary and dismal habitations, as a rule. They were built generally of stone, laid up loosely with clay, and often their only fuel was sage-brush and greasewood—about the last apology for fuel on the earth. The whole region seemed destitute of timber, until you reached the Boisè, and even here there was not much to brag of. Good wholesome water seemed to be equally rare, and even at the stage-stations where they had dug for it, the water was often very unpalatable. We passed three stations, one after the other, one day, where Mr. Halsey knew the water to be bad, without essaying to drink, and finally became so thirsty that when we reached the next station, all hands sung out to the station-keepers :

"I say, men, what kind of water have you here?"

"Wall, strangers," was the reply, "Honor bright, it is not much to brag of! It is a heap alkali, and right smart warm ; but we manage to drink it, when it cools a little. It's altogether, you see, in gitten used to it; you bet!"

But as we hadn't got "used to it" yet, and hadn't time to wait, we concluded to pass on to the next station. At most of the stations, the only persons were two stock-tenders or stable-hands, and sometimes only one. At Maláde, however, as we halted there one cold and blustering night, we were agreeably surprised to find a blazing fire and an excellent meal, that gained all the more by contrast with the forlorn and cheerless stations, that greeted us elsewhere. A neat and tidy woman, with an instinct of true refinement about her, was the simple explanation. But how she came to drop down into that desolate station, with a husband and two or three children, will always remain one of the inexplicable mysteries of the Universe to me.

We were now on the old and well-travelled Emigrant Trail from the Missouri to Oregon. But emigration that way had mostly ceased, and the general unattractiveness of the country was shown, by its leaving no settlements behind. Much of the route had always been a natural road across the plateaus ; but in crossing the "divides" and descending into the abrupt valleys, considerable digging and blasting had been done here and there. We neither saw nor heard of any Indians, and I judge the country as a whole was always too barren and desolate to support any thing but wolves. Night after night we heard these howling around us, and sometimes by day a single cayote would skulk across the road; but they took good care to give our Rèmingtons and Spencers a wide berth. How the cayotes or wolves of these plateaus, and of the Plains, manage to live, it is hard to say. There seems little for them to subsist on ordinarily. And yet camp where you will at night, an hour afterwards the whole surrounding landscape becomes vocal with them. First, it is a solitary yelp, and then a constantly widening chorus, until thousands of the cowards seem to be on the bark. One night we got out to walk, over a piece of extra bad road, and as we rounded a rocky point toward the coming station, suddenly a score or more of them opened on us at once. It was pitchy dark, and the suddenness of their onset certainly startled us; but we sent them our compliments in the direction of the sound, from a Spencer carbine and two revolvers, and that was the last we heard of them. The Indians sometimes counterfeit their howling, in order to take travellers unawares; but otherwise, however startling, there seemed to be little real danger about it, as they seldom or never attack a man.

We crossed Snake River on a rude ferry-boat, stage and all, and found it to be there some two or three hundred yards wide, by perhaps forty feet deep. Its banks were abrupt—its water of the same pea-green, as that at Niagara. It was skirted by narrow bottoms on either side, and then came precipitous basaltic walls, hundreds of feet high, to the plateau above. This plateau again was of the same sterile character, as the country already passed over—devoid of animal and vegetable life, except wolves, sage-brush and grease-wood, and even these didn't seem much inclined to flourish there. The Snake itself seemed to be an abrupt cut, through the heart of a vast volcanic plateau, as if following in the track of some ancient earthquake.

Snake River Station was on the north side, just at the foot of the high basaltic bluff, which here rears its majestic front six hundred feet or more perpendicularly into the air. Half way up, a small river bursts forth, and descends in a beautiful cascade two or three hundred feet, whence it rushes like an arrow down the broken, rocky hillside, and so off to the Snake itself. This fleecy waterfall, against the black basaltic bluff, is the first object that strikes you, as you descend into the valley of the Snake, and is a charming feature of the landscape just there. Our route lay along the Snake for many miles, and at several other points we observed similar cascades, on both sides of the river, though none so large or lofty as this. The conclusion seems inevitable, that subterranean streams, having their sources in the far away Mountains, pervade all this barren region; and could these be tapped and brought to the surface, all these plateaus might be made cultivable and fertile. No doubt a way of doing this, by artesian-wells or otherwise, will be found in the future, when the continent fills up more, and Idaho becomes necessary. But these cascades could be utilized immediately, to irrigate much of the bottoms of the Snake at trifling expense, if anybody chose to settle there. These bottoms, as a rule, appeared very rich; but in the absence of rain there for months, were no better than a dust heap. At Snake River Station, indeed, attempts had been made to raise potatoes, and other garden vegetables, and the results seemed encouraging. No doubt, rye, oats, barley, and flax might be grown there thus very readily; but probably the region is too elevated, and too far north, for the more delicate cereals to succeed well.

The great American Falls of Snake River were twenty miles or so farther up, and, much to our regret, we failed to reach them. Mr. Halsey intended taking us that way, but he was already overdue in Boisè, and as I myself had lost a fortnight by illness at Salt Lake, and the weather was threatening, we concluded to hasten on. These falls have been described by some travellers, as much superior to Niagara; but the station-keeper at Snake River said he had visited them the previous spring, and they seemed to him to be only about a hundred feet or so in height in all. He described them, as consisting of two Falls—the first about twenty-five feet high, with foaming rapids to the second or main fall, which itself then goes down perhaps seventy-five feet or so more. He said, however, that a party of soldiers, from an adjacent post, had measured them only a few weeks before, and they reported them as one hundred and ninety-four feet high in all, by perhaps two hundred yards wide, and with the black basaltic walls of the cañon rising some six hundred feet above them still, on either side. During seasons of high water, this would make them quite worthy, indeed, of their great reputation. But the volume of water there for many months in the year must be so small, that it is to be doubted whether they ordinarily approach the grandeur and sublimity of majestic old Niagara. However, Idahoans set great store by these Falls, as the chief wonder of all that region; and as the country just there has little else to brag of, perhaps it is well not to gainsay them.

From the Snake to the Boisè, as already intimated, the country was, if anything, still more barren and desolate, than the region we had just passed over. In some places, it was strewn thick for miles with black volcanic stones and rocks, glazed and scarred by ancient fires, with no signs of ordinary animal or vegetable life anywhere. In such localities, the wolves disappeared, and even the inevitable sage-brush and grease-wood disdained to grow; or, if they grew at all, only eked out a miserable existence. Once across this high "divide," however, we struck the valley of the Boisè, which soon introduced us to an excellent region again, and as we neared Boisè City we found ranches and farms everywhere thickening up. Horses and cattle were out grazing by the roadside in considerable numbers, and down in the bottoms frequent squads of stacks indicated, that goodly crops of hay and grain had been cut and harvested. Wagons now appeared again on the road, as beyond Bear River, (we had not met a single one since leaving there), and people flocked to the doors and windows as the stage rolled by. Once across the "divide" between the Snake and Boisè, the whole country sloped gently to the Boisè, and we spun along and down these descending grades at a splendid gait. We made one hundred and twenty miles, in the last twenty-two hours out from Boisè City, and rolled up to the Overland House with our last team as fresh and gamey as stallions.

Our general ride from Bear River, however, was hardly an enviable one. There were but three of us —Mr. Halsey, myself, and L. We had mattrasses along, which we carried on top by day, and at night arranged into a passable bed. So, too, we had india-rubber pillows, and robes and blankets in abundance. But the weather was very disagreeable, even for the season, and though convalescent I yet found myself far from strong. We left Bear River about 10 P. M., in an ugly storm of rain and sleet, well tucked in for a night's ride; but in an hour or so were roused up by the stage coming to a dead-halt, and the driver singing out—it sounded half-maliciously—"Good place to walk, gents! Bad place ahead!" Out we got for a dismal walk of a mile or more, through a soft and yielding bottom, where the horses could hardly pull the empty coach through, and then in again with muddy boots and disgusted feelings generally. Just before daybreak, we struck a long and steep "divide," where the sleet had thickened into snow, without stiffening the ground enough to bear the coach up, and here again we had another cheerful walk of a couple of miles or so, to relieve the blown horses. At King Hill, the last serious "divide" before reaching Boisè, we had another promenade of a mile or two, through five or six inches of snow, just after midnight; but I managed to stick by the stage. The weather continued raw and cold, rainy and sleety, by turns, and we found it necessary to keep well wrapped up, except in the middle of the day. At night our mattrasses proved too narrow for three, after all, and Halsey's shoulders or knees were constantly punching into either L. or me. He and L. usually slept right along all night, but I got scarcely a genteel wink from Bear River to Boisè. By sunrise ordinarily we were up, and then came a general smoke and talk over the night's experience. By nine or ten A. M. we halted for breakfast, which usually consisted of chicory coffee, stringy beef or bacon, and saleratus-biscuit. Sometimes we got fried potatoes in addition—which helped the meal out somewhat—but not often. Late at night we stopped for dinner (only two meals a day), which was generally only a poor edition of breakfast over again, with the courses perchance reversed. Bilious and aguish with that accursed mountain-fever still hanging about me, I need scarcely say, I had little relish for such a bill of fare, and indeed scarcely ate a "square meal" from Bear River to Boisè. Fortunately, among other extras, Mr. Halsey had had the forethought to lay in a half a bushel of apples, just fresh from the tree at Salt Lake, and these we all munched *ad libitum* as we journeyed along. They were always juicy and cool, piquant and delicious, when nothing else was palatable; and for my part, I really don't see, how I would have got through without them. We were three days and three nights on the road continuously, never stopping except forty minutes or so at a time for meals. The last twenty-four hours out, the weather was raw and cold even for November; and as we rolled into Boisè, with every joint aching, the lights of a town never seemed more winning and welcome. At the Overland House, they were already full. But they gave us a good hot supper, followed by a "shake-down" in the parlor, and every comfort at their disposal.

A word more about kind Mr. Halsey. A New Yorker by birth, he drifted west when a boy, and at an early age became clerk on a Mississippi steamer. Subsequently, he followed the Army in 1857 to Utah, and was engaged for awhile in the Q. M. Dep't. at old Camp Floyd. Then he passed into Mr. Holladay's employ, and now for several years had been his general superintendent at Salt-Lake, with a handsome salary of course. He was a quick, sharp man, about thirty-five, devoted to business, and sure to make money anywhere, if there was money to be made. Slightly conservative, he was still a strong

Union man, and especially proud of Grant and Sherman, whom he had known before the war. He was a robust and hardy man, of the kind that can chew cast-iron or digest pebble-stones (and hence, Idaho pies and biscuit!), but with a heart as big and tender as a woman's. In the spring of '65, he attempted to stage it from Atchison to Salt Lake, but had to walk most of the way, because of the execrable roads that season. Day after day, he and a single companion pushed on ahead of the coach, frequently fording streams up to their arm-pits, especially among the Mountains, where they must have been icy cold, and never even changed their clothes the whole way. They were never dry, or even comfortably warm, for a day together; and yet they reached Salt Lake all right, and he said, never seemed to mind it. It is of such men, that the Border is made up, and these are the ones that accomplish such miracles out there. Such men are always the pioneers of the race, and the rightful founders of empire. "Natural Selection," I suppose, steps in and duly provides them, by the "survival of the fittest." We were indebted to him for many courtesies, in various ways, and would duly acknowledge this here. Afterwards we met him in San Francisco, and subsequently, I believe, he settled in New York. Stalwart, go-ahead, whole-souled Mr. Halsey, good fortune attend you, wherever you may go!

CHAPTER XIV.

BOISE CITY TO THE COLUMBIA.

IDAHO, one of the latest of our new Territories, was formed by lopping off the eastern prolongations of Oregon and Washington, and calling the incipient state by that euphoneous name. Lewiston, the head of navigation then, *via* the Columbia, was originally its capital; but the "shrieks of locality" demanded a more central position, and so Boisè City secured the honor. We found it (Nov., 1866) a mushroom town of log and frame buildings, but thoroughly alive every way. Three years before, there was nothing there but the Boisè bottoms, and a scattered ranch or two. Now she boasted three thousand inhabitants, two daily newspapers, stage-lines in all directions, and ebullient prosperity. A hotel, of large capacity, that was to "take the shine" out of all the rest, was just being completed. The Episcopalians and Presbyterians already had their churches up, and the Methodists were expecting soon to build theirs, though then worshipping temporarily in the Court House. Excellent free-schools, to accommodate all the children and more, abounded, and the sermon we heard on Sunday was chiefly a "pitching into" Brigham Young, largely for the want of these. The preacher had been down to Salt Lake, spying out the land for missionary purposes, and had returned filled with hearty unction against the whole system of Mormonism. Boisè City was then the centre of the mining regions of Idaho, though not *of* them—like Denver, as related to Colorado. The mines were chiefly miles away, at Owyhee, Ruby, Idaho City, and Silver City; but all business sprang from and converged here at Boisè, as the most central point, all things considered, and most of the "bricks" dropped first into her lap. Mining operations were mostly over for that season, and the streets and saloons of Boisè were thronged with rough miners, *en route* for the Columbia, or even California, to winter and return. They claimed they could save money by this temporary exodus—the price of living was so high in Idaho—and at the same time escape the rigor of the climate. With expansive hats, clad chiefly in red-shirts, and "bearded like a pard," every man carried his bowie-knife and revolver, and seemed ready for any emergency. They were evidently a rougher crowd, than the Colorado miners, and in talking with them proved to be from California, Arizona, Nevada, Oregon, Frazer's River, Montana, and about everywhere else, except Alaska. Your true miner is a cosmopolite, who has "prospected" everywhere, from the British Dominion to Mexico, and he is always ready to depart for any new "diggings," that promise better than where he is, on half a day's notice, no matter how far. His possessions are small, soon bundled up or disposed of, and he mocks at the old maxim, "A rolling stone gathers no moss," though usually he is a good exemplification of it.

The chief business of Boisè, just then, seemed to be drinking whiskey, and gambling. The saloons were the handsomest buildings in town, and were thronged at all hours of the day and night. The gamblers occupied corners of these, and drove a brisk trade unmolested by anybody. The restaurants were also important points of interest, and gave excellent meals at not unreasonable prices, all things considered. Here at Boisè, our U. S. greenbacks for the first ceased to be "currency," and the precious metals became the only circulating medium. It did one's eyes good to see our old gold and silver coins in use once more, though gold and silver "dust" was also a recognized medium of exchange. All the stores, restaurants, and saloons kept a delicate pair of scales, and their customers carried buck-skin or leather bags of "dust," from which they made payment, and into which they returned their change. Disputes now and then arose, from the "dust" offered not being up to the standard; but these were usually settled amicably, unless the "dust" proved basely counterfeit, and then the saloons sometimes flashed with bowie-knives, or rung with revolvers.

Here, also at Boisè, for the first, we met John Chinaman. Quite a number of the Celestials had already reached Idaho from California, *via* the Columbia, and were scattered through the towns, as waiters, cooks, launderers, etc. A few had sought the mines, but not many, as they preferred the protection of the towns. Along with the rest, these Chinese miners were also migrating to the Columbia and beyond; and as they paid their stage-fare and rode, while many others footed it to the "River," of course, we augured well of them. The imbecile, brutal, and barbarous laws of the whole Pacific Coast, where Chinamen are concerned, it appeared, however, were still in force in Idaho. A good illustration of their practical workings had just occurred over in Owyhee, or somewhere there, and should be recorded here. Three or four ruffians over there, it appears, had set upon an unoffending Chinaman at work in the mines, and had first abused and insulted him, and then robbed and killed him. Other miners, hearing of the circumstances, arrested the murderers and took them before an Idaho Dogberry, who promptly liberated them on the ground, that no Anglo-Saxon was present at the transaction, and that the Chinamen (who were) were incompetent as witnesses, as against white men! This was good Idado Law and Justice, no doubt. But it was too strong for the indignant miners, and the same day Judge Lynch amended it, by *hanging* all the miscreants in the nearest gulch. This was rude law, and rough justice, no doubt; but was it not infinitely better, than the absurd and inhuman code of the Pacific Coast?

Idaho, as a whole, seemed then to be at a stand-still, and her merchants, as a rule, were sighing for the flush times of '63 and '64, when our miners were on the rush there. Her total yield of the precious metals for '66 was computed at about $5,000,000, against Montana's $15,000,000. Ross Browne, indeed, with "conspicuous inexactness," reported Idaho at $15,000,000 that year; but nearly everybody seemed to think this at least three times too much — Mr. Halsey, who was a good judge, especially. Her "placer" mines, or "diggings," it was thought, were already well exhausted, and her quartz-mining will always prove very expensive, because of the scarcity of fuel, and the heavy cost of transportation. Railroads, it was hoped, would cheapen both of these items in the future, but as yet they seemed distant. From the Columbia to Boisè City, was only about three hundred miles, and yet the charge then for transportation over this short distance was *more than half* the charge from the Missouri to Salt Lake, some twelve hundred miles. This was explained, as one result of their coin basis, and of the high price of wages, and everything else in Idaho. But the fact remained, as an ugly circumstance, for Boisè to digest.

Fort Boisè, on the outskirts of the town, was headquarters of military affairs in Idaho, but had ceased to be of much importance. The Territorial Legislature had already applied to the proper Department at Washington, for the post buildings, for use of the Territorial Government, and the troops were ready to vacate any day. We stopped there a week, studying Idaho affairs generally, and were delightfully entertained by the post-officers. One of them had been stationed in California, at Benicia Barracks, when the war broke out, and he gave us an interesting account of the attempted Rebel movement there, which the sudden arrival of Gen. Sumner on the Coast so effectually squelched. Another was a Baltimorean, who by reading the *Tribune* had become a staunch Republican, and was one of the intensest Union men I ever met. One day a Paymaster happened along, whose baggage a fortnight before had been robbed of $65,000 in greenbacks, and an equal amount in vouchers, while he was taking supper at Fort Boisè. At first, he was paralyzed to lose such an amount, in that wild region. But subsequently he struck a "lead," and followed it up with the pertinacity of a sleuth-hound, until he recovered most of the money and vouchers, and arrested all the thieves. His success was simply wonderful for Idaho, and his story sounded more like romance than sober reality, as he told of the long chase and final capture, with the finding of his greenbacks in carpet-bags, knapsacks, etc., buried by the roadside, and some even under the ruts of the very roadway. While halting there, the news also reached us by telegraph of the November elections East, and the final outcome of Mr. Johnson's "Swinging round the circle!" Army officers though we were, we could not repress a mild hurrah, and how intensely proud we felt of the loyal North! Surely we were a great and noble people, after all. Step by step—*nulla vestigia retrorsum*—we had overcome all obstacles, in the name of Humanity and Justice; and now, evidently, our reactionary leaders had better take care how they trifled with the Republic! We talked it all over among ourselves, as we sat around the camp-fires, at that distant post in Idaho; and thanked God for America, and that there was "life in the old land yet!"

Recruited up again pretty well by our stay at Boisè, we left there Nov. 19th for Umatilla and the Columbia. Stages ran three times a week, but they were going so crowded, and the roads were reported so heavy, that I deemed it more advisable to proceed by ambulance. It was three hundred miles, and by ambulance it would take three times as long; but this would give me an opportunity of resting at night, and I feared to venture on otherwise, anxious as we were to reach the Columbia before winter set in. Our route lay substantially down the valley of the Boisè, and other tributaries of the Snake, to the Snake at Farewell Bend, and thence across the Blue Mountains to the Umatilla, and down that to the Columbia. The chief tributaries of the Snake just there were the Boisè, Pratt's River, Burnt River, and Powder River, and we traversed the valleys of each of these successively. These valleys were all substantially alike, and consisted usually of bottoms from two to three miles wide, very fertile throughout, but all requiring irrigation, except for grass which grew tolerably well without this. Here and there irrigation had been resorted to, to some extent, with fine crops in return; but only a very little of the land had yet been brought under cultivation. Generally, beyond these bottoms, on either side, were elevated benches or plateaus, from five to six miles in width, extending back to the outlying bluffs or mountains. These were covered chiefly with the inevitable sage-brush and grease-wood; but the soil looked fat and fertile enough, and evidently required only patient irrigation, to become as prolific as the fields of Utah. Water for this might be supplied in part from the rivers mentioned, and in part perhaps from the neighboring cañons, if they be not dry cañons. The chief drawback of the country to the Snake, indeed, seemed to be the scarcity of timber, for fencing and building purposes. For fuel, coal had been discovered, both at Farewell Bend and near Boisè City; but timber for other purposes was everywhere scarce and dear. In the valley of the Boisè, "Shanghai" fences were frequent, such as we had seen in eastern Kansas; but the Idahoans used thongs instead of nails, to fasten the boards or rails to the posts—hides evidently being cheaper there, than hardware.

The valley of the Snake, most sinuous of rivers, as its name well indicates, proved scarcely better, than where we had crossed it several hundred miles farther up, a fortnight or so before. But the Snake itself had now swelled into a broad and majestic river. We travelled down its banks for ten or twelve miles, and found its rocky and precipitous bluffs came quite down to the river generally; and where this was not the case, there were often only great banks of sand, whirled into such sheltered places by the winds of ages. Indifferent timber appeared here and there, but not much to speak of. The road wound along close to the bluffs, and was often quarried out of them, without room for more than one team to pass at a time. We passed one such place by moonlight, with the bluff high above and the river deep below, but fortunately got through safely. We reasoned, that the usual trains would have gone into camp by sundown, and took the chances for any accidental travellers like ourselves. It was a beautiful night, with the moon out in all her glory, walking a cloudless sky and filling the cañon of the Snake with a flood of light; but we were not sorry when we heard the lowing of the cattle, and the wee-hawing of the mules, belonging to the trains in camp beyond. It was eight P. M., (Nov. 20th), when we reached Farewell Bend, and here crossed the Snake again on a stout ferry-boat propelled by the current.

Farewell Bend—a hamlet of half a dozen houses—is so called, because here the Snake makes a sudden turn north, and goes off in a wide circuit through the mountains of Idaho and Oregon, instead of keeping straight on to the Columbia, as it seems it should have done. Here, too, is where the great Emigrant Trail, from the Missouri to the Columbia, finally leaves the Snake, and hence also perhaps the name to this bend. The Snake, or Lewis' Fork of the Columbia, as it is sometimes called, altogether is a right noble stream—by far the largest in all that region—and it seemed would yet be made available for navigation, though now badly beset with reefs and rapids. A steamboat had already been built at Farewell Bend, to run up to the neighborhood of Boisè and beyond; but that was her first season, and the results were yet to be seen. It was said, that by starting early in the season, she could reach a point within about two hundred miles of Salt Lake, and thus communicate with a vast region there, then comparatively isolated. A fine vein of good bituminous coal had just been opened in the overhanging bluff at Farewell Bend, and here was fuel cheap for all the country up the Snake. Below Farewell Bend there were rapids that would have to be circumvented by slack-water navigation or railroad portages, the same as on the Columbia. But with this done, the Snake had long stretches of navigable waters, that needed only population and business to make them teem with commerce. The same Company, that made the Columbia navigable, also built the boat at Farewell Bend, and doubtless intended to push the enterprise, though what they have since accomplished I can not say.

The Snake is the western boundary of Idaho, and, having crossed it at Farewell Bend, we were now fairly in Oregon. We soon struck the valley of Burnt River, and followed it up for many miles. At first, it abounded in wild and rocky cañons, that seemed to have no outlet; but farther on, it widened out, and frequent ranches dotted its broad and fertile bottoms. Powder River valley, the next beyond, was more promising still. This contained thousand of acres of rich grass lands, and hundred of settlers had already pre-empted homes there. Cattle and sheep were grazing along the bottoms in considerable numbers, and the adjacent mountains, we were told, abounded in timber for all necessary purposes. At Baker City, in the heart of Powder River valley, we halted one day for dinner, and found a brisk little town of perhaps five hundred inhabitants or so. It contained two quite respectable hotels, and at one of them we got a plain but excellent dinner. Just in the suburbs, we found a ten stamp quartz-mill in full blast, much to our surprise, yielding —it was said—a clear profit of $4,000 in coin per month. The ores came from a silver mine, ten or twelve miles away in the mountains, and the mill was located here to take advantage of Powder River, which was here really a fine stream.

Farther on, after a long and tedious drive up and across a stony "divide," we came suddenly out on Grande Ronde valley, and were amazed at its beauty and fertility. At first view, it seemed almost circular, and looked like a vast bowl hollowed out of the mountains there. Mountains bristling with pine or fir-trees rimmed it in on all sides, while in their midst the valley reposed, as if a dried up lake. Some thirty miles in length, by twenty-five in width, it contains over six hundred square miles of the very washings of the mountains—the whole as rich and fertile as a garden. Cedar, fir, pine, and oak abound in the embracing mountains; but the valley itself is as bare of timber, as an Illinois prairie. Numberless springs burst out of the mountain sides, and coalescing into streams gridiron the valley—uniting at last in Grande Ronde River, which flows thence to the Snake. In places, we were told, there are hot mineral springs also, but we saw none of these. The edges of the valley—seemingly like the rim of a plate—were already sprinkled well with ranches, while horses, cattle, and sheep by the thousand were grazing off in the bottoms. But few houses appeared in the bottoms yet—the settlers apparently preferring to hug the mountains. The wheat crop of the valley that year alone was computed at half a million of bushels, and large quantities of oats, barley, potatoes etc., had been raised besides. Indian corn, or maize, however, had never flourished well, and it was doubted if it would—it being so far north. Even here, though, irrigation had to be resorted to for most summer crops, but down in the bottoms grass grew luxuriantly without this. Grande Ronde, indeed, resembles the great parks of Colorado, only her soil is far finer, and if cultivated to the full, along with Powder River and Burnt River, would alone supply Idaho with pretty much all she needs. We met old settlers there, who years before had emigrated thither from Missouri and Illinois, tempted by the wondrous beauty and fertility of the place, and one could not wonder at their choice of a home. In all that region we saw nothing like Grande Ronde, and indeed but few places to compare with it from the Missouri to the Columbia. Its only drawback seemed to be the severe winds, which prevail there much of the year. It appeared strange, that a valley so embosomed in mountains should be troubled so with winds. But it seemed to be a sort of funnel, and they said the winds were often fierce and continuous there, for long periods together. Nevertheless, unless these approximate to hurricanes or tempests, we could only say, "Blessed be the man who dwells in Grande Ronde!"

Le Grande, the county-seat, we found to be a thriving town of a thousand or so inhabitants, and the largest and busiest place by far since leaving Boisè. At the foot of the Mountains, where the road from the Columbia debouches into Grande Ronde, it caught a large amount of trade and travel that way, and also did considerable business with several gold and silver mines in the adjacent mountains. These mines, it seemed, were not believed to amount to much; but they helped to sustain and build up Le Grande, and so were welcomed. Just then the town was discouraged somewhat, by the recent transfer of the mail-route to Uniontown. But as the county-seat, with two weekly papers, and Grande Ronde to back her, she would evidently continue to prosper, notwithstanding her loss of the stages. A smart church, and a really fine public-school-house, graced the plateau beyond the town—both of which spoke volumes for Le Grande. The main street, however, was almost impassable for the deep and unctuous mud; but by keeping straight ahead, and a little careful manœuvring, we managed to reach "Our House," the most respectable looking hotel, at last. Here they gave us excellent accommodations for the night, and the next morning we started to cross the Blue Mountains.

We had left Boisè with a four-mule team, but at the end of the first day our lead-mules gave out, and we had to hire a pair of ponies to take their places. These ponies—the only animals we could secure—were bright and active little nags, and with them at the head we posted along, at the rate of forty or fifty miles per day very readily. But at Powder River, one of them becoming lame, we were compelled also to drop the other, and this reduced us to only our original wheel-mules—a pair of large, but antiquated, and sorry-looking donkeys, that entertained grave constitutional objections to any gait faster than a walk. When we struck a bit of extra good road—especially if a little down hill—our driver usually managed, by much pounding and profanity, to persuade them into a mild trot. But when we reached the bottoms, or if a "divide" appeared, they speedily gravitated again into their natural creep. We were all day long making our last twenty-six miles out from Le Grande, and it was clear we would never get over the Blue Mountains with this pokey team, if the roads were as reported. Fortunately, at Le Grande, we succeeded in hiring a fresh team, of four fine and spirited horses, and with these we swung out of the town (Nov. 24th) on a good round trot—a delightful contrast to our snail-like pace on coming in. We had sighted the Blue Mountains—the northern prolongation of the Sierra Nevadas—two days before, soon after leaving Baker City, and all along had got ugly accounts of the condition of the roads there. Their bald summits already showed snow here and there, and for a day or two another snow-storm had been lowering in the sky, much to our anxiety. But as we rolled out of Le Grande, the sun came out bright and clear, and with our ambulance stout and strong, and our high-stepping steeds, all the auspices seemed to change in our favor. We soon struck the Le Grande river, and followed this up for several miles, through wild and picturesque cañons, or along the shelving sides of the mountains, where often two teams could hardly pass. The Le Grande carried us well up and into the Mountains, and every hour the scenery became grander and wilder. Grande Ronde valley soon passed out of sight; but, as we ascended, from various points we caught exquisite views of the wide-stretching ranges and valleys beyond. Farther up, we became environed with hills and gorges, covered thick with gigantic fir-trees, though here and there a clump of cedars or pines appeared. All along we met the wild snow-drop, loaded down with its berries, and in sheltered nooks saw the wild currant, with here and there harebells, though these were rare. The mountain-laurel also occurred frequently; but the great predominating growth was the Oregon fir, from the size of a bamboo cane to the leafy monarch, "fit to be the mast of some great admiral." The road was constructed on the cork-screw principle—much around to get a little ahead—but after countless twistings and turnings, we at length reached the summit, long after noon. Here we found a comparatively level plateau, some two or three miles in width, with only a few scattered fir-trees, swept keenly by the wind, from which we slowly descended over the remains of a once corduroyed road to "Meacham's." We arrived at "Meacham's" about 4 P. M.—only twenty-six miles from Le Grande, after all; but as it was still twelve miles to "Crawford's," the next ranch, at the northern foot of the Mountains, it seemed imprudent to venture on that day.

As to the wagoning, I need scarcely say, it well exemplified, with abounding emphasis, "Jordan's a hard road to travel!" The roads, indeed, as a whole, after we got up into the Mountains, were simply execrable, and our ride in that respect anything but romantic. All along the route, we found freight-trains, bound for Boisè City and the Mines, hopelessly "stalled." Some of the wagons with a broken wheel or axle, had already been abandoned. Others were being watched over by their drivers, stretched on their blankets around huge fires by the roadside, smoking or sleeping, patiently awaiting their comrades, who had taken their oxen or mules to double-up on some team ahead, and would return with double teams for them to-morrow or next day, or the day after—whenever they themselves got through. Snow had already fallen on the Mountains, once or twice that season; we found several inches of it still in various places, and the air and sky both threatened more, as the day wore on. Yet these rough freighters looked upon the "situation" very philosophically, and appeared quite indifferent whether they got on or stayed. If it snowed, the forest afforded plenty of wood, their wagons plenty of provisions, and their wages went on just the same; so where was the use of worrying? This seemed to be about the way they philosophized, and accustomed to the rude life of the Border, they did not mind "roughing it" a little. An old army friend used often to parade a pet theory of his, that a man could not associate much with horses, without directly deteriorating. "The horse," he would say, "may gain largely, but it will only be at the expense of the man. Our cavalry and artillery officers always were the wickedest men in the service, and all because of their equine associations. The animals, indeed, become almost human; but in the same proportion, the men become animals!" I always thought him about half-right; but if this be true as to intimacy with horses, what must be the effect on men of long and constant association with mules or oxen! I thought I saw a good deal of this in mule-drivers in the army, in Virginia and Tennessee; but a harder or rougher set, than the ox-men or "bull-whackers" (as they call themselves) of the Plains and Mountains, it would be difficult perhaps to find, or even imagine. On the road here in the Blue Mountains, with their many-yoked teams struggling through the mud and rocks, of course, they were in their element. *Outré*, red-shirted, big-booted, brigand-looking ruffians, with the inseparable bowie-knife and revolver buckled around their waists, they swung and cracked their great whips like fiends, and beat their poor oxen along, as if they had no faith in the law of kindness here, nor belief in a place of punishment hereafter. And when they came to a really bad place—in crossing a stream, or when they struck a stump or foundered in a mud-hole—it is hard to say whether their prodigious, multiplied, and many-headed oaths were more grotesque or horrible. To say "they swore till all was blue," would be but a feeble comparison; the whole Mountains corruscated with sulphur! Some few of the trains consisted only of horse and mule teams; but ox-teams seemed most in favor, and slow as they were, we took quite a fancy to them—they appeared so reliable. When the roads were good, they averaged ten or twelve miles per day, and subsisted by grazing; when they became bad, they managed to flounder through any how—some way or other. At extra bad places, the teams were doubled or trebled up, and then the wagon was bound to come, if the wood and iron only held together. Twenty or thirty yoke of oxen straining to the chains, with the "bull-whackers" all pounding and yelling like mad, their huge whip-lashes thick as one's wrist cracking like pistols, was a sight to see—"muscular," indeed, in all its parts. The noise and confusion, the oaths and thwacks and splashing of the mud, made it indeed the very hell of animals; but, for all that, the wagon was sure to reach *terra firma* at last, no matter how heavily loaded, or pull to pieces. We had great sympathy for the patient, faithful oxen, and wished for Mr. Henry Bergh and his Cruelty-Prevention Society many a time that day. Here, indeed, was some explanation of the high rates of freight from the Columbia to Boisè; and Idaho would find it to her interest to improve such routes of transportation forthwith.

I need scarcely add, it was a hard day on our noble horses, but they carried us through bravely. Our ambulance was a light spring carriage, with only L. myself and the driver, and could not have weighed over fifteen hundred pounds, baggage and all; yet it was just as much as the four gamey horses wanted to do to haul us along. It was a steady, dragging pull throughout, after we were well into the Mountains, with scarcely any let-up; up-hill, of course, most of the way, with deep mud besides; chuck-holes abounding, and quagmires frequent; in and out, and around freight-trains "stuck" in the road; and on arriving at "Meacham's," our gallant team, though by no means exhausted, yet seemed very willing to halt for the night. How we congratulated ourselves on securing them, before quitting Le Grande! Had we started with our pair of dilapidated donkeys, we would never have got through; but would probably have had to camp out in the Mountains over night, and send back for another team, after all. Once in rounding a rocky hill-side, above a yawning chasm, our "brake" snapped short off, early in the forenoon; and again, in one of the worst quagmires, our drawing-rope by which the leaders were attached broke, and we would no doubt have been hopelessly ship-wrecked, had it not been for our fore-thought on leaving Le Grande. Fortunately, accustomed to army roads on the Peninsula and in Tennessee, we laid in a supply of rope and nails there, with a good stout hatchet, and these now stood us in excellent stead. With these we soon repaired all damages satisfactorily, and went on our way—not exactly rejoicing; but rather with grave apprehensions lest we should break down entirely, far away from any human habitation, and have to pass a supperless night by the roadside, or around a roaring fire, with wolves, bears, and such like "varmints" perhaps uncomfortably near about us.

So, it was, we were glad to be safe at "Meacham's," at last, and to sit down to the generous cheer he gave us at nightfall. Though 8,000 feet or more, above the sea, and built wholly of logs, it was the cleanest, cheeriest, and best public-house we had yet seen in either Oregon or Idaho, outside of Boisè City; and even the "Over-land" there indeed set no better table, if as good. We did ample justice to the luscious venison, sausage, and pumpkin-pies, that they gave us for dinner at 6 P. M. —having breakfasted at 6 A. M., and eaten nothing since. Mr. Meacham himself, our genial host, was a live Ore-gonian, who had come thither from Illinois several years before, and with his brother now owned this ranch, and the road over the Blue Mountains—such as it was. Bad as it was just then, it had cost them a good deal of money, first and last; and being the shortest road from navigation on the Columbia to Idaho and Montana, it had paid well in other years, when there was a "rush" of miners to those regions. But the emigration thither had now fallen much off, and besides a competing road had been opened from Wallula on the Columbia—flanking the Mountains in part—to Uniontown in Grande Ronde valley, and so beyond, which it was believed would hurt the Meacham Road seriously. The mail now went this new road, and trade and travel it was thought would be apt to follow the stage-coaches. Yet Mr. Meacham was not discouraged. He was a plucky, wide-awake man, some forty years of age, with brown hair and stubborn-looking beard, and in general looked like a person who could take care of himself well, travel or no travel. His wife was a really interesting lady, with several well-bred children; and in the evening, when we asked for something to read, he surprised us by producing a file of the *N. Y. Times*, Greeley's American Conflict, and Raymond's Abraham Lincoln. He had been a candidate for the Oregon Legislature at the recent election, and though running much ahead of his ticket, had been beaten by a small majority. He explained, that "the left wing of Price's army" was still encamped in that part of Oregon, and that the Oregon democracy generally were only a step removed from Gov. Price and Jefferson Davis. The early settlers there, he said, had been mostly "Pikes" from Missouri, and they still clung to their old pro-slavery (and therefore Confederate) ideas. In '61, many of them had indeed favored secession, and later in the war when Price's forces were finally routed in Missouri, hundreds of his soldiers deserted and made for Oregon, where they already had acquaintances or friends. We had heard something of this before, and now understood what was meant by the popular expression—even at Salt Lake—that "the left wing of Price's army was encamped" in Idaho and Oregon! Later in the evening, he gathered his little ones about us, and would have us talk about army experiences, during the war and afterwards, and affairs East generally. In return, he gave us his experiences West and incidents of border-life, by the hour together. Thus we spun yarns by his ample fire-side, until the "wee sma' hours" and after—the fir-logs blazing and roaring welcome up his wide-throated chimney—when he showed us to a cosy room, and an excellent bed, clean and sweet beyond expectation even.

During the night, I was awakened by the rain pattering on the roof, just over our heads; but this soon ceased, and the next morning we had several inches of snow, with huge flakes still falling. This was a bad outlook; nevertheless, we decided to go on, as it was impossible to say how long the storm would last, or how severe it would become. We did not want to be "snow-bound" there, and besides we thought we could reach "Crawford's" anyhow, as it was but twelve miles or so, and that would take us well out of the Mountains. We left "Meacham's" accordingly at 7 A. M., with our horses fresh and keen after their night's rest, and got along pretty well for a couple of miles or so, when suddenly, in drawing out of a chuck-hole, one of our wheels struck a stump, and "smash" went our king-bolt. Down came the ambulance kerchuck in the snow and mud; out went the driver over the dash-board *a la* bull-frog, but still clinging to the ribbons; while L. and I sat wrapped in our great-coats and robes on the back seat, at an angle of forty-five degrees or so. Here was a pretty predicament, surely! On top of the Blue Mountains, broken down in a quagmire, the snow falling fast, and no house nearer than "Meacham's!" Fortunately, our gamey horses did not frighten and run away, or we would have been infinitely worse off. Tumbling out, we presently ascertained the extent of our damages, and all hands set to work to repair them. Now it was, that our forethought at La Grande again handsomely vindicated itself. With our hatchet we cut props for the ambulance, and lifted it up on these; and then found, that though part of the king-bolt was broken off and the balance badly bent, it could yet be hammered into shape sufficiently to carry us forward again, with careful driving. It took an hour or more of sloppy and hard work, before we got the bolt back again into its place and every thing "righted up;" and then, as an additional precaution, with our good rope we lashed the coupling-pole fast to our fore axle-tree besides. Altogether it made a rough looking job, but it appeared stout and strong, and we decided to venture it anyhow. The rest of the way out of the Mountains, however, we proceeded very cautiously. The snow continued to fall right along, and concealed the bad places, so that the roads were even worse, than the day before, if possible. At all extra-bad spots, or what seemed so, L. and I got out and walked; and even when riding, we tried to help the driver keep the best track, by a sharp lookout ahead and on either side. Our ambulance, however, rolled and pitched from quagmire to chuck-hole, like an iron-clad at sea; and repeatedly when out walking I stopped deliberately, just to see how beautifully she would capsize, or else collapse in a general spill, like a "One-Horse Shay!" All around us was the dense forest: all about us, that unnatural stillness, that always accompanies falling snow; no human being near; no sound, but our panting horses and floundering ambulance; no outlook, but the line of grim and steely sky above us. "There she goes! This time sure! See what a hole!" And yet by some good luck, she managed to twist and plunge along through and out of it all, in spite of the mud and snow; and at last landed us safely on the high bald knob, that overlooks "Crawford's," and the valley of the Umatilla. We had about ten miles of this execrable travelling, expecting any moment to upset or break down; and when at last we got fairly "out of the wilderness," it was a great relief. We had an ugly descent still, of two miles or more, before we reached the valley; but this was comparatively good going, being downhill, and besides the snow above had been only rain here.

The view from this bald knob or spur, as we descended, was really very fine. Just as we rounded its brow the clouds broke away, and the sun came out for awhile quite brilliantly. Far beneath us, vast plateaus, like those between Bear River and Boisè City, stretched away to the Columbia; and in the distance, the whole region looked like a great plain or valley. To the northeast, we could follow for miles the road or trail to Walla-Walla, as it struck almost in a straight line across the plateaus; to the northwest, we could mark in the same way the route to Umatilla. At our feet, and far away to the west and north, we could trace the Umatilla itself, as it flowed onward to the Columbia. Beyond all these, to the north and west still, a hundred and fifty miles away, sharp against the sky, stood the grand range of the Cascade Mountains, with their kingliest peaks, Adams, Hood, St. Helens, and Rainier, propping the very heavens. On a bright, clear day, this view must be very fine; as it was, we caught but a glimpse or two of it, just enough to make us hunger for more, when the clouds shut in again, and we hastened on. Now that we were out of the forest, the wind blew strong and keen in our faces, with no fir-trees to break it, and for a half hour or so we shivered with the cold; but it also spurred up our gallant horses, and we were soon whirling out of the foot-hills, at a rapid rate. We drew up at "Crawford's" at 1 P. M., and here halted to lunch and to bait our animals—well satisfied, after all, with our morning's work.

An hour afterwards we started again, and now bowled along famously. Our route lay down the valley of the Umatilla, and as the road was a little sandy, the rain had made it just good for travelling. L. and I, with our baggage and driver, were no load at all for four such gamey nags, especially over a descending grade, and soon after dark we rolled into "Wells' Springs"—42 miles from "Meacham's." Here we encountered a motley crowd of teamsters, miners, and others, all very rough, *en route* to Idaho and Montana. "Wells' Springs" was a shabby ranch, and we had no intention of stopping there, but were unable to go on—one of our horses becoming suddenly sick. The house was dirty, and the supper poor and badly cooked; so that we could readily believe the slouchy, slatternly landlady, when in the course of the meal she remarked to one of her rough guests, "O, we never care for puttin' on *style* here! Only for raal substantials!" Supper over, there was a general smoke and talk, and how those rough fellows did talk! At bedtime, we were put into a little closet, partitioned off from the rest, while the main crowd quartered around "loose" on the floor outside. The last thing we heard, two "bull-whackers" were disputing as to who I was—one insisting I was Gen. Grant, and the other contending I was only Inspector-General U. S. A! We soon went heavily to sleep; the next morning, when I awoke, the same chaps were disputing still!

Next morning, our sick horse was better, but still not himself. We left "Wells' Spring," however, at

OREGON INDIAN.

7 A. M. on a walk, but soon achieved a trot, and were getting on quite satisfactorily again, when our ambulance struck a stone and smash went one of the rear springs. Two of its leaves showed old breaks, and it was a mystery how it ever stood the rough and tumble drive across the Mountains. Again our Le Grande rope came into play, and breaking a box to pieces we happened to have along, we soon succeeded in splicing up the spring, so as to make it hold. An hour's drive more, however, over a descending road, took us into Umatilla without further accident, and we hauled up at the *Metropolitan*, at 11 A. M. having come eighteen miles. We were just too late for the tri-weekly boat, down the Columbia to Portland, which we had been aiming at for a week—she having left an hour or so before. If it had not been for our break-down in the Mountains, or for our sick horse, we would have made Umatilla either early in the morning, or late the night before, and thus saved two days. As it was, there was no use lamenting it—we had done our best—and besides a little time for rest and writing was not unwelcome.

After emerging from the Blue Mountains at "Crawford's," our route thence to the Columbia was chiefly down the valley of the Umatilla. This was not over a mile or two in width usually, with high outlying plateaus, that showed only sand, sage-brush and grease-wood, with here and there a rocky butte. Population was very scarce, though we passed a few fine ranches along the Umatilla, that looked to be doing well, and off on the plateaus we saw several large flocks of sheep—thousands in number—grazing under their shepherds. Just beyond "Crawford's," the Umatilla and Walla-Walla Indians have a Reservation twenty miles square, of the best lands in the valley, and the government has agents there, teaching them to farm, raise stock, etc. Their farming did not seem to amount to much, but their horses, cattle, and sheep, by the thousand, all looked well. Both of these tribes together now numbered only about a thousand souls, and were said to be steadily decreasing. We saw scores of them on the road, scurrying along on their little ponies—all of them peaceable and friendly. They were larger and stouter, than our Ute friends on the Rio Grande; but did not seem endowed with half their fierceness and grit. The whole district, from Crawford's to the Columbia, lacked regular rains in summer, and hence farming to be successful required irrigation, as much as in Utah. For this, the Umatilla itself might be made to suffice, a thousand fold more than it did. Draining a wide region of country, it rushed with a rapid descent to the Columbia, and hereafter should be utilized not only to irrigate largely, but also to drive numerous mills and factories, that ought then to throng its banks. Long before reaching the Columbia, it is but little better than a broad raceway; and for miles, as we drove along, it seemed the beau-ideal of a natural water-power. Some day, in the not distant future, when all that region settles up, an Oregon Lowell will yet hum with spindles there, and its woolen-cloths and blankets become world-renowned.

It will be seen, we were seven days and a half in getting through from Boisè City, though expecting to make it in six. The stages advertised to make it in three, but the last one had been out five, with the passengers walking much of the way at that. A party of Irish miners we overtook on the road, footing it from Montana to the Columbia, indeed, raced with us for several days, following us sharply into Le Grande and beating us into "Meacham's;" but after that, we distanced them. At Umatilla, people said, we would have found a better road and made quicker time, if we had come by Uniontown, instead of crossing the Mountains; but our driver insisted "Meacham's" was the best road, and we had been guided of course by his superior wisdom.

This driver of ours, by the way, was something of a character. An Ohioan, so long ago as '49, he had joined the first rush to California, and soon succeeded in picking up $30,000, or so. Thence he went to Frazer River, on the first wave, and in a few months sunk pretty much all he had previously made. Then he mounted a mule, and with pick-axe and wash-pan "prospected" all over the Pacific Coast, landing at last in Idaho. Here he had again picked up a few thousands, and had just concluded a freight contract with a mining company at Owyhee, that he thought was going to "pay big." But it did not commence until spring, and meanwhile he was trying his hand at the livery business in Boisè. While on the coast he had lived in California, Nevada, British America, Washington, Oregon, and now Idaho; had camped out in the mining regions; shot grizzlies in the Sierra Nevadas; trapped beaver on the Columbia; wandered with the Indians for months together; and "roughed it" generally. He had but one eye—had lost the other, he said, in a battle with the Indians, one arrow hitting him there, and another passing through his body; yet he rode seventy miles afterwards on a mule, supported by his comrades—the pure air of that region and his Buckeye grit carrying him through. This was his story, without its embellishments. But he was a person of fine Western imagination; and somewhat, I fear, addicted to "romancing."

But, good-bye, driver—John Wilful, well-named! Good-bye, mustangs and donkeys! Good-bye, stage-coaches and ambulances! Two thousand four hundred miles of their drag and shake, of their rattle and bang, across the Plains and over the Mountains, had given us our fill of them. We had had runaways, we had had break-downs, and about every stage experience, except a genuine upset, and how we happened to escape *that* will always remain a mystery. Our romance of stage-coaching, I must say, was long since gone. There before us now lay the lordly Columbia, with visions of steamboats and locomotives. And looking back on our long jaunt, with all its discomforts and dangers, it seemed for the moment as if nothing could induce us to take it again. Hereafter, we felt assured, we should appreciate the comfort and speed of eastern travel more, and pray for the hastening of all our Pacific Railroads. With a grand trunk line now overland, through Utah, it can not be long before a branch will be thrown thence to the Columbia, substantially by the route we travelled; and when that is done, the ride from Salt Lake to Umatilla will be soon accomplished. The region nowhere presents any serious obstacle to a railroad, except the Blue Mountains; and a Latrobe, or a Dodge, would soon flank or conquer these.

CHAPTER XV.

DOWN THE COLUMBIA.

UMATILLA was then a river town, of two or three hundred houses, mostly frame. It was still the chief point of departure from the Columbia for Idaho and Montana, though Wallula—25 miles farther up—was beginning to compete for this. Trade and travel that season had not been large, and the whole region there complained of dullness and stringency. The *Metropolitan* was a fair hotel, with a goodly supply of eastern and California papers, and seemed like a palace after our long "roughing it" from the Missouri to the Columbia. It was well patronized, especially by babies; and I do think they were the worst *enfans terribles* I ever saw. One doting mamma asked L. if he did not think her red-eyed, puffy-faced youngster "a *dear* little cherub;" and though he smiled approvingly, of course, he subsequently vowed he should think better of King Herod hereafter. The town already boasted one weekly newspaper, a public school-house, and two young churches, with a goodly complement of saloons and restaurants. Of course, the patent-medicine venders had long since reached it. "S. T. 1860 X. Drake's Plantation Bitters," was emblazoned on every dead-wall, "in characters of living light," as it had been from New York there. The year before I had observed it all through the South, in over ten thousand miles of travel there; and here it was again, mysterious and blatant, at the head of navigation on the Pacific Coast. So, we had found it all through the Rocky Mountains, at Salt Lake, and Boisè, as inevitable as the stage-station and post-office; and the design was the same huge cabalistic characters always. Another advertisement accompanied us regularly across the Plains to the Rocky Mountains; but "S. T. 1860 X. etc.," followed us to the Columbia and beyond, and everywhere seemed as universal as the air—as omnipresent as sunlight.

Indians were seen on the streets occasionally, but they were usually in the last stages of dissipation and degradation. They ought to be forbidden all such border towns, as their life there ends only in ruin. The white population consisted chiefly of Oregonians and Californians, of every shade of character. The Micawber type, of course, was not wanting. One afternoon, while writing in my room, a seedy individual, whom we had met at Wells' Springs, sauntered in, and, after some conversational skirmishing, solicited, "the loan of five dollars." He had been keeping a "hotel," he said, up in Owyhee, but the miners hadn't paid up their board-bills, and he was now "dead-broke," on his way back to Puget Sound. He would give his due-bill, and would certainly remit to me at San Francisco, but really couldn't tell exactly when! He claimed to be "a son of old Massachusetts, sir," and from Boston at that. But as he was odorous afar of "needle-gun" whiskey, the Hub, I suspect, would have haughtily repudiated him!

Ding! Dong! Puff! Puff! The steamer had come, and Nov. 28th, we at length embarked for down the Columbia. She was a little stern-wheel boat, scarcely longer than your finger, called *Nez Perce Chief*, Capt. Stump, master. Her fare to Fort Vancouver or Portland, including railroad-portages, was $18 in coin, which at rates then current was equivalent to $25 in greenbacks. Meals were extra, at a cost of $1,50 each, in currency, besides. The distance to Portland was about 200 miles; to the mouth of the Columbia, 100 or so more. We found Capt. Stump a very obliging Oregonian, and obtained much interesting information from him. His boat was part of a line belonging to the Oregon Steam Navigation Company, a gigantic corporation that controlled all the navigable waters of the Columbia, and with far-reaching enterprise was now seeking to connect them with the headwaters of the Missouri. He said, their boats could ascend to Umatilla all the year round, except in mid-winter, when the Columbia sometimes froze over for several weeks together, though not usually. With good water, they could go up to Wallula, at the mouth of the Walla-Walla, 25 miles farther, which they usually did six months in the year. With very high water, they could run up to Lewiston, at the junction of the Snake and Clearwater, about 175 miles more, three months in the year—making about 500 miles from the sea in all. Above Lewiston, there was a bad cañon in the Snake, with shoals and rapids for a hundred miles or so to Farewell Bend; but after that, he thought, a light-draught steamer might get up at least three hundred miles farther, or within about 200 miles of Salt Lake, as stated heretofore.

Clark's Fork of the Columbia, or the Columbia proper, makes a sharp bend north at Wallula, and for 300 miles, he said, was unnavigable, until you reach Fort Colville near the British line, when it trends east and south, until it disappears in the far off wilds of Montana. Just above Fort Colville, it became navigable again, and a small boat was then running up to the Great Bend region, over 200 miles farther, where good placer mines had been discovered (Kootenay) and worked a little This boat could connect with another, already plying on Lake Pond Oreille (a part of Clark's Fork), and this with still another then building, that it was believed with short portages would extend navigation some 200 miles more, or into the very heart of Montana, within two or three hundred miles only of Fort Benton—the head of navigation on the Missouri. These were weighty facts, marrying the Pacific to the Atlantic; but Captain Stump thought the O. S. N. company could accomplish them, or anything else, indeed, it seriously undertook. Just now it was bending its energies in that direction, and he said would beat the Northern Pacific Railroad yet. No doubt we have a fine country up there, near the British America line, abounding in lakes and threaded with rivers, and roomy enough for all enterprises, whether railroad or steamboat.

Puff! Puff! And so we were off down the Columbia, at last. How exquisitely pleasant, how cosy and delightful, our little steamer seemed, after 2,400 miles of jolting and banging by stage-coach and ambulance! The staterooms were clean and tidy, the meals well-cooked and excellent, and we went steaming down the Columbia without thought or care, as on "summer seas." Occasionally rapids appeared, of a serious character; but as a rule the river was broad and deep, majestic in size and volume. On the banks were frequent Indian villages, with their hardy little ponies browsing around—apparently on nothing but sage-brush and cobble-stones. These Indians fancied spotted or "calico" horses, as the Oregonians called them, and very few of their ponies were of a single color. They spend the summer mostly in the Mountains, making long excursions in all directions; but as winter approaches, they return to the

Columbia, and eke out a precarious subsistence by fishing, etc., till spring comes. Timber was scarce, and frequently we saw numbers of them in canoes, paddling up and down the river in search of drift-wood, for their winter's supply of fuel. Past Owyhee rapids and the seething caldron of Hell-Gate, we reached Celilo, eighty-five miles from Umatilla, with its long warehouse (935 feet), and its mosquito fleet of five or six pigmy steamers, that formed the up-river line. Here we disembarked, and took the Railroad around the "chutes" or rapids, some fourteen miles, to still water again below. The shrill whistle of the locomotive and the rattle of the cars were delightful sounds, after our long exile from them, and soon convinced us we were on the right road to civilization again. This portage had formerly been made by pack-mules, and then by wagons; but recently a railroad had been constructed, after much hard blasting and costly wall-work, and now "Riding on a rail," there, with the Columbia boiling and roaring at your side, like the Rapids above Niagara, was exhilarating and superb. At very high water, these "chutes" or rapids somewhat disappear, though they still continue very dangerous. No attempt had been made to ascend them with a steamer; but the spring before, Capt. Stump had safely descended them, much against his will. It was high water in the Columbia, with a strong current, and his boat drifting near the rapids was suddenly sucked in, before he knew it. Clearly, escape was impossible; so he put on all steam, to give her steerage-way, and then headed down stream—neck or nothing. There was a good deal of bumping and thumping—it was a toss and a plunge, for awhile—and everybody he feared was pretty badly scared; but his gallant little boat ran the rapids for all that, and reached still water below safely at last. It was a daring feat, and worthy of this brave Oregonian. Just now, the Columbia was very low, rocks and reefs showing all through the rapids—among, around, and over which the waters boiled and rushed like a mill-race.

The locomotive carried us to the Dalles, at the foot of the Rapids, a town of some two thousand inhabitants, with a maturer civilization than any we had seen since leaving Salt Lake. It was but five or six years old; yet it was already in its decrepitude. A "rush" of miners a few years before, to alleged fine "diggings" near there, had suddenly elevated it from an obscure landing into quite a town; but the mines did not justify their promise, and the Dalles was now at a stand-still, if not something worse. "Mining stock" and "corner lots" had gone down by the run, during the past year or two, and her few merchants sat by their doors watching for customers in vain. The enterprise of the town, however, deserved a better fate. At the Umatilla House they gave us an excellent supper, at a moderate price, and the hotel itself would have been a credit to a much larger town anywhere. The mines on John Day River, and other dependencies of the Dalles, had formerly yielded $2,000,000 per year, and Congress had then voted a U. S. Mint there. We could but sincerely hope it would be much needed, some day or other.

Halting at the Dalles over night, the next morning we took the side-wheel steamer *Idaho*, and ran down to Upper Cascades—some fifty miles—through the heart of the Cascade Mountains. Here we took the railroad again for six miles—to flank more rapids—and at Lower Cascades embarked on the *W. G. Hunt*, a large and elegant side-wheel steamer, that some years before had come "round the Horn," from New York. The Columbia, soon issuing from the Mountains, now became a broad and majestic river, with good depth of water to the ocean all the year round, and larger vessels even than the *W. G. Hunt* might readily ascend to Lower Cascades, if necessary. Our good boat, however, bore us bravely on to Fort Vancouver, amidst multiplying signs of civilization again; and as we landed there, we realized another great link of our journey was over.

To return a little. Our sail down the Columbia, and through the Cascade Mountains, altogether was a notable one, and surpassed everything in the way of wild and picturesque river-scenery, that we had seen yet. Some have compared the Columbia to the Hudson; but it is the Hudson many times magnified, and infinitely finer. It is the Hudson, without its teeming travel, its towns and villas, its civilization and culture; but with many times its grandeur and sublimity. The noble Palisades, famed justly throughout the world, sink into insignificance before the stupendous walls of the Cascade Range, which here duplicate them but on a far vaster scale, for many miles together. Piled along the sky on either side, up two or three thousand feet, for fifty miles at a stretch, with only a narrow gorge between, the Columbia whirls and boils along through this, in supreme mightiness and power; while from the summit of the great walls little streams here and there topple over, run like lace for a time, then break into a million drops, and finally come sifting down as mist, into the far depths below. Some of these tiny cascades streaked the cyclopean walls, like threads of silver, from top to bottom. Others seemed mere webs of gossamer, and these the wind at times caught up and swayed to and fro, like veils fit for goddesses. These Mountains, all through the cañon of the Columbia, abound with such fairy cascades; whence their name. Just below Lower Cascades, where the river-bottoms open out a little, stands Castle Rock, a huge red boulder of comparatively moderate dimensions at the base, but seven hundred feet high. Its walls are so perpendicular they seem inaccessible, and on top it is covered with a thick growth of fir-trees. Its alleged height appeared incredible at first, but on comparing it with the gigantic firs at the base, and those on the summit, the estimate seemed not unreasonable. All along, the vast basaltic walls of the cañon are shaped and fashioned into domes and turrets, ramparts and battlements; and surely in point of picturesque grandeur and effect, the Columbia would be hard to beat. We had not seen the Yosemite yet. But already, we felt, the Columbia compensated us for all our fatigue and danger, in crossing the Continent; and it is not too much to say, that all true lovers of the sublime and beautiful in nature will yet wonder and worship here.

Before reaching the Dalles, and afterwards, we had several superb views of glorious Mt. Hood. All good Oregonians claim Hood is the highest peak in the United States; but Californians boast their Shasta equals, while Whitney out-tops it. A party of savans had recently ascended Hood, and they reported the general range, of which Hood is a part, as 4,400 feet above the sea; above which Hood still shot up 13,000 feet. The summit proved to be crescent-shaped, half a mile long, by from three feet to fifty wide. The north front was a precipice, of naked columnar rock, falling sheer down—perpendicularly—a mile or more at a jump. On the west side was an ancient crater, a thousand feet in depth from which clouds of sulphurous smoke still issued occasionally. On the flanks were true glaciers, with terminal and lateral moraines, the same as among the Alps. Smoke about his summit, just before we reached the Dalles,

MOUNT HOOD.

heralded a smart shock of earthquake there, and no doubt he is the safety-valve of all that region. We had caught a glimpse or two of Mt. Hood in descending the Blue Mountains, and again from Umatilla; but it was only for a moment, and usually with his night-cap on. But in threading the cañon of the Columbia, one morning as we rounded a rocky bastion, suddenly, a hundred miles away, Hood stood before us, a vast pyramidal peak, snow-clad from base to summit, resting in solitary grandeur on a great mountain range—itself black with firs and pines. From the apparent level or slight undulation of the general Cascade Range, Hood quickly shoots up loftily into the sky, individual and alone, and serene and unapproachable dominates the far-stretching landscape. From all points of view, whether descending the Columbia, where the cañon often frames him in like a picture, or at Fort Vancouver, where he stands superb and glorious against the sapphire sky, Hood always gives you the impression of vast loftiness, of serene majesty, of heaven-kissing superiority and power, and Oregonians may well be proud of him. Butman's two pictures of Hood are both good, but neither does justice to his great merits. The White Mountains and the Alleghanies are well enough in their way. The Rocky Mountains are indeed noble and majestic. But once see Hood, and all these pall upon the mind, and he alone rules the memory and imagination afterwards. Up the Columbia and down, off at sea, and pretty much all over Oregon, Hood is a great and magnificent landmark; and, of itself, is well worth a trip across the continent.

Past the Cascade Mountains, we came suddenly out into a new region, and a totally different climate. From Umatilla to the Mountains we had the same clear atmosphere and perfect sky, that we had found everywhere from the Plains to the Columbia, substantially. The country naturally was the same barren and sterile region as at Salt Lake, abounding only in sage-brush and grease-wood; and, indeed, the whole internal basin of the continent, from the Rocky Mountains to the Sierra Nevadas, and from British America down to Mexico, appeared to be of this same general character—from want of regular rains in summer. Over most of this vast region, there had been no rains for weeks, or indeed months; and for days together as we journeyed along, we had never seen a cloud or mist even, to mar the absolute ultramarine of those perfect skies. But now, in descending the Columbia, as we approached the Mountains, we descried the clouds on their western slope ever trying to float over, but never apparently succeeding, their white discs gleaming in the sun; and when we drew nearer, we beheld a fleecy mist drifting up the Columbia, and streaming eastward like a pennon. Nearer still, we encountered a stiff breeze sweeping through the cañon, as through a funnel; and when we got well down into the jaws of the gorge, it needed all our steam, as well as the strong westward current to carry us forward. Sometimes, it was said, the Columbia just here becomes so rough, because of this conflicting wind and current, as to cause real sea-sickness on the boats, and occasionally indeed they have to cast anchor, unable to descend. Farther down, this mist thickened into rain, and when we got fairly through and out of the Mountains, (it raining most of the way), we debouched into the Coast Region, where it was still raining steadily, as it had been for many days, and continued to for weeks together afterwards. As soon as we struck the rain, trees and herbage at once made their appearance, clothing the mountains and bottoms everywhere; lichens and mosses again decorated all the rocks; and when we got well out of the Mountains, behold such forests of fir, pine, cedar, oak, etc., as never appear East. In half a day, you may thus pass from a comparatively rainless to a thoroughly rainy region; and in winter from a severely cold, to a comparatively moderate climate. The contrast is very striking, and you soon feel it keenly in every sense. Your eyes glaze, your skin becomes moist, and if there is a weak spot about your lungs, you will find it out very quickly. The proximity of the Pacific, of course, explains it all—the warm, humid winds from which sweep up against the Cascade Range, but find in their lofty crest an insurmountable barrier. If light enough to ascend, their wealth of moisture is condensed as rain or snow along the mountain sides or summit, by the cold of the upper regions, as with your hand you squeeze a sponge; and, consequently, they topple over the Range dry and clear—to curse a vast region beyond with their sterility. If unable to ascend, they career along the western slope of the Mountains, and hover over the Coast Region generally, literally deluging Western Oregon and Washington, at certain seasons of the year, with rains and fogs. The year before, at Fort Vancouver, they had had one hundred and twenty consecutive days of rain, in one year, without counting the intervening showers; and they said, it wasn't "much of a year for rain" either! Another year, they didn't see the sun there for eighty days together, without reckoning the occasional fogs. No wonder the Oregonians are called "Web-Feet." They do say, the children there are all born web-footed, like ducks and geese, so as to paddle about, and thus get along well in that amphibious region. Perhaps this is rather strong, even for Darwinism; but I can safely vouch for Oregon's all-sufficing rains and fogs, whatever their effects on the species.

Our fellow-passengers down the Columbia were chiefly returning miners, going below to winter and recruit; but rough as they were and merry at times, they were, as a rule, self-respecting and orderly. Our Fenian friends, who had raced with us down Powder River and Grande Ronde Valleys and across the Blue Mountains, turned up here again—"Shanks," "Fatty," and all—and subsequently embarked on the same steamer with us at Portland for San Francisco. A few Chinamen also were on board; but they behaved civilly, and were treated kindly.

CHAPTER XVI.

FORT VANCOUVER TO SAN FRANCISCO.

FORT VANCOUVER is an old Government Post, established in 1849, when Washington Territory was still a part of Oregon, and all the great region there was yet a wilderness. The village of Vancouver, a parasite on its outskirts, had grown up gradually; but had long since been distanced by Portland, across the Columbia in Oregon. A fine plateau, with a bold shore, made the Post everything desirable; but back of the post-grounds, the unbroken forest was still everywhere around it. It was now Headquarters of the Department of the Columbia, and the base for all military operations in that section. Here troops and supplies were gathered, for all the posts up the Columbia and its tributaries; though Portland, rather, seemed to be the natural brain of all that region. So, too, it controlled and supplied the forts at the mouth of the Columbia and the posts on Puget Sound; and, indeed, was of prime importance to the Government in many ways.

Gen. Steele, in command of the Department, was an old Regular officer, who during the war commanded first in Missouri, afterwards around Vicksburg, then in Arkansas, and always with ability. He is now no more (dying in 1868), but some things he related in speaking of the war seem worth preserving. He said, Gen. Sherman was undoubtedly a great soldier; but he owed much to the rough schooling of his first campaigns, and improved from year to year. He said, Sherman in '62 was "scary" about Price's movements in Missouri and cited as an instance, that he once ordered the depot at Rolla broken up and the troops withdrawn, for fear Price would "gobble up" everybody and everything. He (Steele) then a Colonel, but in command at Rolla, appealed to Gen. Halleck, and was allowed to remain; and subsequently Sherman, with his customary frankness, admitted his mistake. So, he said, Sherman in '63, when campaigning around Vicksburg, had little confidence in Grant's famous movement to the rear, *via* Grand Gulf and the Big Black, though the results were so magnificent. He said Sherman was somewhere up the Yazoo, with Porter and the gun-boats, and from there wrote him (Steele), in command of the Corps during Sherman's absence, that the proposed movement was perilous, and would probably fail, ruining them all; but, "nevertheless," he added, right loyally, "We must support Grant *cordially* and *thoroughly*, dear Steele, whatever happens." Subsequently, after they had landed at Grand Gulf—repulsed Pemberton and hurled him back on Vicksburg—cleaned Joe Johnston out of Jackson and chased him out of the country—and were crossing the Big Black in triumph, the movement now apparently a sure thing, Sherman and he were lying down to rest a little, at a house near the bridge, while the troops were filing over. Presently, an orderly announced Gen. Grant and staff riding by, when Sherman instantly sprang up, and rushing out of the house bareheaded seized Grant by the hand, and shaking it very warmly exclaimed, "I congratulate you, General, with all my heart, on the success of your movement. And, by heaven, sir, the movement is *yours*, too; for nobody else would endorse it!" He added, he never heard of Sherman's "protesting" against the movement, as reported afterwards in the newspapers, and didn't believe he ever had —"was too soldierly, by far, for that"—but he (Steele), knew all the facts at the time, and the above was about the Truth of History.

Poor Steele! He was a true Army bachelor, fond of horses and dogs, and a connoisseur in both. He was besides a man of fine intelligence, and after dinner told a camp-story capitally. I remember several he told, with great gusto, while we shared his cosy quarters at Vancouver; but have not space for them here. Afterwards, we met him again in San Francisco, on leave of absence, the beloved of all army circles, and the favorite of society. May he rest in peaee!

But to return to Fort Vancouver. We spent several days there very pleasantly, getting the bearings of things from there as a centre, and were loath to leave its hospitable quarters. It was now the first week in December; but the grapes were still hanging on the vines at Maj. N.'s quarters, and all about the post the grass was springing fresh and green, as in April in the East. We had fog or rain, or both together, about every day; no heavy down-pours, however, but gentle drizzles, as if the Oregon-Washington sky was only a great sieve, with perpetual water on 'tother side. They said, this was their usual weather from fall to spring, and then they had a delightful summer; though sometimes occasional snow-storms, sweeping down from the Mountains in January or February, gave them a taste of winter. Such snows, however, were light, and never lasted long. It seems, the Gulf Stream of the Pacific, sweeping up from the tropics, bears the isothermal lines so far north on this coast, that here at Fort Vancouver in the latitude of

Montreal, they have the climate of the Carolinas in winter, with little of their excessive heats in summer. Walla-Walla, in latitude 46°, boasts the range of Washington, D. C. in 39°; and San Francisco, on the line of New York, claims the climate of Savannah. One evening while there, after a day of weary rain, the clouds suddenly broke away, and just at sunset we caught another noble view of Mount Hood again. A thin, veil-like cloud enrobed his feet, extending much of the way up; but above, his heaven-kissing head rose right regally, and his snowy crown became transfigured through all the changes—from pink to purple, and into night—as the day faded out. He looked still loftier and grander, than we had yet seen him, as if piercing the very sky, and was really superb. Aye, *superbus.* Haughty, imperial, supremely proud—which is about what the Romans meant, if I mistake not.

A ride of six miles down the Columbia, on the little steamer *Fanny Troup*, and then twelve miles up the Willamette, landed us at Portland, Oregon, the metropolis of all that region. The distance from Fort Vancouver, as the crow flies, is only about six miles, but by water it is fully eighteen, as above stated. Here we found a thrifty busy town, of eight or ten thousand people, with all the eastern evidences of substantial wealth and prosperity. Much of the town was well built, and the rest was rapidly changing for the better. Long rows of noble warehouses lined the wharves, many of the stores were large and even elegant, and off in the suburbs handsome residences were already springing up, notwithstanding the abounding stumps nearly everywhere. The town seemed unfortunately located, the river-plateau was so narrow there; but just across the Willamette was East Portland, a growing suburb, with room plenty and to spare. A ferry-boat, plying constantly, connected the two places, and made them substantially one. Portland already boasted water, gas, and Nicholson pavements; and had more of a solid air and tone, than any city we had seen since leaving the Missouri. The rich black soil, on which she stands, makes her streets in the rainy season, as then, sloughs or quagmires, unless macadamised or Nicholsoned; but she was at work on these, and they promised soon to be in good condition. Several daily papers, two weekly religious ones, and a fine Mercantile Library, all spoke well for her intelligence and culture, while her Public School buildings and her Court-House would have been creditable anywhere. The New England element was noticeable in many of her citizens, and Sunday came here once a week, as regularly as in Boston or Bangor. The Methodists and Presbyterians both worshipped in goodly edifices, and the attendance at each the Sunday we were there was large and respectable.

Being the first city of importance north of San Francisco, and the brain of our northwest coast, Portland was full of energy and vigor, and believed thoroughly in her future. The great Oregon Steam Navigation Company had their headquarters here, and poured into her lap all the rich trade of the Columbia and its far-reaching tributaries, that tap Idaho, Montana, and even British America itself. So, also, the coastwise steamers, from San Francisco up, all made Portland their terminus, and added largely to her commerce. Back of her lay the valley of the Willamette, and the rich heart of Oregon; and her wharves, indeed, were the gateways to thousands of miles of territory and trade, in all directions. Nearer to the Sandwich Islands and China, by several hundred miles, than California, she had already opened a brisk trade with both, and boasted that she could sell sugars, teas, silks, rice, etc., cheaper than San Francisco. Victoria, the British city up on Puget Sound, had once been a dangerous rival; but Portland had managed to beat her out of sight, and claimed now she would keep her beaten. It was Yankee Doodle against John Bull; and, of course, in such a contest, Victoria went to the wall!

It seemed singular, however, that the chief city of the northwest coast should be located there—a hundred miles from the sea, and even then twelve miles up the little Willamette. Your first thought is, Portland has no right *to be* at all, where she now is. But, it appears, she originally got a start, from absorbing and controlling the large trade of the Willamette, and when the Columbia was opened up to navigation rapidly grew into importance, by her heavy dealings in flour, wool, cattle, lumber, etc. The discovery of mines in Idaho and Montana greatly invigorated her, and now she had got so much ahead, and so much capital and brains were concentrated here, that it seemed hard for any new place to compete with her successfully.* Moreover, we were told, there are no good locations for a town along the Columbia from the ocean up to the Willamette, nor on the Willamette up to Portland. Along the Columbia, from the ocean up, wooded hills and bluffs come quite down to the water, and the whole back country, as a rule, is still a wilderness of pines and firs; while the Willamette up to Portland, they said, was apt to overflow its banks in high water. Hence, Portland seemed secure in her supremacy, at least for years to come, though no doubt at no distant day a great city will rise

* Though since scourged severely by fire, (1873), she has vindicated herself well by prompt and general rebuilding, like Chicago.

on Puget Sound, that will dominate all that coast, up to Sitka and down to San Francisco. From want of time, we failed to reach the Posts on Puget's Sound; but all accounts agreed, that—land-locked by Vancouver's and San Juan islands—we there have one of the largest and most magnificent harbors in the world. With the Northern Pacific Railroad linking it to Duluth and the great lakes, commerce will yet seek its great advantages; and the Boston, if not the New York, of the Pacific will yet flourish where now are only the wilds of Washington. The Sound already abounded in saw-mills, and the ship-timber and lumber of Washington we subsequently found famed in San Francisco, and throughout California. She was then putting lumber down in San Francisco, cheaper than the Californians could bring it from their own foot-hills, and her magnificent forests of fir and pine promised yet to be a rare blessing to all the Pacific Coast.

The Portlanders, of course, were energetic, go-ahead men, from all parts of the North, with a good sprinkling from the South. Outside of Portland, however, the Oregonians appeared to be largely from Missouri, and to have retained many of their old Missouri and so-called "conservative" ideas still. All through our Territories, indeed, Missouri seemed to have been fruitful of emigrants. Kentucky, Indiana, Illinois, were everywhere well represented; but Missouri led, especially in Idaho and Oregon. This fact struck us repeatedly, and was well accounted for by friend Meacham's remark (top of the Blue Mountains), "the left wing of Price's army is still encamped in this region." The tone of society, in too many places, seemed to be of the Nasby order, if not worse. No doubt hundreds of deserters and draft-sneaks, from both armies, had made their way into those distant regions;

and then, besides, the influence of our old officials, both civil and military, had long been pro-slavery, and this still lingered among communities, whom the war had not touched, and among whom school-houses and churches were still far too few. Of course, we met some right noble and devoted Union men everywhere, especially in Colorado; but elsewhere, and as a rule, they did not strike us as numerous, nor as very potential. In saying this, I hope I am not doing the Territories injustice; but this is how their average public opinion impressed a passing traveller, and other tourists we met *en route* remarked the same thing.

Here at Portland, John Chinaman turned up again, and seemed to be behaving thoroughly well. At Boisè, we found these heathen paying their stage-fare, and riding down to the Columbia, while many Caucasians were walking, and here at Portland they appeared alike thrifty and prosperous. Their advent here had been comparatively recent, and there was still much prejudice against them, especially among the lower classes; but they were steadily winning their way to public favor by their sobriety, their intelligence and thrift, and good conduct generally. Washing and ironing, and household service generally, seemed to be their chief occupations, and nearly everybody gave them credit for industry and integrity. Mr. Arrigoni, the proprietor of our hotel (and he was one of the rare men, who know how to "keep a hotel"), spoke highly of their capacity and honesty, and said he wanted no better servants anywhere. One of them, not over twenty-one, had a contract to do the washing and ironing for the Arrigoni House, at a hundred dollars per month, and was executing it with marked fidelity. He certainly did his work well, judging by what we saw of the hotel linen. In walking about the town, we occasionally came upon their signs, over the door of some humble dwelling, as for example, "Ling & Ching, Laundry;" "Hop Kee, washing and ironing;" "Ching Wing, shoemaker;" "Chow Pooch, doctor;" etc. As far as we could see, they appeared to be intent only on minding their own business, and as a class were doing more hearty honest work by far, than most of their bigoted defamers. We could not refrain from wishing them well, they were so sober, industrious, and orderly; for, after all, are not these the first qualities of good citizenship the world over?

We left Portland, Dec. 11th, on the good steamer *Oriflamme*, for San Francisco. For a wonder, it was a calm clear day, with the bracing air of our Octobers in the east, and as we glided out of the Willamette into the noble Columbia, we had a last superb view of Mts. Jefferson, Hood, Adams and St. Helens all at the same time. Sometimes Rainier also is visible from here, but ordinarily only Hood and St. Helens appear. We thought this the finest view of these splendid snow-peaks that we had had yet, and it seemed strange no artist had yet attempted to group them all in one grand landscape, from the mouth of the Willamette as a stand-point. Or, if he could not get them all in, he might at least combine Hood and St. Helens. The breadth and scope, the grandeur and sublimity of such a picture, with the Columbia in the foreground, and the great range of the Cascade Mountains in the perspective, would make a painting, that would live forever. We watched them all, with the naked eye and through the glass, until we were far down the Columbia, and to the last, Hood was the same

> "Dread ambassador from earth to heaven!"

How he soared and towered, beyond and above everything, as if communing with the Almighty! Lofty as were the rest, they seemed small by his majestic side. St. Helens, however, though not so imperial, was perhaps more simply and chastely beautiful. An unbroken forest of fir, deep green verging into black, girt her feet, while above she "swelled vast to heaven," a perfect snow sphere rather than cone, whose celestial whiteness dazzled the eye. She looked like a virgin's or a nun's white breast, unsullied by sin, and standing sharply out against the glorious azure of that December sky, seemed indeed a perfect emblem of purity and beauty. Farther down the river, we detected a light smoke or vapor, drifting dreamily away from her summit, and Capt. Conner of the *Oriflamme* said this was not unusual, though St. Helens was not rated as a volcano. He thought it steam or vapor, caused by internal heat melting the snow, rather than smoke; but the effect was about the same.

We reached the mouth of the Columbia, the same evening; but Capt. Conner thought it risky to venture over the bar, until morning. The next morning early, we lifted anchor, and steamed down to Astoria — a higgledy-piggledy village, of only four or five hundred inhabitants still, though begun long before prosperous Portland. Her anchorage seemed fair; but ashore the land abounded in a congeries of wooded bluffs and ridges, that evidently made a town or farms there difficult, if not impossible. A short street or two of straggling houses, propped along the hillsides, was about all there was of Astoria; and yet she was a port of entry, with a custom-house and full corps of officials, while Portland with all her enterprise and commerce was not, and could not get to be. What her custom-officials would have to do, were it not for the business of Portland, it seemed pretty hard to say. A venture of John Jacob Astor's a half century before, as a trading post with the Indians, she had never become of much importance, because lacking a good back country; and it appeared, had no future now, because wanting a good town-site. This was unfortunate perhaps for Oregon, and the whole Columbia region; but over it Portland rejoiced, and continued to wax fat.

Of course, it had begun to rain again, and by the time we had passed the ordeal of the custom-house at Astoria, the weather had thickened up into a drizzly fog, that caused Capt. C. much anxiety—especially, when he observed the barometer steadily going down. The bar of the Columbia, always bad, is peculiarly rough in winter, and only the voyage before the *Oriflamme* had to lay to here, nearly a week, unable to venture out. Her provisions became exhausted, and she had to "clean out" Astoria, and all the farm-houses up and down the river for miles, before she finally got away. Our company of four hundred passengers had no fancy for an experience of this sort, and "dirty" as the weather promised to be, Capt. C. at last decided to try the bar, even if we had to return, hoping to find better skies when fairly afloat in blue water. Our engines once in motion, we soon ran down past Forts Stevens and Cape Disappointment, at the mouth of the Columbia, on the Oregon and Washington sides respectively, with the black throats of their heavy cannon gaping threateningly at us. Both forts seem necessary there, as they completely command the mouth of the Columbia, and so hold the key to all that region. But life in them must be an almost uninterrupted series of rains and fogs, with the surf forever thundering at your feet, and one can but pity the officers and men really exiled there. Gathered about the flag-staff or lounging along the ramparts, they gazed wistfully at us as we steamed past; and already in the distance we could see the white-caps, racing in over the dreaded bar. Heading for the north channel, we put all steam on, and once out of the jaws of the Columbia were soon fairly a-dancing on the bar. The wind and tide both strong, were both dead ahead, which made our exit about as bad, as could well be. The sea went hissing by, or broke into huge white-caps all about us. The engines creaked and groaned, and at times seemed to stand still, as if exhausted with the struggle. The good ship *Oriflamme* pitched and tossed, battling with the waves like a practiced pugilist, yet ever advanced, though sometimes apparently drifting shoreward. At one period, indeed, Capt. C. feared we would have to about ship and run for the Columbia—we progressed so slowly; but something of a lull in the wind just then helped us on, and at last we saw by the receding head-lands, that we were fairly over the bar and out into the broad Pacific. We congratulated ourselves in thus getting speedily to sea; but our tussle on the bar had been too much for the majority of our passengers, and soon our bulwarks were thronged with scores "casting up their accounts" with Father Neptune. Sea-sickness, that deathliest of all human ailments, had set in, and our "rough and tumble" with the waves had been so sharp, that many began to suffer from it, who declared they had never been attacked before. A notable New Yorker, a brawny son of Æsculapius at that, bravely protested, that sea-sickness was "Only a matter of the imagination. Anyone can overcome it. It only requires a vigorous exercise of the will." But, unfortunately for his theory, soon afterwards he himself became the sickest person on board, not excepting the ladies. My own experience ended with a qualm or two; but the majority of our passengers suffered very much, for several days. Our steamer really had accommodations for only about one hundred passengers; but some four hundred had crowded aboard of her at Portland, mostly miners eager to get "below" to winter, and those who had no state-rooms now "roughed it" pitiably. They lay around loose—on deck, in the cabin, in the gang-way, everywhere—the most disconsolate-looking fellows I ever saw, outside of a yellow-fever hospital. The few ladies aboard were even sicker; but these all had state-rooms, and kept them mostly for the voyage.

The weather continued raw and the sea rough, most of the way down the coast, and our voyage of eight hundred miles from Portland to San Francisco, as a whole, could hardly be called agreeable. We had fog, and rain, and head-winds all the way down, and with the exception of a day or two, it was really cold and uncomfortable. The steam-heating apparatus of the vessel was out of order, and the only place for us all to warm was at a register in the Social Hall—a narrow little cabin on deck, that would not accommodate over thirty persons at the farthest. There was a similar place for the ladies, but they usually filled this themselves. Groups huddled here all day, smoking and talking, and when the weather permitted also swarmed about the smoke-stacks. And then, besides, as already stated, our ship was badly overcrowded. Of our 400 passengers, less than a quarter had state-rooms, and the rest were left to shift for themselves. After the sea-sickness began to abate, we filled two or three tables every meal; and when bed-time came, mattrasses thronged the cabin from end to end How it was down in the steerage, where the miners and Chinamen mostly congregated, one need not care to imagine. Fortunately great-coats and blankets abounded, or many would have suffered much. We found many choice spirits aboard, and in spite of wind and weather enjoyed ourselves, after all, very fairly. When it did not rain too hard, we walked the deck and talked for hours; and when everything else failed, we always found something of interest in the gulls that followed us by hundreds, and the great frigate-birds with their outstretched pinions, and the ever-rolling boundless sea. Our table-fare was always profuse and generally excellent, especially the Oregon apples and pears they gave us for dessert; and had it not been for our broken heating apparatus, no doubt we would have got along very satisfactorily after all, all things considered.

We arrived off the Golden Gate, late at night, Dec. 14th, only four days out from Portland; but the sea was still so rough, that we feared to venture in. Next morning, however, when the mist broke away a little, we up steam and headed again for San Francisco. We had a tough time getting in, nearly as bad as getting out of the Columbia. We had to combat a strong wind dead-ahead, and to wrestle with a heavy sea. But, nevertheless, our good ship held on her course bravely; and at last, weathering Point Reyes, and rounding Fort Point, we steamed up past frowning Alcatraz, and with booming cannon dropped anchor at the Company's wharf. The storm we had encountered was reported as one of the worst known on the coast for years, and we were glad once more to touch *terra firma*, and strike hands with a live civilization. In a half hour we were ashore and at the *Occidental*, a hostelry worthy of San Francisco or any other city.

And so, we had reached California at last. All hail, the Golden Gate! And 'Frisco, plucky, vain young metropolis, hail! Bragging, boasting, giddy as you are, there is much excuse for you. Surely, with your marvellous growth, and far-reaching schemes, you have a right to call yourself the New York of the Pacific Coast, if that contents you!

CHAPTER XVII.

SAN FRANCISCO.

GEOGRAPHY demonstrates the matchless position of San Francisco, as metropolis of the Pacific coast, and assures her supremacy perhaps forever. The Golden Gate, a strait six miles long by one wide, with an average depth of twenty-four fathoms—seven fathoms at the shallowest point—is her pathway to the Pacific. At her feet stretches her sheltered and peerless bay, fifty miles long by five wide, with Oakland as her Brooklyn just across it. Beyond, the Sacramento and the San Joaquin empty their floods, the drainage of the Sierra Nevadas, and afford channels for trade with much of the interior. Her system of bays—San Pablo, Suisun, and San Francisco proper—contain a superficial area of four hundred square miles, of which it is estimated, eight feet in depth pour in and out of the Golden Gate every twenty-four hours. On all that coast, for thousands of miles, she seems to be the only really great harbor; and then, besides, all enterprise and commerce have so centred here, that hereafter it will be difficult, if not impossible, to wrest supremacy from her. Until we reached Salt-Lake, New York everywhere ruled the country, and all business ideas turned that way; but from there on, the influence of Gotham ceased, and everything tended to "'Frisco," as many lovingly called her. This was her general name, indeed, for short, all over the Pacific coast; though the

Nevadans spoke of her, as "the Bay" still. The city itself stands on a peninsula of shifting dunes or sand-hills, at the mouth of the harbor, much the same as if New York were built at Sandy Hook. It was a great mistake, that its founders did not locate it at Benicia, or Vallejo, or somewhere up that way, where it would have been out of the draft of the Golden Gate, had better wharfage, and been more easily defended. But, it seems, when the gold fever first broke out, in 1849, the early vessels all came consigned to Yerba Buena, as the little hamlet was then called ; and as their charter-parties would not allow them to ascend the Bay farther, their cargoes were deposited on the nearest shore, and hence came San Francisco. It took a year or more then to hear from New York or London, and before further advices were received, so great was the rush of immigrants, the town was born and the city named. Benicia tried to change things afterwards; but 'Frisco had got the start, and kept it, in spite of her false location. Her military defences are Fort Point at the mouth of the Golden Gate, Fort San Josè farther up the harbor, and Alcatraz on an island square in the entrance, which with other works yet to be constructed would cross-fire and command all the approaches by water, thus rendering the city fairly impregnable.

From the first, she seems to have had a fight with the sand-hills, and she was still pluckily maintaining it. She had cut many of them down, and hurled them into the sea, to give her a better frontage. Her "made" land already extended out several blocks, and the work was still going on. With a great *penchant* for right-angles, as if Philadelphia was her model city, she was pushing her streets straight out, in all directions, no matter what obstacles intervened. One would have thought, that with an eye to economy, as well as the picturesque, she would have flanked some of her sand-hills by leading her streets around them; but no! she marched straight at and over them, with marvellous audacity and courage, like the Old Guard at Waterloo, or the Boys in Blue at Chattanooga. Some were inaccessible to carriages; still she pushed straight on, and left the inhabitants to clamber up to their eyrie-like residences, as best they could. Many of these hills were still shifting sand, and in places lofty fences had been erected as a protection against sand-drifts; just as our railroads East sometimes build fences, as a protection against snow-drifts. The sand seemed of the lightest and loosest character, and when the breeze rose filled the atmosphere at all exposed points. And yet, when properly irrigated, it really seemed to produce about everything abundantly. While inspecting one of the harbor forts, I saw a naked drift on one side of a sand-fence, and on the other a flower-garden of the most exquisite character, while just beyond was a vegetable and fruit-garden, that would have astonished people East. A little water had worked the miracle, and this a faithful wind-mill continued to pump up, from time to time as needed. Towards the south, the sand-hills seemed less of an obstruction, and thither the city was now drifting very rapidly. Real-estate there was constantly on the rise, and houses were springing up as if by magic in a night. The city-front, heretofore much confined, was now extending southward accordingly. It was about decided to build a sea-wall of solid granite, all along the front, two miles or more in length, at a cost of from two to three millions of dollars. This expenditure seemed large; but, it was maintained, was not too great for the vast and growing commerce of the city.

But a few years before, it was a common thing for ships to go East empty or in ballast, for want of a return cargo; but in 1867 San Francisco shipped grain alone to the amount of thirteen millions of dollars, and of manufactures about as much more. Here are some other statistics that are worth one's considering. In 1849, then called Yerba Buena, she numbered perhaps 1,000 souls, all told; in 1869, nearly 200,000. In 1868, 59,000 passengers arrived by sea, and only 25,000 departed, leaving a net gain of 34,000. The vessels which entered the bay that year, numbered 3,300, aud measured over 1,000,000 tons. She exported 4,000,000 sacks of wheat that year, and half a million barrels of flour. Her total exports of all kinds were estimated at not less than $70,000,000, and her imports about the same. Her sales of real-estate aggregated $27,000,000, and of mining and other stocks $115,000,000, on which she paid over $5,000,000 of dividends. The cash value of her real and personal property was estimated at $200,000,000. She sent away six tons of gold, and forty tons of silver every month, and in all since 1849 had poured into the coffers of the world not less than $1,030,000,000.* Her net-work of far-reaching and gigantic enterprises already embraced the whole Pacific Coast, northward to Alaska and southward to Panama, while beyond she stretched out her invisible arms to Japan and China, and shook hands with the Orient.

One cloudless morning, after days of dismal drizzle, an enthusiastic Forty-Niner took me up Telegraph Hill, and bade me "view the landscape o'er!" I remembered when a school-boy reading Dana's "Two Years before the Mast," in which he speaks so contemptuously of Yerba Buena, and its Mexican Rip Van Winkles.

* See Appendix.

What a change here since then! Off to the west rolled the blue Pacific, sea and sky meeting everywhere. Then came Fort Point, with its formidable batteries, commanding the Golden Gate; and then the old Presidio, with the stars and stripes waving over it. Farther inland were the stunted live-oaks and gleaming marbles of Lone Mountain Cemetery, with the Broderick Monument rising over all. Then came the live, busy, bustling, pushing city, with its quarter of a million of inhabitants nearly, soon to be a million, its wharves thronged with the ships of all nations, but with harbor-room to spare sufficient to float the navies of the world. Beyond, lay Oakland, loveliest of suburbs, smiling in verdure and beauty, with Mount Diabolo towering in the distance—his snow-crowned summit flashing in the sunlight. The Sacramento and Stockton boats, from the heart of California were already in. Past the Golden Gate, and up the noble bay, with boom of welcoming cannon, came the Hong Kong steamer fresh from Japan. The Panama steamer, with her fires banked and flag flying, was just ready to cast off. While off to the south, a long train of cars, from down the bay and San Josè, came thundering in. A hundred church spires pierced the sky; the smoke from numberless mills and factories, machine-shops and foundries, drifted over the harbor; the horse-car bells tinkled on every side—the last proofs of American progress—and all around us were the din and boom of Yankee energy, and thrift, and go-ahead-ative-ness, in place of the old Rip Van Winkleism. I don't wonder, that all good Pacific Coasters believe in San Francisco, and expect to go there when they die! Her hotels, her school-houses, her churches, her Bank of California, her Wells-Fargo Express, her Mission Woollen Mills, her lines of ocean steam-ships, and a hundred other things, all suggest great wealth and brains; and yet they are only the first fruits of nobler fortune yet to come. She is what Carlyle might call an undeniable fact, a substantial verity; and, in spite of her "heavy job of work," moves onward to empire with giant strides. She contained already fully a third of the population of the whole state of California, and was "lifting herself up like a young lion" in all enterprises—at all times and everywhere—on the Pacific slope.

Her faulty location, however, gives her a climate, that can scarcely be called inviting, notwithstanding all that Californians claim for their climate generally. It is true, the range of the thermometer there indicates but a moderate variation of temperature, with neither snow nor frost, usually. But her continual rains in winter, and cold winds and fogs in summer, must be very trying to average nerves and lungs. We found it raining on our arrival there in December, with the hills surrounding the bay already turning green; and it continued to rain and drizzle right along, pretty much all the time, until we departed for Arizona in February. Sometimes it would break away for an hour or two, and the sun would come out resplendently, as if meaning to shine forever; and then, suddenly, it would cloud over, and begin to drizzle and rain again, as if the whole heavens were only a gigantic sieve. Really, it did rain there sometimes the easiest of any place I ever saw—not excepting Fort Vancouver. Going out to drive, or on business, we got caught thus several times, and learned the wisdom of carrying stout umbrellas, or else wearing bang-up hats and water-proof coats, like true Californians. Once, for a fortnight nearly, it rained in torrents, with but little intermission, and then the whole interior became flooded—bridges were washed away, roads submerged, etc. In the midst of this, one night, we had a sharp passage of thunder and lightning—a phenomenon of rare occurrence on that coast—followed by a slight earthquake, and then it rained harder than ever. But at last, the winter rains came to an end, as all things must, and then we had indeed some superb weather, worthy of Italy or Paradise. Californians vowed their winter had been an unusual one; that their January was usually good, and their February very fine; but, of course, things must be reported as we found them. As a rule, nobody seemed to mind the perpetual drizzle, so to speak; but with slouched hats and light overcoats, or infrequent umbrellas, everybody tramped the streets, as business or pleasure called, and the general health of the city continued good. The few fair days we had in January and early February were as soft and balmy, as our May or June, and all 'Frisco made the most of them. The ladies literally swarmed along Montgomery street, resplendent in silks and jewelry, and all the drives about the city—especially the favorite one to the Cliff-House and sea-lions—were thronged with coaches and buggies. Meanwhile, the islands in the harbor and the surrounding hills and country, so dead and barren but a few weeks before, had now become superbly green, and the whole bay and city lay embosomed in emerald.

We left there the middle of February for Arizona, and did not get back until late in May. Then, when we returned we found the rains long gone, the vegetation fast turning to yellow—grain ripening in the fields—strawberries and peas on the table—and the summer winds and fogs in full vogue. At sunrise, it would be hot, even sultry, and you would see persons dressed in white linen. By nine or ten A. M., the wind would rise—a raw damp wind, sometimes with fog, sweeping in from the Pacific—and in the evening, you would see ladies going to the Opera with full winter furs on. How long this lasted, I cannot say; but this was the weather we experienced, as a rule, late in May and early in June. Heavy great-coats, doubtless, are never necessary there. And so, on the other hand, thin clothing is seldom wanted. Many indeed said, they wore the same clothing all seasons of the year, and seldom found it uncomfortable either way. The truth seemed to be, that for hardy persons the climate was excellent—the air bracing and stimulating—but invalids were better off in the interior. Consumptives could not stand the winds and fogs at all; and it was a mooted question, as to whether the large percentage of suicides just then, was not due in part to climatic influences. The really healthy, however, appeared plump and rosy, and the growing children promised well for the future. Had 'Frisco been built at Benicia, or about there, she would have escaped much of her climatic misery. Even across the bay, at Oakland, they have a much smoother climate. But she *would* "squat" on a sand-spit, at the mouth of the Golden Gate, where there is a perpetual suck of wind and fog—from the ocean, into the bay, and up the valley of the Sacramento—and now must make the most of her situation.

Montgomery Street is the Broadway or Chestnut Street of San Francisco, and California her Wall Street. Her hotels, shops, and banking-houses are chiefly here, and many of them are very handsome edifices. The Occidental, Cosmopolitan, and Lick-House hotels, the new Mercantile Library, and Bank of California, are stately structures, that would do credit to any city. Their height, four and five stories, seemed a little reckless, considering the liability of the Coast to earthquakes; but the people made light of this, notwithstanding some of their best buildings showed ominous cracks "from turret to foundation stone." So long as they *stood*, everything was believed secure; and commerce surged and roared along the streets, as in New York and London. Brick, well strengthened by iron, seemed to be the chief building material in the business parts of the city, though stone was coming into use, obtained from an excellent quarry on Angel Island. The Bank of California had been constructed of this, and was much admired by everybody. The private residences, however, seemed chiefly frame, and were seldom more than two and a half stories high. Doubtless more heed is given to earthquakes here, though your true Californian would be slow to acknowledge this. Nevertheless, deep down in his heart—at "bed-rock," as he would say—his household gods are esteemed of more importance, than his commercial commodities. In the suburbs, Mansard roofs were fast coming into vogue, and everywhere there was a general breaking out of Bay-Window. Brown seemed to be the favorite color, doubtless to offset the summer sand-storms, and the general prevalence of bay-windows may also be due partly to these. Convenience and comfort—often elegance and luxury—appeared everywhere, and to an extent that was surprising, for a city so young and raw. Shade-trees were still rare, because only the native scrubby live-oaks, with deep penetrating roots, can survive the long and dry summers there. But shrubbery and flowers, prompted by plentiful irrigation, appeared on every side, and the air was always redolent of perfume. The most unpretending homes had their gems of flower-gardens, with evergreens, fuchsias, geraniums, pansies, and the variety and richness of their roses were a perpetual delight. A rill of water, with trickling side streams, made the barren sand-hills laugh with verdure and beauty, and gaunt wind-mills in every back-yard kept up the supply. The wind-mill in California rises to the dignity of an institution, and is a godsend to the whole coast. In winter, of course, they are not needed. But throughout the long and rainless summer, when vegetation withers up and blows away, the steady sea-breeze keeps the wind-mills going, and these pump up water for a thousand irrigating purposes. The vegetable gardens about the city, and California farmers generally, all patronize them, more or less, and thus grow fruits and vegetables of exquisite character, and almost every variety, the year round. The markets and fruit-stands of San Francisco, groaning with apples, pears, peaches, plums, pomegranates, oranges, grapes, strawberries, etc., have already become world-renowned, and the Pacific Railroad now places them at our very doors.

Montgomery street repeats Broadway in all but its vista, but with something more perhaps of energy and dash. The representative New Yorker always has a trace of conservatism somewhere; but your true Californian laughs at precedent, and is embodied go-ahead-ativeness. In costume, he is careless, not to say reckless, insisting on comfort at all hazards, and running greatly to pockets. Stove-pipe hats are an abomination to him, and tight trowsers nowhere; but beneath his slouch-hat are a keen eye and nose, and his powers of locomotion are something prodigious. Cleaner-cut, more wide-awake, and energetic faces are nowhere to be seen. Few aged men appear, but most average from twenty-five to forty years. Resolute, alert, jaunty, bankrupt perhaps to-day, but to-morrow picking their flints and trying it again, such men mean business in all they undertake, and carry enterprise and empire in the palms of their hands. The proportion of ladies on Montgomery street, however, usually seemed small, and the quality inferior to that of the sterner sex. Given to jewelry and loud colors, and still louder manners, there was a fastness about them, that jarred upon one's Eastern sense, though some noble specimens of womanhood now and then appeared. Doubtless, the hotel and apartment-life of so many San Franciscans had something to do with this, as it is fatal to the more modest and domestic virtues; but it must be doubted, whether this will account for it entirely. Evidently, California is still "short" of women, at least of the worthier kind, and until she completes her supply will continue to over-estimate and spoil what she has. At least, this is the impression her Montgomery street dames make upon a stranger, and unfortunately there is much elsewhere to confirm it.

Respect for the Sabbath seemed to be a growing virtue, but there was still room for much improvement. Many of the stores and shops on Montgomery and Kearney streets were open on Sunday, the same as other days; and it seemed to be the favorite day for pic-nics and excursions, to Oakland and San Mateo. Processions, with bands of music, were not infrequent, and at Hayes' Park in the Southern suburbs the whole Teuton element seemed to concentrate on that day, for a general saturnalia. On the other hand, there was a goodly array of well-filled churches, and their pastors preached with much fervency and power. The Jewish Synagogue is a magnificent structure, one of the finest in America, and deserves more than a passing notice. It is on Sutter street, in a fine location overlooking the city, and cost nearly half a million of dollars. The gilding and decoration generally inside, viewed from the organ-loft, are superb. But few of the large choir were Jews, and scarcely any could read the old Hebrew songs and chants in the original; so these were printed in English, as the Hebrew *sounds*, and thus they maintained the ancient custom of singing and chanting only in Hebrew! Their music, nevertheless, was grand and inspiring, and it would be well for our Gentile churches, to emulate it. This was called the Progressive Synagogue. The congregation had recently shortened the ancient service from three hours to an hour and a half, by leaving out some of the long prayers—"vain repetitions," it is presumed—and the consequence was, a split in this most conservative of churches. The good old conservative brethren, of course, could not stand the abbreviation. They were fully persuaded, they could never get to Paradise, with only an hour and a half's service. So, they seceded, and set up for themselves. Very prosperous and wealthy are the Jews of San Francisco; and, indeed, all over the Pacific Coast, our Hebrew friends enjoy a degree of respectability, that few attain East. They number in their ranks many of the leading bankers, merchants, lawyers, etc., of San Francisco; and more than one of them sits upon the Bench, gracing his seat. Poor Thomas Starr King's church is a model in its way, and the congregation that assembles there one of the most cultivated and refined on the Pacific Coast. Their pastor, Dr. Stebbins, though not equal to his great predecessor, in some respects, is a man of marked thought and eloquence; and, by his broad christian charity, was doing a noble work in San Francisco. So, Dr. Stone, formerly of Boston, was preaching to large audiences, and declaring "the whole counsel of God," without fear or favor. His church is plain but large and commodious, and was always thronged with attentive worshippers. Dr. Wadsworth, lately of Philadelphia, was not attracting the attention he did East; but his church was usually well-filled, and he was exerting an influence and power for good much needed. The Methodists, our modern ecclesiastical sharp-shooters, did not seem as live and aggressive, as they usually do elsewhere; but we were told they were a great and growing power on the Coast, for all that, and everybody bade them God speed. The Episcopalians, as a rule, I regret to say, appeared to make but little impression, and were perhaps unfortunate in their chief official. The Catholics, embracing most of the old Spanish population and much of the foreign element, were vigorous and aggressive, and made no concealment of the fact, that they were aiming at supremacy. In this cosmopolitan city, the Chinese, too, have their Temples, or Josh-Houses; but they were much neglected, and John Chinaman, indeed, religiously considered, seemed well on the road to philosophic indifference.

During the past decade, however, things on the whole had greatly improved, morally and religiously, as the population had become more fixed and settled; and all were hoping for a still greater improvement, with the completion of the Railroad, and the resumption of old family ties East. The drinking-saloons were being more carefully regulated. The gambling-hells, no longer permitted openly, were being more and more driven into obscurity and secrecy. Law and order were more rigidly enforced. The vigilance committees of former years still exerted their beneficent example. The *Alta*, *Bulletin*, and *Times*, then the three great papers of the city and Coast, all noble journals, were all open and pronounced in behalf of good morals and wholesome government; and it is not too much to say, that the prospect for the future was certainly very gratifying, not to say cheering. "Forty-Niners," (Bret Harte's *Argonauts*) and other early comers, declared themselves amazed, that they were getting on, as well as they did. "Yes," said one of the best of them, a man of great shrewdness and ability, "I grant, we Californians have been pretty rough customers, and have not as many religious people among us yet, as we ought to have; but then, what we have are *iron-clad*, you bet!" I suspect that is about so. A man, who is really religious in California, will likely be so anywhere. The severity of his temptations, if he resist them, will make him invulnerable; and all the "fiery darts of the wicked one," elsewhere, will fall harmless at his feet. Faithful Monitors are they, battling for Jesus; and in the end, we know, will come off more than conquerors. With all our hearts, let us bid them God speed!

CHAPTER XVIII.

SAN FRANCISCO (*continued*).

HERE in San Francisco, our National greenbacks were no longer a legal tender, but everything was on a coin basis. Just as in New York, you sell gold and buy greenbacks, if you want a convenient medium of exchange, so here we had to sell greenbacks and buy gold. A dime was the smallest coin, and "two bits" (twenty-five cents) the usual gratuity. A newspaper cost a dime, or two for twenty-five cents—the change never being returned. Fruits and vegetables were cheap, but dry-goods, groceries, clothing, books, etc., about the same in gold, as East in greenbacks. The general cost of living, therefore, seemed to be about the same as in New York, *plus* the premium on gold. California and the Pacific slope generally had refused to adopt the National currency, and it was still a mooted question whether they had lost or gained by this. At first, they thought it a great gain to be rid of our paper dollars; but public opinion had changed greatly, and many were getting to think they had made a huge mistake, in not originally acquiescing in the national necessity. The prosperity of the East during the war, and the pending sluggishness of trade on the Coast (still continuing), were much commented on, as connected with this question of Coin *vs.* Greenbacks; but it was thought too late to remedy the matter now. This hostility to our Greenbacks did not seem to arise from a want of patriotism, so much as from a difference of opinion, as to the necessity or propriety of their using a paper currency, when they had all the gold and silver they wanted, and were exporting a surplus by every steamer. If there was a speck of Secession there at first, California afterwards behaved very nobly, especially when she came with her bullion by the many thousands to the rescue of the Sanitary Commission; and Starr King's memory was still treasured everywhere, as that of a martyr for the Union. The oncoming Pacific Railroad was constantly spoken of, as a new "bond of union," to link the Coast to the Atlantic States as with "hooks of steel;" and, evidently, nothing (unless it may be the Chinese Question) can disturb the repose of the Republic there, for long years to come. The people almost universally spoke lovingly and tenderly of the East, as their old "home," and thousands were awaiting the completion of the Railroad to go thither once again.

Their great passion, however, just then, was for territorial aggrandizement. Mr. Seward had just announced his purchase of Alaska, and of course, everybody was delighted, as they would have been if he had bought the North Pole, or even the tip end of it. Next they wanted British Columbia and the Sandwich Islands, and hoped before long also to possess Mexico and down to the Isthmus. The Sitka Ice Company, which for some years had supplied San Francisco and the Coast with their only good ice, was proof positive, that there was cold weather sometimes in Alaska; nevertheless, they claimed, the Sage of Auburn had certainly shown himself to be a great statesman, by going into this Real Estate business, however hyperborean the climate. It was soon alleged to be a region of fair fields and dimpled meadows, of luscious fruits and smiling flowers, of magnificent forests and inexhaustible mines, as well as of icebergs and walrusses; and straightway a steamer cleared for Sitka, with a full complement of passengers, expecting to locate a "city" there and sell "corner lots," start a Mining Company and "water" stock, or initiate some other California enterprise.

Christmas and New Year in San Francisco were observed very generally, and with even more spirit than in the East. The shops and stores had been groaning with gifts and good things for some time, and on Christmas Eve the whole city seems to pour itself into Montgomery street. Early in the evening, there was a scattering tooting of trumpets, chiefly by boys; but along toward midnight, a great procession of men and boys drifted together, and traversing Montgomery, Kearney, and adjacent streets, made the night hideous with every kind of horn, from a dime trumpet to a trombone. New Year was ushered in much the same way, though not quite so elaborately. On both of these winter holidays there happened to be superb weather, much like what we have East in May, with the sky clear, and the air crisp, and the whole city—with his wife and child—seemed to be abroad. The good old Knickerbocker custom of New Year calls was apparently everywhere accepted, and thoroughly enjoyed. Every kind of vehicle was in demand, and "stag" parties of four or five gentlemen—out calling on their lady friends—were constantly met, walking hilariously along, or driving like mad. Quite a number of army officers happened to be in San Francisco just then, and their uniforms of blue and brass made many a parlor gay. Of names known east, there were Generals Halleck, McDowell, Allen, Steele, Irvin Gregg, French, King, Fry, etc., and these with their brother officers were everywhere heartily welcomed. Indeed, army officers are nowhere more esteemed or better treated, than on the Pacific Coast, and all are usually delighted with their tour of duty there. In former years, many of them married magnificent ranches—encumbered, however, with native señoritas—and here and there we afterwards met them, living like grand seignors on their broad and baronial acres. Ranches leagues in extent, and maintaining thousands of cattle and sheep, are still common in California, and some of the best of these belong to ex-army officers. Their owners, however, do but little in the way of pure farming, and are always ready to give a quarter section or so to any stray emigrant, who will settle down and cultivate it—especially to old comrades.

The great feature of San Francisco, of course, is her peerless bay. Yet noble as it is for purposes of commerce, it avails little for pleasure excursions; and 'Frisco, indeed, might be better off in this respect. A trip to Oakland is sometimes quite enjoyable, and the ride by railroad down the peninsula, skirting the bay, to San Josè, is always a delight. But the bay itself is fickle and morose in winter, and in summer must be raw and gusty. The suck of wind, from the Pacific into the interior, through the Golden Gate, as through a funnel, always keeps the bay more or less in a turmoil; and during the time we were there, it seemed quite neglected, except for business purposes. One day, in the middle of January, however, we had duties that took us to Alcatraz and Angel Island, and essayed the trip thither in a little sloop. On leaving the *Occidental*, the sky was overcast, and we had the usual drizzle of that winter; but before we reached Meigg's Wharf, it had thickened into a pouring rain, and as we crossed to Alcatraz squalls were churning the outer bay into foam in all directions. After an hour or two there, on that rocky fortress, the key of San Francisco, with the wind and rain dashing fitfully about us, we took advantage of a temporary lull to re-embark for Angel Island. We had hardly got off, however, before squall after squall came charging down upon us; and as we beat up the little strait between Angel Island and Socelito, the sloop careening and the waves breaking over us, it seemed at times as if we were in a fair way of going to the bottom. Just as we rounded the rocky point of the Island, before reaching the landing, a squall of unusual force struck us athwart the bows, wave after wave leaped aboard, and for awhile our gallant little craft quivered in the blast like a spent race-horse, as she struggled onward. An abrupt lee shore was on one side, the squall howling on the other; but we faced it out, and in a lull, that soon followed, shot by the landing (it being too rough to halt there), and weathering the next point dropped anchor in a little cove behind it, just in time to escape another squall even fiercer than the former. Had we been off either point, or out in the bay, when this last one struck us, no doubt we would have gone ashore or to Davy Jones' locker; and altogether, as our Captain said, it was a "nasty, dirty day," even for San Francisco. Returning, we had skies less treacherous and a smoother run; but were glad to reach the grateful welcome and spacious halls of the *Occidental*, best of hotels, again. It may be, that the bay was a little ruder that day, than usual; but it bears a bad name for sudden gusts and squalls, and San Franciscans give it a wide berth generally. Sometimes, in summer, it is afflicted by calms as well as squalls; we heard some amusing stories of parties becalmed there until late at night, unable to reach either shore; so that, altogether, however useful otherwise, it can hardly be regarded as adding much *per se* to the pleasures of a life in 'Frisco.

As an offset to this, however, all orthodox San Franciscans, swear by the Cliff-House and the sea-lions. To "go to the Cliff," is the right thing to do in San Francisco, and *not* to go to the Cliff-House is not to see or know California. In the summer, people drive there in the early morning, to breakfast and return before the sea-breeze rises, and then hundreds of gay equipages throng the well-kept road. Even in winter, at the right hour, you are always sure to meet many driving out or in. Of course, we went to the "Cliff"—wouldn't have missed going there for anything. Past Lone Mountain Cemetery, that picturesque city of the dead, the fine graveled road strikes straight through the sand-hills, for five or six miles, to the Pacific; and when you reach the overhanging bluff, on which the hotel perches like an eagle's nest, you have a grand view of the Golden Gate and the far-stretching sea beyond. On the very verge of the horizon hang the Farallones, pointing the way to Japan and China, and the white sails of vessels beating in or out the harbor dot the ocean far and near. Just in front of the hotel are several groups of high shelving rocks, among which the ocean moans and dashes ceaselessly, and here the seals or "sea-lions," as 'Frisco lovingly calls them, have a favorite rendezvous and home. The day we were there, there appeared to be a hundred or more of them, large and small, swimming about the rocks or clambering over them, while pelicans and gulls kept them company. Some were small, not larger than a half-grown sturgeon, while others again were huge unwieldy monsters, not unlike legless oxen, weighing perhaps a thousand pounds or more. "Ben Butler" was an immense, overgrown creature, as selfish and saucy, apparently, as he could well be; and another, called "Gen. Grant," was not much better. They kicked and cuffed the rest overboard quite indiscriminately, though now and then they were compelled to take a plunge themselves. Many contented themselves with merely gamboling around the water's edge; but others had somehow managed slimily to roll and climb forty or fifty feet up the rocks, and there lay sunning themselves in supreme felicity, like veteran politicians snug in office. Sometimes two or three would get to wrangling about the same position, as if one part of the rocks were softer than another, and then they would bark and howl at each other, and presently essay to fight in the most clumsy and ludicrous way. "Ben Butler," or "Gen. Grant," would usually settle the squabble, by a harsh bark, or by flopping the malcontents overboard, and then would resume his nap with becoming satisfaction. Uncouth, and yet half-human in their way, with a cry that sometimes startled you like a distant wail, we watched their movements from the piazza of the hotel with much interest, and must congratulate 'Frisco on having such a first-class "sensation." May her "sea-lions" long remain to her as a "lion" of the first water, and their numbers and renown never grow less! In former years, they were much shot at and annoyed, by thoughtless visitors. But subsequently the State took them under her protection, and now it was a penal offence to injure or disturb them. This is right, and California should be complimented, for thus trying to preserve and perpetuate this interesting colony of her original settlers.

Returning, we had a superb drive down the beach, with the surf thundering at our wheels; and thence, by a winding road over and through the hills, reached the city again. It was a glorious day in February, after a fortnight of perpetual drizzle—a June day for beauty, but toned by an October breeze—the sun flashing overhead like a shield of gold; the road, over and between the hills, gave us from time to time exquisite glimpses of the sea or bay and city; every sense seemed keyed to a new life and power of enjoyment; and the memory of that "drive to the Cliff," is something wonderfully clear and charm ing still. It would be surprising, if Californians did not brag considerably about it. They are not famed for modesty, and would be heathens, if they kept silence.

Californians are proverbial for their ups and downs, and we heard much of their varying fortunes. You will scarcely meet a leading citizen, who has not been down to "hard-pan" once or twice in his career, and everybody seems to enjoy telling about it. In former years, many had been rich in "feet" or "corner-lots," who yet had not enough "dust" to buy a "square-meal;" and men with Great Expectations, but small cash in hand, were still not infrequent. I ran foul of an old school-mate one day, who arrived in California originally as captain of an ox-team, which he had driven across the Plains. But now he was deep in mining-stocks, and twenty-vara lots, and was rated as a millionaire. I met another who for years lost all he invested in "feet." But luckily, at last, he went into Savage and Yellow Jacket, and now he owned handsome blocks on Montgomery and California streets, and lived like a prince at the *Occidental.* Another still, named O., an eccentric genius, came out to California early, and his uncle (already there) secured him a place in a dry-goods house. In a few months, the house failed, and O. fell back on his uncle's hands again. Then he was given a place in a silk-house, but in a short time this also failed. A fatality seemed to accompany the poor fellow. Wherever he went, the houses either failed, closed up, or burned out; and thus, time after time, he came back to his uncle, like a bad penny. Once he was reduced so low, he went to driving a dray, glad to get even that; and again, turned chiffonier, and eked out a precarious living by collecting the old bones, scraps of tin, sheet-iron, etc., that lay scattered about the suburbs. Finally, he wisely concluded he had "touched bottom," and that California was no place for him. So, his kind-hearted uncle bought him a ticket home by the "Golden City," and supposed when he bade him good-bye on her gang-way, that that would be the last he would see of O. in California. But a week or so afterwards, early one Sunday morning, he was roused up by some one rapping lustily at the door, and opening it lo! there was his hopeful nephew again—"large as life and twice as natural!" It seems, the ill-fated steamer, when two or three hundred miles down the Coast, had caught fire and been beached, with the loss of many lives; but O., strange to say, had escaped scot-free, and now was on hand again. He now tried two or three more situations, thinking his "luck" perhaps had turned, but failed in all of them or they soon failed; and finally set out for the East again, but this time across the Plains, driving a "bull-team." He got safely back to New York, and taking hold of his father's business—grain and flour—for a wonder, made it prosper. He pushed ahead with this swimmingly for awhile, until he had made fifty thousand dollars or so, when he concluded to go into a flour speculation on his own account. He did so, buying largely, when suddenly the bottom dropped out of the market, leaving O. penniless again, with a large deficit—he meanwhile, disappearing. Some years afterwards he turned up in Minnesota, where he had married a border maiden, and gone to farming, and at the last accounts was doing tolerably well again.

Californians will spin you such "yarns" by the evening

—half humorous, half pathetic—and it is upon such romantic histories, that the Golden State has advanced to empire.

But the day of her adventurers is passing away, and society there is fast settling down to its normal conditions. Fewer and still fewer of her people return East, to spend their hard-earned fortunes; and the generation now growing up there regard the Coast as their natural home, and love it dearly. Proud of the soil and enamored of the climate, they expect great things of the future, and surely all the world should wish them well. There are no better or braver men, than our citizens there generally, and the Pacific slope is safe in their hands and brains, beyond peradventure. "Who helps himself, God helps," is a wise old French maxim; and California believes in it, fully and thoroughly, from the Sierras to the sea.

CHAPTER XIX.

SAN FRANCISCO (*Concluded*).

THE Chinese Question, we had an opportunity of looking into considerably, first and last, and here are some conclusions. Striking the orientals at Boisè City, in Idaho, we had followed them down the Columbia and the Coast to San Francisco, and here endeavored to learn all we could about them. We found them everywhere on the streets and in the houses, in pretty much all occupations except the very highest, and were constantly amazed at their general thrift and intelligence. Out of the hundred thousand or so on the Coast, perhaps half were massed in San Francisco and its suburbs; so here was the place to see and study John Chinaman in America, if anywhere. All wore the collarless Chinese blouse, looped across the breast, not buttoned—that of the poorer classes of coarse blue stuff, but of the richer of broadcloth. Otherwise, they dressed outwardly chiefly as Americans. Here and there a Chinese hat, such as you see in the tea-prints, appeared, but not often—the American felt-hat being the rule, stove-pipes never. A Chinaman with a stove-pipe hat on would truly be an anomaly, a violation of all the unities and proprieties at once. A good many still wore the Chinese shoe, wooden-soled, with cotton uppers; but the American boot and shoe were fast supplanting this, especially among the out-door classes, such as mechanics and laborers.

Pig-tails were universal, generally hanging down, but often coiled around the head, under the hat, so as to be out of the way and attract less attention. In features, of course, they were all true Mongolians; but here and there were grand faces, worthy of humanity anywhere. Their food consists chiefly of fish and rice; but the wealthier classes indulge freely in poultry and beef, and the Chinese taste for these was constantly on the increase. The old stories of their dog and rat diet are evidently myths, at least here in America, and no doubt are equally so in China, except in very rare instances, among the poorest classes, and even then only under the direst necessity. Intelligent Californians laugh at such reports as antediluvian, and say their Chinese neighbors are only too glad to eat the very best, if they can only get it. Everybody gave them credit for sobriety, intelligence, and thrift, the three great master qualities of mankind, practically speaking; and without them the industry of the Pacific Coast, it was conceded, would soon come to a stand-still. All are expert at figures, all read and write their own tongue, and nearly all seemed intent on mastering English, as quickly and thoroughly as possible. When not at work or otherwise occupied, they were usually seen with a book in their hands, and seemed much given to reading and study. Their chief vices were gambling, and opium-smoking; but these did not seem to prevail to the extent we had heard, and appeared really less injurious, than the current vices of other races on the Coast, all things considered. The statistics of the city and Coast somehow were remarkably in their favor, showing a less percentage of vagrancy and crime among these heathens, than any other part of the population, notwithstanding the absurd prejudices and barbarous discriminations against them. Their quickness to learn all American ways, even when not able to speak our tongue, was very surprising They engaged in all household duties, ran errands, worked at trades, performed all kinds of manual labor, and yet as a rule, their only dialect was a sort of chow-chow or "Pigeon English," of which the following is a good specimen. It is Longfellow's "Excelsior" done into Pigeon-English, and speaks for itself.

"TOPSIDE GALAH.

"That nightee teem he come chop chop,
One young man walkee, no can stop;
Colo maskee, icee maskee;
He got flag; chop b'long welly culio, see—
Topside Galah!

"He too muchee solly; one piecee eye,
Lookee sharp—so fashion—alla same mi;
He talkee largee, talkee stlong,
Too muchee culio; alla same gong—
Topside Galah!

"Inside any housee he can see light,
Any piecee loom got fire all light;
He look see plenty ice more high,
Inside he mouf he plenty cly—
Topside Galah!

"'No can walkee!' olo man speakee he;
'Bimeby lain come, no can see;
Hab got water, welly wide!
Maskee, mi must go topside—
Topside Galah!

"'Man-man,' one galo talkee he;
'What for you go topside look-see?'
'Nother teem,' he makee plenty cly;
Maskee, alla teem walkee plenty high—
Topside Galah!

"'Take care that spilum tlee, young man;
Take care that icee!' he no man-man;
That coolie chin-chin he good night;
He talkee, 'mi can go all light'—
Topside Galah!

"Joss pidgin man chop chop begin,
Morning teem that Joss chin-chin,
No see any man, he plenty fear,
Cause some man talkee, he can hear—
Topside Galah!

"Young man makee die: one largee dog see,
Too muchee bobbery, findee he;
Hand too muchee colo, inside can stop;
Alla same piecee flag, got culio chop—
Topside Galah!"

"Pigeon" is said to be the nearest approach a Chinaman can make to "*business*," and hence "Pigeon English" really means *business* English. Most of the above words are English, more or less distorted; a few, however, are Chinese Anglicised. They always use *l* for *r*—thus *lice* for "rice;" *mi* for "I," etc.; and abound in terminal "*ee's*." *Chop-chop* means "very fast;" *maskee*, "don't mind;" *Topside Galah*, "*Excelsior, hurrah!*" If you call on a lady, and inquire of her Chinese servant, "Missee have got?" He will reply, if she be up and about, "Missee hab got topside;" or, if she be still asleep, "Missee hab got, wakee sleepee." Not wishing to disturb her, you hand him your card, and go away with, "Maskee, maskee; no makee bobbery!"

We had seen a good deal of the Chinese generally, but on the evening of Dec. 31st were so fortunate as to meet most of their leading men together. The occasion was a grand banquet at the *Occidental*, given by the merchants of San Francisco, in honor of the sailing of the

Colorado, the first steamer of the new monthly line to Hong-Kong. All the chief men of the city—merchants, lawyers, clergymen, politicians—were present, and among the rest some twenty or more Chinese merchants and bankers. The Governor of the State presided, and the military and civil dignitaries most eminent on the Coast were all there. The magnificent Dining-Room of the *Occidental* was handsomely decorated with festoons and flowers, and tastefully draped with the flags of all nations—chief among which, of course, were our own Stars and Stripes, and the Yellow-Dragon of the Flowery Empire. A peculiar feature was an infinity of bird-cages all about the room, from which hundreds of canaries and mocking-birds discoursed exquisite music the livelong evening. The creature comforts disposed of, there were eloquent addresses by everybody, and among the rest one by Mr. Fung Tang, a young Chinese merchant, who made one of the briefest and most sensible of them all. It was in fair English, and vastly better than the average of post-prandial discourses. This was the only set speech by a Chinaman, but the rest conversed freely in tolerable English, and in deportment were certainly perfect Chesterfields of courtesy and propriety. They were mostly large, dignified, fine-looking men, and two of them—Mr. Hop Kee, a leading tea-merchant, and Mr. Chy Lung, a noted silk-factor—had superb heads and faces, that would have attracted attention anywhere. They sat by themselves; but several San Franciscans of note shared their table, and everybody hob-nobbed with them, more or less, throughout the evening. These were the representatives of the great Chinese Emigration and Banking Companies, whose checks pass current on 'Change in San Francisco, for a hundred thousand dollars or more any day, and whose commercial integrity so far was unstained.

There are five of these Companies in all, the Yung-Wo, the Sze-Yap, the Sam-Yap, the Yan-Wo, and the Ning-Yung. They contract with their countrymen in China to transport them to America, insure them constant work while here at fixed wages, and at the expiration of their contract return them to China again, dead or alive, if so desired. They each have a large and comfortable building in San Francisco, where they board and lodge their members, when they first arrive, or when sick, or out of work, or on a visit from the interior. Chinese beggars are rare on the Coast, and our public hospitals contain no Chinese patients, although John before landing has always to pay a "hospital-tax" of ten dollars. This is what it is called out there; but, of course, it is a robbery and swindle, which the Golden State ought promptly to repeal. These great Companies also act, as express-agents and bankers, all over the Coast. In all the chief towns and mining districts, wherever you enter a Chinese quarter or camp, you will find a representative of one or more of them, who will procure anything a Chinaman needs, from home or elsewhere; and faithfully remit to the Flowery Kingdom whatever he wants to send, even his own dead body. Both parties appear to keep their contracts well—a breach of faith being seldom recorded. Here, surely, is evidence of fine talent for organization and management—the best tests of human intellect and capacity—and a hint at the existence of sterling qualities, which the English-speaking nations are slow to credit other races with. Such gigantic schemes, such far-reaching plans, such harmonious workings, and exact results, imply a genius for affairs, that not even the Anglo-Saxon can afford to despise, and which all others may ponder with profit. A race that can plan and execute such things as these, must have some vigor and virility in it, whatever its other peculiarities.

Some days after the Banquet, we were driven out to the Mission Woolen Mills, where Donald McLennan, a Massachusetts Scotch-Yankee, was converting California wool into gold. The climate being so favorable to sheep, the wool-product of the coast was already large, and everywhere rapidly increasing. In 1867, California alone yielded ten million pounds, and the rest of the coast fully two millions more. Of this amount, about one-half was consumed on the Pacific Coast, and the balance exported to New York and Liverpool. The average price per pound in San Francisco was about seventeen cents, coin; but this was lower, than it had usually been. * There were several other Woolen Mills on the Coast; but the Mission-Mills were the largest, and had a great reputation for honest work. They were then doing a business of about a million dollars per year, coin, in cloths, cassimeres, blankets, flannels, shawls, etc., and the demand for their goods was constantly on the increase. Their work, on the whole, was of a superior character, and Californians were justly very proud of it. They were supplying all the Army blankets in use on the Coast, and what a contrast they were to the "shoddy" webs, issued to our Boys in Blue east during the war! The troops transferred from the east now threw their old Army blankets away, on arriving in San Francisco, and gladly furnished themselves with these Mission blankets, at their own expense, before leaving for the wilds of Washington and Arizona. Some extra specimens, intended for the Paris Exposition, as white as new-fallen snow and soft as satin, had the American and French coats of

* In 1873, she yielded 36,000,000 pounds, which she sold for about twenty cents per pound, or say $7,000,000.

arms embroidered very handsomely on them. Another pair, meant for General Grant, were lustrous with the Stars and Stripes, and traditioual eagle, and now no doubt help to furnish the White House. A pair sent to Gen. M. in the east, a noted connoisseur in blankets, he declared the finest he ever saw, and added, "My daughter would make one of them into an opera-cloak, they are so elegant, if she hadn't one already." I mention all these things thus particularly, in order to emphasize the fact, that out of the 450 persons then employed about these Mills, 350 were Chinamen. For the heavier work, Americans or Europeans were preferred; but the more delicate processes, we were assured, Chinamen learned more quickly and performed more deftly, besides never becoming drunk, or disorderly, or going on a "strike." We saw them at the looms, engaged in the most painstaking and superb pieces of workmanship, and they could not have been more attentive and exact, if they had been a part of the machinery itself. And yet, these one hundred Anglo-Saxons were paid $2,95 per day, coin, while the three hundred and fifty Chinamen received only $1,10 per day, coin, though the average work of each was about the same. Without this cheap labor of John Chinaman, these Mills would have had to close up; with it, they were run at a profit, and at the same time were a great blessing and credit to the Pacific Coast in every way. So, also, the Central Pacific Railroad was then being pushed through and over the Sierra Nevadas, by some ten thousand Chinamen, working for one dollar per day each, in coin, and finding themselves, when no other labor could be had for less than two dollars and a half per day, coin. It was simply a question with the Central directors, whether to build the road or not. Without John, it was useless to attempt it, as the expense would have bankrupted the company, even if other labor could have been had, which was problematical. With him, the road is already a fact accomplished; and in view of possible contingencies, nationally and politically, who shall say we have completed it an hour too soon? Here are practical results, not shadowy theories—of such a character, too, as should give one pause, however anti-Chinese, and ought to outweigh a world of prejudices.

Not long afterwards, we were invited to join a party of gentlemen, and make a tour of the Chinese quarter. Part were from the East, like ourselves, bent on information, and the rest Pacific-Coasters. We started early in the evening, escorted by two policemen, who were familiar with the ins and outs of Chinadom, and did not reach the *Occidental* again until long after midnight. We went first to the Chinese Theatre, an old hotel on the corner of Jackson and Dupont streets, that had recently been metamorphosed into an Oriental playhouse. We found two or three hundred Chinese here, of both sexes, but mainly males, listening to a play, that required eighty weeks or months—our informants were not certain which—to complete its performance. Here was drama for you, surely, and devotion to it! It was a history of the Flowery Kingdom, by some Chinese Shakespeare—half-tragedy, half-comedy, like most human history—and altogether was a curious medley. The actors appeared to be of both sexes, but we were told were only men and boys. Their dresses were usually very rich, the finest of embroidered silks, and their acting quite surprised us. Their pantomime was excellent, their humor irresistible, and their love-passages a good reproduction of the grand passion, that in all ages "makes the world go round." But it is to be doubted, if the

Anglo-Saxon ear will ever become quite reconciled to John's orchestra. This consisted of a rough drum, a rude banjo or guitar, and a sort of violin, over whose triple clamors a barbarous clarionet squeaked and squealed continually. Japanese music, as rendered by Risley's troupe of "Jugglers," is much similar to it; only John's orchestra is louder, and more hideous. Much of the play was pantomime, and other much opera; some, however, was common dialogue, and when this occurred, the clash and clang of the Chinese consonants was something fearful. Every word seemed to end in "ng," as Chang, Ling, Hong, Wung; and when the parts became animated, their voices roared and rumbled about the stage, like Chinese gongs in miniature. The general behavior of the audience was good; everybody, however, smoked—the majority cigars and cigarritos, a very few opium. Over the theatre was a Chinese lottery-office, on entering which the proprietor tendered you wine and cigars, like a genuine Californian. He himself was whiffing away at a cigarrito, and was as polite and politic, as a noted New York ex-M. C, in the same lucrative business. Several Chinamen dropped in to buy tickets, while we were there; and the business seemed to be conducted on the same principle, or rather want of principle, as among Anglo-Saxons elsewhere.

Next we explored the famous Barbary Coast, and witnessed scenes that Charles Dickens never dreamed of, with all his studies of the dens and slums of London and Paris. Here in narrow, noisome alleys are congregated the wretched Chinese women, that are imported by the ship-load, mainly for infamous purposes. As a class, they are small in stature, scarcely larger than an American girl of fourteen, and usually quite plain. Some venture on hoops and crinoline, but the greater part retain the

Chinese wadded gown and trousers. Their chignons are purely Chinese—huge, unique, indescribable—and would excite the envy even of a Broadway belle. They may be seen on the street any day in San Francisco, bonnetless, fan in hand, hobbling along in their queer little shoes, perfect fac-similles of the figures you see on lacquered ware imported from the Orient. They are not more immodest, than those of our own race, who ply the same vocation in Philadelphia and New York; and their fellow-countrymen, it seemed, behaved decently well even here. But here is the great resort of sailors, miners, 'long-shoremen, and the floating population generally of San Francisco, and the brutality and bestiality of the Saxon and the Celt here all comes suddenly to the surface, as if we were fiends incarnate. Here are the St. Giles of London and the Five Points of New York, magnified and intensified (if possible), both crowded into one, and what a hideous example it is for Christendom to set to Heathendom! San Francisco owes it to herself, and to our boasted civilization, to cleanse this Augean stable—to obliterate, to stamp out this plague-spot—to purge it, if need be, by fire—and she has not a day to lose in doing it. It is the shameful spectacle, shocking alike to gods and men, of a strong race trampling a weaker one remorselessly in the mud; and justice will not sleep forever, confronted by such enormities.

The same evening we took a turn through the Chinese gambling-houses, but did not find them worse than similar institutions elsewhere. Indeed, they were rather more quiet and respectable, than the average of such "hells" in San Francisco. They were frequented solely by Chinamen, and though John is not averse to "fighting the tiger," he proposes to do it in his own *dolce far niente* way. They seemed to have only one game, which consisted in betting whether in diminishing steadily a given pile of perforated brass-coins, an odd or even number of them would at last be left. The banker with a little rod, drew the coins, two at a time, rapidly out of the pile towards himself, and when the game was ended all parties cheerfully paid up their losses or pocketed their gains. The stakes were small, seldom more than twenty-five or fifty cents each, and disputes infrequent. A rude idol or image of Joss, with a lamp constantly burning before it, appeared in all these dens, and indeed was universal throughout the Chinese quarter.

The Chinese New Year comes in February, and is an occasion of rare festivities. It began at midnight on the 4th that year, and was ushered in with a lavish discharge of fire-crackers and rockets, to which our usual Fourth of July bears about the same comparison as a minnow to a whale. The fusilade of crackers continued, more or less, for a day or two, until the whole Chinese quarter was littered with their remains. It takes them three days to celebrate this holiday, and during all this period there was a general suspension of business, and every Chinaman kept open house. Their leading merchants welcomed all "Melican" men who called upon them, and the Celestials themselves were constantly passing from house to house, exchanging the compliments of the season. I dropped in upon several, whom I had met at the Banquet, and now have lying before me the unique cards of Mr. Hop Kee, Mr. Chy Lung, Mr. Fung Tang, Messrs. Tung Fu and Co., Messrs. Kwoy Hing and Co., Messrs. Sun Chung Kee and Co., etc. Several of these understood and spoke English very well, and all bore themselves becomingly, like well-to-do gentlemen. Like the majority of their countrymen, many were small; but some were full-sized, athletic men, scarcely inferior, if at all, to our average American. Their residences were usually back of their stores, and here we everywhere found refreshments set out, and all invited to partake, with a truly Knickerbocker hospitality. Tea, sherry, champagne, cakes, sweetmeats, cigars, all were offered without stint, but never pressed unduly. For three days the whole Chinese quarter was thus given up to wholesale rejoicing, and hundreds of Americans flocked thither, to witness the festivity and fun. John everywhere appeared in his best bib and tucker, if not with a smile on his face, yet with a look of satisfaction and content; for this was the end of his debts, as well as the beginning of a new year. At this period, by Chinese custom or law, a general settlement takes place among them, a balance is struck between debtor and creditor, and everybody starts afresh. If unable to pay up, the debtor surrenders his assets for the equal benefit of his creditors, his debts are sponged out, and then with a new ledger and a clean conscience he "picks his flint and tries it again." This is the merciful, if not sensible, Bankrupt Law of the Chinese, in force among these heathen for thousands of years—"for a time whereof the memory of man runneth not to the contrary"—and its humane and wise provisions suggest, whether our Christian legislators, after all, may not have something to learn, even from Pagan codes.

The Chinese temple, synagogue, or "Joss-House," of which we had heard such conflicting reports, stands near the corner of Kearney and Pine streets, in the heart of the city. It is a simple structure of brick, two or three stories high, and would attract little or no attention, were it not for a plain marble slab over the entrance, with "Sze-Yap Asylum" carved upon it, in gilt letters, and the same repeated in Chinese characters. It was spoken of as a "Heathen Synagogue," a "Pagan

Temple," etc., and we had heard much ado about it, from people of the William Nye school chiefly, long before reaching San Francisco. But, in reality, it appeared to be only an asylum or hospital, for the unemployed and infirm of the Sze-Yap Emigration Company; with a small "upper chamber," set apart for such religious services, as to them seemed meet. The other companies all have similar hospitals or asylums, but we visited only this one. The first room on the ground-floor seemed to be the business-room or council-chamber of the company, and this was adorned very richly with crimson and gold. Silk-hangings were on the walls, arm-chairs elaborately carved along the sides, and at the end on a raised platform stood a table and chair, as if ready for business. The room adjoining seemed to be the general smoking and lounging room of the members of the company. Here several Chinamen lay stretched out, on rude but comfortable lounges, two smoking opium, all the rest only cigarritos—taking their afternoon siesta. Back of this were the dining-room, kitchen, etc., but we did not penetrate thither. A winding stairs brought us to the second floor, and here was the place reserved for religious purposes,—an "upper chamber" perhaps twenty by thirty feet, or even less. Its walls and ceiling were hung with silk, and here and there were placards, inscribed with moral maxims from Confucius and other writers, much as we suspend the same on the walls of our Sunday-school rooms, with verses on them from *our* Sacred writings. These mottoes, of course, were in Chinese; but they were said to exhort John to virtue, fidelity, integrity, the veneration of ancestors, and especially to admonish the young men not to forget, that they are away from home, and to do nothing to prejudice the character of their country in the eyes of foreigners. A few gilded spears and battle-axes adorned either side, while overhead hung clusters of Chinese lanterns, unique and beautiful. Flowers were scattered about quite profusely, both natural and artificial—the latter perfect in their way. At the farther end of the room, in "a dim religious light," amid a barbaric array of bannerets and battle-axes, stood their sacred Joss—simply a Representative Chinaman, perhaps half life-size, with patient pensive eyes, long drooping moustaches, and an expression doubtless meant for sublime repose or philosophic indifference. Here all orthodox Chinamen in San Francisco, connected with the Sze-Yap company, were expected to come at least once a year, and propitiate the deity by burning a slip of paper before his image. There was also some praying to be done, but this was accomplished by putting printed prayers in a machine run by clock-work. Tithes there were none—at least worth mentioning. Altogether, this seemed to be a very easy and cheap religion; and yet, easy as it was, John did not seem to trouble himself much about it. The place looked much neglected, as if worshippers were scarce, and devotees infrequent. A priest or acolyte, who came in and trimmed the ever-burning lamp, without even a bow or genuflection to Josh, was the only person about the "Temple," while we were there. The dormitories and apartments for the sick and infirm, we were told, were on this same floor and above; but we did not visit them. This Joss-worship, such as it is, seemed to be general among the Chinese, except the handful gathered into the various Christian churches; but it did not appear to be more than a ceremony. The truth is, John is a very practical creature, and was already beginning to understand, that he is in a new land and among new ideas. Surely, our vigorous, aggressive California Christians stand in nc danger from such Pagan "Temples," and our all-embracing nationality can well afford to tolerate them, as China in turn tolerates ours. The hospital and asylum part of them, we might well imitate; and as for the rest, is it not Emerson, who says:

> "*We* are owners of the sphere,
> Of the seven stars and solar year,
> Of Cæsar's hand and Plato's brain,
> Of Lord Christ's heart, and Shakespeare's strain?"

Our own religion and civilization are too potent, or ought to be, to be affected by such a worship; and if its simple rites comfort or content John in his rough transition to the nineteenth century, let him practice them in peace. If treated wisely, it will not be long before he discards them forever.

So much for the Chinese in San Francisco. Elsewhere, throughout California and Nevada, subsequently, we saw them at work in vineyards, on farms, in the mines, and their industry, fidelity, and skill were conceded substantially by everybody. This Chinese Problem, of course, has its embarrassments; but it is already looming into importance, and must be met. Already we have nearly a hundred thousand of these almond-eyed strangers on the Pacific Coast, and the number swells monthly. In spite of obstructions and discouragements, this yellow stream sets steadily in, and seems as irresistible as the tide, if not as inexhaustible. China, with her teeming population of four hundred millions of souls, or one-third of the human family, has already overflowed into all the countries adjacent to her, and now seeks further outlet here in America. To her, it is simply a question of increase and subsistence. And here, fortunately, from Alaska to the Isthmus, we have room enough and to spare, for all her surplus millions. With her, labor is a drug, the cheapest article she has, and so she exports it. With us, it is largely in demand, and everywhere rising in value. The Pacific slope, and the great internal basin of the continent, to-day absolutely need millions of cheap workers—men, who can deftly handle the pick-axe and the spade, the plow and the hoe, the shuttle and the loom, and, it is plain, must get them from Asia, or not get them at all; for the Atlantic slope, and our great West, stand ready to absorb all Europe can spare, and more. With John, their mines will be opened, their forests cleared, their fields irrigated and tilled, their railroads built, their cotton and woollen-mills erected and run, and in short every avenue of industry and trade made busy and prosperous. Without John, a vast expanse of matchless territory there must remain practically a wilderness and a desert, for long years to come. Is it wise, then, would it be humane and sensible—to turn aside from and reject these patient, industrious, orderly, frugal, labor-seeking, business-loving strangers, whom Providence just now seems to tender us, as a mighty means for subduing and civilizing the continent; or should we not, rather, accept them thankfully, as God's instruments for good, and make the most of their brain and muscle? The inexorable, all-prevailing law of supply and demand, it would seem, has already settled this question, or is in a fair way to settle it; and it but remains to consider, what we shall *do* with them.

In the first place, John nowhere aspires to vote, nor even to be a citizen. So far, his sole claim has been for the right to work, and to receive " a fair day's wages for a fair day's work." With the imperturbability of fate, he has settled down on this, and calmly awaits our answer, not doubting the result. If you object, that he persists in being a foreigner, all expecting some day to return to China, his answer is all immigrants to a new country are more or less of that mind; and, besides, as yet nothing has been done to induce him to Americanize himself. Their leading men said, no doubt many of their countrymen would bring their wives and children here, and settle down among us, if they could be sure of safety and protection; but that now California was "no place for a China *woman*—hardly safe for a China*man!*" They said, they had found America very good for work, and "muchee" good for business; but they had to pay odious taxes, not exacted of other persons—were not permitted to testify in court, except for or against each other—were abused and maltreated from one end of the Coast to the other—were at the mercy of white ruffians, who might rob and even kill them, with impunity, unless Caucasians were present—and, in short, that as yet Chinamen here "had no rights that Melican men were bound to respect." Now, I say, let us change all this. Let us do justice, even to the poorest and humblest of God's children. Let us give John, too, "a *fair* start and an *equal* chance in the race of life," the same as every other human being on American soil; and we shall soon check the re-flow to the Flowery Kingdom, and build up an empire on the Pacific Coast, worthy of our matchless soil and climate there. Existing labor and skill might suffer somewhat at first, as in all industrial changes; but, in the end, they would become employers, and supply the brains to guide the Mongolian hand and foot. The first generation passed away, the next de-Chinaized, Americanized, and educated, would soon become absorbed in the national life, and known only as model artisans and workers. As the ocean receives all rains and rivers, and yet shows it not, so America receives the Saxon and the Celt, the Protestant and the Catholic, and can yet receive Sambo and John, and absorb them all. The school-house and the church, the newspaper and the telegraph, can be trusted to work out their logical results; and time, our sure ally, would shape and fashion even these into keen American citizens.

There were indications, that the Coast had fallen to thinking seriously of all this, and somehow meant to deal more justly with the Chinese hereafter. The anti-Chinese mobs in the cities and towns were passing away, and even among the mining-camps Vigilance Committees were beginning to execute rough justice on thieves and murderers, when their treatment of John became too flagrant and notorious.* Capital, always keen-sighted, was getting to see the necessity for their labor and skill, and the culture and conscience of the Coast were already on their side. Gov. Low, (since Minister to China, most fittingly) presided at the *Occidental* Banquet, and in his remarks there took strong ground in their favor. He said, among other good things:

"We must learn to treat the Chinese who come to live among us decently, and not oppress them by unfriendly legislation, nor allow them to be abused, robbed and murdered, without extending to them any adequate remedy.

"I am a strong believer in the strength of mind and muscle of the Anglo-Saxon race, which will win in the contest for supremacy with any people, without the aid of unequal and oppressive laws; and the man, who is afraid to take his chances on equal terms with his opponents, is a coward and unworthy the name of an American.

"Were I to sum up the whole duty imposed upon us, I should say, let us be honest, industrious and frugal, be persevering and progressive, and remember Raleigh's

* See p. 225.

maxim, that "Whoever commands the sea commands the trade of the world, and whoever commands the trade of the world commands the riches of the world, and consequently the world itself."

So, the pulpit, and the press, as a rule, omitted no opportunity to speak a kind word for them, and to denounce the barbarism, and absurdity, of existing statutes against them. In San Francisco, a public-school had been established for their benefit, and was crowded day and night with adult Chinamen striving to learn English. The public-school fund running short that year, (1867) the Chinese merchants promptly volunteered to eke out the appropriation, rather than have the Board of Education close the school. Since then the Rev. Dr. Gibson, (formerly a Methodist missionary to China, and a man of great energy and force), has started his Sunday-Schools, expecting to plant them all over the Coast, and there seems a marked uprising in John's behalf generally. True, Mr. Senator Casserly, himself a catholic foreigner and the negro-hating democracy, are just now essaying a crusade against them; but this is because the XVth Amendment has ended the "nigger," and they are sadly in want of political capital. Our churches have certainly, now and here, a noble opportunity for effective and valuable missionary work. Instead of having to go half round the globe, across the sea, into malarious regions, among Pagan influences, to seek out the lost sheep of the House of Israel, we here have the heathen at our back-door, and ought to unfurl the Banner of the Cross to them, in every town and from every hillside. The story of the Yankee, who gave a missionary-collector a quarter of a dollar, and when he was leaving called him back, and gave him a dollar more, "to send that quarter along," has it not some grains of truth in it? Here the whole dollar and a quarter may be made immediately effective, and our missionary money should be forthcoming without stint. Not only would we thus more readily and cheaply evangelize the Chinese on our shores, but their returning thousands in turn would evangelize their countrymen at home; and we would thus accomplish a hundredfold more for China, than our missionaries there now seem to be doing, judging by their statistics, all put together. And not only do our Chinese themselves call for this, but the harmony and purity of the national life demand it, and may our churches awake to their great responsibility. Here is their true field for instant and aggressive missionary work, and they should occupy it overwhelmingly.

From a full survey of this *quæstio vexata*, I must conclude, if "God made of one blood all the nations of men to dwell upon the earth," if we are children of a common Father, redeemed by a common Saviour, and bound for a common eternity; if the good old rule, "whatsoever ye would that men should do unto you, do ye even so unto them," (which the Chinese had in a negative form a thousand years before the Sermon on the Mount), is not yet effete; if we believe with Thomas Jefferson, that "all men are created equal, and endowed by their Creator with the inalienable rights of life and liberty;" then, we are bound as a nation to accord justice and fair-play even to these poor Mongolians, yellow-skinned, pig-tailed, and heathen though they be. Now, as heretofore, and always, we shall find our reward as a people in right-doing. Right is always politic. Justice is never wrong. And let us as a nation do right, even to the humblest of God's creatures, and leave the consequences with Him, who holds in his hands the destinies alike of individuals and of races. This is not always an easy road; but the Republic has already travelled it so far, and so courageously, we can not now afford to depart from it. Justice, if the sky falls. But, we may be sure, it will not fall. Rather, it will stand all the firmer and broader, for the Justice done and Humanity saved.

CHAPTER XX.

SAN FRANCISCO TO LOS ANGELOS.

WE left San Francisco, Feb. 9th, on the good ship *Orizaba*, for southern California and Arizona. She was a first-class side-wheel steamer, with good accommodations, and belonged to the California Steam Navigation Company—a corporation that then monopolized or controlled all the navigable waters of California, besides running coast-wise lines North and South. She was one of a line, that ran semi-monthly to San Diego and return, touching at Santa Barbara and San Pedro, and seemed to be paying very well. We might have gone southward from San Francisco to San Josè by railroad, and thence by stage to Los Angelos and Fort Yuma; but our long stage-rides, from the Missouri to Salt Lake and thence to the Columbia, had worn the romance off of stage-coaching, and we infinitely preferred to proceed by steamer. It was a superb day, with sea and sky both "darkly, deeply, beautifully blue" —a day of the kind Californians always mean, when they brag about their climate—as we flung off our lines at San Francisco, and steamed down the harbor broadside with the Golden Age *en route* for Panama. We passed by Alcatraz and through the Golden Gate neck and neck, with the decks of both vessels crowded with excited passengers; but once across the bar, the *Orizaba* drew steadily ahead, and long before sunset we left the *Golden*

Age hull down astern. I don't say this was a race, indeed. Perhaps their leaving together was quite accidental. But the *Orizaba* soon showed her mettle, all hands were eager and excited, and her officers were in ecstacies at the results.

Once fairly at sea, our steamer turned her prow sharply south, and all the way down followed the coast from headland to headland. Usually we steamed along some five or six miles off shore, with the land itself always in view, and the ocean everywhere like a mill-pond. From the Columbia to the Golden Gate in December, we had found the Pacific to belie its name; but now steaming farther south, we saw it in its calmness and beauty, and felt like christening it anew. Most of the way, the sky was magnificently clear, the weather moderate, the air bracing and stimulating, while the whole Coast was a shifting panorama of beauty and grandeur. The ocean too smooth for sea-sickness, we strolled about the deck by twos and fours, or lolled for hours on the settees, inhaling life and vigor at every breath, until we almost seemed to be navigating fabled seas or voyaging into paradise. The Coast itself, never out of sight, rose generally in abrupt hills or mountains, and these were now green and gold to their summits. In places, whole hillsides seemed alive with wild-flowers of every hue, while here and there flocks and herds dotted the landscape far and near. Now and then an adobe house gleamed out of some sheltered nook; but, as a rule, houses were infrequent, and trees and shrubbery very scarce. A few stunted oaks and cedars fringed the ravines here and there, but as a forest they were nothing to speak of. The Coast Mountains lifted themselves everywhere, smooth to the summit as if shaven, with no glory of trees to shelter or crown them; and in summer, when their verdure dries up and blows away, they must seem very bald and desolate.

At Santa Barbara, some three hundred miles down the Coast, we touched for an hour or two, and put ashore several passengers, and some thirty tons of freight. While discharging the latter, we sauntered up into the town, and found it to be a pleasant place of some fifteen hundred inhabitants—county-seat to a county of the same name. The buildings were mostly adobe, of course, and all quite old; but the town had an appearance of comfort and respectability, if not of thrift, and the few Americans we met were sanguine of its future. The Santa Barbara plains, just back of the town, consist of a broad and beautiful valley, enclosed by two imposing mountain ranges, that here jut obliquely into the ocean, and they have a climate that is no doubt seldom equalled even on the Pacific Coast. As a sanatarium, Santa Barbara was already being much resorted to by invalids, and doubtless will become more so when better known. With great evenness of temperature the year round,* without either snow or frost, or intense heat, the grape, fig, orange, peach, pomegranate, olive, all flourish here in the open air; and Nature is so prodigal of her gifts, the Santa Barbarans appear exempted from the primal curse, "In the sweat of thy face shalt thou eat bread, etc." Mountain streams from the neighboring ranges, they had, however, trained into irrigating ditches, and by these cultivated a considerable breadth of land. They said, they had water sufficient to irrigate thousands of acres more, and needed only capital and population to build up a prosperous and thriving community. In old times—"before the flood," as a Forty-Niner would say—the Jesuit Fathers had one of their most flourishing

* See Appendix.

Missions here, and their old Mission Church on a plateau back of the town was still standing, though now used chiefly as a school. Dr. O. formerly of the Army, but now married to a señorita and settled at Santa Barbara, escorted us through the town, and afterwards regaled us with wine from his own vineyard, of an excellent brand. He pronounced Santa Barbara, with its fruits and its flowers, a second paradise, the only place fit to live in—where one would about never die—and half persuaded some of us to the same way of thinking. The petroleum wells near there, as yet, had produced but little; but there seemed no doubt of the petroleum being there in large quantities. We had noticed it floating on the sea for miles before reaching Santa Barbara; and, if it issues beneath the sea sufficient for this purpose, it ought to be struck somewhere in that vicinity in paying quantities. The Santa Barbarans by no means despaired of doing this yet, and thus hoped to add another item to their already large and growing products.

At San Pedro, the seaport of Los Angelos, a hundred miles or so farther down the Coast, we put off some four hundred tons of freight, and parted with the bulk of our passengers. Of this place, more hereafter. Thence, past Anaheim, a settlement of German wine-growers, we steamed on down a hundred miles farther, and halted at last at San Diego. A stiff breeze, freshening into a gale, and a rough swell, followed us into San Diego; but once inside the jaws of the harbor, we found the bay almost unruffled, while all outside was wild and threatening. The harbor, indeed, is quite land-locked, and after San Francisco is the finest on the Pacific Coast, below Puget Sound. But a few hundred yards in width at the entrance, it soon spreads out into a broad and handsome bay, one or two miles wide by ten or twelve long, and with a depth of water close in shore sufficient to float the largest vessels. A bold promontory running obliquely into the sea, as all the headlands on this coast do, shelters the harbor perfectly from all north and northwest winds, and contributes much to make San Diego what it is. In the old Mexican times, before the days of '49, San Diego was a leading Mission on the Coast, and the chief seaport of California, whence she shipped wool, hides, etc., and where she received supplies. San Francisco, gushing young metropolis now, was then only sterile Yerba Buena, and practically nowhere.* When the rush of miners to California came in '49, San Diego still held her own for awhile, quite courageously. The Panama steamers then touched here in going and coming. A large city was projected, and built—on paper, with "water-fronts," "corner-lots," and the like, quite *in extenso.* But there was no sufficient back country—no mines or agricultural resources to speak of—to support a town, and so in the end San Diego incontinently collapsed. Poor Derby of the engineers,

* In those days, it appears, the Jesuits had over a score of Missions in California, and some thirty thousand half civilized-Indians living in their communities. Their horned cattle numbered four hundred and twenty-four thousand; their horses, mules, and asses, besides the wild ones that scoured the plains in troops, sixty-two thousand five hundred; their sheep, goats, and swine, three hundred and twenty-one thousand; and the wheat, barley, maize, and other grains they raised measured one hundred and twenty-two thousand five hundred bushels annually. The richest in cattle and horses, and the greatest grain-producer, was San Gabriel, now a modest hamlet Next to it in everything else, and ahead of it in sheep, was San Luis Rey, now even modester, which also had the most Indians. The Mission Dolores, now San Francisco, stood low on the list, with its five hundred Indians shivering in the wind and fog, five thousand horned cattle, sixteen hundred horses and mules, four thousand sheep and swine, and other things in proportion.

immortal as John Phœnix, flourished here in those days, and afterwards used to say in his own inimitable style, he "Thanked heaven his lot was not cast in San Diego; it *had* been, but was sold for taxes!" We anchored off the old wharf, then fallen to decay, where in other days the Panama steamers had floated proudly, and after rowing well in were carried ashore on the shoulders of Mexican peons. The U. S. barracks and corral, now empty and without a watchman even, and a score or so of other buildings, were grouped near the landing, constituting New San Diego; but the main town, or Old San Diego, was three miles off up the bay. A rickety old ambulance, once U. S. property, but long since condemned and sold, carried us up to the town, where we spent several hours. Formerly numbering two or three thousand inhabitants, and a pretty stirring place, it now had only about two or three hundred, and was a good illustration of some of California's changes. Its buildings, of course, were all one-story adobe, but partly inhabited, and these were grouped about a squalid, Plaza, that reminded one of Mexico or Spain, rather than the United States. Being the county-seat, of course, it had a court-house and a jail—the one, a tumble-down adobe—the other, literally a cage, made of boiler-iron, six or seven feet square at the farthest. The day we were there three men were brought in, arrested for horse-stealing, or something of the sort; but as the jail would accommodate only two—crowded at that—the judge discharged the third, with an appropriate reprimand. At least, we supposed it "appropriate;" but as it was in Californicè, and the judge a native, we could make nothing of it. In hot weather, this iron jail-cage must be a miniature tophet; but, no doubt, it remains generally empty. On a hill just back of the town, commanding it and the harbor, were the remains of Fort Stockton, which our Jersey commodore of that name built and garrisoned with his gallant Jack-Tars, during the Mexican war, and held against all comers. Beyond it still, were the ruins of the old Mexican Presidio, with palm and olive trees scattered here and there, but all now desolate and forsaken. The general broken-down, dilapidated, "played out" appearance of the town, was certainly most forlorn. And yet, the San Diegoans, like all good Californians, had still a profound faith in their future, and swore by their handsome bay as stoutly as ever. They knew San Diego would yet be the western terminus of the Southern Pacific Railroad, whenever this got itself built; and with this, they fondly believed, would come population, prosperity, power (the three great *p's* of modern civilization), and come to stay. With the exception of a handful of Americans and Jews, engaged chiefly in merchandizing, the inhabitants consisted mainly of native Californians, in all stages of impecuniosity. Being steamer-day, several Americans—most of them ex-army officers—had galloped in from their neighboring ranches, some coming ten and twenty miles for this purpose, and all were as hospitable and warm-hearted, as men leading such a life usually are. They laughed and chatted over their California experiences, predicted great things for San Diego yet, and offered a hundred acres or more from their leagues-square ranches, to any American who would come and settle among them. All united in pronouncing the climate simply perfect, though a little warm in summer; and, I must say, it really seemed so, when we were there. They declared the thermometer never varied more than twenty degrees the year round, and maintained people never died there, except from the knife or bullet. When reminded of a Mr. S. who had died that morning, they replied, he came there too late—a confirmed consumptive; otherwise, he would have got well, and in the end have shrivelled up and evaporated, like the rest of their aged people.

As to business, the town really seemed to have none, except a little merchandizing and whiskey-drinking, and these only gave signs of life, because it was "steamer-day." The country immediately about the town was dull and barren, from want of water to irrigate and cultivate it. The great ranches were at a distance, and these depended on streams from the Coast Range, that mostly disappeared before reaching the harbor. Here horses, cattle, and sheep were raised in considerable numbers; but the breadth of valuable land was not considered large, and the population of the section seemed to be on the stand-still, if not decrease. A railroad from the Atlantic States, and another north to San Francisco, would of course soon change all this; but these were yet in the future. The splendid harbor, however, is there—the second as I have said, on the California Coast—and it will be passing strange, if the future does not evolve something, that will give it vitality and importance. Its noble waters, surely, cannot lie idle forever. With its superb anchorage and far-stretching shores, it seemed already the prophecy of great things to come, and I sincerely trust the San Diegoans may speedily realize them.*

Down by the mouth of the harbor, were several fishermen's huts, whose owners, it was said, gained a precarious living by whaling. Off the harbor, for miles

* Since the above was written, I believe, the Panama steamers have resumed their calls at San Diego, and doubtless the town is again looking up. So, also, the Arizona trade and travel now start mainly from here, and a railroad to the Colorado at least seems inevitable.

up and down the coast, we noticed a heavy growth of kelp or sea-weed, and this we were told the whales frequented in certain seasons of the year, as a feeding ground. We kept a sharp lookout for them, both coming down and returning; but were rewarded by seeing only a single dead one, which had been harpooned and left floating near shore, with a buoy attached. Capt. Thorne, of the *Orizaba*, reported these whales as quite numerous off the coast sometimes, and thought this business might readily be made much more lucrative, than it was.

Here at San Diego, we were about five hundred miles south of San Francisco, and less than one hundred and fifty from Fort Yuma. We had expected to find a stage thence to Fort Yuma; but the line had recently been withdrawn,* from want of business, and we were compelled to return again up the coast to San Pedro and Los Angelos. On the evening of Feb. 14th, we accordingly bade good-bye to San Diego, and the next morning, when we came on deck, found the Orizaba at anchor again off San Pedro. This, as I have before said, is the old seaport or landing for Los Angelos, and all the country about there, whence supplies were then wagoned into Arizona, Southern Nevada, and even Utah. The Salt Lake merchants, then barred from the East in winter by the heavy snows on the Rocky Mountains, were in the habit of eking out their stocks by purchases in San Francisco, which they shipped 400 miles down the coast to San Pedro, and from here wagoned them *via* San Bernardino and Cajon Pass, through Southern Nevada, 800 miles more to Great Salt Lake. Of course, the completion of the Pacific Railroad has changed all this. San Pedro itself, unfortunately, has no harbor, but

* See foot-note page 329.

is a mere open roadstead, where vessels may ride at anchor in fine weather, but when storms come must slip to sea. From here a slough or gut of the sea sets up to Wilmington, some six miles through a tide-water marsh, where we found a Mr. Phineas Banning doing his "level best"—and it was a big "best"—to build up a nascent city. Formerly, everything was lightered ashore at San Pedro; but recently, Mr. Banning had introduced steam-tugs, and with these at high tide he carried everything to Wilmington, where he had wharves, store-houses, shops, stages, wagon-trains, and about everything else, on a large scale. He was an enterprising Delawarean, but without much regard for "the eyes of Delaware;" had failed two or three times, but was still wide-awake and keen for business; had come to California a common stage-driver, but now ran lines of stages and freight-wagons of his own all over southern California and Arizona, for eight hundred and a thousand miles; had married a native señorita, with several leagues of land, and made her a good husband; was now state senator on the Republican side, and talked of for governor; and, in short, was a good second edition of Mr. Ben Holliday, yet without his bad politics. His town of Wilmington consisted of a hundred or two frame buildings, in true border style, with perhaps five hundred inhabitants, all more or less in his service, or employed at Drum Barracks, the U. S. military post there. A man of large and liberal ideas, with great native force of character and power of endurance, he was invaluable to Southern California and Arizona, and both of these sections owe him a debt of gratitude, which they never can repay. His "latch-string" was always out to all strangers in that latitude; there was no public interest with which he was not prominently identified; and from San Pedro to Tucson, and back again, *via* Prescott and Fort Mojave, through some fifteen hundred miles of border travel, there was scarcely a day in which we did not see his teams or stages, or touch his enterprises somewhere.

Here at Wilmington, in the village barber, we found another good illustration of the adaptativeness of the average American. Originally from Independence, Mo., he had emigrated thence to Oregon, thence to San Francisco, and thence to Wilmington. In Missouri, he was a farmer by occupation; in Oregon, a cattle-drover; in San Francisco, a teamster; in Wilmington, he was now regularly a barber, but occasionally cobbled shoes, or worked as a blacksmith, and on a pinch also practiced medicine. He had not preached, or edited a newspaper yet; but doubtless would have had no objection to trying his hand at either or both of these, should opportunity offer or necessity occur! But such men, after all, are our Representative Americans—real pioneers of empire and champions of civilization—and history will not forget to recognize and respect them accordingly.

Back of Wilmington, some thirty miles wide by seventy-five long, from the Pacific to the Mountains, stretch the great Los Angelos plains, than which there are few finer sights on the Coast, at the proper season. Just now they were green with herbage and gemmed with wild flowers in all directions, from the Mountains to the ocean, a perfect sea of verdure, with flocks and herds roaming over them at will, under the guidance of native rancheros. The latter, mounted on gamey little horses, full-blooded mustangs, with saddles that nearly covered their steeds, and tinkling spurs that almost swept the ground, galloped hither and yon as occasion needed, or lolled for hours on the ground, basking in the sun, while their cattle and sheep fed peacefully about them. The landscape one day, when Gen. Banning drove us over to Los Angelos, to see the vineyards and orange-groves there, with the Pacific rolling in the distance, the Mountains towerering before us, and the Plains stretching all about us, in green and purple and gold, was a perfect idyllic scene, which lingers in my memory yet, as one of the fairest recollections of a life-time. Just then, the marshes about Wilmington, and the Plains beyond, were a halting place for vast flocks of wild-geese, on their annual migration north, and they thronged the country in countless thousands. Off on the Plains, where they were feeding on the young and succulent grass, they whitened the ground sometimes for acres, and were so careless of danger, you might knock them over with a club. Gen. Banning said, they were even more numerous in former years, but even as they were, we had never seen anything to equal them. As we drove along, they rose up by the roadside in flocks of thousands, and fairly deafened the air with their multitudinous konkings. Further on, we found the grass rank and luxuriant, and it seemed impossible to believe, that when summer came, all this wealth of vegetation would wither up, and substantially blow away. Yet this seemed to be the fact—these broad and beautiful Plains, beneath their then rainless sky, becoming everywhere a barren desert, save where *acequias* (Mexican for "water-ditches") regularly irrigate and vitalize them.

We struck the acequias several miles out from Los Angelos, and followed them into the town, our road winding about among and crossing them several times. They are simply water-ditches, four or five feet wide by one deep, the same as those at Salt Lake, but most of them far older. They were begun a century ago, by the old Spanish Jesuits, who formerly had one of their largest and most flourishing Missions here, and are kept in repair and regulated by the city corporation—the water being farmed out, at fixed rates. Their source of supply is the Los Angelos river, a little stream that issues from the Coast Range some miles away, and sinks again, I believe, before reaching the ocean. If husbanded properly, with the same care exercised at Salt Lake, it might be made to irrigate many times the present breadth of land, it would seem; but as it is, it suffices to vitalize hundreds, if not thousands, of acres about the town, where they grow wheat, barley, oats, the grape, the orange, the lemon, citron, olive, peach, pear, and almost everything else, in great profusion and of the finest character. Along the road, and skirting all the main acequias, willows have been planted, and these growing rapidly serve for both fencing and fuel. Here and there wild flowers also have been planted, or have sprung up naturally among the hedges, and these shower their wealth of bloom and fragrance almost the year round. The robin, the blue-bird, the oriole, abounded here; and the whole air seemed vocal with song, as we whirled along through the suburbs, and up into the town.

Los Angelos itself proved to be a brisk and thriving town. It is the county-seat of a large county of the same name, and probably contained then some five thousand inhabitants—about one-third Americans and Europeans, and the balance native Californians and Indians. The Americans seemed to own most of the houses and lands, the Europeans—chiefly Jews—to do the business, the native Californians to do the loafing, and the Indians to perform the labor. It had mail communication with San Francisco twice a week by stage, and twice a month by steamer *via* San Pedro, and telegraphic communication *via* San Francisco with the whole coast and country.

It boasted two or three very fair hotels, a fine old Spanish church, and quite a number of brick and frame residences, that would have been called creditable anywhere. The town seemed steadily increasing in wealth and population, as more and more of the surrounding Plains were brought under cultivation, and already had a substantial basis for prosperity in its vineyards and fruit-orchards, aside from its flocks and herds. It was also doing a considerable business with Utah, Arizona, and Southern California, for all which regions it was then largely a mart and entrepot. Its climate was mild and equable, reminding one more of Italy and the Levant, than America, and already it was quite a resort for invalids from all parts of the Coast. Then in February, and again in May, when we returned there from Arizona, the air really seemed like the elixir of life, and quickened every sense into new life and power of enjoyment. As in all Spanish American towns, however, Sunday seemed to be the chief day for business and pleasure. A few stores and shops were closed; but the majority kept open, the same as any other day. The native Cailfornian and Indian population of the surrounding country flocked into town that day, in holiday attire and, after a brief service at the old church (dedicated "To the Queen of the Angels,") assembled in the Plaza, to witness their customary cock-fights. There were several of these, which men and women, priests and people—alike eager and excited—all seemed to enjoy; but to us, Eastern-bred, they seemed cruel and barbarous. The poor fowls pecked away at each other, until some fell dead, and others dropped exhausted, when the survivors were borne away in triumph.

A ride across the breezy Plains, ten miles to the south, brought us to the ranch and vineyard of Mr.

Ben. D. Wilson, noted over all the Coast for his excellent fruits and wines. "Don Benito" Wilson, he is called out there, and the name is a good one. Without much urban polish, he is nevertheless one of nature's noblemen, and a fine Representative Californian. A Tennessean by birth, long before the acquisition of California, he had hunted and trapped across the continent, living for years among the Utes and Apaches, and finally marrying a California señorita, with three leagues square of land, had settled down here. His noble ranch lies at the foot of the Coast Range of mountains, with their snow-clad summits towering above, the Los Angelos plains in front stretching away to the ocean, while an intervening roll of hills shuts out the raw winds and fogs of the summer and autumn. Two or three dashing rivulets, that issue from the mountains like threads of silver, have been caught up and carried by *acequias* all along the slopes, whence they are distributed wherever the thirsty soil in summer needs them. Here he has orange, lemon, peach, olive, almond, and English walnut groves, by the many acres, while beyond are his vineyards by the hundred acres—part planted by himself, but many a half century ago by the Jesuit Fathers. Just now, his vineyards, trimmed closely as they were, looked for all the world like a Delaware or Jersey field of old peach-trees, with the tops sawn off, as we sometimes see them here. Without trellis or support of any kind, these aged vines stood stiff and gnarled, in rows five or six feet apart, themselves about as many inches thick; but in summer, they throw out runners, that form a leafy wilderness, loaded down with the purpling clusters. In addition, he had great herds of horses, and cattle, and flocks of sheep by the thousand, that roamed over his outlying broad acres and the Los Angelos plains at will. In sauntering through his orange-groves, he showed us trees, from which he had gathered twenty-five dollars' worth of the golden fruit each, that season, and one that yielded him forty dollars' worth. A few of his oranges, dead ripe, were still gleaming amid the rich, deep green of their peculiar foliage, and we had some of these fresh and luscious on the table each meal we took with him. In his wine-cellars, back of the mansion, he showed us two hundred thousand gallons of wine, the product of that year's vintage alone, and it hadn't been much of a year for wine either. This he reported to be worth only fifty cents a gallon then, but as increasing in price, of course, with age. He made both white and red wine, of a superior brand, and had branch houses in San Francisco and New York, that disposed of the bulk of it at fair figures. It all had the peculiar sharpness and alcoholic qualities of the California wines generally; but, he thought, with more careful culture, and increasing age, their wines would improve in this respect. He computed the wine-product of California then, at not less than three millions of gallons annually, and rapidly increasing. The Mission grape was the one mostly grown, as yet; but he thought some foreign varieties, of a finer quality, would gradually supplant this. The white wines were the pure juice of the grape; the red the same, but with the color of the skins added. Farther North, the Sonoma and Sacramento wines were lighter and milder, resembling claret and hock; but these Los Angelos wines were heavy and strong, with a body like those of Spain, whence no doubt the Mission vines originally came. The expressed juice was first put into large casks, holding a hundred and forty gallons or more each, whence after due fermentation it was bottled and sent to market. He said at the end of a year and a half, the wine usually became clear and less alcholic; but it continued to mellow and soften with age for twenty years, when its delicacy of flavor and oiliness of consistency culminated. Brandy was made from indifferent or miscellaneous grapes, skins and all, and from what we saw of its effects, was as fierce and fiery a liquid, surely, as Jersey lightning, or Nebraska needle-gun.

Mr. Wilson lived rather plainly, in anything but a palatial mansion; but he had a fine library, well-selected, and took most of the leading magazines and newspapers, from San Francisco to Boston. We were really surprised at the extent and variety of his periodical literature. He said he had been intending for years to build himself a new house, on a grander scale; but the old one was very roomy and comfortable, and he had never found time to pull it down. We found him a very bright and intelligent old gentleman, well versed in the world's affairs, with an eye keenly alive to passing events both at home and abroad, notwithstanding his seclusion. He was a warm friend of Gen. Banning's; for they naturally comprehended, and appreciated each other, to the full.

Land just about Los Angelos, and adjacent to the acequias, was held at a good figure; but a few miles from the town, it was selling at only five and ten dollars per acre, and a great stock or fruit ranch, it would seem, could be built up here, at small expense, in a few years. The soil and climate are certainly all anybody could desire; the chief drawbacks seemed to be the absence of good schools and churches. These, however, will come with time and sufficient Yankees; and it is not too much to say, that the Plains and City of the Angels will yet become widely known, and well-peopled. California, rich in so many things, may yet well be vain of them.

CHAPTER XXI.

WILMINGTON TO FORT YUMA.

WE had intended to go by stage from Los Angelos to Fort Yuma, to save time, though we knew it would be a "weariness to the flesh;" but the route had just been changed there from San Diego, and as it would take a fortnight to transfer the stock, and get things to working smoothly again, we decided to proceed by ambulance. To this end, we returned to Wilmington, or Drum Barracks, the military post there, whence we left for Arizona, Feb. 19th. Our "outfit," furnished by the quartermaster there, consisted of a substantial vehicle, half-ambulance and half-Jersey wagon, loaned for the trip by Gen. Banning, equipped with four stout mules and a plucky driver. A fifth mule was also added, to meet contingencies; but this was only as a led mule. The vehicle was a contrivance of Gen. Banning's own, with a boot before and behind, capacious boxes under the seats, pockets for books and periodicals, slings for rifles, pistols, etc., which he was accustomed to use in his own long trips through Southern California and Arizona, looking after his widely extended business. Originally, we designed using this only as far as Fort Yuma; but afterwards it proved to be our home for two months, through fifteen hundred miles or more of long and desolate land-travel. A gentleman from San Francisco, connected with the Post-Office department, (Hon. B. T.), accompanied me, and relieved the tedium of many an hour by his rare wit and humor. Our baggage consisted only of a light valise and roll of blankets each, a box of writing-materials and official orders, a sack or two of barley and oats, and some packages of canned fruits and vegetables. For lodgings and provisions generally, we decided to depend on the scattered ranches and stage-stations, notwithstanding vague rumors we would be likely to "rough it," in doing so. With "Adios!" and "Good luck to you!" from broad-shouldered, big-hearted Gen. Banning, we rolled out of Wilmington one day toward noon; and crossing numerous sloughs and quicksands, past countless flocks of wild-geese, arrived the same evening at Anaheim.

Here we found quite a settlement of Germans, fresh from Rhineland, engaged chiefly in wine-making. It appears, they had clubbed together in San Francisco, and bought a thousand acres of the Los Angelos Plains, bordering on the Santa Anna river, whose waters they now used for irrigating purposes. This they divided into twenty-acre lots, with a town-plot in the centre and convenient streets, each lot-holder being also owner of a town-lot of half an acre besides. Here were some five hundred or more Germans, all industriously engaged, and exhibiting of course their usual sagacity and thrift. They had constructed acequias, and carried the hitherto useless Santa Anna river everywhere—around and through their lots, and past every door; they had hedged their little farms with willows, and planted them with vines, orange, lemon, and olive trees; and the once barren plains in summer were now alive with perpetual foliage and verdure. Of course, there had consequently been a great rise in values. The land had cost them only two dollars per acre in 1857; but now in 1867, it was rated at one hundred and fifty dollars, with none to sell. We drove through the clean and well-kept avenues or streets, scenting Rhineland on every side; and, indeed, this Anaheim itself is nothing but a bit of Germany, dropped down on the Pacific Coast. It has little in common with Los Angelos the dirty, but the glorious climate and soil, and was an agreeable surprise every way. We halted at the village-inn, which would have passed very well for a Wein-Haus in Fatherland, and were entertained very nicely. The proprietor was also the village-schoolmaster, and his frau was one of the brightest and neatest little house-keepers, we had seen on the Coast. They gave us bologna sausage and native wine for supper, as well as excellent tea; and when bed time came, we were conducted to apartments unimpeachable every way. In the course of the evening, half the village seemed to drop in for a sip of wine or glass of beer (they kept both, of course), and the guest-room became so thick with smoke, you could have cut it with a knife. The next morning they gave us some wine for our trip, five years old, that had lost much of its alcoholic properties, and so soft and oily, it would have passed for tolerable Hockheimer, or even Johannisberger, almost anywhere.

Here we bade good-bye to civilization, and at last were fairly off for Arizona. The distance from Wilmington to Yuma is about three hundred miles, and we hoped to make it in ten days at the farthest. We got an early start from Anaheim, and crossing the Santa Anna river through a congeries of quicksands rode all day, with the Coast Range to the right of us, and another serrated ridge ten or twelve miles off to the left, through what was mostly an arid and sterile plain, though here and there it was broken up into ravines and "arroyas," or dry water-courses, abounding in cottonwood and live-oaks. Just at sunset, we crossed a divide, and before us lay a sheet of water, five miles long by two wide, reposing like a sea of silver, skirted by wide plateaus, and these in turn flanked by outlying ranges of mountains. This was Laguna Grande, the pet lake of all that region. Draining a wide extent of country, it always remains a large body of water, though in summer much of it disappears, and the balance becomes brackish from alkali. It continues palatable, however, for horses and cattle, and accordingly here we found a great hacienda, one of the largest south of Los Angelos. The proprietors were two brothers Machado, who here owned leagues square of land, from the summit of one mountain range to the other, including the Laguna. They lived in a rude adobe hut, with three rooms, that no common laborer East would think of inhabiting; but they numbered their live-stock by the thousand, and esteemed their rude home a second paradise. They raised a little barley and some beans on a few acres, bordering on the lagoon; but devoted the great bulk of their broad acres to stock-raising. Señor Dolores Machado met us at the door, as we drove up; but as he could speak no English, and we no Spanish, there seemed to be a predicament. Before leaving Los Angelos, we had anticipated this, knowing the old Mexican or Spanish-speaking population still prevailed over most of Southern California and Arizona, and had provided ourselves with "Butler's method of learning to speak Spanish quickly," accordingly. We had conned this over several days, selecting the phrases that would apparently be most useful, and now assailed Señor Machado with everything we could summon. Imagine our disgust, when he looked wild at our attempted Spanish, and responded to every phrase, "No sabe, Señors!" Our driver, Worth, at last came to our rescue, with some mongrel Spanish he had picked up, when soldiering formerly down in Arizona; and when Señor M. understood we only wanted entertainment for the night, he smilingly replied, "O, Si! Señors! Si! Si!" "Yes! Yes!" with true Castilian grace, and invited us into his abode. He gave us a rough but substantial meal, of coffee, frejoles, and mutton; and when bedtime came, allowed us the privilege of spreading our blankets on the softest part of the only board floor in the house. He and his wife occupied a rude bed in one corner of the same room, while his brother slept on one in another. There was not, and never had been, a pane of glass in the house, notwithstanding they were such large-landed proprietors. The breeze stole in at the broken shutter, that closed the only window in the room, and all night long we could count the stars through the dilapidated roof.

Thence to Buena Vista, we passed through a succession of small valleys, between the same general mountain ranges before mentioned. Though wanting in water, yet these all had small streams of some sort flowing through them, which if carefully husbanded could be made to irrigate thousands of fertile acres all through here. Cottonwoods occurred frequently, and along many of the bottoms there was a goodly growth of scrubby live-oaks, that looked particularly green and inviting amidst those arid landscapes. Buena Vista valley seemed to be the outlet of several others, all of which might be largely reclaimed, with proper industry and effort. The soil is rich, the water there, and the climate matchless apparently the year round. Warner's Ranch stands in the midst of Buena Vista valley, and consists only of an adobe hut or two, that answer for grocery and road-side inn. We were detained here a day, by a severe rain that set in at nightfall, just after our arrival, and continued for twenty-four hours; but as it gave us and our team a bit of rest, we did not greatly regret it. Thence to Villacito, the valley opened broader and wider, and the grand San Bernardino peak—which day after day had dominated the landscape off to the north—its outlines sharply defined against that exquisite sky—dropped gradually out of sight.

Here we struck the southern California or great Colorado Desert, and thence on to Yuma—one hundred and fifty miles—we might as well have been adrift on the Great Sahara itself. Until we reached this point, the country consisted chiefly of arid plains, it is true; but broken, more or less, into ravines and valleys, with some semblance of life, or at least capacity for supporting life hereafter, should sufficient intelligence and labor ever drift that way. But as we approached the Desert, all this ceased, and the very genius of desolation seemed to brood over the landscape. We descended into it through a narrow rocky cañon, so rough and precipitous, that T. and I both got out and walked down, leaving the driver to navigate the empty ambulance to the foot, the best he could. Jolting and jumping from rock to gully, now half upset, with wheels spinning in the air, and now all right again, he got down safe and whole at last, and we augured well of our wheels and springs, after such a rugged experience.

Quitting Villacito, we found the road sandy and heavy, the air sultry and hot, and the nearest water eighteen miles off at Carissa Creek. The country was one dreary succession of sand and gravel, barren peaks and rocky ridges, with arroyas now and then, but no signs of humidity anywhere. It was not, however, such a perfect desert, as we had anticipated; for here and there were clumps of chemisal, mescal, and cactus, and these somewhat relieved the general dreariness of the landscape, poor apologies as they are for trees and shrubbery. The chemisal grows in clumps, something like our alder-bushes east, but with rods straighter and slenderer, bearing a pale-green leaf. The mescal seems to be a bastard variety of aloes, much similar to what is popularly known as Eve's Thread, though on a larger scale. The Mexicans and Indians distil a villainous liquor from it, which they also call "Mescal," that is worse in its effects than even fusil-oil or strychnine-whiskey. The cacti appeared to be of several varieties—many the same as we have in conservatories east, but all vastly larger here. The flora, as we proceeded southward, constantly became sparser and thornier; but the fauna continued about the same—the chief species being jack-rabbits and California quails — the latter a very handsome variety, with top-knots, never seen east. The rabbits were numerous, and the quails whirred across our road in coveys quite frequently, until we were well into the Desert, when both mainly disappeared. We reached Carissa Creek, with its welcome though brackish water, about 2 P. M.; but as it was thirty-three miles yet to the next certain water, at Laguna, with only uncertain wells between (dug by the Government), concerning which we could get no definite information, we concluded to halt there till morning.

From there on, the first few miles were about the same as the day before. Then we ascended an abrupt bluff, that looked in the distance like an impassable castellated wall, and suddenly found ourselves on an elevated *mesa* or table-land, the very embodiment of dreariness and desolation. On all sides, it was a vast, outstretched plain, of coarse sand and gravel, without tree, or shrub, or living thing—even the inevitable mescal and cactus here disappeared. Behind us, to the north and east, there was a weird succession of grand terraces and castellated mountains, reminding one of portions of Wyoming. On our right, to the west, the ever-present Coast Range loomed along the landscape, barren and ghostly. To the south, all was a dead level, panting and quivering beneath the sun, as he neared the zenith, except where here and there a heavy mirage obscured the view, or vast whirlwinds careered over the desert, miles away—their immense spirals circling upward to the very sky. These last, on first sight, we took for columns of smoke, so erect and vast were they. But soon they rose all along the southwestern horizon, one after another, like mighty genii on the march, and our driver bade us look out for a Yuma sand-storm. We had already here and there found the sand drifted into ridges, like snow-banks, where sand-storms had preceded us, and had heard ugly accounts of them before leaving Wilmington; but, fortunately, we escaped this one—the whirlwinds keeping away to the southwest, where they hugged the Coast Range, and in the course of the afternoon obscured the whole landscape there. This was now the Colorado or Yuma Desert in earnest, without bird, or beast, or bush, or sign of life anywhere—nothing, in fact, but barrenness and desolation, as much as any region could well be. A large portion of it is so low, that the overflow of the Colorado often reaches it during spring freshets, and remains for weeks. In travelling over this portion, now baked dry and hard beneath the sun, we had frequent exhibitions of mirage, on a magnificent scale. One day in particular, we had been driving since early morning, over a heavy sandy road, with the sun blazing down upon us like a ball of fire, with no water since starting, our poor mules panting with heat and thirst, when long after noon we observed—apparently a mile or so ahead—what seemed like a great outspread pond or lake, with little islands here and there, their edges fringed with bushes, whose very images appeared reflected in the water. The scene was so perfect, that the driver and T. both insisted it must be water; however, I inclined to believe it mirage, as it afterwards turned out, but the optical illusion was so complete in this and other instances, that when later in the day we really did approach a veritable sheet of water at the Laguna, we all of us mistook this for mirage also. Here, however, we found a body of water a mile long by half a mile wide, surrounded by a rank growth of coarse grass, and covered with water-fowl—a perfect oasis in the desert. This was also a part of the overflow of the Colorado, there being a depression in the Desert just here, which holds the water like a cup. The quantity is so large, that it lasts for two seasons; but after that, is apt to dry up, if the overflow does not come. But as this usually happens every year, this Laguna (Spanish for *lagoon* or *lake*) becomes a perfect god-send to the traveller here. On its southern margin, a Mr. Ganow from Illinois had established a ranch, and already was acquiring a comfortable home. His horses and cattle found ample subsistence in the brakes, on the borders of the lagoon, and the passing travel to and from California and Arizona made him considerable patronage in the course of the year.

Thence past Alamo to Pilot Knob, where we rounded the corner of the mountains, and struck the valley proper of the Colorado, the country continued more or less an unbroken desert. The roads were heavy and dusty, the air hot and stifling, the landscape barren and monotonous; and when, at last, we made Pilot Knob and struck the river, eight or ten miles below Fort Yuma, we rejoiced heartily, that the first stage of our tour was so nearly over. The Colorado flowed by our side, red and sluggish, but of goodly volume; the breeze came to us cool and moist across its broad bosom; and as we neared the post, the garrison-flag floating high in air seemed to beckon us onward, and welcome us beneath its folds. Starting long before daylight, and lying by in the middle of the day, we had driven fifty-three miles that day, over a country that equals, if it does not surpass Bitter Creek itself (see p. 150–3); and when at last we drew rein at Fort Yuma, we were thoroughly jaded ourselves, and our poor animals quite fagged out. We had made the distance from Wilmington in nine driving days, instead of ten; but they seemed the longest we had ever driven.

Of the intervening country as a whole, especially from Villacito, it may justly be said, not only is it practically a desert, but even what streams it has seem to be slowly but surely disappearing. There were evidences frequently, that the country had formerly been much better watered than now, and the population—sparse as it was—appeared to be diminishing. After leaving Anaheim, there was only a scattered ranch here and there, every ten or twelve miles apart, of the rudest character—sometimes not even these—where coarse groceries, canned fruits and vegetables, and whiskey and mescal, were kept for sale to Indians and passing travellers. These had mostly been stage-stations on the great Butterfield Overland Route before the war, and when this broke that up, these ranchmen still remained, hoping something would "turn up." The station at Carissa Creek was a good representative of this, and likewise of many others. "Carissa

Creek" itself is one of southern California's "blind" streams, like so many in Arizona, beginning and ending nowhere in particular—without either source or mouth apparently. Issuing from a sand-heap, it terminates in another a few miles away; but just here at the station is a shallow creek—a few yards wide, by six inches deep—tainted, of course with alkali. The station itself is the adobe remains of an old stage-station, whose roof was all gone, and as a substitute the enterprising proprietor had thrown some poles across, and covered them with willows and coarse grass. This turned the sun somewhat, and the easy-going proprietor said, "'Twer'nt no use, no how, to roof agin rain; 'cause, you bet, stranger, no rain ever gits yer!" His forlorn structure, part of which was used for a chicken-roost, also served its owner as bar-room, grocery, kitchen, parlor, bed-room, etc., and yet contained only one rude apartment, altogether.

"Mine host" here was a Texan, who somehow had strayed away out here, and dropped down at Carissa Creek—he hardly knew how. He "didn't think it much of a place, that's a fact; no how, stranger! But then, you see, I'm yer; and it's a heap of trouble to move elsewhar! Besides, yer know, I couldn't recommend nobody else to buy me out, no how! Somebody has got to live at Carissa Creek, anyhow; and why not me?" His philosophy, under the circumstances, seemed delicious, worthy of Mr. Mark Tapley himself, and, of course, we had not the heart to disturb it.

For meals and lodgings *en route*, we did indeed have to "rough it" pretty generally, nearly everywhere—especially after passing Villacito. Salt pork fried, saleratus biscuit hot, and coffee plain, came again into vogue, as in the famous Bitter Creek region; but we supplemented them this time with some excellent canned fruits and vegetables, that we had the foresight to bring along. Our evenings usually ended in long "yarns," after which, spreading our blankets in the hay-corral, or on a sand-heap, we went cosily to sleep beneath the stars. We always slept with our revolvers under our heads, and our rifles by our sides; and though a bit nervous sometimes when we reflected how much we were at the mercy of the rough customers we met *en route*, yet we slept well, and went through safely.

At Porte de la Cruz, before reaching the Desert, we passed an Indian village; but they all seemed quiet and peaceable. They belonged to the Dieganos, a tribe extending from the Coast Range to the Colorado, and wandering over much of the country we had passed through. A score or more of them lay basking in the sun, as we drove by, and they seemed to be about as helpless and idiotic a people, as human nature could well furnish. They are said to subsist chiefly on snakes, lizards, grasshoppers, mescal, etc., and appeared to be worse off than any Red Skins we had encountered yet. At Laguna, in the midst of the Desert, we chanced upon another party of them. As we drove up to Mr. Ganow's, the station-keeper there, we observed quite a crowd of them running around the corner of the lagoon, and making for the station. We supposed, at first, that our arrival was the sensation that attracted them; but as they drew nearer, we saw they were angry and excited, and Mr. Ganow presently explained, that one of them had been robbed of a knife and a silver dollar by a white man at Indian Wells—some four miles farther on—and, when afterwards he remonstrated, the white man had tied him up and flogged him. The poor wretch, still bruised and bleeding, now came with twenty or thirty of his comrades, from their camp beyond the Laguna, to Mr. Ganow—to report the outrage and seek redress. Ganow said the white man referred to was a mean fellow, bad enough for anything, who made a living chiefly by gambling with the Indians, and selling them mescal and needle-gun whiskey, and that he kept the countryside in a constant turmoil. He advised his copper-colored friends to return to the Wells, and demand their property again, and say a U. S. officer was at his ranch, and would be along next day and look after him, if he did not give it up. This seemed to satisfy them, and they all started off on a long trot, kicking a ball before them as they ran, and were soon out of sight. One of them, rejoicing in the name of Charley, was dressed in cast-off army-clothing, and spoke broken-English pretty well. We gave him a handful of cigarritos and matches, in return for his broken talk, and he went trotting off with the rest.

That night we spread our blankets as usual, in the corral, at the foot of a hay-stack, and before going to sleep fell to talking about this affair, and its possible consequences—perhaps even to Ganow and his family themselves. He had a smart wife and two bright children, and it seemed strange a man like him would expose them thus, in such a remote and dangerous locality. From this we strayed to other topics, and talked far into the night, as was often our wont on this trip—the stars were so brilliant, and the night-air so inviting. Near midnight, while T. was spinning one of his longest yarns, and I was lazily listening—on my back, with my hands under my head, and knees at an angle—suddenly an Indian, half naked, loomed up just at our feet, with bow and arrows in hand, and a revolver at his waist. To seize my Spencer was the work of an instant, and the next I demanded:

"Who's there? What do you want this time of night?"

T. stopped talking, and quickly fished up his revolver from the hay, not seeing the Red Skin till after I challenged him. Back jumped the Indian, exclaiming excitedly:

"Ugh! No shoot! Me friend! Me Charley!"

"Well, what are you doing here at this hour? What do you want now?"

"Me been down to Indian Wells. 'Tother fellow got him knife and dollar. Good! Dieganos much friend to Gen-e-ral. Heap!"

"Well, then, Charley, why don't you go home, with the others? What are you loafing here for?"

"Me been playin' cards, till now! Charley gamble a heap! *Mucho! O mui mucho!* Lost all. Coat, hat, shirt, all gone. Me beggar now; got nothing. Charley want Gen-er-al and fat friend (T. *was* a little stout) give him one dollar. Win um all back, quick! Heap more!"

We pitied the poor fellow, but bade him leave till morning. He still lingered, reluctant to go, but presently walked slowly off muttering to himself, and we both became uneasy, as we knew there were a hundred savages close within his call. However, after lying awhile undisturbed, we concluded there was no use borrowing trouble, and T. agreed to keep watch, if I would try to sleep. Once or twice he woke me up with a "hist," and we fancied we heard the stealthy tread of Red Skins about us; but none molested us, and morning broke at last much to our relief. We breakfasted and were off too early for Indian habits, so that Charley missed his "dollar," after all; but we left him a plentiful supply of matches and "smoke-tobacco," which doubtless served him far better. This experience, altogether, was rather exciting at the time; and it is not too much to say, that our friend Charley just escaped getting a bullet or two through him.

As to travel, we met but little, and this was chiefly Mexicans *en route* to California. At Carissa Creek, as we drove up, we found quite a party of these, resting there during the heat of the day. The men were lounging about the station, or sleeping in the sand; the women, washing clothes in the little creek. Their animals—a heterogeneous herd of horses, mules, and bronchos—were browsing by the roadside, on chemisal, mescal, or whatever they could pick up. The entire party consisted of imperialists, who were now fleeing from the vengeance of the just triumphant liberals in Sonora. When Maximilian first came, the liberals had to leave; but now Juarez was in the ascendant, and the imperialists had Hobson's choice of emigration or the halter. Our host there said, that in the past four months about twelve hundred imperialists had passed California-ward, while during the same period only about two hundred liberals had returned Sonora-ward; so that California seemed to be the gainer, by this exodus. We essayed some talk with the party, in our hobbling Spanish, which daily improved, and one who seemed to be the leader responded, as follows:

"Si, Senor! Imperialists we, all; Maximiliani! Sonora no good place for imperialists now, Jesu, no! Liberals just take one knife, this way (and he drew his hand significantly across his throat); or one lariat, this way (and he twirled his fingers around his head); or else, one carabina—bang! Carahu! We vamose to California!"

He said this, with such wild grimaces and mad gesticulations, as only a Mexican can achieve; and presently, to our delight, the whole banditti cut-throat looking crew moved off, with a friendly chorus of "Adios! Senors! Adios!"

The few Americans we met *en route*—but a handful—all reported themselves as going "inside," and smiled at us bound "outside." By *inside*, of course, they meant California and civilization; by *outside*, Arizona and something else! Of all the Borderisms we had heard yet, these seemed the strangest, until we got well "outside" ourselves, and thoroughly comprehended them; and then they appeared the aptest, indeed, of any. How much so, this chapter suggests in part already; and others will further disclose, when we get well into Arizona. "Inside" and paradise, "outside" and purgatory—these were the opposing ideas constantly expressed, and we learned not to wonder at them.

CHAPTER XXII.

FORT YUMA TO TUCSON.

FORT YUMA is popularly believed to be in Arizona, but is in reality in the extreme southeastern corner of California. The fort itself stands on a high bluff, on the west bank of the Rio Colorado, which alone separates it from Arizona, and is usually occupied by two or three companies of U. S. troops. Directly opposite, on the east bank of the Colorado, stands Arizona City, a straggling collection of adobe houses, containing then perhaps five hundred inhabitants all told. Here and at Yuma are located the government store-houses, shops, corrals, etc., as the grand depot for all the posts in Arizona. Hence, considerable business centres here; but it is chiefly of a military nature, and if the post and depot were removed, the "City" as such would speedily subside into its original sand-hills. Being at the junction of the Gila and Colorado, where the main route of travel east and west crosses the latter, it is also the first place of any importance on the Colorado itself; and hence would seem to be well located for business, if Arizona had any business to speak of. The distance to the mouth of the Colorado is one hundred and fifty miles, whence a line of schooners then connected with San Francisco two thousand miles away *via* the Gulf of California. From the head of the Gulf, light-draught stern-wheel steamers ascend the Colorado to Yuma, and occasionally to La Paz, and Fort Mojave or Hardyville—one hundred and fifty, and three hundred miles, farther up respectively. Sometimes they had even reached Callville, some six hundred miles from the Gulf, but this was chiefly by way of adventure, as there was no population or business sufficient to justify such risks ordinarily.

The Rio Colorado itself, or the great Red River of the west, although rising even beyond Fort Bridger, in the very heart of the continent, and draining with its tributaries the whole western slope of the Rocky Mountains for two thousand miles, was yet pronounced an unnavigable stream, after the first few hundred miles, and rather a hard river to navigate even that distance. Much of the way it runs through a comparatively rainless region in summer, and the last few hundred miles it ploughs its course along through a sandy alluvium, where its channel is constantly shifting, and sand-bars everywhere prevail. The tiny river-steamers reported the channel never in the same place for a week together, and they always tied up when night came, for fear of running ashore or grounding in the darkness. The current, moreover, was usually very swift; so that between the sand and water together, voyaging on the Colorado was regarded generally as a slow kind of business. These boats usually took from three days to a week, to make the one hundred and fifty miles, from the mouth of the river to Arizona City, and from ten to twenty days more to ascend to Hardyville—three hundred miles farther—whence, however, they descended to the Gulf again, with water and sand both to help them, in a tithe of the time. In all, there were three boats then on the Colorado, supported chiefly by a contract they had to transport government stores. Without this, there was not enough travel or freight, apparently, to keep even one running, though it was hoped the development of mines in Arizona would soon make business more brisk.

As a means of a water communication, from the Gulf of California into the very heart of the continent, it would seem, that this great river ought to have become more useful to cizilization, than it has. But the difficulties of navigating it, even to Callville, were reported great; and beyond that, was the insuperable obstacle of the Big Cañon of the Colorado, which nobody then knew anything about, except as a geographical mystery, but which Prof. Powell has since explored so gallantly. At Yuma, the river was a turbid, rolling flood, broad and deep; and, judging by what we saw of it there, it would seem, that steamers of proper draught and build ought to be able to stem its current, and be of great service hereafter to all the upper country. The rates then current on the river were as follows: From the mouth of the Colorado to Yuma or Arizona City, 150 miles, twenty-dollars per ton, coin; to La Paz, 300 miles, forty dollars per ton; to Fort Mojave or Hardyville, 450 miles, sixty dollars per ton. The rates from San Francisco to the mouth of the river, some 2000 miles, were then from twelve to fifteen dollars per ton, coin, besides; so that every load of freight put down at Arizona City or Hardyville, cost say thirty-five dollars and seventy-five dollars per ton, coin, respectively, for transportation alone. This may have been good business for the transportation companies; but it was death to mining, and other private enterprises, and operated practically as a prohibition to business, over most of the country there, It made Arizona substantially inaccessible, to population and trade, by this route (and there was no other so advantageous), and the whole country was hoping against hope, with prayers without ceasing, for a sometime oncoming railroad.

March 2d, while still at Arizona City, inspecting the depot there, we saw something of a Yuma sand-storm. The whirlwinds we had observed in the distance, when crossing the Colorado Desert a day or two before, seemed to have been only its precursors. It struck Yuma on the 2d, and promised to be only a passing blow, lulling away at eventide; but on the 3d, it resumed its course, with increased violence, and all day long rolled and roared onward furiously. We had heard much of these Yuma sand-storms, and on the whole were rather glad to see one, disagreeable as it proved. The morning dawned, hot and sultry, without a breath of air anywhere. Along about 9 A. M., the wind commenced sweeping in from the Desert, and as it increased in power uplifted and whirled along vast masses of sand, that seemed to trail as curtains of tawny gossamer from the very sky. As yet, it was comparatively clear at Yuma, and we could see the sweep and whirl of the storm off on the Desert, as distinctly as the outlines of a distant summer shower. But, subsequently, the Desert itself seemed to be literally upborne, and sweeping in, on the wings of the wind. The heavens became lurid and threatening. The sun disappeared, as in a coppery fog. The landscape took on a yellowish, fiery glare. The atmosphere became suffocating and oppressive. Towards noon, the wind rose to a hurricane; the sand, if possible, came thicker and faster, penetrating into every nook and cranny; the air became absolutely stifling, until neither man nor beast could endure it passably. People kept within doors, with every window closed, and animals huddled in groups with their noses to the ground, as if the only place to breathe. As night approached, the tempest gradually ceased, as if it had blown itself out; but it followed us on a minor scale, for a day or two afterwards, as we journeyed up the Gila. The ill-defined horror, and actual suffering of such a day, must be experienced to be appreciated. Out on the Desert, in the midst of the storm, the phenomenon no doubt would amount much to the same thing as the simooms of the Sahara. Travellers or troops caught in these sand-storms have to stop still, and instances are not rare where persons have lost their lives, in attempting to battle with them. They obliterate all signs of a road, where they actively prevail, whirling the sand into heaps and ridges, like New England snow-drifts; and the next travellers, who chance along, have either to go by the compass, or employ a guide, who understands the lay of the mountains, and country generally. Col. Crittenden, of the 32d Infantry, who crossed the Desert with a portion of his command some time after, was detained two days by such a storm, and his men suffered greatly, especially for want of water.

These sand-storms, it appears, are pretty much the only *storms* they ever get at Yuma, and they would not be unwilling there to dispense with even these. In the spring and summer, they frequently prevail there, sweeping in from the south and southwest, and it is not too much to say, that they are simply execrable. They have done much to make the name of Fort Yuma proverbial on the Pacific Coast, as the hottest place in the Union; and in San Francisco there was a story current about a soldier, who died at Yuma in a customary spree, and of course went to tophet. Subsequently, however, the story ran, his ghost came back for his blankets, because as alleged he had found the climate there much *colder* than Yuma—a sort of Alaska to California! The Post stands on a high gravel bluff, facing to the east and south, exposed to the blazing sun throughout the day; and, consequently, becoming saturated through and through with heat, retains it for months together. Hence, in the summer months, for weeks together, the thermometer there ranges from 100° to 125° in the shade, and the chief end of the garrison becomes an effort to keep cool, or even tolerably so. A tour of duty there was commonly regarded on the Coast, as a kind of banishment to Botany Bay; and yet we found the officers a very clever set of gentlemen, and spent some days there quite delightfully. Col. W., the commandant, proved to be an old acquaintance of the Army of the Potomac; and Dr. J., the surgeon, an old school-mate.

The Post here was established about 1857 to overawe the Yumas, then a stalwart and numerous tribe of Indians, occupying both banks of the Colorado for a hundred miles or more. Though much reduced, they still numbered over a thousand souls; and physically speaking, were the finest specimens of aborigines we had seen yet. They cultivate the river-bottoms to some extent, and raise barley, wheat, beans, melons etc.—for their surplus of which, when any, they find a ready market at Fort Yuma and Arizona City. Some chop wood for the river-steamers, and others indeed we found employed on the steamers themselves, as deck-hands, firemen, etc. Altogether, these Yümas seemed to have more of the practical about them, than any savages we had met yet, and no doubt they might be saved to the race for generations to come, were proper efforts made to protect and care for them. They had been peaceable for years, and scores of them thronged the Post and the depot, every day we were there. The men wore only a breech-cloth, with long ends fluttering fore and aft; the women but little more, though some of them affected a rude petticoat. Both sexes, as a rule, were naked from the waist up, and many of each were superb specimens of humanity; but all seemed corrupted and depraved, by contact with the nobler white race. The open and unblushing looseness and licentiousness of the riff-raff of Arizona City, with these poor Indians, was simply disgusting, and it is a disgrace to a Christian government to tolerate such orgies, as frequently occur there, under the very shadow of its flag. Great blame attaches to the army, in former years, for ever admitting these poor creatures within the precincts of the Post there at all. Some time before, it was said, the commanding officer sent for Pasquol, their head-chief, and bade him order his squaws away.

"*My* squaws?" he indignantly responded; "no *my* squaws now! White man's squaws! Before white man come, squaws good—stay in wigwam—cook—fish—work in field—gather barley—heap good. But now squaws about Fort all day—City all night—and Yumas no want 'em. White man made squaws a heap bad. White man keep 'em!"

And with this, old Pasquol, a stately old savage, wrapped his blanket about his shoulders, and strode haughtily away. As far as we could learn, there had never been a missionary, or teacher of any kind, among these poor Yumas; and to all who feel a call in that direction, we would suggest the place as a superb field, for earnest missionary work. Will not some of our religious organizations, now that they have got the Red Man so fully in their hands, make a note of this, and try to look a little after these splendid savages, degraded though they be, as well as the Cheyennes and Sioux, and other more eastern tribes?

At Fort Yuma we overhauled Gov. McCormick and

wife, who had left San Francisco in advance of us, and who were now about to leave for Prescott, then the capital of Arizona. On reflection, however, rather than lose such good company, they decided to journey with us to Tucson, and thence somewhat back to Prescott; whence we designed returning to Los Angelos again, *via* Fort Mojave. Accordingly, we left Arizona City, March 4th, our route lying up the Gila easterly two hundred miles to Maricopa Wells, and thence southerly one hundred miles to Tucson, the oldest and most considerable town in the Territory, and now again the capital. Much as we had "roughed it," while *en route* from Wilmington to Fort Yuma, according to all reports we would have to rough it much worse before reaching Tucson, if we trusted to the wayside ranches; and, therefore, before setting out, we secured a joint cook, and provided ourselves with a tolerable larder. Our "outfit" consisted of two four-mule ambulances, into which and outside we stowed and strapped ourselves, baggage, rations, forage, cooking utensils, etc., as best we could. Expecting to "camp-out" at night, we also took along two extra wagon-sheets, to pitch as tents, if necessary; but never found occasion to use them, except as beds, beneath those exquisite skies. There was no cavalry then at Yuma, and the road as far as Maricopa Wells being reported comparatively safe, we decided to proceed thither without escort, depending upon our own courage and vigilance. Nevertheless, we took the precaution before starting to arm our cook and both drivers with Springfield muskets, while we ourselves were equipped with a Spencer or Remington rifle apiece, as well as our revolvers.

With a host of "adios" and "good-byes," from our Yuma friends, we swung out of Arizona City late that morning, through sand knee-deep, and thus were fairly off for Tucson. The roads proved heavy all that day, and the remains of the sand-storm kept us company; yet we succeeded in making thirty-one miles, and went into camp before night-fall on the banks of the Gila. Some twenty miles out we passed Gila City, consisting of two adobe huts and an abandoned mine, then famous as the spot where Gen. McD., and some San Francisco friends, had recently made rather "permanent investments." Thence on to Maricopa Wells, indeed all the way from Arizona City, the road ascends the south bank of the Gila, and confines itself pretty closely to it, except here and there where it strikes across the mesas, to avoid some bend in this most tortuous of streams. The Gila itself ordinarily is an insignificant river, apparently famed more for quicksands than water; but just now its banks were full with the spring freshet, and its usual fords dangerous if not impassable. Its valley is of uncertain breadth, from one to five miles, though its river bottoms—its only really valuable land—are of course much narrower. Beyond the valley, on either side, are high mesas or plateaus, covered often with barren volcanic rocks, like the table-lands of Idaho; and, beyond these still, are substantial mountain-ranges. The range on the north, day after day, was a constant wonder and delight. Instead of ridges and peaks, it seemed to be rather a succession of domes, and towers, and castellated ramparts, sharp and well-defined against a peerless sky, chief among which was Castle Dome—a superb dome-like mountain, that dominated the landscape for two or three days together. These dome-shaped mountains are a feature of Arizona, and abound everywhere in the Territory, especially in the northern part of it.

As already intimated, we found the Gila very high and still rising. In several places, it had just washed the banks away, destroying the road, and we had to pick our way across the bottoms, through the chemisal and mesquite, to the connecting part, the best we could. In this way, it seems, its channel is constantly shifting, and this was said to be one of the chief drawbacks to constructing acequias, and cultivating its fine bottom lands by irrigation. The head of an acequia to-day, tapping the river well, a month hence may be three feet or more out of water, and then all the work of excavating ditches, damming the river, etc., has to be done over again. The bed of the Gila itself, in the main, seems to be pure quicksand. At one point, a station-keeper showed us where a year before piles had been driven down fifty feet, in making a wing-dam to divert a portion of the river into an acequia; but at the first freshet, the cross currents had underbored everything, and left the head of the acequia high and dry. No doubt the river-bottoms are all exceedingly fertile, and would produce well, if irrigated; but not otherwise. Of these, there is a considerable breadth, at many points along the Gila, and, here and there, there had been some attempts at cultivation, but scarcely any worth mentioning.

These bottoms nearly everywhere abound with bunch-grass and mesquite-timber—the one the delight of horses and cattle, the other invaluable in that treeless region. The mesquite has but little height; but its trunk is often two and three feet in diameter, though only about as many high, from which point it throws out great, sturdy, black, gnarled limbs for a distance of thirty or forty feet all around. We saw many of them, that I think could not have been more than five or six feet in height, the bend of the branches included; nevertheless, with their crooked and gnarled limbs, they sprawled over the ground for a diameter of fully seventy-five or one hundred feet. At first they strike you as dwarfs, puny in aspect and purpose; but afterwards, as stunted giants, massive in strength and power, writhing in very anguish, because unable to tower higher. For lumber purposes, the mesquite amounts to but little; but for fuel, it is invaluable, and the future settlers on the Gila will prize it highly. It occurs pretty much all through Arizona, on the best river-bottoms, and everywhere seems a providential institution. It makes a fire-wood scarcely inferior to oak or hickory, and bears a bean besides, which constitutes a large part of the subsistence of the Mexicans and the Indians there. These mesquite beans make a very sweet and palatable dish, and horses, mules, cattle, etc. are especially fond of them. The Mexicans we met *en route* to California, were subsisting upon them almost entirely, and subsequently in wandering through a Pimo village, we found them in every storehouse. A Pimo belle, for a bundle of cigarritos, cooked us a dish of them, and we have eaten worse things in New York and Washington. Said an old Arizonian one day, "Wherever you see mesquites, strangers, look out for good land, you bet!" and we found it so invariably. Indeed, with a moderate amount of enterprise, and a small amount of capital, we saw no good reason why the valley of the Gila should not eventually be dotted with excellent farms. The land is all there, and plenty of water to irrigate it (if only the Gila can be subdued, and surely it *can*), and the climate the year round must be delicious. But, as a rule, we found the country desolate and forsaken, with the exception of a starving ranch here and there, whose dirty and dilapidated proprietor cared more to swear at his snarling half-cayote dogs, and sell an occasional glass of mescal or whiskey, than to do an honest hard day's work. The truth is, the most of these settlers, as well as too many throughout Arizona generally, were exiles or emigrants from Arkansas and Texas, with little in them of the kind of stuff that founds states and builds empires. They knew how to drink, and swear, and "shoot a Red Skin, sir, on sight;" but were strangers to honest toil and steady industry, and therefore missed their logical and golden fruits—prosperity and thrift. Of course, like all such everywhere, they were opposed to "Chinese cheap labor;" and, like the good William Nye, hated the "Heathen Chinee," even worse than the negro.

At Gila Bend, some fifty miles from Maricopa Wells, the river makes a sharp curve north, and the road leaves it, for a direct course across the Bend to Maricopa Wells. This embraces what is known mainly as the Maricopa Desert—a wide circuit of level country, practically a waterless desert, though with some good land here and there. In wet seasons and during rainy months, water remains in a few holes near the middle of the Desert; but we found all long since dry. The distance is usually made in two stages, water being carried along for drinking and cooking purposes; but our "outfit" was light, and taking an early start and driving late, we pushed through in one. The Desert itself, as level as a house-floor, is covered with a sort of fine gravel, that makes an excellent road, over which our wheels rolled easily. Near its eastern borders, a range of barren mountains crosses the Desert from north to south, apparently blocking the way; but the road climbs along through a narrow cañon, that opens as you approach, and makes the plains beyond very readily. This cañon is a noted resort of the dread Apaches, and several attacks had recently occurred here. Before leaving Fort Yuma we had been told we would find hostile Indians here, if anywhere. But we took the precaution to dismount from our ambulances, and skirmish through on foot; and consequently, Señors Apaches failed to show themselves, if there. Our experience was the same all the way to Tucson. Subsequently, while *en route* thither, we passed several other places, where we had been warned to look out for Apaches, especially at Picacho, where the mountains crowd down to the road, and form something like a cañon again. But a prudent vigilance by day, and a few simple precautions by night, carried us safely through; and we were more than ever convinced, that the great majority of Indian attacks come from carelessness and neglect, on the part of the attacked.

A few miles west of Gila Bend, between Berk's Station and Oatman's Flat, we passed a group of rocks, that interest everybody, but which nobody seemed to know much about. They stand near the roadside, and consist of smooth red porphyry, or some such stone, curiously carved with figures of men, birds, beasts, fishes, etc. Many of the figures are now quite indistinct, but sufficient remain to show what they were, and their very indistinctness—coupled with the hardness of the stone—proves their great antiquity. The rocks themselves, when struck, ring like genuine clink-stones; and, it would seem, only the sharpest and hardest instruments could make much impression on them. The place is called "Painted Rocks," and we had only time for a cursory examination; but the sculpturing seemed too remote for Spanish times, and was generally attributed to the days of the Aztecs. However this may be, they appeared to be there as a species of hieroglyphics, and doubtless have a story to tell, that some future Champollion may unfold. It may be, that the ancient travel for Mexico left the Gila here, or about here, and struck across the country for the Santa Cruz and so south, flanking the Maricopa Desert, and that these sculptured rocks record the place as the starting-point—as a sort of finger-board or mile-stone. This is only a conjecture; but here, at least, is work for the archæologist and antiquarian, as well as at so many other points in Arizona.

With the exception of some mesquite, iron-wood, and palo-verde trees, scattered here and there along the Gila and its bottoms, the whole country from Yuma to Tucson is practically treeless, and must continue so from want of rains. Sage-brush and grease-wood abound, as in Utah and Idaho, and throughout the great internal basin of the continent generally; and on the uplands, you find the great columnar cactus in full vigor and maturity. Indeed, from the time we struck the Colorado Desert, we were fairly into the cactus region of the continent, but the varieties were few, and the size moderate, till we got well into Arizona. Here they increased in height and bulk, until we reached the Maricopa Desert, where we found them thirty and forty feet high, by two or three feet in diameter, with perpendicular branches halfway up, nearly half as large as the main stem. This variety is a green fluted column, with its edges armed with semi-circular thorns, and bears a cluster of apples on top, from which the Indians extract a rude molasses or sugar. Inside, it is a frame-work of reedy poles, that serve many useful purposes in that woodless region. These immense cacti dot the country over to Tucson, and beyond—indeed, down to Mexico, and largely through it — and are a leading feature of southern Arizona. Sometimes you miss them altogether; but, as a rule, they occur more or less on the *mesas* or plateaus nearly everywhere, and seem in the distance like monumental columns. Their clustering groups and varying heights, when seen from afar, have all the effect of a rural cemetery; only here the shafts are emerald green, instead of marble white. In fights with the Indians, they often prove of value as a defence, and their huge trunks secrete a fluid much akin to water, that has saved the life of many a thirsty traveller, when lost amid these arid wastes. How such a gigantic vegetable or immense plant can thus flourish here, where nothing else comparatively will grow, is a continuing mystery and perpetual astonishment. It would seem more fit for a luxuriant soil and a tropical climate. Yet here it is, *magnum opus*, mocking the naturalist apparently to scorn.

At Maricopa Wells, and thence up the Gila, we found a large settlement of the Maricopa and Pimo Indians. The Maricopas, it seems, are an offshoot of the Yumas, and number less than a thousand souls. The Pimos foot up five or six thousand, and from them are sprung the Papagos—a great tribe dominating all southern Arizona. The Maricopas and Pimos have a Reservation here together, some twenty-five miles long by four or five wide, embracing both sides of the Gila, and live in twelve different villages scattered over it. Two of these are occupied wholly by Maricopas—the rest, by Pimos. Both tribes are a healthy, athletic, vigorous-looking people, and they were decidedly the most well-to-do aborigines we had yet seen. Unlike most Indians elsewhere, these two tribes are steadily on the increase; and this is not to be wondered at, when one sees how they have abandoned a vagabond condition, and settled down to regular farming and grazing. They have constructed great acequias up and down the Gila, and by means of these take out and carry water for irrigating purposes, over thousands of acres of as fine land as anybody owns. Their fields were well fenced with willows, they

16*

had been scratched a little with rude plows, and already (March 9th) they were green with the fast springing wheat and barley. In addition, they raise corn, beans, melons, etc., and have horses and cattle in considerable numbers. One drove of their live stock, over two thousand head, passed down the road just ahead of us, subsequently when *en route* to Tucson, and we were told they had many more. The year before, these Indians had raised and sold a surplus of wheat and corn, amounting to two millions of pounds, besides a large surplus of barley, beans, etc. The most of this was bought by Indian traders, located at Maricopa Wells and Pimo villages, at from one to two cents per pound, coin, in trade; and then resold to the government, for the use of troops in Arizona, at from six to seven cents per pound, coin, in cash. This is a specimen of the way in which the old Indian Ring fleeced both the Indians and the government, and I give it as a passing argument in favor of the new policy. These Indians, it appears, have practiced agriculture somewhat from time immemorial, and they should be encouraged in it, as there is no surer way of "pacifying" or civilizing them. During the rebellion, they furnished two companies to the Union volunteers in Arizona, and the most of these had just re-enlisted, to serve as scouts against the Apaches. These wore a mongrel uniform, half Indian, half soldier; but the rest, only the traditional breech-cloth.

Their wigwams are oval-shaped, wicker-work lodges, made of poles, thatched with willows and straw, and this in turn overlaid with earth. An inverted wash-bowl, on an exaggerated scale, would not be a bad representation of one of them. They are usually five or six feet high in the centre, by fifteen or twenty in diameter, and would be very comfortable dwellings, were it not for their absurd doors. These are only about thirty inches high, by perhaps twenty wide, and consequently the only mode of entrance is on your hands and knees. While halting at the Pimo villages for a day, we managed to crawl into one, for the sake of the experience; but the smoke and the dirt soon drove us out. There was a dull fire in the centre, but with no means of exit for the smoke, except the low doorway. Rush or willow mats covered the rest of the floor, and on these three or four Pimos lay snoozing, wrapped in hides and blankets. Various articles of rude pottery, made by themselves, were stowed away under the eaves of the roof; and at the farther side, suspended from a roof-pole in a primitive cradle, was a pretty papoose sound asleep. As we crawled in, the venerable head of the family, raising himself on his elbow, saluted us with:

"Ugh! White man?"

To which, we, in true Arizona dialect, responded:

"How! Buenos dias, Señor!"

His dignified and elegant answer was:

"Heap good! 'Bacco? Matches?"

We gave him some of each, and shook hands all round, when the aged aborigine was pleased to add:

"Pimos! Americanos! Much friends! *Mui Mucho!*"

These Indians had long been quiet and peaceable, and it would seem are already on the road to civilization. What they need is school-houses and religious teachers. They had an Agent, an ex-officer of volunteers, who seemed honest and capable. But his hands were tied, as to many essential things, and as a rule he was powerless for good. The Indian Bureau, with its then accustomed wisdom, continued to send him fishing-lines and fish-hooks, although there was not a palatable fish in the Gila—I suppose, because the Indians formerly on the

Ohio and the Mississippi needed these; but persistently refused him carts and wagons, although these were constantly called for, to enable them to haul their crops and fuel. As it was, we found the poor squaws gathering their scanty fuel as best they could—often miles away—and lugging it home to their villages, on their backs and heads, from far and near. A single cart or wagon to a village would be invaluable to these poor creatures, and would do more to ameliorate their condition, than a car-load of fish-hooks, or a cargo of trinkets and blankets. Religiously, their ideas seemed confused and vague, except that they believed, in a general way, in some sort of a supreme being, whom they call Montezuma. On the mountains to the west of them, clear-cut against their azure sky, is a gigantic human profile, which they claim is Montezuma asleep. It bears, indeed, a striking resemblance to our own Washington, and is a marked feature of the landscape for many miles.

Thence on to Tucson, nearly a hundred miles south, we found the country much the same as up the Gila, and across the Maricopa Desert. There was a great want of water everywhere, and often we would travel for twenty and thirty miles, before we came to a stream or spring. Our road was almost a dead level, generally free from sand, along which our teams trotted gaily, and it really seemed, as if specially designed for a natural highway here forever. A railroad could want no better route; and here is surely the predestined pathway of our future Arizona Southern, or some such road, into Sonora. Of population there was even less than on the Gila, until we struck the Santa Cruz near Tucson, when ranches again thickened up, and flocks and herds on a moderate scale were not infrequent. The chief characteristic of the country everywhere was the columnar cactus, the gigantic species spoken of on page 368. The farther we got south, the larger it grew and the more it branched out, until it became indeed quite a tree, after a clumsy sort. Sage-brush and grease-wood, of course, constantly occurred, and here and there superb bunch-grass abounded, which will prove invaluable hereafter for grazing purposes, when the country settles up. The mountains usually gave us a wide berth; occasionally, however, they crowded quite down to the road, as at Picacho and Point of Mountains, and as we neared Tucson they shot up into a bold, castellated front off to the east, that would be very surprising outside of Arizona. Here, however, such dome-like peaks, and castellated walls, are frequent features of the scenery.

The weather proved delicious all the way down, and our ride throughout a delightful one. We heard of Apaches at one or two points, but it was always a fortnight before or several miles ahead, and we went through unmolested. Before leaving Maricopa Wells, we were warned of Apaches *en route*, and as a prudent precaution accepted an escort of three infantry-men, whom we mounted on our ambulances—there being no cavalry on hand. These stood guard in turn at night, and were vigilant by day. But we saw no enemy, and their only service was to arrest an insubordinate and drunken teamster, who afterwards escaped from them, but the next morning returned and resumed his mules. He was a queer genius, indigenous to the Border; but, subsequently, proved himself a brave and gallant fellow—one of the best teamsters I ever knew.

CHAPTER XXIII.

TUCSON TO PRESCOTT.

TUCSON we found to be a sleepy old town, of a thousand or so inhabitants, that appeared to be trying its best to take things easy, and succeeds in doing so. It was formerly, and is now again, the capital of Arizona, and the largest town in the territory. It is reputed to be some two hundred years old, and its appearance certainly justifies its reputation. It sort of half awoke from its lethargy one day, when news arrived that our party were *en route*, at Point of the Mountains, and would reach Tucson next morning. Arrangements were hastily made to organize a procession, and give their distinguished visitors a grand reception, with music, speeches, etc. No doubt it would have been a curious performance, all things considered. But while its projectors were agitating, and discussing, and deciding what hour to start, lo! our dusty and jaded teams trotted into town, and Tucson missed one of its biggest sensations. No doubt the honorable Committee and their selected orator were much put out; but others, it is certain, secretly rejoiced.

The town itself is built wholly of adobe, in thorough Mexican or Spanish style, and its population fluctuated. During the rule of Maximilian in Mexico, there was a considerable influx of Liberals here from Sonora, so that the town at one time numbered perhaps fifteen hundred souls. But with his "taking off," and the rise again of Jaurez, many had returned thither; so that the population was then only about a thousand or so, as above stated, of whom fully two-thirds or more were Mexicans, originally or by descent. Its streets are unpaved, and all slope to the middle as a common sewer, as in Spain. It boasted several saloons, one rather imposing, and some good stores; but had no bank, newspaper, school-house, or church, except a rude adobe structure, where a Mexican padre officiated on Sunday to a small audience, with much array of lights, images, drums and violins, and afterwards presided at the customary cock-fight. As specimens of ruling prices, grain (barley and wheat) sold at $3 per bushel, hay at $40 per ton, lumber at $250 per thousand, all coin, and other things in proportion. The lumber came from the Santa Rita Mountains, fifty miles away, and was poor and scarce at that.

The basis of Tucson's existence, it appears, is the little Santa Cruz river, which flows along just at the edge of the town, and irrigates some hundreds of surrounding acres, green just then (March 13th–18th), with wheat, barley, oats, etc. There is a good breadth of fine land here, and near here, and the river ought to be made to irrigate the whole valley. No doubt with proper husbanding and utilizing of the little stream, thousands of acres might be cultivated, and the whole region, both above and below Tucson, be made to produce largely. Peach-trees were in bloom down by the river side when we were there; the grape, the orange, and the olive appeared in many gardens; and both climate and soil seemed all the most fastidious could wish. But Tucson lacks energy and capital, and besides, it seemed, the Apaches claim original, and pretty much undisputed, jurisdiction over most of the country there. Merchants complained that the Apaches raided on their teams and trains *en route*, and ranchmen that the wily rascals levied contributions regularly on their live stock, as soon as it was worth anything, and did not hesitate to scalp and kill, as well as steal, if it came in their way. Farming or grazing under such circumstances, it must be conceded, could hardly be called very lucrative or enticing, and the Tucsonians are entitled to the benefit of this explanation.

The livest and most energetic things, however, that we saw about Tucson were its innumerable blackbirds, that thronged the few trees about the streets, and awoke us every morning with their multitudinous twittering and chattering. How those birds did chatter and sing, from daylight well on into the morning; and what a relief they were to the dull and prosy old town! The men and women, wrapped in their serapes or blankets, sunned themselves by the hour in the doorways. The dogs and cats, the goats and pigs, slept on in the streets, or strolled lazily about at will. But these plucky birds sung on and on, with all the heartiness and abandon of the robin or mocking-bird in the East; and Tucson should emulate their intrepidity, and zeal. She should shake off somewhat of the spirit of Rip Van Winkle, and remember she is under Yankee Government now, and in the latter half of the nineteenth century.

Tucson already drove a considerable trade with Sonora, and expected to increase this much, now that Maximilian had subsided. Its main importance, however, just then, arose from its being the headquarters of the Military District there, and the chief depot for the several posts comprising said District. The stores for Camps Lovell, Cameron, Wallen, Bowie, Goodwin, and

Grant, were all received here from Fort Yuma by contractors' trains, and then re-distributed by army teams to these posts, respectively, as needed. This made considerable business, first and last, and rendered the Quartermaster at Tucson quite an important personage. The route was by sailing-vessels, semi-occasionally, down the Pacific Coast and up the stormy Gulf of California to the mouth of the Colorado; thence by cockle-shell steamers up the aggravating Colorado River to Fort Yuma; and thence by contractors' teams to Tucson—at a total cost, from San Francisco, of about *twenty cents per pound, in coin,* for every load of Government freight thus put down at Tucson. The time consumed was anywhere from two to four months, depending on the head-winds and "borers"* in the uncertain Gulf, the amount of water or sand in the Colorado River, and the condition of the roads and Indians generally up the valley of the Gila. Private freight, of course, largely followed the same route, *ex necessitate,* and the rates were simply ruinous to Tucson. Merchants and freighters there claimed, that the same work could be done, *via* either Libertad or Guaymas, instead of Yuma, at a cost of not exceeding seven or eight cents per pound, coin, and in not more than from twenty to thirty days, from San Francisco, at the farthest. This, of course, meant steamers from San Francisco to the Gulf; but a coast-wise line already touched semi-monthly at Guaymas, and it was thought would also put in at Libertad, if inducement offered. Libertad lies two hundred miles off, to the southwest of Tucson, on the Gulf of California, and is a port not equal to San Francisco or San Diego, indeed; but yet it is not much behind San Pedro or Santa Barbara, and it seems is of sufficient advantages most of

* Huge tide-waves at the head of the Gulf.

the year round. It is an open roadstead like the latter, but is well sheltered from all but southwest winds, and when these come, there is the broad Gulf for an offing. Guaymas, farther south, and a hundred miles farther away, is one of the best ports on the Pacific Coast; and the roads to both are excellent natural highways, unsurpassed as such in America.

True, both of these ports are in Mexican territory, which was one of the blunders of our treaty of cession there; but the Mexican authorities, it was said, were willing and anxious to have us make use of them, and now that the Imperialists had left Sonora, there was no difficulty in traversing the country, except from occasional Indians. Individuals, it was said, already travelled everywhere alone there, camping out at night with safety; and a train of teams, with armed teamsters, it was believed, would be invincible against any aborigines, that would be likely to turn up. At least, this was Tucson's oft-told story, and the burden of her griefs, when we were there. What she wanted was to get "inside," or secure access to civilization, cheap and quick. She had rich copper mines and fair silver ones, as we ourselves witnessed, only a few miles off; but these were now all lying idle, because of Apaches, and the excessive cost and slowness of transportation. This last item, of course, was the chief one. For cheap and quick transportation would bring population, stimulate enterprise, develop the country, re-open her mines, "pacify" or extirpate the Apaches, and release the military for duty elsewhere. What she specially wanted, just then, was to get the Government contractors' teams to select either the Libertad or Guaymas route, instead of *via* Fort Yuma and the Gila—she did not care much, which. The wagons returning thither would take her ores, and surplus grain and wool, down to the coast "and a market" cheap, rather than go back empty; and thus solve the problem of her prosperity and growth. Of course, she looked forward to a transcontinental railroad in time; but, as yet, this was in the dim future. The chief object of my trip thither was to look well into these facts, and they were duly reported to the proper Department at Washington, for its information and action. This change of routes, it really seemed, would result in a saving of at least *two hundred thousand dollars, in coin*, to the Government annually; but it may not have been thought advisable, notwithstanding that, to trust our line of supplies thus to foreign soil.

South of Tucson, some ten miles, on the road to Tubac and Mexico, on the banks of the Santa Cruz still, is the famous church of San Xavier Del Bac, a venerable relic of the former Spanish rule in Arizona. The road thither leads through dense mesquite and palo verde bottoms, with water enough in the Santa Cruz to irrigate them all; but, as yet, they were unbroken by the husbandman. The church itself seems to have been built about a hundred years ago, and, though abandoned, is still in a good state of preservation. It is not of adobe, but of large, red, kiln-burnt brick, rough-coated with a yellowish cement, that seems well-nigh indestructible. It is cruciform in style, with thick and solid walls, and its antique front and towers have originally been profusely decorated with saints, angels, griffins, etc., in niche or bas-relief, though many of these are now mutilated or destroyed. Inside it is handsomely frescoed, and was no doubt once rich in paintings, ornaments, relics, etc., though these have now mostly disappeared. Its roof seems to be a sort of asphaltum or concrete, and appears as tight and firm, as when first laid. In one of the towers, there is still a fine chime of bells, that came no doubt originally from Castile or Arragon. The age of this church is variously reported, but from a cursory examination it appeared to have been erected about the year 1797, although we were shown a mutilated register of marriages, births, deaths, etc., that began in 1752. This last, however, seemed to antedate the church, as if it had been in use by the Spanish settlement here in early times, before they were able to achieve such an edifice. This church was no doubt a link in the chain of Spanish Missions, that the Jesuits a century or more ago established, from the City of Mexico to Northern California, and was abandoned like the rest of them, with the subsequent collapse of their priestly power. No doubt, in its time, it was the centre of a considerable community there; but now, only a squalid village of Papago Indians crouches at its feet, who regard the aged structure with a superstitious reverence, and will not permit its fine chime of bells to be removed to Tucson, for fear of Our Lady's displeasure. The padre at Tucson comes down and says mass occasionally, and baptizes their young children; but he cannot cajole them out of their bells, and doubtless they would fight, rather than lose them. Altogether, this church is now the best and oldest civilized structure to be found in Arizona. Very slight repairs would fit it for occupancy and worship again; but, unfortunately, there are no inhabitants there now to occupy and worship in it, except the Papagos aforesaid—and as specimens of good clean Christians, they don't amount to much now-a-days, whatever they were once.

From Tucson, we retraced our steps to Maricopa Wells, reaching there again March 21st, *en route* to Prescott; and here had every prospect of being detained a month or more, by the spring freshets in the Gila and

Salado. While down at Tucson, there had been heavy rains, and a great melting of snows, on the mountains to the east; and the usually sluggish, half-dry rivers were now all alive, and booming. The Gila, especially, had overflowed its banks, and its whole valley below in many places was inundated. Ranch after ranch had been swept away, and in several instances the scant inhabitants had barely escaped with their lives, from its treacherous waters. The fine mesquite bottom at Gila Bend was reported four feet under water, and Mr. James' house, corral, etc. there—the finest we saw coming up the Gila—were all gone. The freshet was said to be the highest known there for years, and inflicted a loss on the Gila valley alone, it was alleged, of many thousands of dollars. The road was submerged or washed out in many places, and all travel to and from Yuma was interrupted for weeks, except such as could make its way around over the hills and mesas, by the old Indian trails. Col. Crittenden, with a column of three hundred men, *en route* to Tucson and Southern Arizona, succeeded in getting through to Maricopa Wells in fifteen days, though we had made it in five. He was accompanied by his wife, a brave lady and true-hearted Kentuckian, who deserved and received much praise, for the long and arduous trip she was thus making, rather than separate from her gallant husband.

These two rivers, the Gila and Salado, lay directly across our path to Fort Whipple and Prescott, for which we were now bound—Gov. McCormick and wife to return to their home there, and T.* and I to look after U. S. post-office and military affairs there generally. They were both, swollen and turbid; nobody had forded them, for a month; and they were still at freshet height, and rising—without bridge or ferry.

As nothing better could be done, we decided to halt at Maricopa Wells for a few days, as we could neither get forward to Prescott nor backward to Yuma, though the delay was most vexatious at such an out-of-the-world place, where the mail was so intermittent, and their freshest newspaper more than a month old. We spent the time in writing up our note-books, and in studying the Pimas and Maricopas; but the days wore heavily on, with small prospect of the waters subsiding. Finally, after waiting nearly a week, chafing at the delay, we heard of a little row-boat owned by a German, down at the McDowell crossing of the Gila, which it was reported would suffice to ferry us over, if we took our ambulances well to pieces. We would then have to mount the boat on a wagon and transport it thirty miles or so, overland to the Salado, and there repeat the operation; but this was better, than halting indefinitely at the Wells. We had been told, there was no boat, available for such a purpose; but I determined to see what we could do, with this one. Of course, it would be slow work, and perhaps dangerous, ferrying over two swollen rivers, by piecemeal thus. But it seemed better, than being embargoed and flood-stayed here—practically five hundred miles away from everywhere—and with no news from "inside" or civilization, for over a month now. As to whether we would succeed, we could only say *nous verrons*, or *quien sabe;* but meant to try, anyhow.

Accordingly, early March 25th, we said "adios" to our good friends at the Wells, and, with many thanks for their hospitality and kind wishes, drove down to the Gila, some six miles away. We found it at freshet height, perhaps a hundred yards wide, by ten or twelve feet deep, and running like a mill-race—its tawny waters tossing and whirling, hither and yon, and overflowing its thither bank for a long distance. Now and then, as if to enliven the scene further, a floating mesquite or an uprooted cottonwood would come rushing by, sweeping all before it. Altogether, I confess, the Gila was not a very inviting stream, just then, to navigate. But Louis Heller was there, with his little boat; Prescott was before, and the Wells behind us; and we resolved to venture over, if possible. His boat was a mere cockle-shell affair at best, a rude canoe, ten feet long by three wide, and clumsy at that; but Louis, nevertheless, with true German grit and skill, managed to make it ferry both us and our "outfit" safely across, in the course of the day. First, went our baggage and forage, with the Governor and his lady; then the vehicles, after being taken well to pieces; then, with much hallooing and shouting, we forced the mules into the stream, and made them swim for it. Only two or three got across at first, though the boat led with a mule swimming behind it, held by a lariat; but these served as decoys, and the next trip the rest ventured over. There was a great struggling and whee-haw-ing in the water for awhile, and now and then a donkey would whirl over or go under, and some landed far down stream; nevertheless, we lost none, and soon after we ourselves got safely across. The little tub of a canoe tossed and tumbled very shakily, when she got out into the current, and for a few minutes shot wildly down stream; but the strong arm of our sturdy Teuton mastered the wild waters, and at last brought us safely ashore.

It was nightfall, before we got over, and our ambulances together again. The next morning early, we put Louis and his boat on a wagon, and started for the McDowell Crossing of the Salado, some thirty-five miles away. The Prescott Crossing, several miles below, was reported impracticable, even with the boat, because of the wide overflow of the banks there; but we hoped to get over at the McDowell Crossing, and then follow down the north bank of the Salado, until we struck the Prescott road again. It was late in the afternoon when we reached the McDowell Crossing, and the condition of the Salado there was anything but encouraging. We found it at least three times the size of the Gila, and with its waters even more swollen and turbulent. Nevertheless, it was perceptibly falling, and Louis predicted a much better state of things next morning. This proved to be true; so, early on the 27th, we began to ferry over again, as at the Gila. But it was a tedious and delicate operation. The river, as I have said, was three or four times as wide, and the swollen flood so swift, that the boat usually landed a quarter of a mile or more below where it went in. Then we had to drag and pole it back along the opposite bank, half a mile or so above, whence we could row it diagonally across to the place of starting again.

It took us two days, to cross the Salado thus, and I need scarcely say, they were long and anxious ones. We were now in a region infested by Apaches, and we had to be constantly on the alert to guard against surprise. Late in the afternoon of the second day, leaving our teamsters and little escort to get the ambulances together and repack them, we proceeded up the Salado to Fort McDowell—the commandant there having heard of our approach, and sent an ambulance to bring us. It was some fifteen miles, part of the way through a dreaded Apache cañon; but we passed safely on, though we did not reach the post until after nightfall. We found the post — the largest and finest in Arizona — short of rations, and wholly out of forage, as it had been for several weeks, because of the spring freshets, as it was alleged, though there was plenty at Maricopa Wells, which it would seem might have been got there, if we could. This was suggested to the officer in charge, and no doubt was well heeded. We remained there until the next afternoon, inspecting the post and its bearings (it seemed admirably located for its work, well into the Apache country, protecting the valley of the Salado and the Gila), and then returned to our ambulances at the Crossing. The next morning, by sunrise, we were up and off, for the Prescott road—if we could find it. At Fort McDowell, they told us, we could never reach it. Some said it was thirty miles off—others claimed it was fifty or sixty, with an impassable country between. The only thing known definitely was, that there was no road at all down the north bank of the Salado, though we were sure to strike the regular Prescott road, if we kept along down that bank of the river far enough, and could get through. We might meet Apaches anywhere, they said, for it was one of their favorite tramping grounds, or we might go through unmolested, depending on circumstances. We had expected to get an escort of a dozen cavalry-men here, to accompany us to Prescott; but six cavalry-men, and six mounted infantry-men, were all the post could spare. The horses of these, though the best on hand, were so broken down for want of forage, that part were sent back before we got three miles out; and of the balance, only five went through to Prescott with us, by extra care and regular feeding with the grain, which we had taken the precaution to bring along from Maricopa Wells. An army wagon, with a six-mule team, also from Fort McDowell, furnished transportation for our escort, as the cavalry-horses successively gave out.

For the first fifteen miles or so, after leaving the

Crossing, we found a well-broken road, used the year before as a hay-road from the river-bottoms to Fort McDowell. But, ultimately, this ended in a bend of the Salado, and from there on all was wild and unbroken—a veritable *terra incognita.* We found the Salado crookeder than a ram's horn, or a mesquite tree, or anything else that is most crooked and involved. Laying our course partly by the compass, and partly by the Salado's fringe of cottonwoods, we struck across from bend to bend of the river, sure only of one thing, and that was—keeping near to water. We found the river bottoms, as a rule, thick with chemisal, relieved here and there by dense mesquite groves, looking in the distance like old orchards, through which it was almost impossible to penetrate with ambulance or wagon. Now and then we had to flank a slough, or flounder through a quicksand, and sundown still found us pushing along through these bottoms, though we had made fully thirty miles since morning. We went into camp by the riverside just at dusk, thoroughly worn out, and not without a degree of anxiety, as we had crossed a number of Indian trails during the day, though none seemed fresh. Our animals were well blown, especially the cavalry horses, and the best we could do for them was a bite of corn, as we had no hay along, of course, and it was too late to graze them.

The night passed wearily away, but without cause for alarm, and early next morning we were again on the move. A drive, or rather struggle, of three miles or so through the mesquite and chemisal, brought us out to an ill-defined track, bearing away in the supposed direction of Wickenburg (and so to Prescott), and we resolved to take that, though certain it was not the regular road. We had heard of a "cut-off," or by-road somewhere there, made by a Lt. Du Bois some months before, and we concluded this must be his road. At all events, we were desperately tired of struggling through the mesquite and chemisal, and concluded we would follow this track up for a while anyhow. It was lucky we did; for, after rather too much easting for the first few miles, it finally struck directly across the Agua Frio, and came into the true Prescott road near White Tanks. This Agua Frio, usually one of Arizona's "dry rivers," we found with three feet of water in it, and bad quicksands beneath that. However, we discovered a practicable crossing, and soon after nightfall reached the vicinity of White Tanks, some thirty miles, since morning.

Here we camped by the roadside, glad to have struck the regular Wickenburg or Prescott road at last, and went supperless to sleep—for fear our fire, if made, might disclose us to the Indians. We could find no water for our poor animals, and the next morning would have missed our accustomed coffee even, had we not taken the precaution to keep our water-kegs well filled. Of course, we broke camp early, and moved wearily on to the Hassayampa, some ten or twelve miles, where we halted to water up and lunch. This Hassayampa, ordinarily, is another "dry river," like the Agua Frio, but we found three feet or more of water in it, and bottomless quicksands nearly everywhere. Our road, then the only road from Southern to Northern Arizona, ran directly up the Hassayampa, for some twelve or fifteen miles here, using the river-bed as a roadway, as the only practicable route through the mountains, and nobody had ventured through for a month or more.

The Hassayampa itself flows through a wild and rocky cañon, with high precipitous walls on either side; and it was soon apparent, that our only alternative was either to flounder through its quicksands, or retrace our steps to Maricopa Wells. The latter was out of the question, as our rations and forage were both about exhausted, and, besides, our improvised ferry-boat had returned to the Gila; so that the only thing left for us was to try the Hassayampa, and get through, somehow, at all hazards. We had heard of a trail, across the ridge and over the mountains, by the Vulture Mine, and so into Wickenburg, by a roundabout course; but a careful reconnoissance revealed no trace of it. We called a "council of war," and discussed the "situation," pro and con, with due gravity, and finally decided that there was nothing for us to do, but to ascend the Hassayampa; and so, into it we plunged. And, verily, it was a *plunge*. Nothing but a prolonged flounder, and plunge, from ten A. M. to six P. M.! Now into the stream; now out on a sand-bank; now deep into a quicksand; crossing and recrossing, from side to side, to take advantage of any land—not less than fifteen or twenty times in the course of the twelve miles! Sometimes a cavalry-man on horseback, "prospecting" the way for the ambulances, would go down, until it seemed impossible to extricate him and his horse. Again, an infantry-man, on foot, would suddenly sink in to his armpits, and call out to his comrades to come and rescue him. Then an ambulance would slip to one side, and half of it commence sinking, while the other half remained on solid ground. Then our six-mule team would go in, and half of the mules would flounder over the tongue, or turn a summerset out of the harness, and, perhaps, come near drowning, before they could be extricated, while the rest would be all right. Now we would be all ashore, clambering along the rocky walls of the cañon, to give the ambulances a better chance; and now, all hands would be out into the water, to start a stalled team, and then such a whooping and shouting, such a whipping and tugging at the wheels, one seldom sees equalled. I campaigned with McClellan, on the Peninsula; I was with Burnside in his Mud Campaign, after Fredericksburg; we had bad roads down in Tennessee and Georgia, when after Joe Johnston and Hood. But this tedious and toilsome drive, through the cañon and quicksands of the Hassayampa, beat all these; and we never would have got through, had we not had light loads, and skilful, plucky, magnificent drivers.

As it was, we just managed by good luck to struggle through, and got into Wickenburg about dusk, with our animals thoroughly blown, and ourselves pretty well used up. It had taken us just a week, to come through from Maricopa Wells, usually a drive of a day or two —or three, at the farthest. But the Gila and Salado were still unfordable, and we would have been detained at the Wells, probably, for a fortnight or more yet, had it not been for Louis' boat. We found we were the first party through in a month, and nobody was expected to venture the Hassayampa either way, for a month or so to come. Of course, with such rivers and roads—rivers without either bridges or ferries, and roads that follow the beds of rivers—our only conclusion was, that Arizona was in no hurry, for either population or business; and, I judge, *this* is about so. She must bridge her streams, and construct good substantial roads—at least between all chief points—before she can expect to grow and prosper. This is fundamental in all civilized communities, and she would have recognized it long since, had her population been more from the busy North, than from the indolent, happy-go-lucky South.

CHAPTER XXIV.

TUCSON TO PRESCOTT (*continued*).

WICKENBURG, much longed for and at last reached, we found to be an adobe hamlet, of perhaps one or two hundred inhabitants, depending chiefly on the Vulture Mine. We were all so thoroughly jaded and worn out, by our rough ride through the country, from Maricopa Wells, that we decided to halt there for a day or two to rest and recruit. This afforded us an opportunity to visit the Mine, which we gladly embraced, as we had heard so much about it. It is really a fine mine of gold-bearing quartz, off in the mountains, some fifteen miles west of Wickenburg, whence the ore was then wagoned to the mill, on the Hassayampa at Wickenburg. It consists of a fine vein of free quartz, from five to fifteen feet wide, and mostly devoid of sulphurets, or other refractory substances. Seventy or eighty men—half of them or more Mexicans—were hard at work, sinking shafts and getting out ore; and already a large amount of work had been done there. One shaft was already down a hundred feet, and another half as far—it being intended to connect the two by a lateral gallery, to insure ventilation, etc. Unfortunately, no water could be found near the mine, and all used there then was transported from Wickenburg, at a cost of ten cents per gallon. So, all the ore taken out had to be wagoned, from the mine to the mill at Wickenburg, at a cost of ten dollars per ton. The cost of everything else was about in the same proportion. Nevertheless, we were told the mine paid, and that handsomely, and I sincerely trust it did.

The mill at Wickenburg, belonging to the same company, was a fine adobe structure, roofed with shingles, and had just gone into operation. They had previously had a small five-stamp mill, which paid very well; but this new mill ran twenty stamps, and would crush forty tons of quartz per day, when worked to its full capacity. Their ore was reputed to average from fifty to seventy dollars per ton, though of course "assaying" much more, and we were assured would pay for working, if it yielded only from twenty to thirty dollars per ton. If so, we thought, stock in the Vulture Company must be a "gilt-edged" investment; and their noble mine certainly was the best-looking enterprise, we had yet seen in Arizona. It appeared, however, to be a sort of "pocket" vein, as prospecting on either side of it, as yet, had failed to discover other points worth working. Fine as it was, the mine was embarrassed by financial difficulties, and was then in the hands of creditors, authorized to work it until their claims were met, though these troubles it was thought would soon end.

Thence on to Prescott, *via* Skull Valley, some eighty-four miles, we passed without further mishap. We made the distance in two and a-half days, and rolled into the capital, just as the last rays of the setting sun were purpling the triple peaks of the distant San Francisco Mountains. The road generally was naturally a good one, but here and there developed a peculiarity seldom seen elsewhere. For example, on a perfectly good road, apparently, even dry and dusty, suddenly a mule would go in to his girth or a wheel to the hub, and there seemed no bottom to the execrable quicksands. In other places, there had been surface-water or mud, that served as a warning. But between Skull Valley and Prescott, when trotting along as usual, we often struck spots, where the dust was blowing, and yet when we ventured on, our vehicles seemed bound for China or Japan, rather than Prescott. Skull Valley itself proved to be a narrow little vale, of perhaps a thousand or two acres, but devoid of timber, and inaccessible in all directions, except over bad mountains. A few ranches had been started here, and a petty Military Post was there to protect them; but this last had already been ordered away, the location was so faulty, and with its departure, Skull Valley, as a settlement, seemed likely to collapse.

Here and at Wickenburg were the only settlements, and, indeed, the only population, we found between Maricopa Wells and Prescott—a distance of nearly three hundred miles, by the way we came. The whole intervening country, as a rule, was barren and desolate, and absolutely without population, except at the points indicated, until you neared Prescott. There were not even such scattered ranches, or occasional stations, as we found in crossing the Colorado Desert, and ascending the Gila; but the whole district seemed given over, substantially, to the cayote and the Indian. The Apaches and Yavapais are the two main tribes there, and were said to infest the whole region, though we saw nothing of them. In the valley of the Hassayampa, and across the Aztec Mountains, they certainly had an abundance of ugly-looking places, that seem as if specially made for ambuscades and surprises. If they had attacked us in the cañon of the Hassayampa, while floundering through the quicksands there, they would have had things pretty much their own way — at least, at first, vigilant as we were. They had killed a wandering Mexican there, only a few days before; but we did not know it, until we reached Wickenburg, and came through ourselves unscathed.

Perhaps the worst place was Bell's Cañon, a long, tortuous, rocky defile — diabolical in every respect — a few miles south of Skull Valley. Here a Mr. Bell and others had been killed by Apaches, some two years before; and here also the Indian Agent, Mr. Levy, and his clerk, had lost their lives, but a few weeks previously. For miles there, the rocks have been tossed about in the wildest possible confusion, and their grouping in many instances is very extraordinary. A small band of Indians there, ensconced among the rocks, would be able to make a sharp fight, and nothing but cool heads and steady courage would be likely to dislodge them. From the peaks on either side, they can descry travellers a long way off, through the clear atmosphere of that rainless region; and should they decide to attack, nothing would be easier than to conceal themselves behind the massive boulders, that bristle along the cañon. We expected trouble here, if anywhere in Arizona, and, as we approached it, "governed ourselves accordingly." But the "noble Red men" allowed their "Pale-face brothers" to pass in peace. Arizonians spoke of this villanous-looking place, as rather dangerous, and didn't care to venture through it alone; but parties of two and three travelled it frequently, and it seemed safe enough, if they went well armed, and kept a sharp look out. The trouble is, travellers in Arizona, and in all Indian districts, as a rule, *see* no Indians, and so after a few days believe there are none—become careless, wander on ahead, or straggle along behind, *without their arms*—when presto! suddenly arrows whiz from behind gigantic rocks or down shadowy cañons, and men are found dead in the road, with their scalps gone. In all such regions, the only safe rule is the rule of our western Borderers, to wit: "Never unbuckle your six-shooter, and never venture from your camp or train without your Spencer or Henry!"

As I have already said, we found the intervening country substantially unsettled, and much of it will never amount to anything for agricultural purposes. Its mineral resources may be great; but, as a rule, it lacks both wood and water, and much of it is a barren desert, given over forever to chemisal and grease-wood. On the Agua Frio and Hassayampa, however, there are considerable bottoms, that might be successfully irrigated; and between the Gila and the Salado there is a wide district, that deserves some further notice. As you come up out of the Gila bottoms, you pass through scattered mesquite trees, and at length enter on a broad *mèsa* (Spanish for "table-land"), ten or fifteen miles wide by thirty or forty long, which bears every evidence of having once been well cultivated, and densely populated. Instead of mesquite, you here find clumps of chemisal two or three feet high, and bits of broken pottery nearly everywhere. Farther on, some eight or ten miles from the Salado, you find immense ruins in various places, and soon strike a huge *acequia* winding up from the Salado, in comparison with which all the *acequias* we had yet seen in Utah or California were the veriest ditches. It must be, I should think, thirty feet wide by ten or twelve deep, and seems like a great canal of modern times. Just where the road to Fort McDowell crosses this, it subdivides into three or four lesser *acequias*, and these branch off over the *mèsa* indefinitely. This great *acequia* heads just above where we crossed the Salado. The river has a considerable descent or "rapids" there, and the ancient constructors of this gigantic water-course, apparently, knew well how to take advantage of this. They have tapped the river there by three immense mouths, all leading into one common channel; and this they have coaxed along down the bottoms, and gently up the bluff, until at a distance of miles away it at last gained the level of the *mèsa*, and there distributed abroad its fertilizing waters. So, there are other ancient *acequias*, furrowing the bottoms of the Salado on either side, though we observed none so large as this.

The ruins of ancient buildings, thoroughly disintegrated, are scattered widely along these bottoms, and in some places there must certainly have been large cities. The rectilinear courses of the walls, and the dividing lines of the rooms, are all plainly visible still, though nothing remains but the cobble-stones and pebbles, out of which they seem to have been mainly constructed, and here and there a bit of cement or mortar. The ancient builders and occupiers of these could not have been our present Indians there, because they use different forms and materials. They could not have been Mexicans or Spaniards, because they invariably use brick or adobe. Who they were, where they came from, when they disappeared and *why*—these are knotty problems for the antiquarian, which it is to be hoped time will soon solve. One thing is certain, these ancient builders—Aztecs (as popularly believed) or whoever they were—were at least good architects and engineers, and they must have peopled much of Arizona with an industrious and dense population, such as it will not see again—I was going to say—for centuries to come. But the Salado, in those days, must have been a larger river than it is now, or probably ever will be again; because two or three of these old *acequias* would carry off all its present waters, and leave none for the others, whose remains yet furrow the country there everywhere.

However, the larger *acequias* may have been used only as receiving reservoirs, to husband the spring freshets, and for this purpose they might soon be utilized again. However this may be, there are fine lands all along the bottoms of the Salado, and enough water flowing there yet to irrigate many thousands of acres. Indeed, the best lands we saw in Arizona are here in the heart of it, on the Gila and Salado, and in time no doubt there will be flourishing settlements there. What the region needs, is a railroad to connect it with "inside," or civilization; and this the "Texas and Pacific," it seems, will eventually furnish. Now, like so much of Arizona, it is inaccessible, or practically five hundred miles across a desert—from about everywhere. A railroad will remedy all this, and stimulate Arizona wonderfully in many ways. The whistle of the locomotive will end her Indian troubles, and many others, and may she hear it echoing and re-echoing among her mountains and cañons very soon! A railroad, indeed, is a great blessing everywhere; but in our western territories it means civilization as well, and without one Arizona will evidently continue to slumber on, as she has for so many years.

CHAPTER XXV.

PRESCOTT, THE APACHES, ETC.

PRESCOTT had been described to us, as resembling very much a "New England village." We were told so in San Francisco. It was repeated at Fort Yuma. It was hinted at Tucson. Well, perhaps, it did, except as regards school-houses and churches, white paint and green blinds, general thriftiness, and a wholesome respect for law and order. Eliminating these, Prescott, perhaps, *was* quite New-Englandish; but, otherwise, it resembled rather some country cross-roads in Missouri, or Arkansas. In brief, there was not a school-house, or church, or bank, in the place. Business we found at a general stand-still, because of absolute stagnation among the mines. And the peaceable and quiet population had just shown their New-Englandlike disposition, by robbing and beating a squad of United States soldiers—a part of those recently sent out better to protect that region—mortally wounding one, and severely injuring several others. Of course, the Blue-Coats were off duty, or the cowards wouldn't have assailed them.

Said I to an old acquaintance I met, an ex-Army of the Potomac officer:

"I hear you have quite a New England village here?"

"Yes, indeed, it is very New-Englandlike! Last night I was in our billiard-saloon here. A game of monte was going on in one corner, brag-poker in another, and a couple of dogs were having a free fight under the billiard-table. I lived in Boston once for some time, but have no recollection of seeing anything exactly like that!"

"But you have a good class of population, have you not, as a general thing?"

"O yes! Excellent! Less than five hundred, altogether! But we have ten drinking-saloons, and a dozen gambling-hells, more or less! What kind of a population that implies, judge for yourself!"

I think my friend was, perhaps, somewhat prejudiced. He had, probably, invested in mining "feet," and found out he had made a "permanent investment," with slight prospect of "dividends." Nevertheless, Prescott had been much overrated and bepraised, and, consequently, suffered somewhat in the estimation of strangers. We found it well laid-out, on a scale of Magnificent Distances, like its illustrious prototype, the National Capital, and lacking only—buildings and people to be a fine city. Its site, though nearly six thousand feet above the sea, is a good one, along the undulating bottoms of Granite Creek, about a mile or so from Fort Whipple, then the chief military-post in northern Arizona. Its houses were grouped mostly around a spacious plaza, after the old Spanish custom, though a few straggled off into ragged streets either way. They were chiefly of logs and rough lumber, and guiltless of paint, though some brick and adobe structures appeared here and there. The population seemed to be between four and five hundred. The autumn previous, it had been largely increased by a notable immigration from Montana, which came to Prescott with the expectation of finding rich placer mines, from what they had seen published about the region. But the most of these had already left, cruelly disappointed, and others would follow, if they had the means. The barber, who shaved me one day, proved to be a Montanian, from Helena City. I asked him, casually, what he thought of Arizona.

"Why, you see, stranger, I pays for this yer room eight dollars a month, in "dust." For a room in Helena City, of the same size, I paid last summer seventy-five dollars per month."

"You mean *that* for a fair comparison of Arizona, with Montana?"

"Sartin! Thet's about it naow, you bet! Our fellers, who come down yer with me last fall, most all gone; others leavin' every week. I'm goin' to vamose, too, 'fore long, you bet!"

These placer mines were scattered over a district of ten or twelve miles around Prescott, and the truth seemed to be, that as a general thing they had produced poorly. It appeared, there were two or three hundred men, in all, engaged in them still, but these were making only indifferent wages, and many were quite discouraged. The quartz mines covered a much wider area, and beyond question were very rich in the precious metals; but the ores were sulphurets, of the most refractory character, and there was no known "process" to work them at a profit. Eleven mills, of from five to twenty stamps each, had been erected, at mines whose ores assayed from one hundred to two hundred or more dollars per ton—an excellent yield, of course. But, of all these, only one five-stamp mill was then running—the Ticonderoga—and that was reported as only about paying expenses. Instead of two hundred dollars, or more, per ton, as per assay, the mills in fact could only stamp out and save from ten to twenty dollars per ton; and this was a losing business. A new "process" was just being tried at the Eureka Mill, which did excellently well, as per assay in the laboratory; but it was uncertain what would be the result, when applied to large quantities of ore in the mill. The Bully-Bueno and Sterling lodes seemed to be the most in favor. Specimens from the Sterling, that were shown, were indeed wonderful in richness, and there seemed to be no doubt that the ledges around Prescott abound in mines, which will yield very largely, if only a process can be found to treat successfully such obstinate and refractory sulphurets. For the present, however, mining operations about Prescott were very "sick," with poor prospect of speedy recovery. The region had indeed two advantages, very rare in Arizona, to wit, good fuel, and sufficient water. The breadth of timber here, however, had been much overstated. An area of ten miles square or so embraced the bulk of the pine, which was an exceptional growth just there; the rest consisted chiefly of scrawny juniper and scraggly cedar, fit only for fuel and fencing.

The Territorial capital was still at Prescott, but its permanent location was yet to be decided on. Maricopa Wells and Tucson were both contending for the honor, and the latter it seems has since won it. Ultimately, however, it is probable, the Territory will divide on the line of the Gila, and Prescott again become the capital of the northern part of it. Arizona naturally and geographically subdivides on that line, and the interests of the two sections are usually quite divergent. The population of the territory was variously computed at from three to four thousand only, of whom the major portion by far were Mexicans and their descendants. The other whites were mainly Arkansans and Texans, many of them no doubt exiles from the East, "for their country's good." Of course, this was not a very promising basis for a commonwealth, and the Territory, it appeared, was about at a stand-still. As evidence of this, there was not then a bank, or banking-house, or free-school, or Protestant church, or missionary even, throughout the whole of Arizona—a region some four or five times as large as the great State of New York. The Indian population was estimated at about twenty thousand, of whom ten thousand were regarded as friendly, five thousand as hostile, and five thousand as half and half—that is, sometimes friendly, and sometimes hostile, depending on circumstances. To offset and antagonize these, the Government had then about twenty-five hundred regular soldiers in Arizona, which would seem sufficient, if well handled, though the people of course were clamoring for more. The great controlling tribe in Arizona, and extending into New Mexico, and the terror of the Mexican border, were the Apaches. Those that we saw gave one the impression of a fierce, sinewy, warlike race, very different from the Plains Indians, and it was plain there would be no peace in Arizona, nor much hope for its development, until these Apaches received a thorough chastisement. This they had never yet had, from either Mexicans or Americans, and consequently they despised and hated the Pale Faces, as we hate (or ought to hate) Satan himself. They inhabited the mountains chiefly, though they often descended into the plains, and in bands of two or three, or more, scoured the country far and near, as it suited them. About Tucson and Tubac they stole stock, and occasionally killed travellers, often within a mile or two of the towns. Sometimes, for months together, they would leave a road unmolested, and then, suddenly, attacking it at different points, clean out all the ranches. A few miles from Camp McDowell, on the road between there and Maricopa Wells, they infested a rocky cañon on the Rio Salado, and mockingly defied all attempts to expel them. A fortnight before we reached Maricopa Wells, *en route* to Tucson, a party of them crossed the Salado and Gila, and stole ten head of stock from a ranch only three miles from the Wells. About the same time, another party of three lurked around the station at Blue Water, on the road to Tucson, some fifty miles south of the Wells, and, failing to find anything they could steal, vented their spleen by shooting an arrow into a valuable horse that was stabled safely from their reach. This done, the same night they struck across the country, some fifteen or twenty miles, to the peaceable Pimo settlements on the Gila, where they each stole a couple of horses apiece, and made good their escape with them to the mountains.

Some of their exploits were very amusing, as well as very daring, worthy of the best days of Osceola or Tecumseh. We heard one of a party, that had just preceded us in Arizona. They camped at a station for the night, and thought their animals thoroughly secure, when they had put them into an adobe corral, with a wall four or five feet high by two thick, and then lay down themselves across the only entrance, with their rifles by their sides. The stealthy Apaches waited until their pale-face friends were well asleep, and then with a piece of dry cow-hide, hard and thin, sawed out a section of the adobe wall, at the other end of the corral, and in the morning *Los Americanos* found themselves horseless and muleless. We may "fancy their feelings," when they discovered the opening! Just then, I fear, they would have made poor Peace Commissioners! Especially, as they had to foot it fifty miles, back to the next station, for new animals!

There was another story told of a gallant army officer, who had been out on a scout the year before, and was determined not to lose a favorite horse he had along. The Apaches were about thick, and the night before had stolen several animals, in spite of the utmost vigilance. To guard against what he supposed even the possibility of loss, the officer picketed his horse with a lariat to a troe, and then spreading his blankets camped down under the tree—at the same time posting a sentinel over his horse, with strict orders to watch faithfully. Toward morning the sentry thought the horse was a little farther from the tree than he should be; still, as he saw nothing suspicious, he supposed he must be mistaken as to the length of the lariat. After walking a few more beats, he thought the horse was still farther off; but it seemed so little, and the horse was so quiet, he did not think it right to make an alarm. A few beats more, however, convinced him that something must be wrong, as the horse was evidently still farther away. But now, simultaneously with his challenge, lo! an Apache sprang lithely upon the steed, and in a twinkling he was galloping off through the chaparral and cactuses, with a yell of defiance at the astonished Blue Coat! Creeping stealthily up in the dark, with a more than cat-like caution and silence, he had severed the lariat, and edged the horse off little by little, until at last his capture was sure.

If a party were strong, or not worth cleaning out, or killing, the Apaches usually gave them a wide berth. But woe to those whom they marked for their prey, if not well armed, and ceaselessly vigilant. They would dog a party for days, with the tireless energy of the sleuth-hound, watching for an unguarded moment in which to attack, and then suddenly pounce upon them, like fiends, as they were. As a rule, they used bows and arrows still; but many had fire-arms, and knew how to handle them with deadly effect. We were shown several of their children, captured in different fights, and they were the wiriest, fiercest little savages imaginable. Sullen, dogged, resolute little Red Skins, they lacked only maturity and strength to "make their mark" on somebody's head; and this they seemed quite likely to do yet, unless their Apache natures were thoroughly "reconstructed." They had a peculiar and pleasant *penchant* for setting fire to hay-stacks and ranches, and on the whole were a species of population, that nobody but an Arizonian would care much to fancy. They were held as servants in different families, and their service in too many instances approximated to downright slavery—so much so, indeed, that the attention of the Territorial authorities was already being directed to the matter.

As if to give us some proof of their enterprise and audacity, a band of these Apaches made a raid near Prescott, the very day we arrived there. They attacked a ranch only three miles east of "this New-England-like" village, and seized several cattle and drove them off. A mounted scout was at once sent out from Fort Whipple, and though they marched seventy-five miles in twenty-four hours, they failed to come up with the Red Skins. The officer in command reported the bold marauders as strong in numbers, and fleeing in the direction of Hell Cañon—an ugly, diabolical-looking place, some forty miles east of Prescott. Gen. Gregg, then commanding the District of Prescott, immediately ordered out two fresh companies of cavalry, and, himself at their head, made a forced march by night, in order to surprise them in their reported stronghold. Next morning at daybreak, he was at Hell Cañon, but no Apaches were found there, nor any traces of them. After a brief halt, he ordered the cavalry to follow down the cañon to its junction with the Verde, and after scouring all the cañons centering there, to return by a wide detour to Fort Whipple. The General himself now returned to Prescott, and I cheerfully bear witness to his vigor and chagrin, having accompanied him out and back. A detachment of the cavalry, a day or two afterwards, succeeded in finding a rancheria of Apaches in a villainous cañon, miles away to the southwest of the Verde—a thin curling smoke in the mountains revealing their presence. The troops pushed boldly in, and came suddenly on the rancheria, or village, before they were discovered. Dismounting from their horses, they poured in a rapid volley from their Spencer carbines, that killed five Apaches, and wounded twice as many more. The rest fled, but in a few minutes bravely rallied, and soon came swarming back, down the cañon and along its rocky cliffs, in such numbers and with such spirit, that the officer in command deemed it prudent to fall back on the main column. This he succeeded in doing, but it required a march of several miles, as the column had moved on; and when he rejoined, it was thought best for the whole command to return to Fort Whipple, as their rations and forage were about exhausted. Subsequently, Gregg sent them out again, and this time they succeeded in damaging the Apaches very considerably; but it was not long before they were lurking about the country again.

The rough ride to Hell Cañon and back, despite occasional snow-squalls, was not unpleasant, and not without its interest. Our route in the main was down the valley of Granite Creek, and past the site of old Fort Whipple, now called Postle's Ranch. Here was a fine plateau of several hundred acres, with acequias and a petty grist-mill, the whole used formerly by the troops; but occupied now by only a family or two. The truth is, population was too sparse, and the Apaches too plenty, to make farming an agreeable occupation just there. We saw several men at work in the fields, as we rode along, all with rifles slung across their backs, and the infrequent settlers protested they meant to quit the country, as soon as their harvests matured. The last ranch eastward—the one most remote from Prescott, and, consequently, the very edge of the frontier there—was owned and occupied by what may justly be called a typical American emigrant. Born in New Jersey, the nephew of an eminent minister there, he early emigrated to Canada, and thence to Michigan. Here he married, and soon afterwards emigrated to Illinois. Thence he went to Kansas, and thence to New Mexico. Subsequently, he emigrated to California, and when he grew weary there, as he could "go west" no farther, concluded to remove to Arizona. Here he had been for two years, with his family, on the very edge of the border; but was now tired of the West, and meditating a return East. He said his children were growing up, and needed school-houses and churches, and he meant to sell out and leave as soon as practicable.

The country as a whole proved barren and sterile, like so much of Arizona elsewhere, though here also the Aztecs (or whoever the ancient population were) had left their marks, as on the Salado and Gila. The remains of edifices, or fortifications, and acequias, were still quite visible in various places, and no doubt the ancient settlers had followed up the rivers, and their tributaries, nearly everywhere. They seem to have been a pushing, progressive people, bent on conquest and civilization, after their kind, and doubtless swayed the whole interior of the continent. At Point of Rocks, on Willow Creek, we halted for an hour or two, to explore the wonderful rock-formations there; and subsequently dined with a settler on a wild turkey, that stood four feet high and weighed forty-three pounds, when first shot, and about thirty pounds dressed. We were tired and hungry, from long riding and light rations, and you may be sure enjoyed our meal to the full.

Fort Whipple, already alluded to several times, was situated on Granite Creek, a mile and a half east of Prescott, near the centre of a Reservation there a mile square. It consisted of a rude stockade, enclosing the usual log quarters and barracks of our frontier posts, and was then Headquarters of all the district north of the Gila. Its garrison was small, and dependencies few and petty; but the cost of maintaining it seemed something enormous. Here are a few of the prices then current at the post: hay cost about sixty dollars per ton; grain, about twelve dollars per bushel; lumber, from fifty to seventy-five dollars per thousand; freight on supplies, from San Francisco (and about everything had to come from there *via* the Gulf of California and the Colorado), two hundred and fifty dollars per ton; and these all in coin. The flag-staff alone, quite a respectable "liberty-pole," was reported to have cost ten thousand dollars; and District Headquarters—a one-and-a-half story frame house, surrounded by verandas, but barely comfortable and genteel—was said to have cost one hundred thousand dollars. This last, plain as it was, was then about the best modern edifice in Arizona, but was used as the Post Hospital — Gen. Gregg ("Cavalry Gregg" of the Army of the Potomac) in the true spirit of a soldier, declining to occupy it, until his sick and disabled men were first well sheltered, and provided for. Himself and staff, as yet, shared the log cabins of the Post proper, through whose open crannies the wind and rain had free course to run and be glorified, during every storm. We were there during a wild tempest of rain and hail, as well as for a week or more besides, and learned well how to appreciate their infelicities and miseries. All honor to this chivalrous and gallant Pennsylvanian, for his courtesy and humanity. A Bayard and a Sydney combined, surely he deserves well of his country; and the Army may justly be proud of such a representative soldier.

CHAPTER XXVI.

PRESCOTT TO LOS ANGELOS.

PRESCOTT, as already intimated, was not Paradise, and we left there April 13th, for Los Angelos, *via* Hardyville and Fort Mojave, on our return "inside," with real rejoicing. Our first stage was to Fort Mojave, on the Colorado, distant one hundred and sixty miles, and this we made in five days. Of course, we travelled by ambulance, and "camped out" every night, as elsewhere mostly in Arizona. The road was a toll-road, but its general condition was hardly such, as to justify the collection of tolls ordinarily. As a whole, it was naturally a very fair road, though there were some bad points, as at Juniper Mountain and Union Pass, where considerable work had been required to carry the grades along. At Williamson's Valley, twenty miles out from Prescott, we found one of the best agricultural and grazing districts, that we had yet seen in Arizona. There were but two or three settlers there then, though there were apparently several thousands of acres fit for farms. The hills adjacent abounded in scattered cedars and junipers, that would do for fencing and fuel, and game seemed more abundant near there, than in any place we had yet been. Quails, found everywhere in Arizona to some extent, here soon thickened up; the jack-rabbits bounded more numerously through the bushes; even pigeons and wild-turkeys were heard of; and as we

18

rattled down through a rocky glen, at the western side of the valley, a herd of likely deer cantered leisurely across the road—the first we had seen in Arizona, or indeed elsewhere in the West.

Thence across Juniper Mountain to Rock Springs, some fifty miles, the country was wild and desolate, with a scraggy growth of cedars and junipers much of the way. A few scattered oaks and pines grew here and there, but they could scarcely be called good timber, or much of it. At Rock Springs was a fine bottom of several hundred acres, but not a single inhabitant. Thence on to Hardyville, through Cottonwood Cañon, past Hualapai Springs, Beale's Springs, etc., for nearly a hundred miles, there were no ranches, and no cultivable lands, indeed, worth mentioning. The country, as a whole, seemed a vast volcanic desert—of mountains, cañons, and mesas—and what it was ever made for, except to excite wonder and astonishment, is a mystery to the passing traveller. Even at the high elevation we were travelling, usually four or five thousand feet above the sea, the sun was already intensely hot by day, though the air grew bitingly cold at night, before morning. The principal growth, after leaving Rock Springs, was sage-brush and grease-wood, and in many places it proved difficult to secure sufficient for fires of even these. Water was found only at distances of ten and twenty miles apart, and in the dry summer months it must be still scarcer. Our poor animals suffered greatly, and one day we came near losing several—two of them continuing sick far into the night. Now and then we found an Indian trail crossing the road, but the Red Skins either did not see us, or else kept themselves well under cover, intimidated by the half-dozen cavalrymen, that accompanied us as escort.

The prevailing hues of the landscape were a dull red

and brownish gray, and these produced at times some very singular and striking effects. The one thing, that relieved our ride from utter dullness and monotony, was the weird and picturesque forms, in which nature has there piled up her rocks, and chiseled out her mountains. Domes, peaks, terraces, castles, turrets, ramparts—all were sculptured against the cloudless sky; and we fell to interesting ourselves sometimes for hours, as we rode along, in tracing out the strange resemblances to all sorts of architecture and animals, ancient and modern, that nature, in her silent sublimity, has perpetrated there. At sunset, when parting day lingered and played upon the surrounding or distant mountains, it bathed their rock-ribbed sides and summits in the most gorgeous tints of purple and maroon, and filled the imagination with all that was most sublime and mysterious. What Milton must have thought of in portraying Hell, or Dante imagined in delineating the weird and sombre landscapes of his awful Inferno, may well be realized in passing through this singular region, where Desolation seems to have outstretched her wings, and made up her mind to brood gloomily forever.

At Union Pass, we crossed the last mountain range, at an elevation of fully five thousand feet, whence we caught welcome sight again of the ruby waters of the Colorado. Debouching into the valley, we presently struck the river at Hardyville. Here it winds its sinuous course, through a broad valley of volcanic mesas and mountains, and has no bottoms worth mentioning, except those occupied of old by the Mojave Indians. These are fertilized by the annual overflow of the Colorado, like the bottoms of the Nile, and no doubt might be made to produce very largely. As it was, the Mojaves scratched them a little, so as to plant some corn and barley, and raise a few beans, vegetables, etc., the surplus of which they sold chiefly at Hardyville, for Mr. Hardy to re-sell to the Government again—of course, at a profit. It seemed, on the whole, that they did not usually raise enough, off of all their broad acres, to feed and clothe themselves comfortably; and we were told they would often go hungry, were it not for the gratuitous issues of flour, meal, and other supplies occasionally made to them by the commanding officer at Fort Mojave. We rode through their villages one evening, while halting at Fort Mojave, and found they numbered about a thousand or so just there; but farther down the Colorado, at La Paz, there was said to be another branch of them, even more numerous. They were usually a shapely, well-made race, and seemed to take life even more easy, if possible, than their red brethren elsewhere. Their women made a rude pottery ware, that seemed in general use among them, and the men themselves sometimes labored commendably, in gathering drift-wood for fuel for the petty steamers, that occasionally ascended to Hardyville. These Mojaves had been quiet and peaceable for years, and it seemed very moderate efforts would put them on the road to civilization, as readily as the Choctaws and the Cherokees. But they complained, and quite justly, that the Government did not furnish them implements, tools, seeds, etc., to enable them to work their lands and support themselves, while the savage Hualapais, Pai-Utes, and other hostile tribes, were being constantly bribed with presents and annuities. This, however, was only another instance of the stupidity and blundering of our Indian Department at that time, whose policy, or rather impolicy, seemed to be to neglect friendly Indians, and exhaust its money and efforts on hostile ones, under the plea of "pacifying" them! As if "gifts" and "annuities" ever really pacified or civilized a Red Skin yet, or ever will! No; the only true policy with our Indians, then as now, is to encourage and reward the friendly, in every right way; while the hostile ones should be turned over to the Army, for chastisement and surveillance, to the uttermost, until they learn the hard lesson, that henceforth they must behave themselves.

Fort Mojave, some four miles or so below Hardyville, on the east bank of the Colorado, was a rude post, most uncomfortable every way. It had been established originally in 1860, abandoned in 1861, but re-occupied in 1864, and maintained since then. We found it hot, and dusty, and miserable, even in April; and could well imagine what it must be in July and August. At Prescott, we were some six thousand feet above the sea; but here we had got down to only about eleven hundred, and the change was most perceptible. Here were a handful of troops, and two or three officers, all praying for the day when they might be ordered elsewhere, assured that fortune could send them to no worse post, outside of Alaska. One officer had his wife along, a lady delicately bred, from Pittsburg, Pa., and this was her first experience of Army life. When we first arrived, she tried to talk cheerily, and bore up bravely for awhile; but before we left, she broke down in tears, and confessed to her utter loneliness and misery. No wonder, when she was the only white woman there, no other within a hundred miles or more; and no newspaper or mail even, except once a month or fortnight, as things happened to be.

Hardyville itself was then more of a name than place, consisting chiefly of a warehouse and quartz-mill, with a few adobe shanties. Near Hardyville, some ten or twenty miles away in the outlying mountains, there were several mines—gold, silver, and copper—of more or less richness, and the mill was located here to take advantage of the two great essentials, wood and water. The mill, however, was standing idle, like most enterprises in Arizona, and but little was doing in the mines. Mr. Hardy himself, a hard-working energetic man, and the Ben Holliday or Gen. Banning of that region, controlling all its business, including Government contracts, from the Colorado to Prescott and beyond, was getting out some ore, and specimens we saw at his store were certainly very handsome. He said there were "leads" in the neighboring mountains of exceeding richness, and indeed here and at other similar points along the Colorado, as at La Paz, Aubrey City, El Dorado Cañon, etc., there seemed the best chances for mining of anywhere in Arizona. Here were wood (drift-wood, in which the Colorado abounds) and water, the two great needs, usually wanting elsewhere in Arizona; and the Colorado itself, it would seem, ought to afford reasonably cheap and quick transportation, if the steamboats on it were constructed and run with proper enterprise and efficiency.

The great drawback to Arizona then, overshadowing perhaps all others, not excepting the Apaches, was the perfectly *frightful and ruinous cost of transportation*. To reach any mining-district there from California, except those along the Colorado, you had to travel from three to five hundred miles through what are practically deserts; and for every ton of freight carried into or out of the Territory, you were called on to pay from three to five cents per pound, per hundred miles, in coin. Golconda, itself, could not flourish under such circumstances, much less Arizona—which is scarcely a Golconda. The patent and palpable remedy for all this, was either a railroad or the speedy and regular navigation of the Colorado. It seemed nonsense to say that the Colorado could not be navigated, and that too at rates reasonably cheap. It looked no worse than the Ohio and the Missouri, and like western rivers ordinarily; and there appeared but small hope for Arizona very speedily, until she availed herself to the full of its actual advantages. With the alleged mines along the Colorado, from Ft. Yuma to El Dorado, in good operation, her population, as it increased, would naturally overflow to other districts; and, in the end, arid Arizona would become reasonably prosperous. But, like all other commonwealths, she must have a base to stand on and work from. That base seemed naturally and necessarily the Colorado River, indifferent as it was. And all attempts to develop herself, except from that, in the absence of a railroad, seemed likely to end like the efforts of the man, who tried to build a pyramid with the apex downward. History declares it was *not* a "success."

Bidding good-bye to our friends at Fort Mojave, we crossed the Colorado on a rude flat-boat, on the evening of April 18th, and proceeded three miles to Beaver Lake where we camped for the night, in order to get a good start next day. We dismissed our escort at Fort Mojave, as no longer necessary; and, Gov. McCormick and wife having left us at Prescott, our little party was now reduced to two and our drivers. Col. Carter, Secretary of the Territory, had accompanied us from Prescott to Mojave; but here he left us for a trip up the Colorado, intending to push into the Big Cañon, if possible. Subsequently, I learned, he failed in doing this; but the fault was not his, and, for the present, we bade him speedy success and a safe return.

From Fort Mojave, on the Colorado, to Los Angelos was still about three hundred miles, and this we accomplished in eight days. The valley or great basin of the Colorado extends most of the distance, and of the intervening country, as a whole, the most that can be said of it is, that it is an absolute desert of extinct volcanoes and outstretched sand-plains, fit only for tarantulas and centipedes, rattlesnakes and Indians. As far as could be seen, I think this a fair and truthful statement of pretty much all that region to Cajon Pass, and don't see how it can well be objected to, by any honest mind. Its changes of elevation are, indeed, something very curious. At Fort Mojave, on the banks of the Colorado, you are only about a thousand feet above the sea. Thence, for ten or twelve miles, you steadily ascend, until you get where the view of the Colorado Valley proper becomes something really sublime—a barren ocean, a sea of desolation, with a line of living green meandering through the centre—and at Pai-Ute Hill, only some thirty miles from the Colorado, you reach an elevation of some four thousand feet. At Government Holes, indeed, you get up to 5,204 feet; but at Soda Lake, about a hundred miles from Fort Mojave, you descend again to 1,075 feet, or seventy-four feet lower than the Colorado itself.* From here you climb back to 1,852 feet at Camp Cady, some forty miles from Soda Lake; 2,678 feet at Cottonwood Ranch, some eighty miles from Soda Lake; and gradually get up again to 5,000 feet at Cajon Pass, about one hundred and twenty miles from Soda Lake. These ascents and descents usually are not sudden, nor indeed much perceptible; but gradually you roll up and down over a vast desert region,

* Hence the recent proposition to turn the Colorado thither and convert all this district, including the Yuma or Colorado Desert, into a great lake or inland sea. It seems hardly feasible in this generation; but, possibly, may happen in the future.

where the sun was already (in April) intensely hot by day, and getting to be fairly warm at night.

In the long drives by day, sometimes forty and fifty miles—to reach water—the heat and glare from the sand became terrible to the eyes, and twice we drove all night, lying by in the day, to avoid this. By day, we usually saw no live thing, except here and there a stray buzzard, or scampering lizard, or horned toad. By night, we would hear the rattlesnakes hiss and rattle, as we drove along—our "outfit" as we rattled by, I suppose, disturbing their quiet siestas, or moonlight promenades. It was too early in the season, however, to be troubled much with such interesting acquaintances as rattlesnakes, tarantulas, centipedes, etc. They were but just beginning to come out of their holes, and we were glad to escape from the country before they ventured forth much. We saw, indeed, some centipedes, and killed several rattlesnakes. One night one of the party woke up, and found something reposing snugly on the outside of his blankets. Giving it a kick and sling from underneath, it proved to be a snake, and answered him back from the place where it landed, with the usual inevitable hiss and defiant rattle. Another night, at Soda Lake, while sleeping by the rocks there, a rattlesnake crawled under the bottom blankets, and in the morning when the owner of them began to yawn and stretch himself, preparatory to getting up, his snakeship from beneath hissed, and rattled, and protested, as badly as a northern copperhead or a southern rebel at the Proclamation of Emancipation, or the Reconstruction measures of Congress. Of course, we all slept on the ground every night, *ex necessitate;* but, after this, we usually retired with all our clothes and tallest boots on!

Pai-Ute hill, so-called (before spoken of), is really a

sharp and ugly little mountain, up which we toiled slowly and wearily. In rounding an angle of the road, soon after beginning the ascent, one of our ambulances sliding struck a rock, and soon like the famous "One Hoss Shay," ended in a "general spill!" There could hardly have been a more thorough collapse of spokes and felloes —everything seemed to go to pieces—and it could hardly have occurred in a worse place. It was a wild and desolate cañon, barren and rocky, miles away from every human habitation; yet there was nothing for it, but to leave the driver in charge, and the rest of us proceed on to Camp Rock Springs, whence we sent an army-wagon back to gather up the remains and bring them on. Camp Rock Springs itself was a forlorn military post, consisting of one officer and perhaps a dozen men, guarding the Springs and the road there. The officer was quartered in a natural cave in the hillside, and his men had "hutted" themselves out on the sand the best they could. No glory there, nor much chance for military fame; but true patriots and heroes were they, to submit to such privations. Too many of our frontier posts are akin to this, and little do members of Congress east, who know only "the pomp and circumstance of glorious war," imagine what army-life out there really is. It is a poor place for fuss and feathers, gilt epaulets and brass buttons; and our "Home Guard," holiday Militia east, so fond of parading up and down our peaceful streets, with full rations and hotel quarters, would soon acquire for soldiering there only a rare and infinite disgust. Yet these are the nurseries of the Army, and from such hard schools we graduated a Grant and Sherman, Sheridan and Thomas.

Soda Lake, already mentioned, is simply a dried-up lake, or sea, whose salts of soda effloresce and whiten the ground, like snow, for miles in every direction. The country there is a vast basin, rimmed around with desolate hills and mountains, and during the rainy season a considerable body of water, indeed, collects here. Soon, however, evaporation does its work, and the Lake proper subsides to little or nothing, worth speaking of. When we were there, it was said to be twenty miles long, by four or five wide, though of course everywhere very marshy or shallow. Skirting the borders of it, we reached a rocky bluff on (I think) the northern shore, and there found a noble spring of excellent water, welling up of from unknown depths, within a stone's throw of the soda deposits. Here was the usual halting-place, and as we had driven all night, we went into camp on arriving there, soon after sunrise. It was Sunday, April 21st; there was no house or even hut there; no person or living thing; and what with the heat, and glare, and awful desolation—our weariness, fatigue, and sense of isolation—I think it was about the most wretched and miserable day I ever spent anywhere. To crown all, during the night before, while jogging along, we had descried what we supposed to be an Indian camp-fire, off to the south of the road some distance; we had driven quietly but hastily on, getting the utmost out of our jaded mules; but whether the Red Skins were asleep, or had discovered and were now dogging us, awaiting their opportunity, we were blissfully ignorant. We passed the hours away, as best we could, sleeping and watching in turn; but the next morning, bright and early, we were up and off for Camp Cady. We would have departed, indeed, by night; but the route lay largely up the disgusting cañon of the Mojave, and was impracticable in the dark. This was the only sign of hostile Indians we saw *en route* from the Colorado. We could hardly call it a genuine "scare;" and yet were not greatly grieved, when we found they had given us a wide berth.

Some fifteen or twenty miles beyond Soda Lake, we struck the Mojave River, so-called, which there runs for several miles through a narrow and rocky cañon, much similar to that of the Hassayampa, though its walls are not so high. The road itself leads up this cañon, for lack of a better route over and through the mountains there, and on first view, it promised to be the Hassayampa over again; but, fortunately, the bottom is chiefly gravel and rock, and therefore has not the same disagreeable habit of "dropping out," when you venture over it. We found from one to two feet of water in the Mojave here, and crossed it, I suppose, at least thirty or forty times between there and Camp Cady—within say twenty miles. Two days afterward, when we crossed it for the last time, farther up, at what is called the Upper Crossing of the Mojave, we found it two feet *deeper* than it had been a hundred miles below, and with more than *twice* the volume of water. Our famous Pathfinder, in one of his great expeditions, struck it near here, at freshet height, and it is said reported the Mojave as "an important tributary of the Colorado, navigable for light-draft steamboats several months in the year." He would have been partly right, perhaps, if the Mojave indeed continued on to the Colorado. But unfortunately, it sinks in the desert, long before it gets there; and the enthusiastic explorer's "light-draft steamboats" would have to go paddling across a broad expanse of sand and rock, if they wanted to voyage from the Mojave to the Colorado, or *vice versa!* The Mojave, in fact, although draining the snow-capped San Bernardino Mountains, and a wide stretch of country there, is only another of the many strange anomalies that one meets with in

Southern California and Arizona. Said a ranchman in that region :

" Dis yer's a quar country, stranger, you bet ! All sorts of quar things out yer. Folks chop wood with a sledge-hammer, and mow grass with a hoe. Every bush bears a thorn, and every insect has a sting. The trees is pretty nigh all cactuses. The streams haint no water, except big freshets. The rivers get littler, the furder they run down. No game but rabbits, and them's big as jackasses. Some quails, but all top-knotted, and wild as greased lightning. No frost; no dew. Nobody kums yer, unless he's runnin' away. Nobody stays, unless he has to. Everybody 'vamoses the ranch,' 'cuts stick,' 'absquatulates,' as soon as he kin raise nuff 'dust' to 'git up and *git*' with. You *bet*—ye ! Sure !"

It is due to truth to say, that our friend had just got up from the "break-bone" fever, and was still troubled with the "shakes." His mine had "petered out," and his "outfit" was about "gone up." In fact, he looked, and I have no doubt felt, slightly dismal—not to put too fine a point upon it. But I give his opinion, as he gave it to us; and the reader must take it *cum grano salis*—as much or little as he chooses. In truth, we have a vast region there, that as a whole is simply barren and worthless, and that will never be utilized or seriously amount to much, until the rest of the continent is well occupied and settled up. We may, of course, regret it; but that is about the truth of things, and emigrants thither soon discover it.

Beyond Camp Cady, another rude post, much like Rock Springs, we found a few ranches scattered here and there along the Mojave; but they were importing grain and hay fifty and a hundred miles, from San Bernardino and Los Angelos, for sale to passing teams and travellers, which looked as if their prospects were not very flattering. There ought, however, to be some good farms there, if the Mojave were properly utilized; and doubtless this will be done soon, if it has not been already.

At Cajon Pass, through the lofty Coast Range, you quickly run down from five thousand feet above the sea, to about one thousand feet at San Bernardino, or even less. The descent is through a wild and picturesque cañon, that almost equals in grandeur and sublimity the far-famed Echo Cañon of Utah. We camped all night near the foot of the Pass, sleeping so soundly that several mounted deserters * from Fort Mojave passed us unheeded, and the next morning, bright and early, we rolled into San Bernardino. Here was a well-laid out and tolerably built town, of a thousand or so inhabitants, with a newspaper, telegraph, and most modern improvements. It reminds one of Salt Lake City, and was, indeed, patterned after that gem of the mountains, being settled originally by the Mormons many years ago, when they planned a route through here to the Pacific at San Diego. We remained here but a few hours, and, as the weather was already becoming warm, started the same evening for Los Angelos, some sixty miles north, where we arrived late next morning.

The country just now (April 26th), between Cajon Pass and Los Angelos, was beautiful and glorious beyond description. I scarcely know how to speak of it in fitting terms, but I remember well how it impressed us at the time. The Los Angelos Plains, seventy miles long by thirty wide, were one wild sea of green and yellow, pink

* They were our escort from Prescott, whom we had dismissed at Mojave, with orders to return as soon as rested. But, it seems, the poor fellows were tired of Arizona, and as they were so far on their way "inside," concluded to continue thither!

and violet—herbage and flowers everywhere. Thousands of lusty cattle and contented sheep roamed over them at will; but not one herd or flock, where there ought to be a score or hundred. The vineyards were all putting forth their leafy branches, and preparing for their purple clusters. The fields were heavy with barley and wheat. The olive and walnut orchards were clad in foliage of densest green. The orange groves were everywhere filling the air with their delicate and delicious fragrance, so exquisitely sweet and ethereal it seemed as if distilled from heaven. Ten thousand "beautiful birds of song" flitted and twittered, from bush to tree, as we drove along. On the west rolled the blue Pacific; on the east rose the noble Coast Range; and over all, like a celestial benediction, hung the California sky—a superb sapphire we never see East. The setting sun lit up the distant hills, as we gazed, and now clothed with crimson and gold—an ineffable glory of splendors—the snow-clad peaks, that towered to the north and east. Up there was the frozen zone, most of the year round; but down on the Plains, the balmy zephyrs of the tropics, and nature literally one wild scene of beauty and of glory.

The transition from the Mojave Desert, and Arizona generally, to this delightful region, was like coming into Eden—seemed like "Paradise Regained," in very truth. As we emerged from the mountains at Cajon Pass, and drove down into it, we could scarcely refrain from shouting for joy. Our animals whinnied, pricked up their ears, and, jaded as they were, trotted along with a new-found speed. Poor beasts, faithful donkeys, we had driven some of them fully fifteen hundred miles, "outside" and "inside," forth and back. Just to think of it once, plenty of good water, fresh green grass, and a moist and fragrant atmosphere once more! No more blazing sun; no more glaring sand; no more alkali streams; no more thorny mesquite and prickly cactus; no more Apaches and Hualapais, Pai-Utes and Chemehuevis; no more scanning every bush and rock by day, and listening intently to every sound by night; no more riding with rifles in our hands, no more sleeping on our arms; no more bottomless quicksands; no more fear of rattlesnakes and centipedes; no more freshets, and no more sand-storms. No! The long drag of fifteen hundred miles was over, and once more we struck hands with civilization and school-houses—touched steam-ships and telegraphs.

Verily, we had a right to sing "Out of the Wilderness," and "Home again," with infinite gusto; and it is not surprising, that with these and other jolly airs we did, indeed, make the welkin ring. Once more we had the newspapers—we hadn't seen one in a month before—that is, less than a month old—and to fair and hospitable Los Angelos, ever and truly the City of the Angels, we were welcomed as ones from the desert, if not from the dead. We had, indeed, been reported several times, as waylaid and captured by the Indians; but here we were *in propriis personis*, brown and hearty, though dusty and fatigued. Our good friend Banning and Don Benito Wilson were among the first to congratulate us; and their kindness and courtesy during the next three days, and until we left by steamer for San Francisco (April 30th), when shall we forget?

CHAPTER XXVII.

SAN FRANCISCO TO VIRGINIA CITY.

A SOJOURN of a fortnight or so, at San Francisco, sufficed for rest and bringing up back Reports, and on the evening of May 16th, we took the good boat, Chrysopolis for Sacramento, and thence on to Virginia City. There were posts in Nevada I was ordered to inspect, and this was then the best route to reach them. The weather was raw at San Francisco, but when we got well up the bay and past Benicia, the air became mild and June-like, and the evening was passed delightfully on deck, under such star-lit skies as only California and the Far West can boast. We had a full complement of passengers, of all grades from New York cockneys to Nevada miners; but the proportion of ladies was small, as usually on the Coast. The few children aboard seemed general pets, and many eagerly seized a moment's chat with them. I saw a rough-looking miner, tall, and "bearded like a pard," entice two of them to his side, and, subsequently wander all over the boat with them, talking with the little folks by the hour, about the machinery and whatever else excited their curiosity. At supper, we had a substantial and excellent meal; at bed-time, we found the berths clean and sweet; and the conduct of the boat in general was all that could be desired.

The Sacramento itself is a noble stream, of which

any commonwealth might well be proud. To Benicia, and beyond, it is navigable for first-class sea-going vessels, and here upon the bold shores and by the deep waters thereabouts, San Francisco ought really to have been built, as elsewhere intimated. But, unfortunately, the metropolis got itself camped down on the sand-hills, near the Golden Gate, and now will remain there forever.

We reached Sacramento City, one hundred and twenty miles from San Francisco, about 2 A. M. next day, and after an early breakfast and a short walk through the town, took the train at 6½ A. M. for Cisco, then the advance station on the Central Pacific Railroad. This ride, of about a hundred miles, was first up the rich valley of the Sacramento, and then through the foot-hills, and up the Sierra Nevadas. At Sacramento the river was still broad and deep, but with low banks that necessitated levees to guard against overflows. Once a clear mountain stream, fresh from the Sierras, it was now tawnier than the yellow Tiber, with the results of mining on its head-waters and tributaries, and, it was reported, was steadily filling up. Sacramento, indeed, may well have an eye to this; but what she can do to correct or prevent it, it seems difficult to say.

As we advanced, the valley of the Sacramento steadily narrowed, but everywhere appeared rich and fertile. Broad farms stretched out on every side, and clumps of live-oaks, with their deep green foliage, everywhere relieved the golden yellow of the ripening wheat-fields. The general lack of timber continued noticeable, but these scattered live-oaks, sturdy and defiant, relieved the landscape, and they seemed preserved with commendable care. As we approached the foot-hills, the soil grew thinner, the lordly wheat-fields gave place to extensive vineyards, and soon the dense pines of the Sierras made their appearance. Here, too, we struck the mines, and on all sides saw evidences of the spade and rocker. In many places, there were only old placers abandoned, with the hills ragged and torn, and the earth generally topsy-turvy with past operations—cabins empty, ditches dry, sluice-ways falling to pieces; but, in others, the washings were still in full operation, and the hills and streams seemed alive with human industry and energy. Little mining hamlets were perched, here and there, on the edge of mountain torrents; and, where the water did not suffice, broad ditches, improvised for the locality, brought it from some far-off point and carried it wheresoever wanted.

Some of these water-ditches are among the wonders of the Pacific Coast, and deserve more than a passing notice. With surprising engineering, they wind down and around and among the mountains, leaping ravines, crossing ridges, and everywhere following the miner, like faithful servants of his will. Wherever necessary, the miner taps them, and either uses the water in his ordinary sluice-way, or else by his hydraulic pipes hurls it against the hills, and literally washes them to the plain. This hydraulic mining seemed to be most in favor there, and the power developed by some of these streams was immense. The momentum acquired by the water in its long descent, sufficed to melt huge hills of clay and gravel very quickly; and instances were reported where men, and mules even, had been killed by being struck by the water, as it issued from the pipes or hose. The men engaged in mining were rough and hirsute, as miners everywhere are; but they looked bright and keen, and as if they believed in California and her future, come what might.

The change in the climate, as we plunged into the foot-hills, and felt our way up into the Sierras, was very apparent, and soon became disagreeably so. At Sacramento, the weather was close and warm; but hour by hour, as we ascended, the thermometer went down, and long before reaching Cisco, only about a hundred miles or so, we were shivering in winter garments. As I have said, this was then the "jumping off" place or terminus of the Central Pacific road, and is well up into the mountains. We reached there soon after noon, and I must say were surprised at the general excellence, as well as audacity of the road. Some of its grades are over a hundred feet to the mile,* and in many places it literally springs into the air, over immense trestle-work bridges or along the dizzy edge of precipices, that seem fraught with peril and destruction; but we reached Cisco safe and sound, and sat down to a smoking dinner, with the snow-drifts still up to the eaves of the roofs of the hotel, and the houses round-about.

Cisco was then a scattered village, of frame tenements, only a few months old; but as the terminus of the road, and depot of supplies for all Nevada, it was bustling with business. The Overland Mail, for Virginia City and the East, left here daily, on the arrival of the train; and, after a hurried dinner, we were off again with the mail. It was now May 17th, and though the advancing summer had melted the snow in the regular roadway, so that wagoning was practicable for some distance, yet the old snow still lay six and eight feet deep on the general level, and our road ran between solid walls of it. We set off from Cisco in

* Above Dutch Flat, the maximum grade of 116 feet per mile has been resorted to, for over ten miles. From Owl Gap to the Summit, a distance of twenty-four and a half miles, the average grade is 81, and the maximum 85 feet per mile. From the Summit to the Truckee, the average is 84, and the maximum 90 feet per mile; but down the Truckee, the grades average less than 40 feet per mile.

stage-coaches (mountain mud-wagons), but soon had to surrender these for sleighs; and then came a long and dreary pull, through slush and mud and ice, for several miles, till we got well across the summit of the Sierras, when we again took coaches and rattled down to Donner Lake, where we arrived at 8½ P. M., having made only eighteen miles since noon. The most of us walked a good part of the way, and found it altogether rather a fatiguing march. The depth of the snow still left on the summit seemed surprising; but a gentleman I met in San Francisco assured me, that when he crossed the Sierras in December previous, he found the telegraph poles, even, in many places snowed under. The stage-people reported the snow as having been fifteen and twenty feet in depth on the level generally, and we could see where they had set up poles and "shakes" long before, to mark out the general course of the road itself.

It was these huge vast snows that the Central Pacific folks had mainly to provide against, and the problem would have appalled most men. But they quietly set to work to board the snows out, and since then have literally housed their road in for thirty miles or more. The surrounding forests furnished them cheap timber, and portable saw-mills shifted from point to point soon converted this into the required lumber. But what a herculean job it really was! These great snow-sheds or snow-galleries consumed in all nearly forty-five million feet, board measure, of sawed timber, and over a million and a quarter feet of round timber, equivalent in the aggregate to fifty-two and a half million feet, board measure, of sawed timber; and nearly a thousand tons of iron and spikes. Two general styles of construction were adopted—one intended for localities where the *weight* of the snow only had to be supported, and the other for such places as were exposed to "slides," and the slower but almost irresistible "glacial movement" of the snow, as on the steep and rocky slopes near the summit. These galleries have proved a great success, and though frequently covered with drifted snow to a depth of ten or twenty feet, and in some places of more than fifty feet, they afford a safe passage for trains at all seasons, without noticeable detentions.

Near the summit, we came upon John Chinaman again, in all his glory. Here was the "Heathen Chinee," five thousand strong, burrowing and tunnelling a way for the road, through the back-bone of the Sierras. It was a huge piece of work, nearly half a mile long, through the solid granite; but John was patiently pegging away at it, from four different faces, and soon afterwards completed it successfully. They all wore their pig-tails, the same as in San Francisco, but usually had these sacred appendages twisted well around their heads, instead of dangling at their heels; and, with the exception of the universal blue blouse, were dressed like ordinary navvies or laborers. Of course, they had American or English superintendents and foremen of gangs; but these all spoke well of the almond-eyed strangers, and praised them, especially, for their docility and intelligence. A more industrious or orderly set of workingmen, were never seen; and though railroad-building was a new employment for Asiatics, they seemed to take to it very kindly. Subsequently, they pushed the Central down the mountains, and through to Ogden City; and the day is not distant, when they will push such roads, with their thousand civilizing influences, all through the Flowery Kingdom.

We crossed the summit just at sunset, and from that proud altitude—seven thousand two hundred feet above the sea—gazed down upon that gem of the Sierras, Donner Lake—a body of crystalline water, five miles long by over half a mile wide, in the very heart of the mountains. The crest of the Sierras lifts itself boldly along the west, but elsewhere the ridges slope down to the Lake, and the hoary peaks and cliffs seem to hold it in their lap, like a sleeping infant. The sunset itself, that evening, was superb. The clouds became gold, the snow burnished silver, while a purple haze sifted down from the sky, and soon veiled exquisitely the lake and its far-stretching cañons. As the night gathered deeper, the lights and shadows became grandly sublime; and then, as a fitting sequel, came one of those glorious skies, ablaze with stars, for which the Coast is so famed. It was blackest marble, gemmed with silver. It seemed to uplift itself into eternity. The whole scene fixed itself indelibly in the memory, and though we saw Lake Tahoe afterwards I preferred this view of Donner Lake.

In the midst of the falling shadows, we passed the snow-limit, and again betook ourselves to mountain mud-wagons, which farther down we again exchanged for Concord coaches. About 9 P. M. we halted for supper, but were soon on the road again, and striking the Truckee, followed it down until long after sunrise. Once out of the mountains, its valley rapidly broadened; but here was the rainless region, and sage-brush again prevailed, as in Idaho and Arizona. Here and there, we passed some fair farms; but irrigation was the secret, and without this, agriculture in Nevada, as elsewhere in the great basin of the continent, will seldom amount to much. The air continued raw and chilly, well into the morning; but the roads had become dusty and superb, and we bowled along down the mountains and up the wonderful Geiger grade, at a swinging pace, that brought us into Virginia City—seventy miles or more from Cisco—at about 10 A. M. Here we stopped at the International, then the "swell" house of Virginia City, and found excellent cheer, for the hungry and the weary.

The next day was Sunday, and though many of the business houses continued open, yet the mines and mills as a rule were silent, and the proportion of church-goers was larger than we expected. Virginia already boasted several creditable churches, and in one of these a noted revivalist from the East (Rev. Mr. E.) was attracting crowds by his zeal and earnestness. His discourse that day was bald to plainness, but direct and searching; and when, at its close, he invited penitents to rise, a score or more stood up—many of them rough and burly men, bathed in tears. He had crossed our path in Oregon in December, and subsequently we had heard of him again in San Francisco, where the press were divided as to his merits. But here in Nevada, he was regarded as a great evangelist, and one enthusiastic journalist asserted that he had added more to the church, during his brief tour on the Coast, than all their parsons before all put together. Some days after, when about to depart for other fields, he was presented with a silver "brick" or two, as appropriate evidence of Nevada appreciation.

As a mining town, Virginia City impresses one very favorably, and her growth seemed steady and real. She already possessed many excellent buildings, and others were fast going up. She sits high and dry, on the side of a silver mountain, six thousand feet above the sea, with a population of some eight or ten thousand souls, with other mountains shouldering away beneath and above her; and, of course, would never have been at all, had it not been for the lucky discovery of the Comstock

Lode. This is *the* great lode of Nevada, from which the bulk of her silver has been taken, and few of her mining operations elsewhere were then paying for themselves. White Pine had not then been discovered (May, '67), and the great enterprises of Nevada, such as Gould & Curry, Yellow Jacket, Ophir, Savage, Crown Point, etc., were all located on the Comstock Lode. This ran along the mountain-side, beneath the town, for two or three miles, varying in width from fifty to one hundred feet, and of unknown depth. The Gould & Curry Company had sunk a shaft nearly a thousand feet, and the argentiferous deposits still appeared, more or less richly. Less than a third of the companies then at work on this great lode, however (some thirty in all), were then paying dividends, and the general product of the State, it was conceded, was falling off. One company had spent over a million dollars, in "developing" its property, without striking "pay-ore," and others were following in its footsteps. But others, again, had paid very handsomely. The Gould & Curry, on an investment of less than two hundred thousand dollars from its stockholders, had paid them back four millions in dividends, and altogether had produced over twelve millions in bullion. In one year, it had yielded nearly five millions, with a clear profit of over one million; but in 1867, it was not promising so well. It had spent vast sums in mining and improvements, with something here and there that looked like extravagance, if not worse. Its magnificent mill, of eighty-stamp power, cost over a million of dollars, and was said to be the largest and finest quartz-mill in the world. This company owned twelve hundred feet of the Comstock Lode, and had dug down nearly a thousand feet in depth, and back and forth fifty times. Its shafts and tunnels measured over two miles under ground, and it had used more lumber in strengthing its walls, it was said, than was embraced in the whole of Virginia City overhead. We spent an afternoon wandering through its drifts and galleries, part of the time nine hundred and fifty feet beneath the surface, and were amazed at the work that had been done.

Another, the Yellow Jacket, had yielded over two millions of dollars, and paid its stock-holders nearly four hundred thousand dollars, or fifty thousand more than all their subscriptions and assessments. The Savage had taken out six millions of bullion, and the Ophir over twelve millions; but, as yet, the stock-holders had realized but little, because of bad management and expensive experiments, that proved failures. This Comstock ore averaged less than forty dollars per ton, more usually only twenty-five to thirty; but it was less refractory than most American ores, and required only to be crushed and amalgamated to extract the bullion. Better "processes" were continually being looked for, as in Colorado, with which it was hoped much poorer ores would pay well. Selected ores, such as averaged a thousand dollars per ton or so, were still shipped to Swansea, Wales, for treatment, though this seemed absurd, considering the distance and expense, and our vast deposits of coal at home. The famous Sutro Tunnel, in behalf of which Congress has since been so earnestly memorialized, is a magnificent scheme to tap this great lode at lower levels, where it may be drained and worked at much better advantage; and, if ever realized, will no doubt result in the Comstock turning out fabulous sums again.*

The most of the mining capital seemed to be furnished by California, and the best-informed people

* See Appendix.

thought, notwithstanding the large yield of many mines, that she had not yet received back the amount of money she had actually invested. A fair estimate was, that she had put fully a hundred millions into Nevada mines and mills, and had taken out only about sixty millions, leaving a balance of forty millions on the wrong side of the ledger yet; but then there were the shafts and tunnels, the mills and machinery, with large added experience, and 'Frisco capitalists were still hopeful of the future.

The fluctuations of mining stocks were great and frequent, and we watched them with interest while on the Coast. A lucky "strike," probably in some rich "pocket," would send Savage or Yellow Jacket high up on the list for a few days or weeks, when the vein would "peter out," and again it would drop to its former figures or below. Our conclusion was, that silver-mining, after all, is a very risky business. There may be money in it, for superintendents and directors; but for stockholders, as a rule, very little. The Mexicans have an adage, and they are old and experienced miners, that "it takes a *mine* to work a mine;" and that seemed to be about the opinion of the best minds we met with. Miners and mining-life, are much the same everywhere; and if the reader wants to know more about them, let him turn to Chapter V., p. 58.

CHAPTER XXVIII.

VIRGINIA CITY TO STOCKTON.

AFTER concluding my duties at Fort Churchill, some thirty miles east on the road to Austin, we returned again to Virginia City, and on the morning of May 22d took the coach for California again. As we had come over by Cisco and Donner Lake, we decided to return by Lake Tahoe and Placerville, and thus see as much of the country both ways as possible. Our route lay first through Carson City and Genoa, and thence across the Sierras by Lake Tahoe to Placerville. The sun shone clear, but cool, as we swung out of the Silver City, amidst rolling clouds of dust; but when we reached the grease-wood and sage plains, it speedily grew warmer. We found Carson a diminutive "city," noted chiefly for its penitentiary, and pushed rapidly ahead all day. We threaded the valley of the Carson, and striking the Sierras skirted their base for miles; but finally turned square west, and zigzagged over the first range, by a splendid turnpike, that is unsurpassed anywhere. The range was so abrupt, and the road so sharp, that the summit seemed higher than it really was; but when we reached there, we were repaid by a magnificent view of the valley of the Carson, and the far-stretching sage and alkali plains of Nevada. So far, we had encountered no snow; but when we approached the second range, or Mother Ridge of the Sierras, we found it snow-crowned still, and prepared ourselves for the worst.

At Yank's Station, where we changed horses just at nightfall, they reported the road ahead as not good enough for sleighs, and too bad for coaches; but concluded, on the whole, we had better risk a coach. So, after a hearty supper, we set off in a Concord coach, being the first one over the Placerville route that spring. We had a full load—nine passengers inside and four outside, including two ladies and three children; but our six horses were fresh and gamey, and for a time we swung along at a spanking pace. Halfway up the range, however, we struck the ice and slush, and soon came to a dead halt, with a request from the driver for all to get out and walk, except the ladies and children. With only these on board, the coach forged ahead for a mile or so more, when again it halted, and these, too, were ordered out. Two of the children were small, only four or five years of age, and these the rest of the passengers chivalrously agreed to shoulder and carry by turns. The road was itself quite steep; its bed, mingled ice and slush; while on either side were still four or five feet of snow, as on the Donner Lake route. It ascended the range by long zigzags, and some who attempted a "short cut" across these, trusting the snow, soon found themselves up to their waists or shoulders in it. It was slow and painful travelling at best, especially with a child on your back; but the coach progressed still slower, and often we heard it floundering along far below us, or wholly stalled in some villainous chuck-hole, worse than the rest.

Reaching the summit at last, near midnight, by such long and toilsome climbing, we there found a rough station, where we dried our feet and clothes, and got fresh horses, after which we pushed on again—now, however, sticking by the coach, and helping to lift it out, and urge it along from time to time as needed. Sometimes, it seemed hopelessly stalled, especially when it got wedged in, besides, against one of the snow-walls; but by lifting and prying, and much faithful shouting, we always managed somehow to pull out, and at last struck *terra firma* again along toward morning. But we were six mortal hours, in making less than ten miles, across this range; and what with trudging through the slush, helping the ladies forward, and carrying the children, it was altogether one of the worst night-journeys I ever experienced. If anybody thinks differently, let him try his hand at carrying fifty pounds of childhood, up a slushy road, six miles more or less across a mountain, through the chilly night air, about midnight and after. When happily we regained the coach, after passing the snow, we supposed our troubles about over; but an ambitious mother from Virginia City, *en route* to San Francisco, left her Gertrude Jane unselfishly to me, while she herself sank gracefully into a corner of the coach, and went deliberately to sleep. It was, perhaps, characteristic of her sex on the Coast, where women are so few, they are over-appreciated; but to the Eastern mind, I confess, it seemed somewhat too much of a good thing, considering the premises.

Once out of the snow, we struck comparatively good roads again, and whirled along down and out of the mountains at a magnificent rate. Our general pace was a good square trot, but we swung around the zigzags usually at a sharp gallop, and often shaved the edge of cliffs so closely, that it made the goose-flesh come and go, or one's hair about stand on end. With the first break of day, I sought the outside of the coach, and revelled in the ride through the breezy pines of the Sierras—

monster coniferæ, ten and twelve feet through, and running up straight as an arrow by the hundred feet—and so down the range to Lake Tahoe. This (Tahoe) is the gem of the Sierras, *par excellence*, according to all good Californians; and one scarcely wonders at their immense pride in it. Itself six thousand feet above the sea, skirted with primeval forests, rimmed about with snow-clad peaks, it stretches wide for ten or twelve miles, and its waters are so pure and clear, that trout may be seen at all depths in it. It had already become a popular resort for all the Pacific Coast, and waited only for the completion of the railroad, to welcome visitors from the East. Here was the limpid heart of the Sierras; and the wild, the picturesque, and the sublime, all combined to enhance its conceded beauty. California herself, ever alive to her own interests, was also entertaining some very utilitarian views with regard to it. A long-headed, broad-minded German engineer proposed to tap it, by tunnelling through the Sierras, and conducting its crystal waters across the State—first utilizing them as water-power and a grand irrigating canal *en route* as wanted, and at the terminus supplying San Francisco with unimpeachable water. It was a gigantic project, involving many millions; but was already much talked of, and was just the kind of scheme to interest the minds, and lighten the pockets, of good Californians.

Past Lake Tahoe, we whirled over and down the mountains at a telling pace—by the side of rushing torrents, amidst aromatic pines, along the dizzy edge of precipices—it was the very romance of stage-coaching—and drew up at Shingle Station, on the Placerville and Sacramento Railroad, at 11 A. M., having come 116 miles since leaving Virginia City, only the day before, despite the snow on the summit. At Placerville, we struck the original gold-fields of California, and saw abundant evidences of past washings on all sides of us. These were now mostly abandoned, except by the Chinese, who here and there were still patiently at work, content to glean what Americans despised. Placerville itself, in the then early spring, was one mass of perfect roses and foliage. The balmy breath of summer seemed everywhere at work, and the climate reminded one rather of Charleston or Savannah in May or June. Her ragged hillsides, abandoned by the miner, were everywhere changing into vineyards and orchards, while skillful irrigation was rapidly converting her waste lands into productive farms. Once out of the foot-hills, we again struck the lordly wheat-fields, and thence on to Sacramento we were never out of sight of broad acres of waving grain.

At Sacramento, we found hearty welcome, and good hotels, and tarried there for a day or so. It was then a city of fifteen or twenty thousand people, and though not prospering as in former years, as capital of the State and the centre of a magnificent farming district, was yet certain of its future. Here, as at Placerville, the wealth of roses was something surprising, and indeed the whole city seemed to be a wilderness of color and perfume. It is difficult for one residing on the Atlantic slope, to realize how richly California is endowed with flowers. To us, here, they were a constant wonder and delight, though this may have partly come from our sudden transition from the snows of the Sierras.

From Sacramento, we rode over to Stockton, some fifty miles, leaving at 6 A. M. and reaching there at 1 P. M. As there were but few passengers, we had the coach pretty much to ourselves, and the ride proved delightful, barring the dust. Our route lay mainly down the valley of the Sacramento proper, and we found the country a dead level or gently rolling, not unlike an Illinois prairie, though diversified here and there with groups of live-oaks, festooned with Spanish moss. Now and then these oaks thickened into respectable groves, but nowhere did they seem to amount to much as timber. The soil was everywhere black and deep, all a farmer's heart could wish, and there appeared to be literally no end to the wide-stretching wheat-fields. They skirted the road for miles, on every side, and our driver was continually pointing out to us this hundred or that thousand acre wheat-field. Wheat seemed too much their main crop, though vineyards and fruit-orchards were not infrequent, and on the "divides" we here and there saw some large flocks of sheep and herds of cattle, quietly feeding under their native rancheros. Evidently their breadth of wheat-land was constantly extending. When California first began to grow wheat, for several years it was thought the bottom-lands were the only ones worth cultivating. But it was found that good crops could also be grown on her uplands, and year by year more of these were now being reclaimed and sown. Unlike other crops, her wheat nowhere requires irrigation; but, sown late in the fall or early winter, it germinates beneath the December rains, grows rapidly all winter, and by May is ready to harvest. Her long and rainless summer affords ample leisure to gather and market it—no granaries or barns being required; and the reported yield—50 to 80 bushels to the acre—seems fabulous to any one, but a Californian.

Her fruit and vegetable fields require regular irrigation, the same as in Colorado and Utah; and wherever these appeared, long-armed windmills wearily beat the air, pumping water to the surface. The steady sea-breeze of the long summer renders these very reliable, and California everywhere had been quick to adopt them. All about Stockton, they stood gaunt and skeleton-like against the sky, like a cordon of ghostly sentinels; but they seemed to serve their purpose admirably well, and this was the main thing. The water they lifted to the surface was conducted by troughs and ditches hundreds of yards away, as needed, everywhere converting the parched and arid earth into bountiful fields and gardens. Stockton seemed literally embosomed in these, foliage and flowers abounding on all sides, and her climate appeared perfect even for California. At the head of steamboat navigation on the San Joaquin, she gathered into her lap the trade and travel of a wide district there, and was already a busy and thriving town of several thousand inhabitants. Of course, she has no great and magnificent future, like San Francisco; but as an important inland city, doubtless she will continue to grow and prosper for many years to come.

YOSEMITE VALLEY (from foot of Mariposa Trail).

CHAPTER XXIX.

STOCKTON TO THE YOSEMITE.

HERE at Stockton, I had expected to find friends from San Francisco, to go through to the Yosemite with me, and return. (*Yo-Sem-i-te*, big-grizzly bear.) But, instead, I found letters, begging off, on the plea, that it was yet too early in the season to venture there. It was, indeed, rather later than usual; but the previous winter had been a severe one, and in San Francisco, they said, the snow was still too deep on the mountains, to reach the far-famed valley. This was all very well for them, being residents on the Coast. But my official duties there were now substantially over; there was only about a fortnight or so left, before the steamer sailed on which I had engaged passage; and the question with me was, whether now, or perhaps never, to see California's (if not the world's) chiefest wonder. I inquired at the Stockton hotels, but could find no one *en route* to the Yosemite; and finally concluded I must go alone, or not at all.* At last, however, I heard of two Englishmen who had just returned, declaring the route practicable *via* Coulterville; but alleging they were the only ones, who had been in and out that season. This decided me,

* Perhaps I should add, my friend Dr. M. had already returned East, *via* Hong Kong and Calcutta, around the world; and L. was in San Francisco, suffering from the ague.

especially as I preferred to be on the move, rather than idling in San Francisco until my steamer sailed.

Accordingly, I took the stage early next morning (May 25th) for Coulterville, and reached there the same evening. My design was to go in by the Coulterville route, and come out by the Mariposa, so as to visit the Mariposa Grove of Big Trees also, if possible; but, failing that, to return by Coulterville. The first twenty-five miles of the road from Stockton was through a sea of lordly wheat-fields, like the ride from Sacramento; but, after that we struck the more barren foot-hills, and settlements soon became fewer and poorer. Our general course was up the valley of the San Joaquin and its tributaries—the Stanislaus and the Tuolomne—with the country gradually rising, and the Coast Range looming always grandly against the west. The latter half of the way was dreary and desolate, the arid hills and plains stretching on all sides around; and we hailed with joy the lovely view of the Merced Valley, that betokened our approach to Coulterville. We had several passengers thus far, evidently men intent on mines or other local business, and Coulterville gave us a kindly evening welcome.

The next morning a guide was found, who guaranteed to take me into the valley and back, if I could stand a little rough riding and walking; and after an early dinner we set cheerily out. He could not promise to bring me out by the Mariposa trail, but he would do the best he *could*, and in this I had faith. The distance to the Yosemite was still some fifty-five miles, too much for one day's journey, and we decided to go no farther than Black's, some eighteen miles on, the first day. The wagon-road terminated practically at Coulterville, and from here we proceeded on horseback, over a wandering mountain trail, that seemed specially designed to bring out all the finest views in the country. My horse was a mustang pony, named Punty, small but sure of foot, and as brave and faithful a little creature as ever lived. The day was glorious. The sky was without a cloud. The atmosphere seemed, indeed, like "wine of airy gold." The pines of the foot-hills and mountains perfumed every breeze, and every sense seemed satisfied and full. As we had ample time, we allowed our horses to take their "own sweet will," and whiled the afternoon away in chat and song. My guide, Capt. Coulter, was a companionable young fellow, who had seen something of army life among the California Volunteers, and we got on together very well.

At Bower Cave, halfway or so along, we halted to give the horses a brief rest, and meanwhile explored the little bijou of a cave there, which is quite perfect in its way. It is a natural cave, several hundred feet in extent, in a limestone bluff there, with a pool of water in one corner, forty feet deep, and clear as crystal. At the bottom of the cave are several petrified trees, while from its mouth uprises a group of stately maples, that spread their umbrageous branches like a canopy over all. At a little distance, they quite conceal the entrance to the cave; but down in the cave, looking up, the light breaks through their multitudinous leaves, and illuminates the cave and pool to the very bottom. Thence, we proceeded on to Black's, in a sheltered nook, well among the mountains, where we found plain but excellent entertainment, and went early to bed, with the roses crowding about our windows, and the irrigating streams that gave life to them murmuring in our ears. Here, as elsewhere in California, irrigation was still essential; but Mr. Black had caught and tamed a mountain rivulet—led it indeed everywhere—and wherever it went, it worked wonders, in that virgin soil and matchless climate.

The next morning, we were up bright and early, though withal a little stiff and sore, and at 6 A. M. were off for the Yosemite again. Like the day before, only hourly more and more so, the trail still wound up, and along, and over the ridges and mountains—now through deep forests of primeval pines, that would be monsters anywhere else, where our horses sank to their fetlocks in mosses of emerald green, and now along some rocky bluff, naked and barren, whence we could gaze for miles on miles across ravine and ridge, wooded mountain and arid plain, to the purple Coast Range beyond. Often I reined Punty in, and gazed with delighted eyes over such glorious scenes and far-away landscapes, as we are never permitted to see East. There was a purity and clearness about the air, that lent long range to the vision; and besides, our elevation above the sea had now become so great, that the foot-hills seemed merged into the plains. At times, there came a feeling of loneliness—only two of us thus together, adrift among the Sierras; but the ever-changing landscape soon banished this again, and throughout the day every sense seemed filled to the utmost. This magnificent horseback ride, through the foot-hills and up the Sierras, over and along their flanks and summits, alone repaid me for all the toil and fatigue of the trip; and then, there was the Yosemite, and other experiences besides.

When we got within five or six miles of the Yosemite, however, we struck the snow, and the remainder of our ride became chiefly a plunge and flounder. The snow still lay several feet in depth, over most of this distance, completely hiding the trail in many places, so that my guide frequently became lost. A pocket-compass, and his own keen eye for topography, however, usually soon put us right again, and so we floundered on—determined to get through, if possible. In places, the snow had a stout crust, which bore both us and the horses up, and here we would mount and ride along quite gayly. But, in an unguarded moment, when we were thinking the worst was over, or that we were almost out of the snow-limit, suddenly our mustangs would go in to their saddle-girths; and then, there was nothing left for us but to dismount (if we were not already sprawling in the snow), and coax them forward the best we could. This kind of travelling told quickly upon our animals, and severely; however, we got along better than we expected, and late in the afternoon, emerging from the snow and pines, we rounded a rocky bluff, and before us in a moment—yawned the Yosemite. At our feet lay the wonderful valley—how sublime and glorious! Before us swayed the Bridal Veil, in all its grace and beauty. To the left was El Capitan, looming up in solemn grandeur. Beyond stood Sentinel Peak, piercing the clouds; and still beyond, the great South Dome, propping the very sky. We reined our horses in for a while, feasting our eyes on the general view; but soon hastened on again, as the day was waning, and the descent into the valley yet to be accomplished.

Soon we struck a brace of foaming torrents, that shot across our pathway like feathery arrows, and sped to join the lovely Merced in the far valley below. Ordinarily, these were but mountain rivulets; but now they were fierce and swollen, because of the melting snows, and as they were unbridged, the only way was to ford them. We tried the usual ford, but found it so deep and swift, and rocky withal, that we were afraid to venture it. Finally, Capt. Coulter suggested, that if I would cross by some fallen trees farther up, that nearly met and made a sort of foot-bridge there, he thought he could make Punty swim the streams, swollen and rocky as they were, when the other horse would be likely to follow suit. So, taking off his saddle and bridle, and shouldering these and my roll of blankets, I cautiously made my way over the tangled trees, and presently succeeded in reaching the other side in safety. From here, I called to Punty to come over, while Capt. C. urged him in. At first, he whinnied, as if he knew what was wanted of him; then ventured into the icy water, and shrank out again, as if uncertain of himself. But, finally, with more coaxing and urging, the plucky little fellow plunged courageously in, and though the current bore him considerably down, and the rocks bruised him cruelly, at length he reached my side in safety. He walked up to me, a wet and dripping thing, but eager for the biscuit with which I rewarded him; and, as he munched it, rubbed his nose familiarly against my shoulder, as if to testify his good-will. An exchange of whinnies, now, soon brought the other horse over, after a little urging; and Capt. C. crossing also by the trees, we quickly saddled up, and were off again. A long and rather perilous descent, over a rocky and precipitous trail, not yet repaired after the spring washings, brought us at last down into the valley; and soon after 6 P. M. we reached Hutchings'. In truth, it was a hard day's ride, after all. We had been twelve hours in the saddle, first and last; but had come thirty-seven miles, over an ugly road, and were the first Americans of the season in the Yosemite.

Here, at Hutchings', I spent three days in the Yosemite; but scarcely know where to begin, or how to speak about it. They were all perfect days in point of weather, and with Mr. Hutchings usually as guide, I made the most of them. He was then one of the only two settlers in the Yosemite, and his house the only real place of entertainment there. An artist and an author himself of considerable merit, more than a man of business, he had chosen the Yosemite out of all the Pacific Coast, as the best place to live and die in; and was content to be shut up here, from October to June of each year, without even a newspaper or a word from the outside world, during that period. From June to the last of September, he always had more or less company, the influx of sight-seers being pretty steady and constant; but, after that, the snows interfered with travel, and with his family he hibernated there the rest of the year. With rare taste for the picturesque and the sublime, he had located his house—only a rough shanty then, but meant to grow into something better—in the very heart of the valley, with huge and massive El Capitan in front, the incomparable Yosemite Falls to the right, and the spire-like Sentinel Peak just off to the left. Standing on his lawn, you take all these grand and majestic features in at one view, and at the same time obtain a general view of the valley from there, I think, unsurpassed elsewhere down in it.

The first day, we took horses and rambled leisurely through the valley, crossing and recrossing from side to side, as the views were finest; and, much as had been anticipated, I confess, I was overwhelmed with admiration and delight. The valley itself, running about east and west, is some five miles long by a half-mile wide, and seems to be a fissure or crevice in the heart of the Sierras there; or rather, as if the bottom had here dropped out of the mountains, and the lofty Sierras had sunk to a level with the plain. The sharp, almost perpendicular, sides of the valley give you this impression further, and it is hard to account for its features otherwise, though some claim it all as the work of erosion, like the glen at Watkins, or the gorge at Niagara. Its walls are often quite perpendicular, half a mile or more in height; and its wonderful South Dome, rearing its crest six thousand four hundred feet above the level of the valley, or a mile and a quarter high, seems split half in two, as if one half had suddenly disappeared, with its northern face so sharp, that a stone dropped from its edge would fall to the bottom without striking. This had never yet been ascended, and probably never will be—its remaining half-dome is so smooth and globular.

The general color of the walls is a grayish yellow, but here and there they are mottled with green and black; and usually in every niche and crevice, where a tree can gain a foothold, great spruces and pines grow luxuriantly. In many places, however, its walls stand sheer and bare, great masses of honest granite, from half a mile to a mile perpendicularly; and, perhaps, I can't give a better impression of them, than by saying, that if either of them was toppled over, in many instances it would fill the valley and more. Up above, on the summit of the range, snow lies more or less the year round; but down below, in the heart of the valley, you have the general climate of California outside, but without its aridity, for here showers prevail in summer, as in the East. When I was there, the snow still lay five and six feet deep on top of the walls and domes; but below, the valley was a June meadow, rich with herbage, with groves of pine and fir scattered here and there, shooting up two and three hundred feet into the air, but dwarfed into saplings apparently by the majestic walls. Birch, willow, and dogwood lined the streams; the primrose, violet, and other early flowers dotted the lawns; the bluebird, the robin, and the bobolink—

"June's bridesman, poet o' the year,
Gladness on wings—"

twittered among the trees; and on every side, wherever we walked or rode, the wild strawberries were ripening in the grass, and perfuming the breeze.

Here and there, plunging over the lofty walls, were waterfalls of surpassing beauty, some a mere line of mist, tossed hither and yon by the passing wind, like a veil of gauze, and others thundering down with a voice approaching even Niagara's. Later in the season, when the snows measurably disappear, these falls of course become much shrunken in size, and visitors behold them then shorn in part of their beauty and sublimity. But just then, so early in the season, they gave one full greeting, and I counted a score or more from different points thundering in chorus. We rode to the foot of the Bridal Veil, usually a sheet of misty gauze, but now a roaring cataract, and gazed up nine hundred feet, to where it leaped from the southern wall. Then we crossed to El Capitan, a massive bastion or angle in the northern wall, of solid granite, rising sheer into the air for three-quarters of a mile without a break, except a niche one-third of the way up, where a tall fir has gained a foothold, and will never be molested by hand of man. Thence, we turned and rode up the valley, to where the Yosemite Fall plunged boldly out from the northern wall, like a thing of life, and thundered headlong down twenty-six hundred feet, or fifteen times the height of Niagara. Above, where it leaped from the cliff, and afterwards, it seemed a goodly river; but long before it reached the bottom, it became a column of mist, which the wind swayed to and fro at will, but whose thunder yet shook the valley. From there, we rode back to Hutchings'; and that night, when the moon rose and from a cloudless sky flooded the valley with her silver light, Nature seemed to be endeavoring to out-do herself in our behalf.

The next day, we rode up the Merced River, which winds through the valley and drains it—a stream ten or twelve feet deep by twice as many yards in width, so pure and clear you may everywhere count the pebbles at the bottom—to the Lake, and Domes. The former is a small sheet of water, of wonderful clearness, that reflects the surrounding mountains and falls, like a mirror; the latter are dome-like masses of naked rock, peculiar to the Coast scenery, crowning the Sierras just there. Of the South Dome, I have already spoken; the North Dome is inferior in size and height, but is complete as a dome, and wonderful to behold. A dozen such domes as crown the capitol at Washington could readily be put inside of it, and there would be room for several more. From here, turning an angle of the South Dome, we caught a superb view of the South Fork of the Merced, as it came tumbling over the mountain wall, a mile or more away, an unbroken mass of foam. At that distance, it seemed a sheet of fleecy whiteness—purest lamb's wool—hundreds of feet in height, and the rocks and trees framed it in as a picture. Returning, we rode again to the grand Yosemite Fall, and tying our horses, started to climb to the foot of the fall, which seemed not very far above us; but again California air deceived us, and after toiling for two or three hours up the mountain-side, from bush to bush and rock to rock, without reaching it, we were forced to retrace our steps by the approach of evening,

The next morning, we saw a thin smoke curling above the trees in the lower part of the valley, and after breakfast had the pleasure of greeting Professor Whitney and party, of the State Geological Survey. They had been out for weeks, geologizing along the Sierras south of the Yosemite, and had entered the valley the evening before by the Mariposa trail, to repeat some triangulations and surveys they were not quite certain of. They reported the Mariposa route as rather rough, but practicable, and this was good news, as they were the pioneers of the season that way. There were five or six in the party, all active, athletic men, as keen to walk and climb as to analyze and cipher. They travelled with a pack-train, and "camped out" invariably, and their Bedouin habits had made them all as brown as berries. Greetings over, our horses were soon at the door, and presently, we all set off together for the Vernal and Nevada Falls. A mile or so above Hutchings', we struck the main branch of the Merced, and turning up its bank soon found the ascent too difficult for horses. Dismounting and turning our animals loose to graze, we proceeded on foot by a narrow trail, that wound along beneath umbrageous pines and firs, just on the margin of the river, which here foamed and roared at our feet a rushing cascade for a mile or more. Rounding a shoulder of the cañon, the spray from the Vernal Fall suddenly wet us to the skin; but exquisite rainbows, perfect in form and color, began to flame and circle around us, until it almost seemed as if you could put their many-colored ends in your pockets. Rainbows—quadrants and semi-circles—may often be seen elsewhere; but these were perfect circles, whirling around and about us, and most intense in color. Moist as we were, we all stopped to enjoy the scene, and were reluctant to move onward.

Here, at the Vernal Fall, the whole mass of the Merced drops 350 feet, without a break, and the volume of water just then was very great. Stairways and ladders carry you to the top, and here a natural wall or breastwork of solid granite enables you to lean out and overlook the Fall, and Cascades, and wild cañon beyond, without a tremor. Above, the river comes shooting like an arrow, over half a mile of polished granite, from the base of the upper or Nevada Fall. There the Merced makes another leap, of seven hundred feet in all; but half-way down, the rock shelves just sufficiently to keep the water on the flow, whence it pours in hurrying sheets of lace-like foam to the bottom. The water here seemed really instinct with life and motion ; the long lines of gauzy foam circled ever downward and onward; and the whole seemed like one vast drapery of living lace, which Nature was here ever weaving to deck the Yosemite. Valenciennes and point-lace capes and collars, were never so airy and exquisite; but here they fell, and flowed, and circled, in snowiest tracery, by the million.

Returning by Mt. Broderick, we rode down to Sentinel Peak and Cathedral Rock, with Prof. Whitney and party, having much interesting and delightful talk by the way, and reached Hutchings' again at nightfall. The day had been a fatiguing one, so much of the route was wild and rocky; and I retired early, foot-sore and leg-weary. Altogether, however, the day was very rich and enjoyable; and I look back upon it now, as one of the noblest and best I spent on the Coast. The views of the Yosemite were everywhere sublime and picturesque; and at sunset, we beheld "parting day" still playing among the Sierras, while the Merced and meadows down below were already in shadowy twilight. In fact, down in the valley, looking up, you never see but a mere ribbon-like line of sky at best, flanked on either side by mountains; and in winter, for half the morning and half the afternoon, the sun is never visible from Hutchings' at all. The Yosemite is simply an open tunnel, so to speak, half a mile or more deep, in the heart of the Sierras, and in winter-time the sunlight cannot have much chance there, except about mid-day. Doubtless the snow and ice there then must be something gorgeous, and sublime—glaciers trailing from the walls, and avalanches now and then thundering from the heights above, to the far depths below.

CHAPTER XXX.

THE YOSEMITE TO SAN FRANCISCO.

THE next morning (May 31st), I bade good-bye to Mr. Hutchings, most hospitable of hosts and gracious of guides, and started to return *via* Mariposa. In addition to Capt. Coulter, I now had Mr. Galen Clark also, who had piloted Prof. Whitney in from the Mariposa Grove of Big Trees. Trotting down through the meadow-like valley, we reached the Professor's camp, and found them just packing up, for their return *via* Coulterville. With a hearty hand-shake all around and mutual promises to meet again at Stockton, if possible, we parted, and continued on down the valley, past El Capitan, sublimest of mountains, the Three Brothers, and Bridal Veil Fall; and, at length, turning to the left, struck the Mariposa trail. One would naturally suppose, that an exit might be found by following the river down; but the Merced passes out between perpendicular walls of vast height, miles in extent, so that the only way into or out of the valley then was by the old Indian trails to Coulterville or Mariposa.*

The Mariposa trail runs by sharp zigzags up the southern wall, taking advantage of every rock and bush where an Indian could find a foot-hold, and we found it a long and

* Now, I believe, a carriage-road has been blasted out, following the Merced. But what it adds in comfort, it must lose in scenery.

toilsome climb, before we got to the top. We were over an hour by the watch; but when, at last, we rounded the last bend, and stood perspiring and breathless on the jutting ledge of Inspiration Point, what a view opened before us! From here, you get, perhaps, the best general view of the Yosemite, as a whole, that can be had; and as the eye sweeps over its peaks and domes, its battlement and towers—its massive walls, its flashing streams, its foaming cataracts—its fragrant groves and sleeping meadows—the soul swells with unutterable joy; or, rather, your whole being bows down in reverence and awe. To the right, the exquisitely beautiful Bridal Veil Fall descends, wreathed in mists and rainbows. Beyond, the Three Brothers and Sentinel Peak pierce the heavens. To the left, in solemn and awful grandeur, stands El Capitan, severe and self-centred—monarch of the vale—dominating all. Beyond, the incomparable Yosemite Fall, as if pouring from the clouds, leaps and sways and thunders—its mist at times streaming like a gorgeous pennon, its deep-toned base a perpetual *Te Deum.* While farther still, towering above all, clear cut and distinct against the sapphire sky, the great South Dome rears its awful front, as if the visage of the Almighty, and bids the universe bow down and worship. Clinging to a gnarled and stunted tree, out-grown from the very granite, we crept far out upon the rocky ledge, and there seemed literally enfolded by the Infinite.

The overwhelming sublimity, the awful loneliness and desolation of the scene — its solemn beauty and grandeur—were simply unutterable. It was a place to make one feel the littleness of all human achievements, and to lead a man out of himself up to God. It was the confrontal of God, face to face, as in moments of great danger, or in solemn and sudden death. It was the perilous edge of battle. It was storm and shipwreck. It was Niagara, many times magnified. It was Switzerland, condensed into a *coup d'œil.* I had stood on the Rocky Mountains; I had descended the Columbia; I had crossed the Sierras. But the Yosemite was all of these, and more, compressed into one view; and, surely, our planet has not its equal. Most fittingly has Congress set the Yosemite apart from the public domain, and consecrated it to mankind, as a National Park and pleasure-ground forever. Let it never be degraded to lower uses. So far it was yet free from debasing associations, and California, as its natural guardian, must keep it so. Beyond the necessary paths and bridges, it had so far escaped our so-called "improvements;" and hereafter, as heretofore, it is to be hoped, Nature will be allowed to work her own sweet will there, unchecked by the hand of man.

But our stay there was over, and lifting our hats we bade the Yosemite a reverent good-bye, and mounting our horses, turned our faces towards Mariposa. A short ride along the well-defined trail, over crackling pine leaves and gigantic cones, brought us to the Hermitage —a huge sugar-pine, ten or twelve feet in diameter, hollow in the centre, where a Californian aforetime had made his home, closing the entrance with a rude door. It afforded him a goodly-sized room, much better than many of the border cabins; and here, in the midst of the gigantic pines, miles away from any human habitation, as he swung his axe or boiled his pot, he must have had Solitude to his heart's content.

Passing on, we soon struck the snow, and for five or six miles again, as when coming into the valley, we again had a decidedly "hard road to travel." To plunge and flounder along so, through snow-field after snow-field, was tedious and toilsome in the extreme; but there was no help for us, and we struggled on. A mile or so from Inspiration Point, in crossing an open glade, where the snow had melted into a pool, we caught sight of grouse and deer; but they were off before Clark, an experienced hunter, could get a shot at them. Some two miles farther on, we came out into a larger opening, and as we lifted our eyes from the blinding snow saw, right across our trail, a hundred yards or so ahead, a huge she-grizzly and two young cubs. We were all on foot, leading our horses over the snow the best we could—Capt. Coulter behind, Clark and I some yards ahead abreast of each other—our only weapons our trusty revolvers, and a long single-barrelled rifle of Clark's. My own good Spencer carbine (seven-shooter), that I had carried so faithfully across the continent, and through Arizona, without occasion to use it, I had left in San Francisco, not thinking it necessary in California. How I wished for it now, with its seven good balls ready for instant use!

Simultaneously with our sight of her, Madame Grizzly also descried us, and Clark at once frankly said we were in great danger, if she showed fight. For a minute or two, she stood with her head raised, snuffing the air, as if calculating the chances, and then deliberately wheeling in her tracks, shuffled off into the forest—her cubs gambolling by her side, like clumsy kittens. Clark instantly threw me his bridle, and decided to try a shot, if he could sight her heart; but she kept herself well under cover, as she moved off, and he was afraid to fire, unless certain of killing her. He said if he missed or only wounded her, we would have to take to the trees, as the attack would make her savage and ferocious; and also, that if her cubs happened to turn and run toward us in play, as they often did, we would have to run or climb for it, as she would take this also for a hostile movement, and assault us fiercely. Under the circumstances, clearly discretion was the better part of valor; nevertheless, Clark wanted the brace of cubs, and when she waddled off through the slush and snow, he followed cautiously after, resolved to try his luck, if she gave him a decent chance. From bush to bush, and tree to tree, for quite a considerable distance, he dodged along after her; but presently returned, without firing, declaring the risk was too great for such a venture, and we were not sorry to be well rid of her. She was, in truth, as big as a small cow, and altogether would have been an ugly customer to deal with, if not killed at the first shot.

Clark said, grizzlies were now rare on this route, although formerly frequently encountered. And indeed on both routes, and in all our travel among the Sierra Nevadas, I was struck with the general absence of animal life—as I had also been among the Rocky Mountains. I doubt whether in either of these ranges, there is anywhere such variety and extent of animal life, as we always find East, in unfrequented forests and mountains. The solemn stillness, the glad silence, the perfect peace and rest of the Sierras, seemed everywhere profound; and nowhere and never more so, than during this day's ride in general.

Once well out of the snow, we remounted our gamey little steeds, and the rest of the day the trail led down and over the ranges—through magnificent forests of pine and spruce, cedar and fir—where to ride along was itself a luxury and delight. The prevailing tree was the California sugar-pine, so called because the Indians obtain a rude sugar from boiling down its sap. These sugar-pines frequently grow ten and twelve feet in diameter, and shoot up two hundred and fifty, and three hundred feet in height. They bear a gigantic cone, four inches in diameter, by sixteen inches in length usually; and lest this may seem like a "California story," perhaps I should add, I myself picked up one, as we rode along, measuring over eighteen inches in length, and have it now in my private cabinet. Their dead leaves carpeted the ground thickly under foot, and often our horses ambled almost noiselessly along. Overhead, their dense shade excluded the sun, which hourly became more uncomfortable, as we descended the range; while the mountain air was everywhere resinous with their perfume.

Late in the afternoon, we crossed the last ridge, and, descending into the valley of the South Merced, halted at "Clark's," the house of our new guide. We had come twenty-two miles since leaving Hutchings'; and here found excellent accommodations for the night. Mr. Clark himself was from the East, I believe Pennsylvania, but was now an enthusiastic Californian. He said he had come to California years before, a confirmed consumptive; but once among the Sierras, inhaling their resinous breath, his lungs soon healed, and here now he meant to abide the remainder of his days. He could not live in San Francisco at all, the air was so raw and sharp there; but here among the Sierras, he was well and strong, and he looked indeed as rugged as the mountains themselves. His house contained several comfortable rooms, and already the tide of Yosemite travel was setting that way, and paying him well.

Six miles from Clark's, on the border of Mariposa and Fresno Counties, is the Mariposa grove of Big Trees. We visited them next morning (June 1st), under the guidance of Clark himself, who regards them as his special wards. They number in all some five or six hundred, scattered over perhaps a mile square, but usually in clumps together. You ride up to them, through an open forest of huge sugar-pines and cedars, that would be regarded as sylvan monsters elsewhere—ten and twelve feet over; but these Big Trees dwarf even such giants, into pigmies. Many of them, indeed, measure twenty-five and thirty feet in diameter, and run up three hundred feet or more in height—the first hundred feet or so without a limb, and scarcely diminishing in size. Six of them are over thirty feet in diameter, and from ninety to a hundred feet in circumference; fifty are over sixteen feet in diameter; and two hundred over twelve feet. The "Grizzly Giant," the largest, is thirty-three feet in diameter, and its first limb—ninety feet from the ground—is itself six feet through. Another, still standing erect and vigorous, but hollowed out by fire, three of us rode *into* on horseback, one behind the other, and there was still room for more. Another, prone on the ground, and with its heart eaten out by fire—reduced to a huge shell—we rode *through* on horseback, for a hundred feet or more, and then passed out—by a small knot-hole!

Among them were some young trees, still coming forward, mere saplings; but as a rule, these Big Trees (*Sequoia Gigantea*, I believe the botanists call them) impress you with their great age, and hoary venerability. With many the mountain-fires in other years have made sad havoc, scarring and half-consuming some of them; but these are now stopped, the Mariposa Grove being also included in the Congressional grant, which sets apart the Yosemite as a National Park and pleasure-ground forever. Their bark, often eighteen and twenty inches thick, is of a pure cinnamon-color, and fluted up and down like a Corinthian column. Their wood is of a

A BIG TREE.

deep red, and much resembles that of the great red-wood trees, that are found everywhere in the Coast Range. Their foliage and cones are much like those of our ordinary yellow-pines East, though their leaves are somewhat smaller.

The trees here are of the same species as those in the Calaveras Grove, though I believe a few of the latter are rather bigger. They are also found elsewhere, along the western slope of the Sierra Nevadas, in scattered groves or clumps; but the whole number is not large. Evidently, they are the lingering survivors of some former geologic period, and no doubt will soon become extinct. Many of them are regarded, as already two thousand years old—some say six thousand; but Professor Whitney assured me, that he had made a very careful inquiry into their age, counting their annual rings and otherwise, and he doubted if any were older than the Christian era. But, at least, here are trees, that were wooing the air, and rejoicing in the sun, when the babe was first laid in the manger at Bethlehem. They have been growing in beauty and majesty ever since, through all the sunshine and storms of nineteen centuries. And to-day, they stand as matchless pillars in God's great temple, to testify of His skill and power—a fit part of

> "That cathedral, boundless as our wonder,
> Whose quenchless lamps the sun and moon supply;
> Its choir, the wind and waves; its organ, thunder;
> Its dome, the sky."

Truly marvels in themselves, in one sense these Big Trees of California are the greatest natural curiosity in the world, because no other country possesses any trees like them. If not really *sui generis*, their like, at least, I believe, has not yet been found. California, at her own request, has been appointed their lawful guardian;

and the nation and mankind expect, that she will watch them well. It would seem like sacrilege, indeed, to raise one's hand against them; and the penitentiary, surely, would be small punishment, for such a miscreant.

Returning to Clark's, we left there at noon, and the same evening reached Mariposa, twenty-five miles distant. The scenery most of the way was superb, vista after vista opening constantly before us, as we descended the mountains; but the sun had already acquired a June fierceness, and the heat seemed doubly oppressive to one just fresh from the snows of the Sierras. We rode up to the Mariposa House, dusty and jaded, travel-stained and weary; but it was now Saturday night, and the most inveterate cynic will concede, the week had been well spent.

We found Mariposa to be a straggling village, of a few hundred inhabitants, with uncertain prospects. It is the centre of what was once Gen. Fremont's magnificent estate—seventy miles square, in the heart of Mariposa County—and formerly was much noted for its mining operations. But its placer-mines were now mostly abandoned, except by John Chinaman; and its famous quartz-mill, that cost over one hundred thousand dollars—perhaps the finest in California—was standing idle. The Mariposans, however, had great faith in their mining resources still, and were expecting their fine mill to resume operations soon. In the interim, the town dozed along, in the Micawberish way common to stagnant mining centres; and welcomed my arrival, as the advance guard of the Yosemite travel, for that summer.

Here, I bade good-bye to Punty, ever-faithful pony, and kindly Capt. Coulter, my companions for a week (good luck to them both!), and took the stage for Stockton again, *via* Honitos. This was a ride of a hundred miles, through varying landscapes—across the divides and down the valleys of the Merced, Tuolomne, Stanislaus, and San Joaquin rivers—and, though hot and dusty, was yet thoroughly enjoyable. In crossing the ridge at Bear Valley, you catch a superb view of the Coast Range and Mt. Diabolo, a hundred miles away; and for the rest of the ride, Diabolo's lofty crest is almost always in view. Much of the way was barren and uncultivated, but the ranches and settlements were yearly pushing farther and farther into the foot-hills; and as we neared Stockton again, the illimitable wheat-fields were everywhere about us.

At Stockton, I had the pleasure of again meeting Prof. Whitney and party, and further comparing notes about California and the Coast generally. Thence, taking the steamer together for San Francisco, we reached there again June 4th—myself somewhat jaded and dilapidated, indeed, but richly repaid for all my toil and fatigue in going to the Yosemite. Kind friends welcomed my arrival, and the fine fare and downy beds of the *Occidental* seemed doubly luxurious. Its proprietor, of course, was a Leland—one of that family of brothers, who beyond all other Americans, know excellently well "how to keep a hotel;" and his thoughtful attentions, his genuine kindness and courtesy to everybody, were the constant remark of strangers on the Coast.

CHAPTER XXXI.

SAN FRANCISCO TO NEW YORK.

A RIDE down the bay (June 8th), through San Mateo and Melno Park, some fifty miles to San Josè, com pleted my wanderings on the Pacific Coast. The air at San Francisco, fresh from the ocean, was raw and rasping; but at San Josè, sheltered by the Coast Range, the thermometer measured over twenty degrees warmer, and the valley there seemed sleeping in summer. The whole ride by railroad is through farms and gardens, and San Josè itself we found embowered in roses and foliage. Here are old Spanish convents and churches, with their surroundings of vineyards, fig-trees, orange-groves, etc., as at Santa Barbara and Los Angelos—only better preserved—and the ride thither is a favorite excursion for San Franciscans and strangers. The sleepy old town is in vivid contrast, with the rush and whirl of the Golden Gate; and its soft and delicious air proves a soothing balm, to the invalid and the weak. A fair hotel furnished good entertainment, and the place seemed indeed like a haven of rest, after "roughing it" so in the interior.

Returning to San Francisco, the last farewells were said, and June 10th, at 11 A. M., the good steamer *Constitution* bore us away for Panama. We had spent six months on the Coast, and would fain have remained longer, especially to visit the "Geysers." But my official work was ended; and besides, I was in receipt of private letters, that required my presence East. The 10th was "steamer-day"—still a recognized event in San Francisco. All business ended then; and from then, began again. There was a bustle about the hotels, and an air of importance everywhere. Hundreds thronged the vessel and wharf, to see their friends off, and tarried till the last moment. But, prompt to the minute, the *Constitution* cast loose, and rounding into the stream, was soon heading down the bay, for the Golden Gate and the Pacific. Past Alcatraz and Angel Island, past Fort San Josè and Fort Point, we reached the bar, and crossed it in a chopping sea, that soon sent most of the passengers to their berths.

In San Francisco, the sun shone bright as we steamed away, but the air was raw and chilly like our later autumn;* and once out at sea, we found an overhanging mist, that often deepened into a winter fog. This uncomfortable weather continued for a day or two, keeping most of the passengers below deck—many of them seasick; but as we passed down the coast, the weather gradually moderated, and soon we were sailing beneath perfect skies, over, indeed, "summer seas." The rest of the way down, what a superb voyage it really was! Looking back on it now, it seems rather a grand picnic excursion, than a *bona fide* journey by sea. The ocean, in the main, proved itself truly Pacific. We were very seldom out of sight of land by day. The purple, and crimson, and golden hues of the Coast Range, were a perpetual wonder and delight. Schools of porpoises, and now and then a vagrant whale enlivened the day; and the phosphorescent waves, wide-spreading from our wake, made our track a blaze of fire by night.

* The evening before, I saw ladies at the opera, with their winter furs on.

And what skies those were! By day, "deeply, darkly, beautifully blue;" by night, one blaze of flaming stars. It was the very luxury of travel—the very poetry of locomotion. Sometimes I would lie for hours on deck, breathing in the balmy air, watching the gulls and frigate-birds as they hovered in our wake, or gazing on far-off hill and mountain, as the shore opened up before us—losing all sense of thought and action, content solely with being. Even novel-reading sometimes seemed a task, and writing a great burden. And when evening came, we would sit and talk far into the night; or, leaning over the guards, would watch the stream as of liquid fire, that boiled, and curled, and rippled away beneath us.

As we got farther down the coast, the climate became warmer; but blue-flannels and white-linens in place of winter-woolens, rendered this endurable, and indeed the change from temperate to tropic—from latitude 38° to 7°—did not seem so great after all, barring the first day or two out from San Francisco. Some, however, who had not provided themselves with such changes of clothing, complained bitterly of the heat and lassitude, though most of us got on very well. We had a thunder-storm one night, and a stiff rain next day, when well down the Mexican coast; but otherwise were favored with uninterruptedly fine weather.

From San Francisco to Panama is somewhat over three thousand miles, and we were fifteen days in making it. Our steamer was a fine specimen of her class, with a burden of 3,500 tons, and a carrying capacity of eleven hundred passengers, besides freight. She measured three hundred and forty feet in length, by forty-five feet in beam, and her great deck morning and evening was a rare promenade. Of passengers, we had only about four hundred; so that all had state-rooms, and to spare. We carried our own beef, and mutton, and poultry, to be slaughtered as wanted; and our fare, as a whole, was excellent and generous. Our company, it must be confessed, was rather heterogeneous, but altogether was social and enjoyable. We had army officers and their wives, going east, on leave or transfer; a U. S. Consul from the Sandwich Islands, *en route* to Washington, on public business; Englishmen from Hong Kong, bound for New York or London; merchants, bankers, and gamblers from San Francisco; red-shirted miners from Nevada and Arizona; and women of all sorts, from fine ladies and true mothers, to dulcineas of dubious character. The general decorum, however, was above criticism; and on Sundays, when a San Francisco divine held service, all were attentive listeners, notwithstanding his High-Church absurdities. The morning promenade on deck, and the evening smoke on the guards, were the great occasions for conversation, and all enjoyed them to the full.

Our first stopping-place was at Cape St. Lucas, the extreme point of Southern California, where we put off two passengers, and took on none. Thence, we crossed the mouth of the Gulf of California, and halted at Manzanillo, Mexico—a little hamlet of two or three hundred souls, the sea-port of the fine town of Colima, some seventy-five miles inland. Here we put off a hundred tons of freight, intended for the interior, and spent several hours. Eight days out, we reached Acapulco, the chief Mexican port on the Pacific Coast, and world-famous in other days, when Spain bore rule here. The harbor is perfectly land-locked, with bold islands off the mouth and deep water close in shore, and here ought to be a great and puissant city. From San Francisco down, not counting San Diego, this is the first really good harbor; and here is the great route for trade and travel, across Mexico, *via* the capital and Vera Cruz, to the Atlantic. Yet we found only a squalid town of two or three thousand inhabitants, mostly half-negro and half-Indian, with a trace of the Spaniard here and there mixed in. A handful of Americans and Germans controlled the business of the town; and as for the rest—they seemed to be a lotus-eating, inert race, not inaptly denominated "greasers." A general look of decadence prevailed everywhere; and if this be a sample of Mexican civilization, after a trial of two centuries, or more, alas for its future! Not a single wagon-road led from the town inland, in any direction; and the only means of transit, to or from the interior, was by horse or mule-back, over winding mountain-trails, the same as in the days of Cortez.

We reached there June 18th, soon after breakfast; and had scarcely rounded to, before the Philistines were —not exactly upon, but—around us. They swarmed about our vessel in bum-boats and dug-outs, of all shapes and sizes, tendering oranges, limes, bananas, shells, etc., for a consideration—sending them up the ship's sides by a cord and tiny basket, trusting us to return the agreed-for coin. When these failed to please, they paraded their skill as swimmers and divers, plunging under like ducks when a coin was tossed overboard, and sure to catch it before it reached the bottom. With little or no clothing, except about the loins, and often not that, they seemed to be an amphibious sort of creatures—equally at home on land, or sea.

As we were to spend several hours here, taking in coal and water to last to Panama, many of us embraced the opportunity to go ashore and see something of the town. When we touched the beach, comely maidens of coffee-colored complexion met us, with baskets and strings of shells, to any of which we were heartily welcome, provided we paid well for them. They always tender their wares as a "gift," a trick of Acapulco's, as also of Manzanillo's and Panama's; but they invariably expect more than their real value, in return. Passing on, we found the town to consist of one-story adobes, with streets hardly more spacious than good foot-pavements East, and with little business to speak of, except what the tri-monthly steamers supplied. The stores were chiefly baskets or boxes on the side-walks or street-corners, and even these were in charge of women, while the lazy-looking men "loafed" or lounged in the shade, sipping their aguardiente or whiffing their cigarritos with infinite content. The flocks of children, from infants to half-grown youths, were usually guiltless of raiment, and all seemed supremely happy, if only sucking an orange or munching a banana.

All gazed at Los Americanos with good-natured curiosity, and a score were eager to show us to the U. S. Consulate, which was already well-designated by the Stars and Stripes drooping idly from its staff. The Consul himself, unfortunately, was absent; but his deputy, Mr. Sutter, gave us kindly welcome, and we spent an instructive hour, listening to his stories of Mexican life and manners. From there, we went to the rude church or "cathedral," on the plaza; and found in its tawdry ornaments and doll-like images—its wax-figure Christs, its tissue-paper angels, and pewter amulets—an easy explanation of the ignorance, and squalor, and stagnation of this people. The fat and jolly priest suspended his devotions, to sell us pewter charms (he swore, by the Virgin, they were silver!) that would insure us against fever and shipwreck on the voyage; and afterwards he invited us round to take a sip of aguardiente and see his favorite game-cock. Thence, we strolled down the beach, between rows of palms and bananas, to the old Spanish fort, and found it a solid and substantial structure still, though a century or two old. True, it would not stand long before one of our modern monitors; but it was a fine work in its day, and showed well yet. A company or two of dirty and ragged soldiers constituted the garrison—their uniforms heterogeneous, and their arms really worthless. We sent our compliments to the commanding officer, hoping to gain an entrance; but he was absent, and his pompous subordinate declined to admit such Northern barbarians.

Returning to the *Constitution*, late in the afternoon we bade good-bye to Acapulco; and thence, following the trend of the continent, across the gulf of Tehuantepec, by Guatemala, by San Salvador, by Nicaragua, by Costa Rica, and finally by New Granada, at last, on the morning of June 25th, we cast anchor at Panama. During all of this week's sail, we were hardly ever out of sight of land, and usually were so near, that we could note the flocks and herds, the houses and trees, and rich luxuriance of this tropical coast generally, as we glided by. Lofty mountain-ranges and cone-shaped peaks—old volcanoes now extinct, rising thirteen thousand and fourteen thousand feet above the sea—were generally in view by day; and at night fitful lightnings, playing apparently from peak to peak, often lit up the whole heavens.

Here at Panama, the key of two continents and two oceans, we again struck the busy currents of modern life, though but little belonged to the natives there. The broad bay itself, with its shapely islands of perpetual green, crowned with the ever-graceful palm and banana, was a delightful scene, tropical thoroughly; but here also were lines of busy steamers, from Chili and Australia, as well as California, and the old harbor gave multiplied signs of life and energy. The railroad to Aspinwall, costly as it was, both in life and treasure, opened up a pathway across the Isthmus to the commerce of the world, and Panama stands at the gate. In another land, or with a better people, she would soon become a mighty metropolis. But we found her much like Acapulco, though with broader streets, better houses, and more population. I believe she claimed four or five thousand inhabitants then; but they were chiefly a mixed race, in which the most of what is really valuable in humanity seemed to be dying out. They had no public schools, and scarcely knew what popular education meant. Their churches, venerable only for their age, but in this dating back to the Spanish conquest, were crumbling to ruins. Their religion was only an ignorant superstition or savage fanaticism. And their government, so-called, was in a state of chronic revolution, so that nobody seemed to know when it was *up* or *down*. Of course, the real business of the town was in the hands of foreigners—chiefly Americans, Germans, and English—and these "pushed things," with much of their wonted skill and energy, notwithstanding the climate. The natives, as a rule, contented themselves with driving a petty traffic in parrots and shells, oranges and bananas; and literally swarmed around us, until we were weary alike of their clamor and dirt.

We reached Panama, as I have said, early in the morning, but did not get off for Aspinwall until about noon. All this time was spent in disembarking passengers, with their baggage, and fast freight; but, at last, the impatient locomotive whistled "up brakes," and we moved slowly off. The ride across the Isthmus is fifty miles, and is usually made in two or three hours; but half-way across, a baggage-car broke down, and we were detained four hours in an impenetrable jungle. It had rained that morning at Panama, and the sun was still obscured; but the air was dense with heat and moisture, that hung as if in strata and folds about you, without a breath to disturb them—and to say we steamed and sweltered, during those four long hours there, would only half express our perspiring experience. All along the road, there was a tropical luxuriance and splendor, which no word-painting can describe, and here in this jungle both seemed to culminate. What we in a sterner clime grow in hot-houses and conservatories, as rare exotics, there rioted in the open air, as well they might, and all nature seemed bursting with exuberance and richness. Underneath, grasses and shrubbery so dense, that only the machete could clear the way, or keep them under. Overhead, the lordly palm and gracious banana, with flowering vines, pendent, interlacing, creeping, and twining everywhere. Bread-fruit and bananas hung everywhere, in clusters as big as half-bushel baskets; and here and there, birds of brilliant plumage flitted to and fro, fit denizens with the chattering monkeys, and screaming parrots, of such a wilderness. The whole ride, indeed, through the heart thus of the tropics, after all, was a rare experience; and the transition from the steamer to the railroad, notwithstanding the heat, a welcome change.

The railroad itself seemed well built, and fairly managed. It was said, indeed, to rest literally on human bodies, so many poor fellows perished in the deadly miasmas, while constructing it. The ties and sleepers were of lignum-vitæ, and the telegraph poles of terra-cotta or cement, as nothing else would withstand the insects and moisture of the Isthmus. The stations were well apart, and seemed maintained solely for the convenience of the road, as hardly a passenger got off or on, except employés of the company. We could see the natives, as we passed along, lolling in their hammocks, or stretched out on mats, in their rude huts of poles and palm-leaves; and their herds of children ran everywhere at will, as naked as when born. Sometimes, a few of the inhabitants clustered about a station; but as a rule, this required too much effort, and they preferred to take their *dolce far niente* in their huts. The taint of the Spaniard seemed to be over them all; or, else, nature was too kindly to them, removing all incentive to exertion, by omitting the necessity for it.

We ran into Aspinwall at 6 P. M., and remained there until 8 P. M. We spent the time in exploring the town, but found little to interest any one. It had no storied past, like Panama; and its future depended on—Pacific Mail. Some found cheap linens, wines, and cigars, as Aspinwall was a free port, and laid in a stock for future consumption, to the damage of our Customs Revenue. But the most of us were sated and weary, with the day's rare experiences, and were glad when the steamer's bell rang "All aboard!" Our High-Church chaplain proved to be our only really useful man, at Aspinwall, after all. He married a couple, while we halted there; and would have married another, had there been time. Both had been waiting several weeks, much-enduring souls—Aspinwall, it seems, not affording a minister.

Our complement of passengers had been swelled, by accessions from Valparaiso and Melbourne; and hence, from Aspinwall to New York, we were rather overcrowded. Our good ship *Rising Star* was staunch and sea-worthy; but without the roomy accommodations of the *Constitution*, or her thorough appointments. Her beef and mutton were all brought from New York on ice, to last for a twenty-day's voyage to Aspinwall and back; and, before we reached New York, were not like Cæsar's wife—above suspicion. But, on the whole, there was little to complain of; and the ship's officers certainly did their utmost, to make everybody content and comfortable.

Our route to New York, distant about two thousand miles, lay across the Caribbean Sea, and thence off the eastern terminus of Cuba, through the West Indies, home. We had some rough weather, with continuous thunder and lightning, as it seemed, for a day or two, while crossing the Caribbean. But, once past that, we entered a region of blue skies and balmy breezes, and sighted New York in eight days from Aspinwall. We passed Cuba so near, that her green hills and mountains seemed within a stone's throw; and, threading the West Indies, struck the Gulf Stream, whence both steam and current hurried us forward. We reached Sandy Hook at sundown, July 3d, where they quarantined us till morning, much to our disgust. But the 4th broke gloriously, over city and bay; and amid ringing bells, and firing cannon, and fluttering bunting, we steamed proudly up the harbor—it never seemed so magnificent before—and touching the pier, thus ended our journey.

To land on such a day seemed a fit conclusion, to such a twelve-month's ramble, across the continent and over the seas; and that evening at home, surrounded by loving friends, seemed doubly dear from the long absence and safe return. How much we had seen of the Great Republic—only a little can be told here! How it enlarged, and dignified, one's conception of the Fatherland! What a magnificent country we really have—washed by two oceans, crowned with mountains, and gemmed with lakes; and yet, evidently, it is only a prophecy of that Greater America, when we shall occupy the continent, from the Arctic down to the Isthmus, with teeming millions, and convert the Pacific practically into a Yankee sea. Well might Whittier, our truest seer, melodiously sing:

> "I hear the tread of pioneers,
> Of nations yet to be;
> The first low wash of waves, where soon
> Shall roll a human sea."

And, best of all, over all this broad land, there shall then be but one flag and one freedom, one law and one liberty, one Right and one Justice, for us and for all men—wherever born and of whatever faith, however poor or however humble. And *to* this end, and *for* this purpose, let us, and all who love the English-speaking race, if not mankind, sincerely pray, God save the Republic!

In conclusion, let me add, to the many friends we met everywhere *en route*, for their numberless kindnesses and unstinted courtesies, we were much indebted; and I would gratefully record my sense of this here. Nobler souls, more generous spirits, than most of the people we encountered, especially in Colorado and California, never breathed; and here is good fortune to them, one and all, wherever they may chance to be! Surely, they have fought a good fight, in their rough life on the border, preparing the way for civilization, and deserve well of their country and their kind.

But, all things must end—this trip included; and so, O reader, in the vernacular of the Coast, "*Adios*," and good-bye! I will simply add to this volume a chapter of advice to emigrants and settlers, which I trust may prove of value to those who would seek a new life in the GREAT WEST.

CHAPTER XXXII.

ADVICE TO EMIGRANTS AND SETTLERS.

HORACE GREELEY'S sage advice to a needy office-seeker was, "Go West, young man, go West!" It was sound advice, and doubtless many people have taken it. Since my return, I myself have often repeated it, and have usually been met with the inquiry, "But *where* shall I go? Where is the *best region* to locate—the *best place* to settle?" To all such inquiries, my answer has been and is, that will depend on circumstances and no one answer will meet all cases. Generally, I would say:

1. If you intend to lead a *city-life*, the chief points now are Omaha, Denver, Salt Lake, Portland, San Francisco, Sacramento, and Virginia City, and these seem destined to remain the chief centres of population and business for many years to come. These are all large and growing cities already, and he who settles there now and maintains himself, will of course grow and prosper with them. The conditions of life there are not greatly different, from what they are in most of our eastern cities. There is less respect paid, however, to "old families" and "blue blood." But little inquiry is made as to one's antecedents. The chief touchstone is *success*. All stand upon an equality, and the "best man" is he who comes to the front oftenest and farthest on the various lines of life he is pursuing. As a consequence,

young men largely predominate in positions, where only old and middle-aged men are found in the East. For mechanics and laboring men, there is always an open door in all these places, with chances for promotion as the years roll by. For lawyers, physicians, merchants, bankers, etc., of course, the competition is keen and sharp, with an asperity perhaps beyond the east; but there is always room for men of worth and mettle, and these are about the only ones that succeed anywhere.

2. If you prefer a *country-life*, and mean to be a *farmer*, then your best region is Kansas, Colorado, or California. For general farming purposes, the Platte Valley is too far north, as likewise is the most of Dakota, Wyoming, Montana, and Idaho. But there is no finer country in the world than Southern Kansas (and the valley of the Arkansas generally), the eastern slope of the Rocky Mountains in Colorado, and the Western slope of the Sierra Nevadas in California. The climate here is almost perfect, and along all the rivers and streams are fertile bottoms and uplands, where you have only to "tickle the earth with a hoe, and she will laugh at you back with a harvest." Corn, wheat, rye, oats, barley, etc., all flourish here, though in California irrigation is generally necessary to grow corn well. So the valley of the Willamette, in Oregon, and other localities there are very inviting; but as a rule, Oregon, the home of the "web-footers," indulges in too much *rain*, to be popular with emigrants. So, too, in Utah and Arizona, are many very fertile districts, particularly in Arizona, along the Colorado and Gila, and their affluents; but the rainless summers there necessitate irrigation, and this is a slow and costly process. The climate, especially in Arizona, is generally superb, and the old irrigating canals of the extinct Aztecs still remain there, and doubtless

will be utilized by thrifty Anglo-Saxons, when the much needed "Texas and Pacific Railway" penetrates thither.

3. If you want to be a *fruit-farmer*, go to Utah for apples, peaches, and plums; to Oregon for apples and pears; and to California for oranges, grapes, strawberries, olives, and almost everything. California abounds in fruits of all kinds, except apples, and when her mines "peter out," as they ultimately will, she is destined to become chiefly a vast wheat-field and fruit farm. Her grapes and wines are already a great feature, and her capacity for increasing these is practically unlimited. Her vineyards and fruit orchards are already spreading all along her foot-hills, with neither snows, nor frosts, nor intense heats to menace them, and what can be more charming than life in such a region? What Arizona may yet become, in this respect, it is too soon to say; but we saw thrifty old peach trees in bloom at Tucson, in March, and doubtless she has many districts well-adapted to the orange, the olive, the grape, etc.

4. If you intend to be a *grazier*, and raise horses, cattle, sheep, etc., then your best localities are Western Texas, Eastern Colorado, and Southern California and Arizona. Of all these, Texas without doubt is the best, as she is free from snows, has regular rains, and her soil is deep and rich. Her prairies are unsurpassed on the continent for stock-feeding purposes; her rivers and streams are abundant; and she has more timber, than most of the prairie states. Her chief industry now is cattle-raising, and this has already assumed gigantic proportions. She has large settlements of thrifty Germans, and a steady stream of northern emigrants is also setting that way. Though a Southern State, slavery never had much foothold there, and her proportion of the African race is very small. She is the paradise of the mustang and the

steer, and the typical Texan is said to eat and sleep, live and die on horseback!

In Colorado, much attention is also being given to stock-raising, and a good deal has already been accomplished there in this line. See p. 487 to 493, where very interesting facts are given. Doubtless this business will succeed well there in most years, but sometimes the winters prove severe, and then her stock suffers greatly. In this respect, Texas is better off. But here, in Colorado, on the Great Plains, is the old Buffalo Range of the continent; and where buffalo once flourished, cattle ought to do well, and as a rule will. Her grass is not the long, luxuriant, prairie grass of Texas, but the coarse grass of her river bottoms, and the short "buffalo grass" of her plains. She has much land, that will never amount to much for general farming purposes, from want of regular rains in summer. But the grazier has a wide field there, and even in the "Parks" of the Rocky Mountains—the very heart of them—they are said to graze horses and cattle all seasons of the year.

In Southern California and Arizona, there are many districts well adapted to stock-raising, but which as yet are almost unoccupied. The climate here is excellent, but there is sometimes a lack of water. The grass is largely the "bunch-grass" of that region, which cures upon the ground, and can always be found ready for use. For sheep, especially, it is very excellent and nutritious, and California already has vast flocks of these. In the rainy season, she grazes these on the plains; when the dry months come, she withdraws them to the river-bottoms, or sends them into the foot-hills, where they find good pasture until the rains come again. Arizona ought to raise sheep by the millions. She has hundreds of square miles admirably adapted to them. And if she ever gets herself settled up, her wool-clip will be enormous. The climate there resembles more the climate of the Orient, and sheep should everywhere abound.

5. If you mean to be a *miner*, of course, you will go to Colorado or Utah, Nevada, California, or Arizona. Colorado and Nevada are perhaps the most promising of these. California is at a "stand-still," in the mining-business, and Utah is too much married to suit ordinary people. But Colorado and Nevada are intensely alive with every human energy, and are progressing at a rate, that will soon push them far ahead of our other mining regions. Arizona, too, abounds in the precious metals, with mines of extraordinary richness, and the day is not distant when she will produce very heavily. All she needs is a Railroad, for access to and exit from her. The truth is, our Western mountains, both the Rocky and the Sierra Nevadas, everywhere abound with gold and silver, copper and iron, more or less, and the question of the future there is chiefly *how to reduce* their ores, so as to make it pay to work them. Here is a wide field for the active, intelligent, energetic young man, and the future there belongs chiefly to him. Chemistry, metallurgy, geology, all these and their kindred sciences he wants to know, and then set to work to unlock the secret of the "sulphurets." The key is somewhere, and it will be given to him, who *thinks the most, studies the hardest, works the best.*

6. In conclusion, let me add, if you go West, if possible, *don't go empty-handed.* It is no place for the poor man, any more than the East—hardly so good; for it lacks rich people with surplus incomes, and organized charities. If possible, have enough to stock your ranche, or start your farm, or begin your store, and to carry you through the *first year*, however pinchingly.

Enthusiastic westerners will, perhaps, tell you this is nonsense, and recount instances where men have made money from the start; but they forget to tell you of the many cases where men have become disheartened, and would give anything to return East again. Remember, it is the *first year* that costs. Weather that successfully and courageously, and usually the future is secure.

If you have a family, leave them East, and go out and try it one year alone. Then, if you like it, send for the wife and babies. If you have a friend or acquaintance there, settle where he is, rather than elsewhere; for his experience and friendship will prove of value to you. Avoid the "grasshopper" regions. Keep clear of the malarial districts. Decide on some honest occupation or business, and *stick to it.* Above all, don't believe more than half the rose-colored romances you hear and read of—the "Rocky Mountain," "Big Indian," and "California" stories—and then you will get somewhere near the truth!

APPENDIX.

APPENDIX.

ON page 51, I speak of the Plains as the great stock-raising and dairy region of America, in the future. As some evidence of how fast this prophecy is becoming fact, I append the following extracts from an article by Dr. H. Latham, in the *Omaha Herald* of June 5, 1870:

"*Demonstrated Facts.*—The season of 1870 has been a memorable one in the stock business on the Plains. It commenced in doubt, but closes with unlimited confidence in the complete practicability and profits of stock-growing and winter grazing.

"*Increase of Cattle in the West.*—The number of cattle in the country west of the Missouri River and east of the Snowy Range, is now double, if not four times larger than in 1869. Its present magnitude and future prospects entitle it to a full share of public attention.

"*Shipments of Beef to Eastern Markets.*—Two years ago our beef and cattle were brought from the East. To-day, cattle-buyers from Chicago and New York are stopping at every station on our railroads, and buying cattle in all our valleys for Eastern consumption. It is safe to predict that 15,000 head of beeves will be shipped from our valleys East the present season. During the past week I have visited some of the great herds on the Plains, and will give your readers an account of them.

"*The Great Herds.*—The herds of Edward Creighton, Charles Hutton, and Thomas Alsop, are grazed on the Big Laramie, which is a tributary of the North Platte. The Laramie Valley is between the Black Hills and the Medicine-Bow Range. It is about one hundred miles long and thirty miles wide. It is about midway in this valley, and six miles from the railroad station at Laramie, that these gentlemen have located their stock ranches. They have extensive houses, stables, and corrals. As we leave the station on a beautiful August morning (which is characterized by the clearest of blue skies and golden sunlight), you see Mount Agassiz directly in

21

front of you, while Mount Dix and Mount Dodge, with snow-covered tops, are respectively on the right and left.

"We follow up the Laramie on a smooth road, which is like rolling the wheels over a floor. We follow the windings of the stream, which is clear as crystal, and pure as the snow from which its waters have just come. We first come to a herd of 4,000, half and three-quarter, breed cows; that is, there are none more than one-half Texan, and many only one-fourth. They are known among cattle dealers as short-horned Texas cattle. There are 3,600 calves in this herd, that are from three-eighths to one-half Durham. These cows have been here on the Plains one winter and two summers. All the dry cows are exceedingly fat, and many of the cows, with calves by their sides, are good beef. In this herd are many two-year-olds and yearlings, all fat for the butcher, so far as their condition is concerned. In all this herd there are as many as 9,000 head of cattle—4,000 cows, 3,600 calves, 1,000 two-year-olds, and 500 yearlings.

"*Their Habits.*—They range over a country fifteen by twenty miles. The cows and calves run together the year around, and, in fact, are never separated, but run in families of four, generally, cow, calf, yearling, and two-year-old. They are to be found on the river bottoms in the middle of the day, where they had come about 11 o'clock for water. They return about 4 o'clock in the afternoon to the high grounds, where the rich bunch and the nutritious gramma grasses are abundant, and feed till night, and lie down on the warm sandy soil till next morning, when they feed till the heat of the day It is interesting to see the habits of these cattle when unrestrained by herders. They travel back and forth to the water and grazing-ground in families and little herds, in single file, like their predecessors of the soil, the buffalo, forming deep paths, or trails, like them. After having spent three or four hours looking at this herd, we pass up the river to the beef herd, which consists of 3,500 fat Texas cattle, in the very highest order at which grass-fed cattle arrive in this world. These cattle have been here one or two seasons, and will weigh, upon an average, live weight, 1,300 pounds. They could all be sold to-day for Eastern markets at good figures. They have yet three months of good weather to fatten this season, when, with 5,000 more, bought by these enterprising men, and on their way here, they will be sold East, or slaughtered and sent East in the quarter.

"There is, still higher up the stream, and nearer the mountains, a stock herd of yearlings and two-year-olds, that occupy our time for an hour or two.

"*Blooded Stock Cattle.*—Then we cross over to Sand Creek, a small branch of the Laramie, and see the herd of American cattle, which, including Hutton's and Alsop's, numbers 400, mostly cows. They are as fine stock as can be found anywhere. Among this herd are several fine-graded Durham bulls, and two thoroughbreds that were bought in Ohio at high prices. These parties are owners of 300 blooded bulls, from which the finest calves are being raised by the cross between them and the graded Texan cow. It is interesting for the stock man to see these calves, which show the Durham so clearly in every instance—another proof of the general law that the stronger and better blooded of the two races will give form and impress to the progeny. This fact is remarkably illustrated in these herds—the second and third crosses leaving no trace of the Texan blood.

"Here, on this ranch, are 300 brood mares, and some young stock, yearling and two-year-old colts, which have been raised here, and have never been fed nor sheltered. They are as large and fine colts as are raised anywhere. These brood mares and colts are herded, but never stabled nor fed winters.

"*Sheep.*—We next proceed to these flocks of sheep, which in all number more than 10,000 head, besides the lambs—of these there are 3,000—making in all 13,000. Some of these are from New Mexico, but the great majority are from Iowa, and are fine Merino sheep. They will average fully five pounds of wool per head. Ample shelters have been provided them in case of storm. Much the larger number of these flocks are ewes. The owners expect to raise 6,000 lambs, and to shear 65,000 pounds of wool next year.

"These parties have about five miles of fence, inclosing hay grounds, pastures for riding stock, and other purposes. They have, in all, more than $300,000 invested here, which is a sufficient commentary upon their enterprise, foresight, and courage. They are the great stock princes of the mountains. Of all living men they have done most to solve this question of winter grazing.

"We next proceed to the Little Laramie, where Messrs. Mautle & Bath have 400 head of American and half-breed stock ; they are at the old stage-road crossing, and have some fine blooded stock. Above them, behind Sheep Mountain, directly under the white top of Mount Dodge, named after General Dodge, on the head of the Little Laramie, is a valley twenty miles long and ten miles wide, divided about equally by the north, middle, and south forks of that stream. These are rapid running streams that never freeze in winter. They have groves of timber on their banks and bottom lands furnishing shade in summer and shelter in winter. This valley is a pocket in the mountains, having only one point of ingress, and no egress but by the same way. Here are 2,900 cattle owned by Lambard & Gray, of New York, Captain Coates of the Army, and the subscriber. Three men are able to herd them, from the nature of the valley, and it is certainly a cattle paradise. Of this herd, 1,200 are cows, 700 two-year-olds, 300 yearlings, and 700 calves. This stock is short-horned Texan, and a good lot of stock cattle.

"*Iliff's Herds on Crow Creek.*—After leaving this herd, we take a three-hours' run on the railroad, which takes us across the Black Hills to Cheyenne, which is the headquarters of J. W. Iliff. His cattle range is down Crow Creek to the Platte, twenty to thirty miles. On this grazing ground he has 6,700 cattle, classed as follows: 3,500 beeves, 2,000 cows, and 1,200 calves. The stock cattle are half-breeds, except yearlings and calves, which he has raised, and which show the Durham cross. The beeves are heavy, fat cattle, ranging in live weight from 1,200 to 1,400 pounds. This whole range down Crow Creek, from Cheyenne to the Platte, affords the best of grasses, and the creek bluffs shelter the stock completely from storms. Mr. Iliff has been the owner of great herds of cattle in the last twelve years, and is firm in the faith that this is the place to raise beef for Eastern markets. His cattle have sold in Chicago market from five to six cents per pound, live weight, this season. The whole 3,500 head of beeves will be shipped East this fall. Mr. Iliff is another of those who have demonstrated to the world that we have winter grazing, and in so doing he has made a fortune. Long may such men live to enjoy their fortunes!

"On the other side of the Platte, on the Bijou, are the herds of the Patterson Brothers, Reynolds, and John Hitson. These herds number 8,000 head of cattle, 6,000 of them being beef-cattle. The Patterson Brothers are great cattle-raisers and dealers. They own ranches on the Arkansas River, at Bent's Old Fort, and on the Pecos River, below Fort Sumner, in New Mexico. They have handled hundreds of thousands of dollars' worth of cattle in the last five years.

"John Hitson is another of the great cattle-raisers and dealers in New Mexico. His herds are numbered by the thousands. His operations are transferred to Colorado now, and so are those of the Patterson Brothers. On Box-Elder Creek, which is a branch of the Caché la Poudre, is the ranch and stock range of Mr. Whitcombe, an old settler of Colorado. He has 2,000 stock cattle and some fine blooded bulls. This range and shelter are perfect.

"Reed & Wyatt, on the Platte, nearer Denver, have 1,000 head of stock and beef cattle. They are about adding largely to their number

"Farwell Brothers, Greeley, have 200 head of fine American cattle.

"Baily, on the south side of the Platte from Greeley, has 400 head of Durham and Devon stock, and 2,000 sheep.

"Geary, on the Platte, has 300 head of American cattle.

"The Lemons, at Greeley, have 400 head of American stock. In this neighborhood, Ashcraft has 400 head of American cattle; Munson has 800 head of cattle and 3,000 sheep. Up the Caché la Poudre are twenty large stock-raisers.

"On the Big and Little Thompson's there are some five herds of blooded stock.

"After you leave Evans and go south towards Denver, the whole country seems one pasture covered with stock. I travelled over this same ground in 1869, and I am sure there are fully three times as many cattle here now as then. There are hundreds of farmers on the Lone-Tree Creek, Caché la Poudre, Big and Little Thompson's Creeks, St. Vrain's, and many other streams which flow from the mountains to the Platte, who have from one hundred to one thousand head of cattle, a description of whose herds and grazing grounds would take too much space in an article of this kind.

"*Shipments of Cattle West.*—Colorado has sold an immense number of cattle this season to Montana, Idaho, Nevada, and Utah. It is safe to say that Montana will receive twenty thousand head of cattle during the season of 1870, four-fifths of which are from Colorado. Many have gone to Utah, Nevada, and Idaho from the same source, and yet, ten years ago, the commercial and stock-growing people of the East did not know that Colorado contained a thousand acres of grass land. To-day they have no idea of the magnitude of her grazing resources.

"Leaving Colorado, we find some herds along the base of the Black Hills.

"*North of Cheyenne.*—H. Kelly, on the 'Chug,' has 500 stock cattle. He sold 100 head of American beeves at $70 per head.

"Messrs. Ward & Bullock, at Fort Laramie, have 200 head of American cattle.

"Adolph Cluny, so long a resident on the North Platte, has a herd of 1,000 stock cattle between Forts Laramie and Fetterman.

"Between Cheyenne and Sidney, on the line of the railroad, there are several small herds. At Sidney are the Moore Brothers, who have 12,000 sheep and lambs, and 1,400 cattle; 400 of the latter are American and very fine. The sheep sheared an average of five pounds of wool per head last spring. They are graded Merinos, and are in fine condition. There is no disease among them. The Moore Brothers were ranchmen on the South Platte, prior to the day of railroads, and are about returning to that stream for grazing. Their place is the Valley Station of olden fame on the stage road. Above them, on the Platte, at the old 'Junction,' Mr. Mark Boughton has 2,500 stock cattle. He has as fine a cattle range as there is in the world, not excluding the Pampas of South America nor table-lands of Australia.

"Farther down the Platte, at O'Fallon's Bluffs, on the north side of the South Platte, Creighton & Parks have 3,500 stock cattle, 400 of which are Durhams. They range twenty miles up and down the Platte. Near them, below, is the herd of Mr. Keith, of North Platte Station, who has about 1,000 head.

"Mr. M. H. Brown has 500 head of stock cattle and beeves near the same place.

"Across the Platte, in the neighborhood of Fort McPherson, the Bent Brothers have 1,000 head of stock cattle, and will add another 1,000 the present season.

"Messrs. Carter & Coe have a large herd near there, which numbers near a thousand.

"Mr. Benjamin Gallagher has 1,200 head at the old Gilman ranch, twelve miles from McPherson.

"*Progress this Season.*—More real progress has been made in stock matters west of the Missouri this season than in all time before. We have not only added to the numbers of our herds and flocks, but we have given confidence to all our stock-growers and to Eastern people in the permanency and profit of grazing in the Trans-Missouri country.

"We are now in easy reach of Eastern markets. The railways are landing the heaviest cattle in Chicago from the Rocky Mountains at $9 and $10 per head; we can sell thousands and tens of thousands annually to the Pacific slope, and there is still an all-absorbing home demand to stock our thousands of valleys.

"*The Future.*—As every country in the West receives a new emigrant, and his plow turns the grass under, that corn and wheat may grow in its stead, the range of the stock-grower is that much contracted, and the area of grazing lessened. By reason of the high value of lands for grain-growing purposes the people of the country east of the Mississippi River are already coming to us for beef and mutton. Chicago and New York people are enjoying the juicy steaks from cattle fattened on our nutritious grasses that grow in our valleys and on our mountain-sides, close up to the perpetual snows of the Rocky Mountains.

"As immigration takes up more and more of the pastures east of us for grain, drovers will be obliged more and more to come to us for beef. Texas, the great hive of cattle, has received three hundred thousand settlers this season. The grazing area of that State has been lessened at least a million acres thereby. Everywhere events point to this Trans-Missouri country as the future dependence of the East for wool, beef, mutton, and horses."

PAGE 60.—The following article, clipped from the *New-York Times*, contains so much valuable information, bearing on the question of Irrigation, as related to the Plains and the great Internal Basin of the Continent, that I venture to insert it here. It seems to be a careful *resumé* of the facts that were brought before the notable Convention of Governors and others, that met in Denver in the autumn of '73, to consider the question of a general and comprehensive system of irrigation for all that region:

WATER SUPPLY FOR THE GREAT PLAINS REQUIRED.

Correspondence of the New-York Times.

DENVER, Colorado, Friday, Oct. 17, 1873.

It is a fact, perhaps not generally considered, that the ninety ninth meridian of longitude west from Greenwich, the meridian of Fort Kearney on the Platte, and Fort Hays, marks a division line in the physical geography of the continent. Here the prairies merge into the great plains, and the abundant rain-fall of eastern meridians ceases. West of this line lies one-half of the area of the United States, all of which, excepting a small strip on the shores of the Pacific, is without sufficient rain-fall for the cultivation of the soil. This great arid region comprises more than two-thirds of Kansas and Nebraska, a large portion of California, Oregon, Washington, and Texas, and nearly all of Colorado, Wyoming, Utah, New Mexico, Idaho, Montana, Arizona, Nevada, and Dakota. Here are one million square miles of barren country, and the question is, What shall we do with it?

The keen interest felt in this matter has been evident from the large attendance upon this convention, and the mass of information and argument presented. Whatever has been done thus far toward reclaiming any portion of these waste lands has been by individual enterprise, except in Utah and New Mexico a system of irrigation has been enforced by legislative enactments. In New Mexico the acequias are the most important features of the country. The subsistence of the people depends upon them, and the laws protecting them fill many pages of the statute books. An overseer of acequias is selected in every precinct, who fixes the number of laborers to be furnished by each land-owner, apportions their work, and distributes the water. Yet not over 300 square miles is under cultivation in that Territory. In Utah, where there is in operation the most complete and successful system of irrigation in this country, only about 140,000 acres are under cultivation. By legislative enactment the counties have power to build canals just as they build roads. Water commissioners are chosen at regular elections, in each county, and their services are paid out of the general tax levy, and they give bonds for the faithful performance of their duties. Subordinate commissioners, or water masters, are selected by neighborhoods, cities, and towns, and they are paid by assessments on the land. There are now over 1,200 miles of irrigating canals in Utah, with a capacity for watering 100,000 acres. The population of the Territory is upward of 150,000. It has 190 prosperous towns and cities. Its farm products are shipped into the neighboring Territories, and even into the Missouri Valley. In Colorado there has been no general plan of irrigation. Private corporations build canals and sell the water therefrom to the ranchmen. Several of the towns are supplied in this way. The colonies have also done much in this respect. But no general system has been adopted in that Territory, nor has the legislature ever taken cognizance of the situation. The same may be said of the other States and Territories interested in this movement. Irrigation has been limited. The few acres that have been reclaimed in the immediate vicinity of the streams and cañons, near the mountains, bear no comparison to the vast body of plain and desert stretching hundreds of miles in every direction.

The cost of constructing irrigating canals varies according to the character of the country. The average in Colorado has been $7 per acre. It is thought by competent engineers that in a general system of canals for the Plains, east of Denver, the cost must run from $10 to $15 per acre. According to careful estimates, Colorado has a water supply sufficient to irrigate 6,000,000 acres, an arable area which, in Egypt, in the times of the Ptolemies, supplied food for 8,000,000 people. The Plains, extending from the foot-hills of the Rocky Mountains eastward nearly 300 miles, comprise about 25,000,000 acres. Of this vast tract there are 1,500,000 acres belonging to the Kansas Pacific Railway Company, lying south of the Platte River, and which a canal from the Platte Cañon to the head-waters of the Republican will cover. Such a canal, 12 feet wide and 3 feet deep, will cost $1,000 per mile. It will make lands that now go a-begging at $2.50 per acre worth from $10 to $15.

The want of water is the one and only drawback to the settlement of the Trans-Missouri country. Farming along the streams has been carried on enough to show that the soil is not only fertile, but extremely so, insuring, with plenty of water, crops surpassing those of the best farming districts elsewhere. The average yield, year in and year out, through the Rocky Mountain region, whenever irrigation is employed, has been found to be as follows: Wheat, 27 bushels per acre; oats, 55; potatoes, 150 to 200; onions, 250; barley, 33. This is far above the average of Illinois or Ohio. It is believed that the mountain streams, if turned into proper channels, will irrigate the greater part of the Plains, both east and west of the Mountains. This is particularly true of Western Kansas and Nebraska, Colorado, Utah, Wyoming, and New Mexico. The great rivers of the Platte, Arkansas, Rio Grande, and Colorado could be divided at or near their source in the mountains, and made to cover vast quantities of land. In Utah, it is proposed to take out canals from the Jordan, Weber, and Bear rivers, diminishing the supply in Great Salt Lake, and distributing it over other adjacent portions of the territory. And in California, engineers have been sent out to turn the Colorado River into the desert of Arizona, and Southern California.

PAGE 279.—Her statistics (San Francisco) for 1873 are equally significant, and foot up about as follows: In that year over 70,000 people arrived there, by land and sea, and less than *half* that number departed. Nearly 4,000 vessels entered her harbor, measuring about 2,000,000 tons. She exported 10,000,000 sacks of wheat, and nearly 1,000,000 barrels of flour; and Californians claimed, it wasn't much of a year for "wheat", either! The total wheat crop of the State, which mostly sought her wharves, was estimated as worth fully

$26,000,000, or nearly $10,000,000 more than in 1872—prices being higher; the wool-clip, say, $7,000,000; the wine product, $2,000,000. Her total exports, of all kinds, was estimated at about $80,000,000; and, best of all, while her exports had largely increased, her imports had considerably decreased. Real estate had been dull for a year or two, and yet her sales that year aggregated about $15,000,000; while her mining stocks sold for $150,000,000, and paid dividends about $14,000,000, as against less than half that amount in 1872. The cash value of her property was estimated at $250,000,000 and of the State at about $600,000,000.

California's yield of the precious metals in 1873 was estimated at about $18,000,000, which was some two millions *less* than in 1872, and was already surpassed by her magnificent wheat crop of $26,000,000. Her total agricultural products for '73 were believed to aggregate $80,000,000; while all her mines and manufactures produced only about $70,000,000, though employing nearly double the number of people. Evidently, with her vast area of 120,000,000 acres of land, of which fully 40,000,000 are fit for the plow, our farmers there have a brilliant future before them, notwithstanding they will have to irrigate to raise some crops.

PAGE 324.—The following is a table of mean temperature at Santa Barbara for the year 1870-1:

April,	average of the	three daily	observations......	60 62°
May,	"	"	"	62.35
June,	"	"	"	65.14
July,	"	"	"	71.49
Aug.,	"	"	"	72.12
Sept.,	"	"	"	68.08
Oct.,	"	"	"	65.96
Nov.,	"	"	"	61.22
Dec.,	"	"	"	52.12
Jan.,	"	"	"	54.51
Feb.,	"	"	"	53.35
March,	"	"	"	58.42

Average temperature for the year, 60.20°.

COLDEST DAY.		WARMEST DAY.	
April 12th	60°	April 16th	74°
May 15th	66	May 23d	77
June 1st	69	June 3d	80
July 26th	76	July 11th	84
Aug. 11th	77	Aug. 8th	86
Sept. 23d	66	Sept. 27th	90
Oct. 23d	60	Oct. 20th	92
Nov. 7th	64	Nov. 20th	87
Dec. 15th	52	Dec. 28th	71
Jan. 11th	56	Jan. 3d	76
Feb. 22d	42	Feb. 28th	71
March 13th	56	March 27th	83

Coldest day in the year, Feb. 22d	42°
Warmest day in the year, Oct. 20th	92
Variation	50

Compare these with the average temperature of the Atlantic Coast, say at Trenton or New York, and what a paradise for invalids Santa Barbara must be!

PAGE 434.—Our yield of the precious metals for 1873 was exceptionally fine, and the following table of the total for that year, from the districts west of the Missouri River, gave immense satisfaction on the Pacific Coast:

California	$18,025,722
Nevada	35,254,507
Oregon	1,376,389
Washington	209,395
Idaho	2,343,654
Montana	3,892,810
Utah	4,906,337
Arizona	47,778
Colorado	4,083,268
Mexico	868,798
British Columbia	1,250,035
Grand total	$72,258,693

The total yield for 1872 was only $62,236,913; so that here is a gain of $10,000,000 or so in one year. This extra increase, however, was chiefly from Nevada, whose total product, it will be seen, about equals that of all the others; and it must be credited mainly to the great Comstock Lode, whose ores, it is now about demonstrated, grow richer and better, the deeper you go down, like the best mines of Mexico and Peru. In 1871 they averaged only $27 per ton; in 1872 they increased to $32; and in 1873 to $40.

These figures well sustain Mr. Sutro's theories, and his Great Tunnel now well under way will soon become a fixed fact. This Tunnel will be several miles in length, when completed, and in both conception and execution must be regarded as one of the greatest triumphs of engineering in America. The famous "Bonanza" silver mines are mainly located on the Comstock Lode, and this tunnel will prove of immense advantage to them, increasing their yield very largely.

Our yield of the precious metals for 1876, from the region west of the Missouri River, was still better than in 1873, and the gain is so marked as to challenge the attention of everybody. The following figures, it is believed, are substantially correct:

California	$18,615,817
Nevada	49,280,764
Oregon	1,500,000
Washington	300,000
Idaho	2,038,000
Montana	4,230,000
Utah	5,850,000
Arizona	1,540,000
Colorado	7,292,000
Mexico	2,213,748
British Columbia	1,441,566
New Mexico	350,294
Total	$94,652,189

Here is a gain of $22,393,496 over the product of 1873, or an increase of over 30 per cent., which certainly must be very gratifying to our mine-owners, if to nobody else. It is surely a very handsome addition to the world's wealth. California, Oregon, Washington and British Columbia, it will be seen, made a very slight increase over their yield for 1873; but Colorado, Utah, Nevada, Idaho, Montana, and Arizona all ran largely ahead, especially Colorado and Nevada. Arizona also has done well, and doubtless will do better.

The total yield it will be observed was $94,652,189, comprising of course both gold and silver. Of this amount, however, nearly *one half* was silver, derived as follows:

California	$ 577,500
Nevada	26,525,000
Montana	1,155,000
Idaho	1,000,000
Utah	5,775,000
Colorado	4,042,000
Arizona	1,000,000
Total	$40,074,500

Here surely is some basis for Resumption. If the product of our mines continues to increase at the same rate, we shall certainly soon be on the safe road to Specie Payments, and the sooner we reach that shining goal the better.

PAGES 279 and 489.—The statistics of San Francisco for 1876 still show a steady growth and increase, that must be very gratifying to the average Californian. In that year about 90,000 persons arrived there, by land and sea, and only about half that number departed, showing a gain of over 40,000 population by immigration alone, to be distributed thence over California and the Pacific coast generally. In 1875 her actual gain was 66,172, and in 1874 it was 67,688; but these were exceptional and extra good years.

The total wheat crop of the State in 1876 was estimated as worth $36,000,000, or a gain of about $10,000,000 over that of 1873. Her wool-clip was computed to be worth $8,200,000; her wine-product $4,000,000. Her total exports, of all kinds, doubtless approximated $100,000,000. Her sales of real-estate footed up $25,000,000; her mining-stocks paid dividends $35,000,000, as against $14,000,000 in 1873. The cash value of her property was estimated at $300,000,000, and of the State at about $700,000,000.

California's yield of the precious metals in 1876 was only $18,077,500, as against $18,025,722 in 1873, so that in this respect she seems to have come to a standstill. But this was more than offset by her enormous wheat crop of $36,000,000. Her total farm products for 1876 were thought to aggregate over $100,000,000. The following statement of the receipts of domestic produce at San Francisco, for the periods indicated, is very significant and speaks for itself:

	July 1, 1875, to Jan. 8, 1876.	July 1, 1876, to Jan. 6, 1877.
Flour, qr sks	1,031,441	1,233,925
Wheat, 100-lb sks	4,662,583	8,825,018
Barley, 100-lb sks	707,729	1,296,161
Oats, sks	181,653	178,391
Potatoes, sks	442,879	474,532
Corn, sks	97,995	113,094
Rye, sks	10,141	17,951
Buckwheat, sks	1,180	6,232
Beans, sks	78,036	80,507
Bran, sks	83,033	142,364
Hay, tons	37,088	49,252
Salt, tons	5,010	4,441
Wool, bales	59,965	80,685
Hides, No	84,677	111,640
Raisins, 20-lb bxs	16,836	23,818
Quicksilver, flasks	30,412	37,070
Hops, bales		6,584

Here, it will be observed, is a marked increase in every item, except oats and salt.

The wool-clip of 1876, as I have said, was estimated to be worth $8,200,000. Her wool interest has developed very rapidly, during the past decade or so, and promises to have a brilliant future. Prior to 1867, her wool-product was less than 9,000,000 pounds; but it had increased from 1,100,000 pounds in 1857, to nearly 9,000,000 pounds in 1865—a gain of about 800 per cent. Since then, there has been a steady growth and a gain of about 460 per cent in the total product. Her exports of wool for the past decade foot up about as follows:

Years.	Pounds.	Value.
1867	7,048,000	$1,215,000
1868	13,225,000	2,420,000
1869	13,274,000	2,454,000
1870	19,010,000	3,506,000
1871	22,323,000	6,697,000
1872	23,430,000	8,185,000
1873	30,144,100	6,450,000
1874	36,088,700	8,120,000
1875	48,189,000	8,450,000
1876	52,588,300	8,200,000
Totals	265,314,100	$55,697,000

The growth of her export trade in late years, as compared with previous decades, is as follows:

	Pounds.	Value.
1857–66..................	41,052,000	$7,481,000
1867–76	265,314,100	55,697,000
Total for 20 years.....	306,366,100	$63,178,000

PAGES 396 and 415. On these pages, allusion has been made to the importance of railroad connections East and West, for Arizona particularly; but the remarks apply equally to New Mexico and Texas. Such connections the "Texas and Pacific Railway" has been designed to furnish, and it will be a blessed day for all that region when its last rail is laid, and the whistle of its locomotives wakes the echoes of the mountains and canōns there. By reference to the Map, it will be seen, that this proposed road with its connections extends from San Francisco South, through Los Angelos to Fort Yuma; thence up the Gila *via* Tucson east, across Arizona to Mesilla and El Paso; thence across New Mexico and Western Texas east, to Fort Worth; and thence by diverging branches to St. Louis, Memphis, Vicksburg, New Orleans and Galveston. At Galveston and New Orleans, it would connect with ships and steamers, *via* the Gulf of Mexico to all parts of the world by sea; at Vicksburg and Memphis with the sea-coast and midland great railroad routes to the north; and at St. Louis with the Pennsylvania Railroad and its great through connections to Chicago, Philadelphia, New York, and the East generally. Its total length, I suppose, from San Francisco say to the Mississippi is about 2300 miles. The western end has already been pushed down nearly to Fort Yuma, by the Southern Pacific Railroad, of California, which is understood to be practically the same as the Central Pacific, and the eastern end or branches have been completed, either by the Texas and Pacific or allied companies, to Fort Worth in Western Texas; so that the work yet to be done is practically the gap of 1200 miles, between Fort Yuma and Fort Worth, or about two-thirds of the whole distance.

The route lies mainly over rolling prairies, high plateaus, and easy mountain grades, and through a region free from obstructing snows at all seasons of the year. The highest elevation on the whole road is only about 5000 feet, at a pass in the Hueca Mountains, just east of El Paso, with a grade of only 66 feet to the mile while the total length of grades between 80 and 105 feet, it is thought will not exceed 45 miles. On the contrary, the Union Pacific, where it crosses the Rocky Mountains, has to climb up to 8,235 feet, and the Central Pacific only gets over the Sierra Nevadas by a climb of 7,042 feet.

A glance at the Map will show the high character, and indeed supreme importance, of such a railroad to all our vast empire there, now practically inaccessible to population and trade, and destined to remain so, until the iron horse opens a way thither. It will open up all Western Texas, with its great flocks and herds, to the East and a market. It will tap New Mexico and Arizona, with their rich mines of gold and silver, copper and iron, and pour into their mining regions an active and busy population. It will shake hands with California again across the continent, through a far better region, and furnish another highway for the trade and travel of China and Japan. Nay, more, at El Paso, or somewhere there, it will ultimately connect with a great trunk line into Old Mexico *via* Chihuahua and the City of Mexico south, and thus rejuvenate and rehabilitate that sick Republic, by bringing her too into harmony with the railroad system—the business and ideas, the activities and energies—of the American Union. In short, it means trade and travel—development, population, civilization—to all that great region to the west and southwest of us. It means the speedy and thorough solution of the Indian Question, and of pretty much all other questions out there. It means another "bond of union," safe and strong, binding the Pacific slope to the Atlantic States. It means prosperity to the south, over which it would pour its streams of wealth. It means another arm of defence, sure and steadfast, in case of foreign war. All these are practical results, certain to follow from the construction of such a road, and their magnitude and significance are simply incalculable.

Of course, such a railroad will cost money, and a good deal of it, both to build and equip, to operate and maintain it. Its original cost is estimated anywhere, from $75,000,000 to $100,000,000. To provide for this in part, the road already has a land-grant of some 13,376,000 acres of superb land in Texas, 14,387,200 acres in New Mexico and Arizona, and 3,456,000 acres in Southern California, making in all, nearly 32,000,000 acres. All of this is valuable for farming or grazing purposes, and much of it is immensely rich in minerals of all sorts, as stated repeatedly in my chapters on Arizona. Ultimately, as the road advances, and settlers, and miners pour in, this magnificent endowment, this princely domain, will prove of very great value to the company; but it is not now materially available, and the burning question with the road is, how to secure present funds.

To this end, in view of the National character of the road, and the great results sure to flow from it, the company hopes for aid from Congress, pleading the precedents of the Union Pacific, the Central Pacific, and the Northern Pacific railroads, all of which were helped in some way, directly or indirectly. But it asks not actual money, or even the endorsement of its bonds, as some or all of them, more or less did; but only a *guarantee of the interest* on its bonds, for a stated period, in return for which it offers the government a first mortgage on the road and equipment, and all its lands and franchises—the whole of its net income, both from sale of lands, and operation of the road, and a proportion of its bonds per mile as issued, until said mortgage is extinguished—and further to provide a sinking fund to meet the bonds as they mature. These terms seem fair on their face, but Congress naturally hesitates, and the country doubts, in view of the hard times, and our picturesque, not to say romantic, experiences with the Credit Mobilier and otherwise.

Of course, the other Pacific roads are hostile to it, because it would break down their monopoly across the continent, and introduce the healthful principle of legitimate competition. But notwithstanding this, it seems clear, that eventually it will secure National aid, to some extent, in some shape or other, and that not distantly. But, however this may be, it is pretty sure to get itself built, and will then certainly prove a mighty instrument for progress in all that region. Bold hands and skillful brains have conceived and executed the project thus far, with consummate ability. That great railroad king, or rather emperor, Thomas Scott, of the Pennsylvania Railroad, a man of imperial grip and boundless resources, is now at the head of it, and should he live, nothing seems more certain, than that he will carry the enterprise speedily through. A greater boon he could not confer upon the Great Southwest, and hardly upon the country generally.

INDEX.

THE END.

www.ingramcontent.com/pod-product-compliance
Lightning Source LLC
LaVergne TN
LVHW021305110826
845150LV00003B/487

* 9 7 8 1 4 2 5 5 5 9 0 2 1 *